Using R in HR Analytics seamlessly bridges the gap between data science and human resources. Brimming with practical examples and case studies, this is an essential guide for understanding and applying statistical techniques in HR. An indispensable resource for anyone looking to enhance their HR practice through the power of analytics.
Sally Smith, Head of People Analytics, National Australia Bank

An essential read for HR leaders and practitioners wishing to deepen their knowledge and capability in analytics. The authors balance the need to present technical concepts and theory with clear and simple solutions to apply within the workplace. This book is full of wisdom for anyone wishing to embrace analytics as a fundamental HR capability.
Caroline van der Feltz, HR Director, Danske Bank UK

Detailed, precise and clearly written, this book isn't just about statistics; it's about the future of HR. Essential reading for everyone in HR.
Professor Binna Kandola OBE, Business Psychologist, Senior Partner and Co-founder, Pearn Kandola

This book is a comprehensive and detailed guide for any professional interested in this exciting new field. It will help you understand what data to analyse, how to interpret it and how different types of models work. Highly recommended for people analytics specialists.
Josh Bersin, global industry analyst and Founder of Bersin by Deloitte

Using R in HR Analytics

A practical guide to analysing people data

Martin Edwards, Kirsten Edwards
and Daisung Jang

KoganPage

Publisher's note
Every possible effort has been made to ensure that the information contained in this book is accurate at the time of going to press, and the publishers and authors cannot accept responsibility for any errors or omissions, however caused. No responsibility for loss or damage occasioned to any person acting, or refraining from action, as a result of the material in this publication can be accepted by the editor, the publisher or the author.

First published in Great Britain and the United States in 2025 by Kogan Page Limited

2nd Floor, 45 Gee Street
London
EC1V 3RS
United Kingdom

8 W 38th Street, Suite 902
New York, NY 10018
USA

www.koganpage.com

Kogan Page books are printed on paper from sustainable forests.

ISBNs

Hardback   978 1 3986 1827 5
Paperback   978 1 3986 1825 1
Ebook   978 1 3986 1826 8

British Library Cataloguing-in-Publication Data

A CIP record for this book is available from the British Library.

Library of Congress Control Number

2024035274

Typeset by Integra Software Services, Pondicherry
Print production managed by Jellyfish
Printed and bound by CPI Group (UK) Ltd, Croydon, CR0 4YY

To Lily and Max

CONTENTS

06 Case study 3: Predicting employee turnover 184

07 Case study 4: Predicting employee performance 228

08 Case study 5: Recruitment and selection analytics 276

09 Case study 6: Monitoring the impact of interventions 309

PREFACE

Origins of this book

This book has been written in response to the evolving nature of the HR analytics field. HR analytics has seen considerable growth, and with this growth comes an influx of analytic experts with different backgrounds, skills and capabilities. While the focus of this book's sister text, *Predictive HR Analytics: Mastering the HR metric,* was on conducting analyses using SPSS, many experts now prefer using R over SPSS. Consequently, this book, which builds upon the foundation laid by *Predictive HR Analytics,* is dedicated to R users.

Who this book is for

This book is an ideal starter guide for those working in any HR analytics team. Whilst the considerable growth in the field of HR analytics means that we are witnessing the creation and development of HR analytics teams more and more, this book is also for anyone working in the Human Resource function, anyone working in a Management Information function, anyone who is studying HR, management or business analytics, and anyone who has to make decisions about people in an organizational context. It also provides a great context through which to learn the R language in a domain that is present and increasingly important in all medium to large organizations.

DIY

The key difference that this book has over other books on predictive HR analytics is that we show you how to actually conduct analyses with different types of HR-related data and we also guide you through the statistical models required for each type of analysis. This book shows you how to conduct the analysis with R, an open-source statistics programming language. Whilst there are books on the market that discuss HR analytics, and ones that show people how to run statistical analyses, few combine both aspects.

Why R?

The main point of this book is to put the open-source statistical language R at its core. There are a number of reasons for this. First is the free and open nature of the R language. Unlike proprietary statistical packages, it can be downloaded and used for free, and thus it lowers the barrier to learning and conducting advanced HR analytics. We hope this book will be adopted widely by practitioners, students and other learners wishing to better understand people at work. A related reason is that, unlike paid statistical packages, R imposes no artificial limits on what users can do – some packages require the user to purchase additional modules to access certain statistical procedures, which is not the case with R.

An additional reason is that R allows users to do more than conduct statistics. Because it is a programming language, its use goes beyond statistical analysis and allows users to engage in enhanced data manipulation and creation of publication-ready tables and graphics. We touch on these abilities in the book and the motivated learner will find all manner of ways to develop their data analytic skills by building on what they learn here. Advanced uses of R beyond the scope of this book include generating interactive dashboards, creating individualized feedback reports, machine learning algorithms, collecting data from the internet, etc. There is little to limit people who want to extend their abilities. Reflecting the combination of free use, extensibility and wide range of possible uses, R is a popular language among data scientists and this book provides an introduction to that world.

Note to instructors

This book is based on and bears a close resemblance to *Predictive HR Analytics* (3rd edition), by the same authors. Both the content and structure of the book are very similar – consider this book an enhanced R edition. As mentioned, *Predictive HR Analytics* uses SPSS as the main vehicle through which to guide the HR analytics journey, while this new text is specifically for those who want to be guided as an R user. While we do include some new analytic methods and content, such as machine learning and developments in artificial intelligence, it is not intended to be an entirely new book to replace *Predictive HR Analytics*. In short, if you like and are comfortable working in SPSS to conduct analyses, *Predictive HR Analytics* is the book for you. If you would like to use the R language, this is the book for you.

How to use this book

This book can be used by anyone who wants to learn statistical analysis techniques, and we use applied HR data here so that the book has authentic relevance and 'real world' application. It is not designed to be *just* a statistics book, but we go through the statistical procedures in enough depth for the reader not to need to buy a statistics book as well (until they get a bit more advanced). However, this book is likely to be most useful for people who want to get some experience estimating statistical models with HR data.

Throughout the book, you will find examples demonstrating how to conduct analyses using R, which involves writing and running code. This code will be provided both within the book pages and in supplementary materials available for download from the Kogan Page website (www.koganpage.com/urhra). While the code itself will be identical across sources, its appearance may vary slightly due to line breaks, as the formatting differs between printed pages and computer screens.

The structure of this book is as follows:

Chapter 1 provides a brief introduction to the field of predictive HR analytics, where we set out how and why the analytic methods used in this book are different from the kind of activity that HR functions and MI teams currently undertake as a norm.

In Chapter 2 we discuss the nature of HR data and demonstrate how to convert HR data into a workable form to analyse with R. We also explain why we use R as the statistical tool.

Chapter 3 is really a reference section; it discusses the aim of statistical models, inferential statistics and significance. It then goes on to describe and outline the main statistical analytic techniques used in this book; it sets out when certain analytic tests should be used and in what context. We also detail the R libraries used to conduct these analyses.

Chapters 4–9 are all case study 'meat and bones' chapters: Chapter 4 – diversity analysis; Chapter 5 – employee attitude and engagement data; Chapter 6 – employee turnover analysis; Chapter 7 – predicting employee performance; Chapter 8 – recruitment and selection analysis; and Chapter 9 – monitoring the impact of interventions. In each of these chapters we give a brief introduction to the issues and topic areas and demonstrate a number of ways that HR-related data can be analysed/modelled in each case. We supply example data sets to be used in each chapter and walk the analyst through how to run a range of possible analytic models in each case. Importantly, we show how to interpret the statistical results and highlight some 'snapshot hidden gems' that the analytic techniques expose in each case. The example data sets can be found on the Kogan Page website (www.koganpage.com) associated with the book.

Chapter 10 is all about applying the predictive models to try to get the most out of the analysis. Here we give examples of the true potential that predictive HR analytics can bring to an organization.

Chapter 11 discusses and introduces a range of different, more advanced analytic techniques that we do not cover, but we feel it is important for the budding analyst to get a conceptual understanding of their potential.

Finally, in Chapter 12 we end the book on a reflective note: the journey of HR analytics is fraught with obstacles and potential sticky problems. This chapter encourages the analyst to reflect and think critically about the predictive HR analytic project, with the aim of ensuring that the analyst does not carry out HR analytics without considering the limitations and ethical challenges that the activity raises.

By the end of the book the reader should have gained considerable experience in applying statistical models to HR data and should be ready to use their analytic capabilities and set sail on their own organization's ocean of people-related data. They will also have developed their skills in the R language in a hands-on way using real business problems.

Bon voyage!

ACKNOWLEDGEMENTS

We would like to thank everyone who helped us in the creation of this book.

Thanks go to Melissa Winnel at Rio Tinto for sharing her extensive knowledge of large language models and generative AI.

Martin would like to specifically thank David, Riccardo, Jon and Mike at King's College London, all of whom showed enough encouragement to get the project underway! Special thanks go to our friend Carl Robinson, solicitor and Managing Director at CMR Advisory Ltd, for thoughtful comments on data protection and GDPR legislation.

Daisung would like to thank Erin Batman for her many hours of patience and support during the writing of this book. We thank Belen Alvarez Werth for her valuable feedback on a draft of this book. Her thoughtful comments have improved it considerably.

We would also like to thank Lucy Carter and Joe Ferner-Reeves at Kogan Page for their guidance and support.

We would also like to thank all the individuals who have kindly provided a testimonial for the book.

01

HR analytics

What is it and why is it important?

Arguably the most practical tool and greatest potential for organizational management is the emergence of predictive analytics.

SOURCE Fitz-enz and Mattox II (2014)

Workforce analytics has the potential to generate new knowledge, leading to improved outcomes at the individual, team, and organizational levels through more effective management of human capital.

SOURCE Levenson, Minbaeva, Huselid and Edwards (2024)

People analytics has matured but still has considerable challenges to overcome, and when done correctly it paves the way for differentiated HR, amplifying the impact of people on business outcomes.

SOURCE Rasmussen, Ulrich and Ulrich (2024)

As discussed in the preface, this book is built on the foundations of the Edwards and Edwards (2016, 2019) and Edwards, Edwards and Jang (2024) *Predictive HR Analytics* book, which guided the readers through an HR analytics journey using SPSS. Since the first edition of Edwards and Edwards was published, the accelerating field of HR analytics has gone from being an interesting novel area with potential, to a mainstream (if not essential) aspect of what should be included in the offering of any sophisticated HR function.

1.1   Plot of internet search interest of HR analytics subject words from 2004–2023

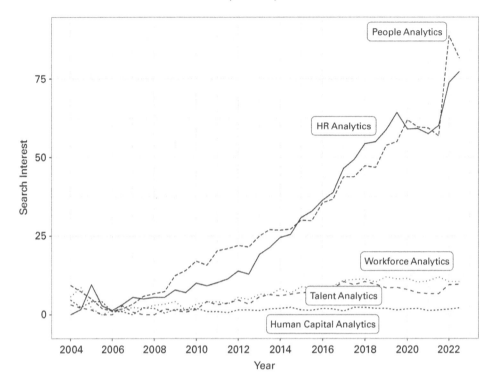

Figure 1.1 shows the growth of interest in the area, based on internet searches; clearly, the plot lines are only going upwards over recent years! A recent LinkedIn report (2023) shows that the demand for HR analytics experts is continuing to rise, with HR Analytics Manager achieving second place in the list of 'LinkedIn jobs on the rise' in 2023 (in the US). There is no doubt that we have witnessed a massive growth in the field in the last 10 years. In the past decade we have witnessed a considerable growth in the number of HR analytics practitioner conferences, training courses, consultancy offerings, books (e.g. Levenson, 2015; Edwards and Edwards, 2016; Guenole et al, 2017; Ferrar and Green, 2021; Edwards et al, 2024) and academic papers (e.g. Angrave et al, 2016; Marler and Boudreau, 2017; Kryscynski et al, 2017; Larsson and Edwards, 2021 and Edwards et al., 2022). The 2014 quote at the start of this chapter is as relevant now as it was ten years ago. We can clearly see from the narrative, blogs and articles that are being published around HR analytics that, as a field, it is becoming an increasingly important part of the HR sphere; and this growth of interest is only accelerating.

Some argue that HR should shift focus from copying practices to actively promoting and advising leadership based on thorough data assessment and research (Rousseau and Barends, 2011). HR analytics, which prioritizes using data and research to address business challenges, aligns well with this goal. However, while many HR professionals grasp the concept of HR analytics, few possess the necessary skills for sophisticated predictive analysis. Although more experts with analytical prowess are entering HR analytics, and the importance of these skills is gaining recognition (Kryscynski et al, 2017), the HR profession still lacks the widespread analytic competency needed to fully exploit HR analytics' potential. This book aims to bridge this gap by equipping readers with the skills needed to understand and apply HR analytics effectively. It seeks to demystify this field, which to many appears veiled in complexity, by providing foundational tools and knowledge. Before delving further into HR analytics, it is crucial to define what we mean by 'predictive HR analytics' and establish our understanding of the concept.

Predictive HR analytics defined

We define 'predictive HR analytics' as:

> the systematic application of predictive modelling using inferential statistics to existing HR people-related data in order to inform judgements about possible causal factors driving key HR-related performance indicators. The results of this modelling can be used (where appropriate) to make tangible predictions about particular results or people outcomes'.

Put simply, predictive HR analytics adapts sophisticated statistical and quantitative techniques used in scientific fields (like predicting heart disease or cancer treatments) to analyse organizational data about people. This allows us to test statistical models and predict factors like high performance drivers or reasons for employee turnover. When appropriate, these predictive models can forecast specific outcomes or behaviours based on given conditions. Effectively applying predictive statistical models to HR data requires knowledge of statistics and the ability to interpret analysis results. Currently, despite processing vast amounts of people-related data, HR functions often do not utilize these advanced statistical techniques for predictive insights. More often than not, whilst HR metrics and HR analytics teams do (at the moment) process and report on vast amounts of people-related data, very few apply statistical techniques that enable predictive inferences to be made. This is as much the case now (2024) as it was at the time of the previous editions of the Edwards and Edwards book (2016 and 2019).

Predictive modelling in HR analytics shares common ground with computational data science techniques and big data analysis. However, many of these applications rely on statistical methods discussed in this book, such as regression analyses that generate algorithms for predictions (see Chapter 10). Understanding these statistical tools and their application to HR data forms a solid foundation for aspiring HR analytics professionals.

Understanding the need (and business case) for mastering and utilizing predictive HR analytic techniques

Historically, HR and management information (MI) teams have dedicated significant time and effort to generating descriptive reports. These reports are meticulously monitored and compared across different geographical locations and timeframes, yet their primary function often stops at their creation and distribution. Descriptive HR reports, typical of those produced by MI teams, provide a snapshot of the organization's current status. While valuable for informing managers about ongoing developments, these reports have inherent limitations. They merely describe what is happening without delving into the reasons behind these occurrences or exploring alternative explanatory factors within the data. Additionally, they often lack rigorous validation of data reliability and fail to offer predictive insights into future trends.

Advancements in HR information systems and analytics technology have led to an increasing adoption of HR dashboards. These dashboards integrate HR information systems data to present sophisticated graphical representations of people-related metrics. Some systems even incorporate basic statistical analysis capabilities. However, their primary focus remains on descriptive, frequency-based data presentations. They rarely integrate predictive analytics, which can forecast future outcomes based on historical data patterns.

Experts like Bersin (2012) emphasize the transformative potential of predictive analytics in enabling organizations to anticipate and comprehend individual or group performance based on historical data trends. This capability allows HR professionals and management teams to make more informed strategic decisions by identifying emerging trends and patterns. Predictive HR analytics facilitates the modelling and analysis of historical data to uncover causal factors influencing organizational behaviour, aligning with Bersin's (2012) and Huselid's (2014) assertions on the strategic value of analytics in workforce management.

Understanding past organizational trends and identifying the underlying drivers behind behaviours such as high performance, increased productivity, retention rates and employee engagement provides valuable insights for strategic decision-making. Armed with this knowledge, managers can prioritize activities that maximize positive employee outcomes effectively.

Human capital data storage and 'big (HR) data' manipulation

To be able to realize the potential of predictive HR analytics, all of us are reliant upon what current and historical data is available. Predictive HR analytics relies completely on good data; we cannot look for patterns in data when the available data is limited and sketchy. Thus the success of HR analytics is completely reliant on the availability of good people-related information. As we discuss in Chapter 2, increasingly HR functions are not necessarily faced with the problem of there being a lack of data available – they are often faced with the problem that there is too much data to know what to do with. Much has been talked about in the popular and practitioner press about 'big data' (we discuss this in Chapter 2). Thus a challenge often faced by an HR analytics team is what to do with all the people-related HR data that is available. Once we have sufficient HR-related data, one of the biggest challenges is getting that data into the right format for analysis (we walk through an example of this in Chapter 2).

Useful HR-related data is made up of many different types of information and might include the following:

- skills and qualifications
- measures of particular competencies
- training attended
- levels of employee engagement
- customer satisfaction data
- performance appraisal records
- pay, bonus and remuneration data

It takes time and considerable manipulation of data files to make sure that the analyses conducted are appropriate to the type of data available, so Chapter 2 talks more about systems and data, and Chapter 3 will help you to determine which analyses to conduct for which circumstance. Ultimately, the data that is available (and the data that is missing) is the key determining factor on what kind of analysis can be carried out and what business questions can be answered. The other important factor is respect for the 'head space' required to be able to fully engage with the data, the analysis and what it all means for the organization.

Predictors, prediction and predictive modelling

By definition, central to the idea of 'predictive' HR analytics is that something can be 'predicted'. One of the critiques sometimes posed at predictive HR analytics is that the 'predictive' part is very rarely realized. Obviously, if the future was known by an organization then this would be extremely useful and managers would be able to make strategic decisions in order to exploit it. Presumably this is one of the reasons why 'predictive analytics' as a term has become so popular. However, in terms of analytics, there are a number of ways that we can use the term 'predictive' and it is worth distinguishing this at the start so that we can be comfortable with our use of the term in this book (and indeed the title of the book!).

One of the ways that we (and others) use the term 'prediction' is related to the idea of identifying 'predictors' or potential 'causal' factors that help explain why a particular feature or measure shows variation (e.g. why performance levels vary amongst employees). As we explain in Chapter 3, some of the analytic techniques that we use aim to explore relationships between many different types of data (or variables) in order to identify 'predictors' of some important HR outcome (such as employee performance or staff turnover). This type of analysis is used to identify trends and relationships between multiple factors with the hope of obtaining information that suggests the possible causes of variation in the phenomenon that we are hoping to predict. Assuming that we find a range of significant features of our people-related data where variation is associated (in a unique way) with an increase or decrease in what we hope to account for, we can say that we have found potential 'predictors'. In this context one can also refer to these predictors as potential 'drivers' of our outcome. Importantly, the use of the word 'predictors' here implies that we seek out and have found potential 'causes' of variation on the feature we are trying to predict (see Chapter 12 for our discussion of causality and challenges of assuming that relationships found in data imply 'causality'). Almost all of our case study chapters (Chapters 4–9) utilize analytics that relate to this form of the word 'prediction'.

A second use of the term in the context of 'predictive HR analytics' is the use of 'predictive modelling'. Here, we take features and findings of our analysis (for example, where we identify a series of factors that were related to variations in staff productivity or sales), then we apply our model to help demonstrate or 'predict' what would happen to our key outcome variable (e.g. staff productivity or sales) if we could do something to change or adjust the key drivers that we have identified. We demonstrate this use of the word 'prediction' in Chapter 10.

Finally, a third use of the term 'prediction' that we can use in the context of 'predictive HR analytics' is that we can translate the findings from our 'predictive models' where we identified 'predictors' of variation in our particular outcome variable (e.g. staff productivity or sales) and use the resulting model to 'predict' how current or future employees (or teams) may behave (e.g. staff productivity or sales) in the future. We also demonstrate this use of the word 'prediction' in Chapter 10 where we show how, through identifying patterns and trends in existing data, you can apply a particular algorithm to newly collected information so as to provide evidence-based predictions of possible future behaviour that can help managers to make a decision.

Importantly, this book can help provide a 'walk-through' and demonstrate to students of HR analytics how they can apply statistics in order to fully utilize all aspects of the promise that the term 'predictive HR analytics' implies.

Current state of HR analytic capabilities
and professional or academic training

As mentioned, the field has moved on considerably since the previous edition of previous editions of the Edwards and Edwards book (2016 and 2019); there now seems to be a much greater availability of HR/people analytics training providers that service the professional HR community. In 2016 there was an obvious scarcity of this, but a number of academic institutions are now including HR/people analytics modules in their teaching (including the two universities that the first author has worked at since the first edition of this book). There has also been a general growth in data analytics and business analytics academic programmes available.

We discussed previously how HR training provision generally does not tend to include either intermediate or advanced level quantitative analyses; ultimately, there are no general expectations that HR should include analytics, and it is often the case that students can get to an HR Masters level without having ever been trained in statistics. Certainly, the vast majority of people who enter the HR profession (in the UK at least) do not have the required skills to be able to carry out any sophisticated predictive HR analytics. The level of analytic skills that HR graduates possess will often be dependent upon the degree that they studied at undergraduate level; for example, an undergraduate degree in a traditional discipline such as economics, mathematics or psychology would have statistics as a substantial part of the degree content. Within many countries, even when students have come from a business or management degree, such students can often sidestep statistics (almost) completely. Up until 2018, HR may have been seen by some students as a 'safe haven' from numbers. In addition to this, many HR professionals move into HR without formal academic training and are unlikely to have had any formal training in statistics. If we take the UK as an example and we look at the competency requirements for membership into the Chartered Institute of Personnel and Development (CIPD) up to and before 2018, even with advanced-level module expectations there was very little requirement that candidates develop numerical abilities (let alone statistical abilities). At the time of writing, the authors have been informed that the CIPD is preparing a new set of professional standards, and quantitative skills will be included in this to a greater degree.

Recent research, however, is beginning to show how important analytic competencies are in the HR profession. Kryscynski et al (2017) showed a positive relationship between ratings of analytic competencies and ratings of performance from a number of stakeholders. However, Minbaeva (2017) reports on a 2015 Deloitte survey that found 75 per cent of companies surveyed indicated 'human capital analytics' was important for business performance but only 8 per cent had strong capabilities. A 2018 CIPD survey of the state of HR analytics in the profession showed considerable geographical variation in HR capabilities with advanced analytics, with only 21 per cent of UK respondents stating that they had confidence in conducting advanced analytics (and only 6 per cent indicating that they use these regularly).

In terms of how an HR team gets the competencies required to conduct advanced analytics, there is a debate about how best to set up an HR analytics offering/team (Rasmussen and Ulrich, 2015; Edwards, 2018) and data scientists/quantitative scientists who do not originate from the field of HR are an important resource to draw upon, to include in the HR analytics team. This is mainly because HR specialists rarely have the requisite skills, even though there is a perceived need for the HR profession to have these capabilities. This skills/capability gap is, however, something that this book hopes to do something about! Whether the HR professional is a generalist, a specialist in one particular area (such as talent, diversity or engagement), or the head of HR for a large multinational organization, the ability to identify and understand trends and patterns, to take bias and gut instinct out of decision making, and to predict organizational challenges is something that will set them apart in becoming a credible, high-performing HR professional (helping the organization to be more successful). This competence gap needs to be addressed if the HR profession is to fully exploit the opportunities that Huselid is alluding to in the quote earlier in this chapter.

Importantly, one of the key aims of this book is to help educate HR students and practitioners so as to help have a positive impact on the profession as a whole by adding to the quantitative literacy of people within it. Of course, in trying to achieve this aim, we will always be confronted with the phenomenon of many people having an automatic 'off switch' when it comes to statistics. This is no doubt why books out there have titles such as *Statistics For People Who Think They Hate Statistics* and *Statistics Without Tears*, etc. We argue, and truly believe, that having a strong quantitative analytic capability and knowledge of statistics will provide a firm foundation for any HR professional. Thus, mastering the HR metric by learning to carry out predictive HR analytics will fundamentally strengthen the skillset of the profession.

Business applications of modelling

Almost all of the analyses presented in this book will have significant business implications and application; sometimes this is obvious, and sometimes it requires a careful consideration of the results of the models tested. One of the things that the HR analytics team will need to be able to do, as a matter of course, is to be able to translate analysis findings to potential business applications. We discuss this in Chapter 10 where we give some examples of translating our predictive models to specific applications. However, we only touch the surface of presenting examples of ways in which the analytics in this book could be translated to specific business applications. Importantly, any HR analytics team should instil a mentality of always looking to answer the 'So what?' question (one that they will inevitably be asked when presenting their analytic results). The analytics team need to be always on the lookout for how their findings could be translated to useful practice knowledge, and whether any particular knowledge gained can help to strengthen and steer the organization's people strategy.

HR analytics and HR people strategy

In learning and applying the methods outlined in this book, it should become obvious to the analytics team that it is possible to use analytical models to help steer, adjust and even drive business strategy. Ultimately, the analytics approaches recommended can provide evidence-based pointers for practice and can help take some emotion and gut instinct out of 'people' decision making. Methods such as those described in all of the case study chapters should be able to help highlight key strategic factors to focus on when devising a people strategy plan, and the methods outlined in Chapter 9 (monitoring the impact of people interventions) will assist the HR function in tracking and monitoring the success of their people plan (proving opportunities for reflection and adjustment to the plan). We discuss how to use predictive models to improve performance, turnover and hiring decisions – essential areas of HR on which the success of the function is measured. Hopefully the methods discussed in this book will assist HR analytics teams and their organizations to make sound, evidence-based people decisions that will help the organization to prosper – and, in doing so, value the HR function.

Becoming a persuasive HR function

The development of HR's strategic role has been an evolution... The next step in the evolution is for HR professionals, and particularly senior HR professionals, to develop what we call analytic literacy.

SOURCE Huselid and Becker (2005: 279)

As you work through this book, you will begin to understand the opportunities that can open up for answering business questions, even those that have not been asked yet! We believe that this 'analytic literacy' will help transform the HR function. An HR function that fully utilizes predictive HR analytics capabilities will be more credible because the function will be able to present robust 'hard' evidence to show that it has a good understanding of what makes its people tick, along with knowledge of who is likely to perform well, who is likely to leave, which parts of the organization are showing race or gender bias, which candidates are likely to be successful in the organization, and which interventions had a significant impact on the organization and which did not. The function will be able to carry out substantial 'what if' scenario modelling to help build solid business cases that help the organization to make decisions around whether particular investments are likely to be worthwhile, and what the return on those investments are likely to be.

By systematically going through this book and the exercises provided, any developing HR analytics team should have increased their capabilities and learnt many things that will help them to become *Masters of the HR Metric*.

References

Angrave, D, Charlwood, A, Kirkpatrick, I, Lawrence, M and Stuart, M (2016) HR and analytics: Why HR is set to fail the big data challenge, *Human Resource Management Journal*, 26, pp 1–11

Bersin, J (2012) *The HR Measurement Framework*, Bersin and Associates Research Report, November

CIPD (2018) People analytics: Driving business performance with people data, CIPD. www.cipd.org/uk/knowledge/reports/people-data-driving-performance (archived at https://perma.cc/UX3X-2ZXB)

Edwards, M R (2018) HR metrics and analytics, in *E-HRM: Digital approaches, directions and applications*, ed M Thite, Routledge, Abingdon, UK

Edwards, M R and Edwards, K (2016) *Predictive HR Analytics: Mastering the HR metric*, Kogan Page, London

Edwards, M R and Edwards, K (2019) *Predictive HR Analytics: Mastering the HR metric*, 2nd edn, Kogan Page, London

Edwards, M R and Edwards, K (2024) *Predictive HR Analytics: Mastering the HR metric*, 3rd edn, Kogan Page, London

Edwards, M R, Charlwood, A , Guenole, N and Marler, J (2022) *HR Analytics: An emerging field finding its place in the world alongside simmering ethical challenges*, Human Resource Management Journal

Edwards, M R, Minbaeva, D, Levenson, A and Huselid, M (2024) *Global Workforce Analytics*, Routledge, Abingdon

Ferrar, J and Green, D (2021). *Excellence in People Analytics: How to use workforce data to create business value*, Kogan Page, London

Fitz-enz, J and Mattox II, J R (2014) *Predictive Analytics for Human Resources*, Wiley, New Jersey

Guenole, N, Ferrar, J, and Feinzig, S (2017) *The Power of People: Learn how successful organizations use workforce analytics to improve business performance*, Pearson FT Press, London

Huselid, M (2014) The corporate mirror, D'Amore-McKim School of Business, web.archive. org/web/20160329115926/http://www.damoremckimleadersatworkblog.com/corporate-mirror-looking-big-data-analytics-workforce-management/#sthash.4qx5y7F3.dpuf (archived at https://perma.cc/P8E5-ZNE6)

Huselid, M A and Becker, B E (2005) Improving human resources' analytical literacy: Lessons from moneyball, in *Future of Human Resource Management*, ed D Ulrich, M Losey and S Meisinger, John Wiley and Sons, New York

Kryscynski, D, Reeves, C, Stice-Lusvardi, R, Ulrich, M and Russell, G (2017) Analytical abilities and the performance of HR professionals, *Human Resource Management*, Online First, doi.org/10.1002/hrm.21854 (archived at https://perma.cc/5FVF-PEMX)

Larsson, A-S and Edwards M R (2021) Insider econometrics meets people analytics and strategic human resource management, *International Journal of Human Resource Management*, 33 (12): 2373–2419

Levenson, A (2015) *Strategic Analytics: Advancing strategy execution and organizational effectiveness*, Berrett-Koehler Publishers, Oakland, CA

Levenson, A, Minbaeva, D, Huselid, M and Edwards, M R (2024) Introduction to global workforce analytics, in *Global Workforce Analytics*, M R Edwards, D Minbaeva, A Levenson and M Huselid, Chapter 1, Routledge, Abingdon.

LinkedIn (2023) LinkedIn jobs on the rise 2023: 25 US roles that are growing in demand, LinkedIn. www.linkedin.com/pulse/linkedin-jobs-rise-2023-25-us-roles-growing-demand-linkedin-news (archived at https://perma.cc/2GUA-TZM4)

Marler, J H and Boudreau, J W (2017) An evidence-based review of HR analytics, *The International Journal of Human Resource Management*, 28 (1), pp 3–26

Minbaeva, D B (2017) Building credible human capital analytics for organizational competitive advantage, Human Resource Management, Online First, doi.org/10.1002/hrm.21848 (archived at https://perma.cc/5FVF-PEMX)

Rasmussen, T and Ulrich, D (2015) Learning from practice: How HR analytics avoids being a management fad, *Organizational Dynamics*, 44, pp 236–42

Rasmussen, T H, Ulrich, M and Ulrich, D (2024) Moving people analytics from insight to impact, Human Resource Development Review, journals.sagepub.com/doi/abs/10.1177/15344843231207220 (archived at https://perma.cc/2W6P-7MZ4)

Rousseau, D M and Barends, E G R (2011) Becoming an evidence-based HR practitioner, *Human Resource Management Journal*, 21, pp 221–35

Van der Laken, P (2018) Data-driven human resource management: The rise of people analytics and its application to expatriate management, PhD Thesis, Tilburg University

02

HR information systems and data

We hope that Chapter 1 has given you a good understanding of the benefits that predictive HR analytics techniques can bring to an organization. Before we get into the actual analysis piece, it is worth taking time out to understand the lay of the land. What type of data do you have in the organization already: what illuminating nuggets of information may be hidden on a spreadsheet in a colleague's personal folder, or the sales database, or the learning and development (L&D) records that could all tell a story when the pieces come together?

To illustrate with a simple example, looking at the customer satisfaction survey results alone can provide some useful information about how our customers feel about our customer-facing staff. It is difficult, though, to determine prescriptive action that should be taken from customer satisfaction survey results by themselves. If the results are poor overall, we may issue a guidance paper to all customer-facing staff. If, however, the data is linked to L&D team records, we might find that staff who attended a relationship management course in the previous quarter obtain the best customer service results. Or if we link it to our client profile information, we might find that it is our underrepresented groups (UG) clients in branches outside major cities that are most dissatisfied, suggesting that we may need to provide some unconscious bias or diversity awareness training. The more relevant information we have linked, the better chance we have of understanding the big picture of what is actually going on, which in turn means the better chance we have of correctly diagnosing a problem and prescribing a solution that will work – we don't want to spend time and money putting a plaster cast on the entire foot if all that is broken is the middle toe.

In this chapter, we look at:

- Information source examples: what you are likely to find and where.
- The software: a short review of analytics software packages.
- Using R: becoming familiar with the R environment.
- Preparing the data: what the data looks like, getting it into R and preparing it for analysis.
- Big data: what it is and why it is valuable to organizations.

While it would be impossible to list all of the possible information sources in all organizations, the next section looks at what many organizations are likely to have and may give you ideas on where to look.

Information sources

The information available in the form of data to be analysed will vary greatly depending on the type of organization. In this book, we look not only at the data typically managed by an HR department, but also important customer satisfaction and operational data that is key to running a successful organization. The key is not to be limited by what is immediately available in the HR department, even if you are in an HR role. It is when the information is expanded, linked together and analysed with rigorous statistical techniques that we find what is truly happening in our organization. Some examples of the types of data we consider in this book are outlined in Table 2.1.

TABLE 2.1 Information source examples

Information Source	Description	Example
HR database (such as SAP, Oracle or Workday)	Information describing the employee across a wide range of people-management activities, including employee personal details, performance, diversity data, promotion information. Further information on data protection and storage of personal data can be found in Chapter 12 (Reflection on HR analytics: Usage, ethics and limitations).	Age, gender, education level, role, salary, performance ratings, disabilities, tenure, sickness absence, leaver information, country location, team leader, etc.
Employee attitude survey data (often stored in survey programmes and exported to Excel)	Survey results from annual employee attitude surveys. Either managed in-house or with an external survey provider organization. Typically containing employee engagement data. The information will depend purely on the questions asked in the survey; however, the examples to the right will give an idea of what can be included. Further information on employee engagement and survey data can be found in Chapter 5 (Employee attitude surveys – engagement and workforce perceptions).	Job-strain level, employee engagement, job satisfaction, person-organization fit and perceptions of justice.

(continued)

TABLE 2.1 (Continued)

Information Source	Description	Example
Customer satisfaction survey data (often stored in survey programmes and exported to Excel)	Often collected by marketing or sales functions, customer satisfaction survey data often provides extremely useful information about customer preferences and, when linked to employee profile and operational data, can help organizations to identify how changes to employee skills and behaviours, as well as any operational or process changes, can have a direct impact on the customer experience. Further information on employee engagement and survey data can be found in the employee engagement case study in Chapter 5.	Customer ratings on specific services, branches and customer-facing employees, customer loyalty, customer preferences, customer satisfaction, likelihood of further business.
Sales performance data	Information usually owned by the sales function, recording details of sales performance and revenues. This information is key to determining organizational revenues and the success or otherwise of salespeople and teams in meeting targets. When linked with employee data and operational information it can also help determine the conditions under which salespeople and teams are more likely to succeed or, put another way, what individual or team characteristics tend to make for a more positive bottom line.	Average monthly sales, number of new customers introduced, meeting or not meeting target, individual or team daily, weekly or monthly sales.
Operational performance data	Information or data measuring the successful running of the business. Usually referring to efficiency.	Supermarket scan rates, call-centre call durations, average number of calls dropped out, average number of queries resolved on first contact, time taken to onboard a new customer, etc.

By linking data sources and thinking broadly across the whole organization, we are able to model organizational patterns of behaviour and link HR and people-management practices directly with revenue and efficiency. In order to link and analyse the information available with ease, we need to use a statistical analysis package, of which there are many available on the market.

Analysis software options

There is no shortage of statistical software programs and, because many of them are prohibitively expensive for individual users, the one you use is likely to be determined by the organization or university you are currently involved with. The good news is that there is lots of overlap between the packages, and the analyses generally produce the same core output; once you learn one, it is relatively straightforward to transfer those skills to another system. So although in this book we only use R for our examples, the skills you learn and the analytic methods we take you through may be applied in most other systems. Here is a sample of some commonly used statistical analysis tools with varying degrees of difficulty. Some come with a cost (Kaur, 2023), while others are open source. Also see Kane (2012) for an earlier discussion of statistical software.

R

In a change from previous editions by Edwards, Edwards and Jang (2016, 2019, 2024), we make the statistical language R the primary statistical tool. This has multiple benefits. R is free to use, has a vast collection of packages that cover the basics and beyond, and is often at the cutting edge – its open nature means a community of developers, statisticians and academics constantly add functionality to it. Importantly, being open source, functions can be examined for anyone to see, so there is little mystery to what is happening with your data.

While there are numerous benefits to using R, it also presents some challenges. Using R means typing out computer code, due to its heritage as a programming language. So you will need to learn to do a little programming to fully utilize the benefits of R. Typing out code means that it is more difficult to learn than SPSS or Minitab, making the learning curve steep. Also, with R, you will not see and manipulate a data file in the same intuitive way as you do with Excel or SPSS. With Excel or SPSS, you see your data all the time and can see any changes that you have made to this. While we are used to seeing the data in front of us all the time, there is a good reason to separate the manipulation of data from the analysis of data. Conceptually, these are two very different tasks that should be done sequentially, not together.

The trade-off for the greater difficulty of R is that it allows you to use a much larger range of statistical procedures. R has a fair amount of statistical utility built into the program. Additionally, one of the stand-out features of R is that you can install additional analytic packages for free (over 20,000 packages at time of writing), which vastly broadens the scope of analytic tools that it can handle. Each package contains a collection of programs that help you accomplish an analytic goal. Thus, once you have learned the basics of R and built a library of code to help you with your analyses, you can keep adding elements that broaden its (and your) capabilities.

You can, for example, conduct social network analyses, create interactive visualizations/dashboards, conduct machine learning, as well as generate print-ready reports.

We will provide examples of R code that enable you to run all of the statistical analyses in the book as a download at www.koganpage.com/urhra. Thus this book will help ease the learning curve. It also enables R users to estimate the models presented in the book with R.

It is worth noting that 95 per cent of users of statistical software packages – and arguably HR analytics professionals – could get what they need from packages such as SPSS and Minitab, which appear to be more intuitive. However they may at some point reach a limit of capability, which generally does not happen with R, as there will often be a package that you could install into the program. Kane (2012) also notes that the graphical output that R produces 'pretty much blow[s] away anything that seems feasible in other packages'. The steep learning curve required to get off the ground can be a big inhibitor (and be intimidating) for those who are learning statistics at the same time as trying to learn R. This book will help ease that learning curve. Having said this, R users tend to get very enthusiastic about the program and there is a big support community of R users on the net that readily share R learning resources.

Julia

Like R, Julia is a statistical programming language. It is newer than R and rapidly evolving. It has some advantages, such as being faster to conduct analyses. But for the kind of tasks that an HR professional is likely to encounter, the speed advantage is minimal. It can conduct most analyses, but does not have the large and enthusiastic set of developers and users. Advanced R users will be well advised to keep an eye on Julia's development.

Python

Python is one of the leading general-purpose programming languages and, similar to R, relies on a command line interface. This means that, unless you have experience with programming languages (in which case you would find it quite easy to learn), there is a steep learning curve to begin with compared to systems with user-friendly interfaces. Its application, however, is wide-ranging and it can be used for traditional statistical analysis as well as for machine learning. Python is also free to download and there are many online communities for experienced and new users alike.

Unlike R, which was designed with specific features to support statistics and data analytics, Python is more of a general purpose programming language and hence its functionality is more wide-ranging. Python is also reported to be much faster than R and the learning curve less steep.

SPSS

SPSS is a user-friendly statistical program with a graphical user interface and a point-and-click menu for running procedures. It is relatively easy to learn and, although it does have the option for coding for the more advanced user, it is the clear leader of all the statistical software packages in its ability to run many complex procedures by using the mouse and menus alone. Although SPSS does not cover all statistical procedures, it does cover what is required by 95 per cent of users (and each new version seems to have more and more options). SPSS is a great package for being able to transfer output to other formats for reports. Although it can sometimes be slow at processing very large amounts of data, SPSS is good for extracting subsets of smaller data for analysis and the process to do this is relatively simple to learn. Once you have the data loaded into SPSS, a great benefit is the ease at which it is possible to manipulate that data (e.g. to relabel and create new variables, etc). The newest versions of SPSS have expanded functionality by allowing the use of programming languages such as R and Python (further discussed below) via plug-ins. This allows use of advanced statistical and data manipulation methods that may not be available otherwise.

Minitab

Minitab also has a user-friendly menu-based user interface for running procedures and has been noted as the simplest package to learn. Like SPSS, Minitab enables users to do most analysis procedures without having to understand the coding syntax. It does not cover all statistical procedures, but does cover what is required by 95 per cent of users. In terms of manipulating data, once the data is in Minitab, it can sometimes be difficult to change (Kane, 2012). It can also be difficult to transfer output to other formats for inclusion in reports.

Stata

Although Stata does have some menus, it is primarily command-line driven and hence takes a bit longer to master. Stata does offer a more comprehensive range of statistical procedures and is often used by economists. It is quite good at being able to manipulate data once it is in the system; however, the user will need to learn the command-line interface systems in the first instance. On the negative side, it can be difficult to transfer data and output to other formats for reports (Kane, 2012).

SAS

SAS is primarily a command-line-driven package with relatively few menu-driven procedures. For this reason it can take some time to master. It is a very powerful package and offers a more comprehensive range of statistical procedures than the others discussed here. It is also the leader in being able to handle large amounts of data, which could be pertinent depending on the type of organization, and particularly relevant considering the section on 'big data' later in this chapter. It is also possible to extract small subsets of large data quickly. Finally, it can also be difficult in SAS to transfer output to other formats for reports (Kane, 2012).

JASP

JASP is another open source/free statistics program which supports many of the classical statistics methods we cover in this book, as well as some Bayesian statistics methods. It is very user friendly and has some nice reporting features as well as helpful videos available to users. Whilst the functionality is somewhat limited, beginners will find this a useful tool. See jasp-stats.org.

Jamovi

Jamovi is another new, very exciting and free statistical program. It mainly has a Windows interface but can also incorporate an R code interface. At the moment there are some limitations to the analytic tools available but the programmers are adding new functions regularly. You can add analytics utilities to it (that are available) and this includes some very useful extensions. There are restrictions to the analyses options in places, which create some limitations, but for a free package you can run many models using a simple user interface.

Using artificial intelligence and large language models to aid analyses

Before we introduce R, a discussion about artificial intelligence (AI) and large language models (LLMs) is necessary. In just a few years, remarkable and visible improvements in AI have produced a number of LLMs, including the well-known ChatGPT. LLMs inspire awe. They allow human-like dialogue with a vast library of human knowledge, providing answers to both common and complex queries. It can pass exams meant for law school (Choi et al, 2023), and MBA programs (Terwiesch, 2023). In classrooms and in the workplace, they are being used to augment and sometimes replace human labour across many tasks. They have potential use in HR analytics because they can be used to analyse data – a paid subscription to ChatGPT gives you access to its data analysis module, where you can upload data and have it analyse it for you, as well as to generate useful tables and visualizations. It can also generate a written report summarizing the findings. The latest versions of its competitor, Claude, can download data from multiple internet sources and aggregate the information to generate a detailed analysis.

You might ask why it's worth bothering to learn analysis methods if it can be done by chatting with an LLM. Having used these tools for ourselves, we find there are several reasons to learn the fundamentals, as we will cover in this book. First, LLMs can be wrong. They can 'hallucinate', or generate plausible-sounding but incorrect information (Cowen and Tabarrok, 2023). It takes a trained person to understand whether responses given by an LLM are correct or not. So, an LLM can help you save time, but we do not think it should dictate your understanding of data and analysis methods. Second, LLMs are limited. At the time of writing, the data analysis functions of ChatGPT were limited in the amount of data they could handle. Those working with large data sets may find that only a portion of their data can be analysed using an LLM, or none at all. Of course, we expect the capabilities of LLMs to improve over time, but it is a current limitation. Third, many LLMs are not private. Uploading data to ChatGPT or other online LLMs may represent a breach of privacy, because the data is being sent to a computer that is not under your or your organization's control. Confidential information like addresses, performance or salary may not be analysable using online LLMs. Finally, LLMs do not have contextualized understanding of data. By default, LLMs do not have the background information about how the data was collected, understanding about norms or important contextual information that may not be immediately apparent. For example, studying the relationship between commission earned in the last three months and sales person gender may reveal a number of people who are outliers, but closer consideration of the individuals might reveal some are on maternity/paternity leave, or one gender predominantly works in areas with more/less competition. Contextual factors such as these are always important to consider, and LLMs cannot always have knowledge of them.

This is not to discount their use in augmenting the analyst's capabilities. The authors of this book have used LLMs to generate R code for data analysis, with the understanding that it may not always be correct and testing the generated code is necessary before using it in proper analyses. LLMs can help if the code you wrote does not work, and troubleshooting is required. A programming language requires sticking to a strict syntax, and an extra space, a missing comma or an unintended capitalization can lead to error. They can also be used to explain what another person's R code does, especially if it is not well documented. If any R code in the book is not clear to you, we encourage you to use an LLM to explain what a particular line of code does. And they can also be helpful for starting an inquiry, such as asking which analyses might be appropriate given a particular circumstance, followed with additional research in more authoritative sources like a textbook. Sometimes we lack the vocabulary to start asking the right questions and LLMs can be helpful in this regard. Overall, we conclude that the more you know, the more that you can get out of LLMs. Greater knowledge can help you reject incorrect suggestions by the LLM as well as help ask questions of greater specificity, which increases LLM response quality (Cowen and Tabarrok, 2023).

Using R

In this book, we have made R the primary statistical tool. Why? Because it is free, powerful and flexible. Although it appears less user-friendly than SPSS, as featured in the sister book, its price is hard to compete with and it allows users to conduct advanced analyses.

But, regardless of the software, the analyses we show throughout the book should be largely replicable with other statistical tools, such as the ones mentioned in the previous section. There may be minor differences across statistical tools, as slightly different default options, labels and computation methods are used by each. So a user familiar with another program should be able to translate these examples in another program and obtain similar results. Thus, the essence of the output should be similar across programs. Once you get to know one statistical software tool, it is much easier for you to learn a second one – because you are essentially trying to do the same thing. The work beforehand – knowing which test or which procedure to run – is where the real skill comes in. Chapter 3 (analysis strategies) will walk you through the steps in determining which statistical test to use in which situation. It is also worth noting that the screenshots and commands used in this book are based on R version 4.3.2, on MacOS.

To use R, you will first need to install it. The homepage for the R statistical project is: www.r-project.org. You will be able to download the latest version there. In addition to R, we highly recommend installing RStudio (posit.co). RStudio is an integrated development environment (IDE). IDEs provide users with a convenient visual interface they can use to write code for analyses, execute it and visualize results. Both R and RStudio are free. While there is a paid version of RStudio, it is not necessary for conducting analyses, and we only recommend using the paid version if your organization cannot use open source software.

Once you have installed R and RStudio, open RStudio. The first thing you will notice about R is that it has multiple windows.

The RStudio interface

The RStudio interface is unlike many programs you have used previously, such as Microsoft Excel or SPSS. There are no clickable menus for analyses or buttons you can press to run functions. Instead, the idea behind an IDE is to help you write code, execute it, and to look at the results.

2.1

The interface is divided into four panes. We'll look at each of those in more detail.

On the top left is the Source panel. This is the panel where we write our code. You can see a tab called 'Untitled1'. That is a blank R document where you can write your code. Similar to modern web browsers, you can have multiple tabs open with different R documents in each one. Although there are other buttons and tools available, we will save explanations for each function until it is needed. If it is the first time you have installed RStudio, you may not see a source pane. In that case, go to the menu bar, select *File >> New File >> R script*. This will make the Source panel visible, with an untitled R script, as in Figure 2.2.

2.2   The Source pane

On the top right, we have the Environment pane. It shows all of the files, data sets and objects that are currently loaded in R and ready to use. You can click on 'Import dataset' to work with a new data set. Note that R can open the common CSV files, in addition to Microsoft Excel, SPSS data files and most major formats.

One important thing to note is that 'opening' a data file in R is not quite the same as 'opening' a file in Excel or SPSS. In those programs, when you open a file and work with it, you are directly interacting with that data file. In contrast, when you import a file into the R environment, R makes a copy of that data and stores it in the environment. Anything you do to the data within the environment does not affect the original file. While making a copy of the data can seem like an extra step, this can have one major benefit. This ensures that the original data is preserved in its original form. Any changes you make along the way can be traced back to reproducible code and inspected for errors at a later stage. From experience, we have encountered many unintended changes to raw data, such as an accidental key press deleting a cell of data; or creating a column of data with a formula we subsequently have forgotten. By leaving the original data untouched and documenting all of the changes in code, we can prevent this from happening.

There are some additional tabs worth mentioning. The History tab shows a running list of all of the code executed, the Connections pane helps you to connect R to local or internet databases, such as ODBC and SQL. Finally, the Tutorial tab has a series of helpful tutorials to help you get started.

2.3   The Environment pane

The Console pane is on the bottom left. You can type code directly into the console and run it there, which is one way to use R. It also shows the results of any code executed. 'Executing code' can mean anything from importing data to transforming a variable or conducting data analyses. Any result from executing code will be shown in the console, and this is where we will see much of the results of our work.

You will also see a Terminal tab, which is a command line interface for working with your computer. While it is useful for general programming it is of less use for data analysis, so we will not mention it further.

2.4   The Console pane

The Help pane is on the bottom right. By default, it focuses on the Packages tab, which shows you the packages that are currently installed. We'll discuss packages in more detail, but these are bundles of programs that extend the capability of R. They can be downloaded for free. The availability of many free packages (over 20,000!) is a benefit of using R. You'll see the Help pane of one of the authors in Figure 2.5 – you'll see lots of packages already listed and this will differ from those who have a fresh installation. People will vary in what they have installed, because they will have different needs. To install a package, you will need an internet connection as R/RStudio will only include a small number of packages by default. From time to time, your packages may need updating and you can do so by clicking the *Update* button in green.

Other tabs are also useful. The Files tab helps to navigate your computer, and can help you to load files into R, the Plots tab displays graphs you generate, the Help tab offers help for each program, the Viewer tab can be used to look at html files or a local web application, and the Presentation tab can be used to look at presentation files created in R. One note is that this description of RStudio is based on default settings – much of the layout can be customized, including colour schemes, the positioning of panes and so forth. For simplicity, we stick to what you will experience with just the default options.

2.5   The Help pane

Files Plots Packages Help Viewer Presentation		
Install Update		
Name	Description	Version
System Library		
abind	Combine Multidimensional Arrays	1.4–5
ACEt	Estimating Dynamic Heritability and Twin Model Comparison	1.9.0
admisc	Adrian Dusa's Miscellaneous	0.34
AER	Applied Econometrics with R	1.2–10
AICcmodavg	Model Selection and Multimodel Inference Based on (Q)AIC(c)	2.3–2
apaTables	Create American Psychological Association (APA) Style Tables	2.0.8
arm	Data Analysis Using Regression and Multilevel/Hierarchical Models	1.13–1
askpass	Password Entry Utilities for R, Git, and SSH	1.2.0
assertthat	Easy Pre and Post Assertions	0.2.1
AzureAuth	Authentication Services for Azure Active Directory	1.3.3
AzureGraph	Simple Interface to 'Microsoft Graph'	1.3.4
backports	Reimplementations of Functions Introduced Since R–3.0.0	1.4.1
base	The R Base Package	4.3.2
base64enc	Tools for base64 encoding	0.1–3
bayestestR	Understand and Describe Bayesian Models and Posterior Distributions	0.13.1
BH	Boost C++ Header Files	1.81.0–1
bigD	Flexibly Format Dates and Times to a Given Locale	0.2.0
binom	Binomial Confidence Intervals for Several Parameterizations	1.1–1.1
BiocManager	Access the Bioconductor Project Package Repository	1.30.22
BiocVersion	Set the appropriate version of Bioconductor packages	3.17.1
bit	Classes and Methods for Fast Memory–Efficient Boolean Selections	4.0.5
bit64	A S3 Class for Vectors of 64bit Integers	4.0.5

A paradigm shift

We anticipate a lot of questions at this stage. People familiar with Excel and SPSS will likely be puzzled about the sparse interface. There's no immediately obvious way to look at and play with data, no buttons or menus to select for analyses, and a lot of different windows to keep track of. Instead, using R means typing out code, which we admit can be intimidating and, at first appearance, time consuming. Let's deal with these concerns one by one.

It is possible to inspect and manipulate data using R, and we will guide you through it in the next section. You will see that R does not make data inspection and manual correction a priority. The implicit assumption is that R will work with data, not be a tool for data entry. The lack of buttons and menu items mean that it is not clear how one should go about conducting analyses. This is partly because of the open nature of programming languages, and the availability of a large number of libraries. Imagine designing a computer interface that has buttons or menu items for each of the 20,000+ libraries currently available. There is simply not enough room, even on the largest of monitors, to squeeze all of that in. Regarding the large number of windows to keep track of (we highlighted four panes and multiple tabs within them), we routinely look at only a few. Finally, regarding the need to type in code, we consider it a major benefit. Clicking on buttons or menu items is quick to do, compared to typing out the equivalent commands. But people often forget which buttons or menu items they clicked in sequence, leading to confusion about exactly what was done. With structured code, there is no such ambiguity. And while typing out code the first time can be slower, you'll notice that once you have mastered code for one kind of analysis, you can copy and paste that code for other uses, which saves you lots of time compared to clicking buttons or menu items.

So working in R requires us to change our mindset. Unlike Excel or SPSS, which is often used for manual data entry and prominently displays data, R and RStudio encourage you to think about what you will do with it, and be more systematic and meticulous about working with the data.

Creating a data set in R

Let us create a simple data set we can use with R. We talk about the different types of variables in detail in Chapter 3, but for now we focus on setting up the data. Let's use an example involving employee performance and compensation.

The annual performance review project manager, Remi, has forwarded you an email he has just received from the marketing team manager containing some key information about performance results of his team. For each of the five employees on the marketing team, the email contains the following information:

- employee ID
- performance rating
- salary adjustment (percentage)

Until you train Remi and the other managers to enter data into a spreadsheet (which you will soon see is much easier) rather than an email, for each manager you will have to go through the exercise set out below. The first step, then, is to create a dataframe and program in the data. Remi has at least promised to be consistent and provide you with the same information from each manager.

First, we will create a dataframe. 'Dataframe' is the technical term in R to describe a data set. This dataframe will have three columns, starting with an employee ID (*emp_id*), performance rating (*perf_rat*), and salary adjustment (*salary_adj*). As a guide when deciding on variable names:

- Make sure each variable name is unique. This makes sense – we would get confused about which one you were talking about if you had duplication. If you try having two identical variable names, R will append a number (.1) at the end of the second identical variable name.

- Try not have any spaces in the variable name. While R tolerates spaces in variable names, it is cumbersome to work with. Instead, use underscores as we have above.

- Stick with the alphabet. If you do use numbers and symbols, make sure they are not the first character.

- R is case sensitive. To save typing, use lowercase letters.

Before we begin, we note a key point of difference from working in SPSS. There are no variable labels in R. This means that long descriptions of variables should be stored in comments in your R file. We recommend including a description of every variable in your R or data files to ensure that both your future self and others will be able to understand what the variables mean. So at the top of your R file, we recommend writing these out as a comment (the code below is available in the file Ch2_1.R file in the supplementary download materials at www.koganpage.com/urhra):

```
# Create an empty dataframe with the following variables:
# emp_id = Employee ID, text values
# perf_rat = Performance rating (1 = very poor performer … 5 = Superhuman)
# salary_adj = Salary adjustment (number in percentages?)
```

The above code is a comment. Any line starting with a '#' will be ignored by R. On your screen, it should appear as green text, which means it will not be treated like computer code. Copy and paste the code above into the Source pane.

We then define a dataframe with the following code:

```
df <- data.frame(emp_id = character(), perf_rat = numeric(), salary_adj = numeric())
```

To explain the code above, we are using the *data.frame* program to define the three variables in the data set. The *character* after the *emp_id* indicates this will be a text variable, and the *numeric* after *perf_rat* and *salary_adj* variables indicates these will be numeric. In most cases in HR analytics, you will be working with numbers (*numeric*) as in the values for a variable measure such as *age* (e.g. 46, 55), or text values such as the variable *employee_first_name* (e.g. Joe, Mary, Bob), or a date, such as *start_date* (e.g. *24/07/2015*). It is important to set these up correctly before entering any data. The left-pointing arrow means that we assign the name *df* to this dataframe. So from now on, we will refer to this dataframe as *df* when working with it.

Copy the code above into the source pane. It should look like Figure 2.6:

2.6

```
O  Untitled1*
          Source on Save  Q  /  ▾                               Run
     1   # Create an empty dataframe with the following three variables:
     2   # emp_id = Employee ID
     3   # perf_rat = Performance rating (1 = very poor performer ... 5 = Superhuman)
     4   # salary_adj = Salary adjustment
     5
     6   df <- data.frame(emp_id = character(), perf_rat = numeric(), salary_adj = numeric())|
```

Now highlight the code by dragging the cursor over the entire line of code as in Figure 2.7 and click the *Run* button, as shown in Figure 2.7.

2.7

```
O  Untitled1*
          Source on Save  Q  /  ▾                               Run
     1   # Create an empty dataframe with the following three variables:
     2   # emp_id = Employee ID
     3   # perf_rat = Performance rating (1 = very poor performer ... 5 = Superhuman)
     4   # salary_adj = Salary adjustment
     5
     6   df <- data.frame(emp_id = character(), perf_rat = numeric(), salary_adj = numeric())|
```

A quick note: R is case sensitive. That means if you try to type in the command *Data.Frame* instead of *data.frame* above, R will give you an error, because, to it, *Data.Frame* is different to *data.frame*. This applies to variable names as well.

You will notice two things have happened. In the Environment pane, there is a new data set called *df*, with '*0 Obs. of 3 variables*'.

2.8

```
Environment  History  Connections  Tutorial
     Import Dataset ▾   155 MiB ▾                                    List ▾
R ▾    Global Environment ▾
Data
 df                          0 obs. of 3 variables
```

And in the Console pane, you will see the code:

2.9

```
Console   Terminal
R   R 4.3.2 · ~/

R version 4.3.2 (2023-10-31) -- "Eye Holes"
Copyright (C) 2023 The R Foundation for Statistical Computing
Platform: aarch64-apple-darwin20 (64-bit)

R is free software and comes with ABSOLUTELY NO WARRANTY.
You are welcome to redistribute it under certain conditions.
Type 'license()' or 'licence()' for distribution details.

  Natural language support but running in an English locale

R is a collaborative project with many contributors.
Type 'contributors()' for more information and
'citation()' on how to cite R or R packages in publications.

Type 'demo()' for some demos, 'help()' for on-line help, or
'help.start()' for an HTML browser interface to help.
Type 'q()' to quit R.

> df <- data.frame(emp_id = character(), perf_rat = numeric(), salary_adj = numeric())
>
```

In Figure 2.9, the chevron to mark a new line means that R is ready for the next command.

Now that we have an empty dataframe with pre-defined columns, we can add data to it. Let's define the first row. This will be employee 'A1234', who has a performance rating of 3, and salary adjustment of 2.

To add this row to the dataframe *df*, we can copy and paste this code into the Source pane:

```
df[1, ] <- c("A1234", 3, 2)
```

The code above says that the values *A1234, 3* and *2* should be assigned to the first row of the dataframe *df*. You can run this code by highlighting it and clicking the *Run* button, or through the keyboard shortcut *Control + Enter* (Windows and Linux) / *Command + Return* (MacOS). You will see now in the Environment pane that the dataframe *df* now has one row. The *c* in front of the brackets is a program that combines values you give it. In the code above, it combines the three elements of data (i.e. *A1234, 3, 2*) into one entity that can fill a row of entries in the *df* dataframe. You will encounter the program *c* a lot throughout your journey with R, as it is a basic tool required for many operations.

We can similarly fill in rows for the remaining four staff:

```
df[2, ] <- c("A3421", 5, 25)
df[3, ] <- c("A7654", 3, 2)
df[4, ] <- c("A5698", 4, 10)
df[5, ] <- c("A7854", 3, 2)
```

The Source pane should now look like Figure 2.10:

2.10

Source on Save

```
1   # Create an empty dataframe with the following variables: emp_id, perf_rat, salary_adj
2   # emp_id = Employee ID, text values
3   # perf_rat = Performance rating (1 = very poor performer _ 5 = Superhuman)
4   # salary_adj = Salary adjustment (number in percentages?)
5
6   df <- data.frame(emp_id = character(), perf_rat = numeric(), salary_adj = numeric())
7
8   df[1, ] <- c("A1234", 3, 2)
9   df[2, ] <- c("A3421", 5, 25)
10  df[3, ] <- c("A7654", 3, 2)
11  df[4, ] <- c("A5698", 4, 10)
12  df[5, ] <- c("A7854", 3, 2)
```

You can run this code by highlighting lines 8–12 (see Figure 2.11) and clicking the *Run* button or by using the keyboard shortcut (*Control* + *Enter*; Windows and Linux / *Command* + *Return* MacOS):

2.11

Source on Save

```
1   # Create an empty dataframe with the following variables: emp_id, perf_rat, salary_adj
2   # emp_id = Employee ID, text values
3   # perf_rat = Performance rating (1 = very poor performer _ 5 = Superhuman)
4   # salary_adj = Salary adjustment (number in percentages?)
5
6   df <- data.frame(emp_id = character(), perf_rat = numeric(), salary_adj = numeric())
7
8   df[1, ] <- c("A1234", 3, 2)
9   df[2, ] <- c("A3421", 5, 25)
10  df[3, ] <- c("A7654", 3, 2)
11  df[4, ] <- c("A5698", 4, 10)
12  df[5, ] <- c("A7854", 3, 2)|
```

You can view the completed dataframe. You can do this in multiple ways. The easiest way is to click on the *df* dataframe in the Environment pane:

2.12

Environment   History   Connections   Tutorial

Import Dataset ▾   161 MiB ▾

R ▾   Global Environment ▾

Data

df   5 obs. of 3 variables

Clicking on the letters *df* will result in a new tab in the Source pane:

2.13

	emp_id	perf_rat	salary_adj
1	A1234	3	2
2	A3421	5	25
3	A7654	3	2
4	A5698	4	10
5	A7854	3	2

While you can see the data, you cannot click on it to change individual values like in Excel or SPSS.

In some cases, we may have some values should be treated as missing data. For example, if Remi did not have the salary adjustment for employee ID *A4698*, we would need something to use as a placeholder. In R, the convention is to use the letters *NA*, like so:

```
df[4, ] <- c("A5698", 4, NA)
```

R will treat the letters *NA* as a special case and treat it as a missing value (i.e. they will be ignored). If you have a data file that treats specific values as missing, you should replace these with *NA* before importing the data.

What you have done so far is conceptually identical to opening an Excel file and typing in these values. And now that the information is in the R environment, you can perform operations with it. If you would like to save your work to a file you can use later, you will first need to decide where you want the data stored. Go to the Help pane on the bottom right and click on the Files tab, as in Figure 2.14.

If you want to save your file in the *Documents* directory, click on the *Documents* text next to the folder icon to open that directory. You can also click on the three dots to the right of the file pane (arrow in Figure 2.14) to open a new window that you can navigate to that directory.

2.14

Once you see the contents of that directory, click on the *More* button and *Set As Working Directory*.

2.15

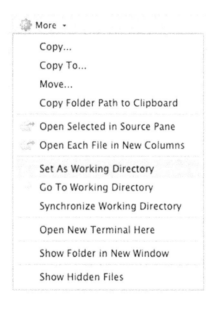

You can then copy and paste this command in the Source pane and run it:

```
write.csv(df,"salary_and_performance_marketing.csv")
```

The command above will save the dataframe *df* as a CSV file in the directory you just chose.

We should discuss the concept of a working directory before moving on. The working directory means the directory in which R looks for data files or stores data files. So setting the working directory as the location where we have all of the data and R files for our analyses can save us a lot of time. If the working directory is not the same as the location where we stored our files, R might complain that it could not find files we wanted to open, or store data files somewhere other than where we expected. If you followed the instructions above, your working directory should be the *Documents* folder. You can see the working directory displayed at the top of the console pane as in Figure 2.16:

2.16

When you work with Excel or SPSS, the concept of the working directory is implicit, but not readily visible. When you try to open a new file through a menu interface, often, the dialogue box shows you the last location from you opened a file from, or, if you have a file open, the location of the file that is currently open. So the program has some memory of the directory you are working in. This is handy and relevant for the program to keep track of. In R, you must be more explicit about setting the working directory.

Importing and merging data

While you can manually enter data using R, it is time consuming to do so. It is much more convenient to import data from existing sources, such as an Excel spreadsheet or an SPSS data file. The example below will walk you through the process of importing data.

Importing data from an Excel spreadsheet into R

Let's say that, the day after Remi sent the initial email above, he has now seen the error of his ways and sent us the remainder of the information from the three remaining departments collated together in a spreadsheet that looks like this (see Figure 2.17):

2.17

	A	B	C
1	emp_id	perf_rat	salary_adj
2	B1234	5	10
3	B4567	3	15
4	B4568	4	4
5	B5907	3	0
6	B8893	3	0
7	C1785	3	0
8	C3893	4	20
9	C7863	5	25
10	C8633	3	2
11	D1134	3	2
12	D2227	5	40
13	D3897	3	5
14	D7736	3	5
15	D8733	4	30
16	D9083	3	5

You can find this file, called 'Ch2 performance and salary spreadsheet.xlsx', at www.koganpage.com/urhra. That website contains all of the data and R code necessary to complete the examples in this book. Download all of the files on to your computer, and then make a note of where you saved the files. You should set the working directory as the location where you downloaded the files.

Once the working directory is set, go to the Environment pane and click on *Import Dataset* as in Figure 2.18:

2.18

And select 'From Excel', which will show this window:

2.19

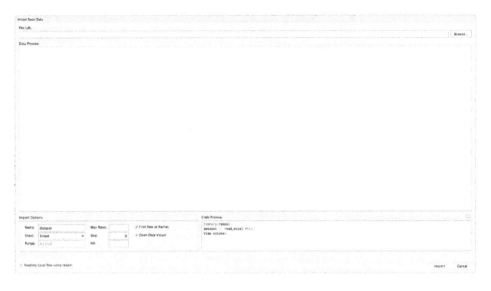

Click the 'Browse' button on the top left and navigate to where you saved the R and data files:

2.20

You will be able to see a preview of the file before importing. Before you click on *Import*, for ease of use, change the name of the data to *df2* in the *Import Options* section (see Figure 2.21). Then click *Import* on the bottom right (see Figure 2.20) to finish.

2.21

Import Options:

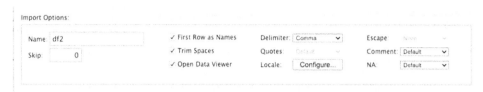

Name: df2   ✓ First Row as Names   Delimiter: Comma ∨   Escape: None ∨

Skip: 0   ✓ Trim Spaces   Quotes: Default ∨   Comment: Default ∨

✓ Open Data Viewer   Locale: Configure...   NA: Default ∨

2.22

	emp_id	perf_rat	salary_adj
1	81234	5	10
2	84567	3	15
3	84568	4	4
4	85907	3	0
5	88893	3	0
6	C1785	3	0
7	C3893	4	20
8	C7863	5	25
9	C8633	3	2
10	D1134	3	2
11	D2227	5	40
12	D3897	3	5
13	D7736	3	5
14	D8733	4	30
15	D9083	3	5

You should now see the new dataframe, *df2*, in the Source pane and in the Environment pane, *as well as the initial dataframe.*

You can combine *df* and *df2* with this command:

```
df_all <- rbind(df, df2)
```

Copy and paste that command into the Source pane, as in Figure 2.23:

2.23

Untitled1*   df2   df

Source on Save

```
1  # Create an empty dataframe with the following variables: emp_id, perf_rat, salary_adj
2  # emp_id = Employee ID, text values
3  # perf_rat = Performance rating (1 = very poor performer ... 5 = Superhuman)
4  # salary_adj = Salary adjustment (number in percentages?)
5
6  df <- data.frame(emp_id = character(), perf_rat = numeric(), salary_adj = numeric())
7
8  df[1, ] <- c("A1234", 3, 2)
9  df[2, ] <- c("A3421", 5, 25)
10 df[3, ] <- c("A7654", 3, 2)
11 df[4, ] <- c("A5698", 4, 10)
12 df[5, ] <- c("A7854", 3, 2)
13
14 write.csv(df, "salary_and_performance_marketing.csv")
15
16 df_all <- rbind(df, df2)
```

Now highlight and run the code. The command above creates a new dataframe, *df_all*, which is the combination of *df* and *df2*. The command we used, 'rbind', stands for *row bind*, and works as intended when the two dataframes being joined have the same number of columns that are ordered in the same sequence.

And *df_all* should now be available to you in the Environment pane:

2.24

| Environment | History | Connections | Tutorial |

Import Dataset ▾   172 MiB ▾

R ▾   Global Environment ▾

Data

df	5 obs. of 3 variables
df_all	20 obs. of 3 variables
df2	15 obs. of 3 variables

So now we have all the data from the performance review into R and have worked through the examples of how to set up variables and enter data manually, as well as how to import a Microsoft Excel file. On reflection, you'll see that it's much easier to enter in all of the data in Excel and import it into R. So we recommend importing data compiled elsewhere rather than entering data using R. While it is possible, RStudio is not an interface where you want to spend a lot of time manually entering data.

Following this example on importing an Excel file, you should be able to import the Excel file called *Ch2 hr profile spreadsheet.xlsx* using the same steps. As the file name suggests, this file contains employee profile information, including employee ID, names, age, gender, start date and the department people work in. *Before you click on import*, you should call this dataframe: *df_profile*. You should be able to see this in the Source pane:

2.25

	emp_id	name	age	gender	start_date	department
1	A1234	Flash	45	M	2010-11-12	Marketing
2	A3421	Diana	41	F	2013-11-24	Marketing
3	A7654	Clarke	19	M	2014-09-03	Marketing
4	A5698	Peter	57	M	2000-03-19	Marketing
5	A7854	Logan	23	M	2012-07-19	Marketing
6	B1234	John	37	M	2001-12-12	Operations
7	B4567	David	31	M	2013-06-30	Operations
8	B4568	Seema	63	F	2012-04-12	Operations
9	B5907	Jemima	42	F	2010-03-14	Operations
10	B8893	Hambel	39	F	1997-07-06	Operations
11	C1785	Big Ted	67	M	2011-05-05	HR
12	C3893	Luke	26	M	1999-03-03	HR
13	C7863	Alison	27	F	2001-11-12	HR
14	C8633	Anais	34	F	2013-10-30	HR
15	D1134	Graham	63	M	2012-09-12	Sales

At this stage, we may want to recode the data for gender so that they are represented as numbers rather than characters. This is because we are able to perform more arithmetic and processes on numbers than we can on character values. To start, let's create a new variable called 'female'. In this variable, 1 = female, and 0 = male. Run this command:

```
df_profile$female <- ifelse(df_profile$gender == "F", 1, 0)
```

The command above tells R to work with the *df_profile* dataframe, and references a variable called *female* within it. While there isn't such a variable, R will create one automatically if it isn't there already. The command also includes the program *ifelse*. This program tells R to follow instructions based on a statement being true or false. Every time R sees the value *F* in the gender variable, the statement is true, so the *female* value will be the first value you give it; every time R doesn't see the value *F*, the statement is false and so the *female* value will be the second value you give it. In other words, for each value of the gender variable it comes across in the *df_profile* dataframe, if the value is *F* (i.e. the person is female), the value of the *female* variable should be a 1. If the value of the variable is not *F*, then the value should be zero. We can see the result of this command in Figure 2.26.

2.26

	emp_id	name	age	gender	start_date	department	female
1	A1234	Flash	45	M	2010–11–12	Marketing	0
2	A3421	Diana	41	F	2013–11–24	Marketing	1
3	A7654	Clarke	19	M	2014–09–03	Marketing	0
4	A5698	Peter	57	M	2000–03–19	Marketing	0
5	A7854	Logan	23	M	2012–07–19	Marketing	0
6	B1234	John	37	M	2001–12–12	Operations	0
7	B4567	David	31	M	2013–06–30	Operations	0
8	B4568	Seema	63	F	2012–04–12	Operations	1
9	B5907	Jemima	42	F	2010–03–14	Operations	1
10	B8893	Hambel	39	F	1997–07–06	Operations	1
11	C1785	Big Ted	67	M	2011–05–05	HR	0
12	C3893	Luke	26	M	1999–03–03	HR	0
13	C7863	Alison	27	F	2001–11–12	HR	1
14	C8633	Anais	34	F	2013–10–30	HR	1
15	D1134	Graham	63	M	2012–09–12	Sales	0

This is similar to performing a search-and-replace. But instead of replacing the original values, we create a new variable that is more descriptive. The variable name *female* strongly implies that a value of 1 represents female, and a value of 0 implies otherwise. The alternative *gender* does not provide a direction about which way the variable is coded. *Gender* is a perfectly fine variable name if we use characters to represent the various genders, but for numeric variables, a name that implies how the numbers should be interpreted makes for more interpretable data.

Another point about the code above is about working with multiple dataframes. In the code you just ran, you saw a dollar sign $ in between the dataframe and variable name. The dollar sign allows you to access a smaller part of a larger object. So *df_profile$female* tells R that you want to do something with the *df_profile* dataframe, specifically the *female* column. Because there are multiple objects we can work with, as in Figure 2.18, we need to be specific about what dataframe we want to work with, and which variable or column we want to work with. In programs like Excel or SPSS, we would need to work with multiple data windows of data to do this. If you have two windows, that may be manageable, but beyond that the process gets cumbersome. Not showing the data in plain view helps us to work more abstractly with the data and lets us work across multiple data sets more efficiently. And if the data sets are large, this saves us a lot of time scrolling trying to find the right column to work with.

Merging two data sets in R using employee ID as a key

So now we have two dataframes in R – one containing performance ratings and another containing people's profile information. We might want to join them together so we can perform some analysis.

Joining two dataframes in R is simple as long as you have a column in each that uniquely identifies people. In our example, and likely in many examples you will come across in HR analytics, that key is the employee ID. As a reminder, the *df_all* dataframe contains employee ID, performance rating, and salary adjustment; and the *df_profile* dataframe contains employee ID, name, age, gender, start date and department.

The following code joins the data together:

```
df_combined <- merge(df_all, df_profile, by = "emp_id")
```

The merge command tells R to merge the *df_all* and *df_profile* dataframes together, by using the *emp_id* variable as the key that matches rows across data sets. It then tells R to name the resulting combined dataframe *df_combined*. You should see a new dataframe in your environment, as in Figure 2.27.

2.27

Clicking on the text *df_combined* should show the data in the Source pane, as in Figure 2.23:

2.28

	emp_id	perf_rat	salary_adj	name	age	gender	start_date	department	female
1	A1234	3	2	Flash	45	M	2010–11–12	Marketing	0
2	A3421	5	25	Diana	41	F	2013–11–24	Marketing	1
3	A5698	4	10	Peter	57	M	2000–03–19	Marketing	0
4	A7654	3	2	Clarke	19	M	2014–09–03	Marketing	0
5	A7854	3	2	Logan	23	M	2012–07–19	Marketing	0
6	B1234	5	10	John	37	M	2001–12–12	Operations	0
7	B4567	3	15	David	31	M	2013–06–30	Operations	0
8	B4568	4	4	Seema	63	F	2012–04–12	Operations	1
9	B5907	3	0	Jemima	42	F	2010–03–14	Operations	1
10	B8893	3	0	Hambel	39	F	1997–07–06	Operations	1
11	C1785	3	0	Big Ted	67	M	2011–05–05	HR	0
12	C3893	4	20	Luke	26	M	1999–03–03	HR	0
13	C7863	5	25	Alison	27	F	2001–11–12	HR	1
14	C8633	3	2	Anais	34	F	2013–10–30	HR	1
15	D1134	3	2	Graham	63	M	2012–09–12	Sales	0

All of the variables are present.

A couple of notes about the joining process. The order of the employer ID variable does not need to be the same across data sets, as R will take care of that for you. But it is important that the employer ID variable is identical across data sets, and that each employee has a unique ID. If this is not the case, you may not be able to join the data sets successfully. As a reminder, R is case sensitive, so 'A1234' is not the same as 'a1234'. In addition, stray spaces in the variable 'A1234 ' (with extra space at the end) make it different to 'A1234' (without extra space at the end).

To save your work to a file, use this command:

```
write.csv(df_combined, "hr_profile_salary_and_performance.csv")
```

All of the code written out above is available in a file called Ch2_1.R in the online supplement. That file will have some additional commentary to explain what each line of code does.

If you want to save it to a different directory, follow the instruction in previous sections on how to change the working directory.

Now, we have created some data in R, learned how to import existing data into R, added additional rows of data to an existing data set, merged two data sets that have different columns and saved our work as a file.

Big data

The term 'big data' is often used to describe sets of data that are so large that traditional methods for storing, analysing and sharing data can be inadequate. Gartner

(2012) defines big data as 'high volume, high velocity, and/or high variety informa-tion assets that require new forms of processing to enable enhanced decision making, insight discovery and process optimization'.

As an organization develops, databases grow in size because information is constantly being gathered. Sometimes hundreds, even thousands, of servers are required to store all of the information required by an organization. So bringing all this together for analysis is not a trivial matter. Because of the sheer size of the data, it is uncommon for predictive analysis to take place across the entire spectrum of big data; most predictive analysis uses data files that can be comfortably stored on a PC (and be files of 'PC-sized' data). Depending on the organization, the term 'big data' could refer to hundreds of gigabytes or hundreds of terabytes.

This concept has grown such that large IT companies such as Google, Facebook and LinkedIn developed multiple technological advancements to manage the vast amount of information they were collecting (Bersin, 2021). Relational databases such as Oracle and Sybase were not originally designed to manage that degree of volume, velocity (frequency of updates) and variety of data.

As already mentioned, however, this is not a book about information manage-ment – but a quick summary of the four types of databases you are likely to come across is as follows:

- Relational databases (e.g. SAP, Oracle or Sybase). These store information in tables. These tables are linked together and information is queried using a struc-tured query language (SQL). Most HR systems use relational databases.

- Multidimensional databases (e.g. Cognos, Business Objects). Also called online analytic processing (OLAP) databases, these take data out of traditional relational systems and create a data warehouse. They store data by 'dimension' (i.e. such as a division, or a year of hire) and precalculate the information so that when you query the database it is quick to respond with answers to queries such as turnover by department or new hires per month.

- Object-oriented databases (e.g. Workday). These store data as 'objects'. So the 'employee object' would store data about employees such as name, address, start date, etc. It also stores 'rules' or 'methods' such as 'gender must be M or F' or 'start date must be after 1900'. With object-oriented databases, the analyst can change an object and the entire system changes along with it. So, if you added a new field to the employee object, such as 'languages spoken', then the other parts of the system could use this field as well, immediately. Without getting into the details, suffice to say that object-oriented databases are far more flexible and easy to change than traditional relational databases.

- Big data databases or NoSQL databases (e.g. Hadoop). These databases are designed specifically to handle enormous amounts of data, going up to hundreds of terabytes or even thousands of terabytes (called petabytes). They break down data into small pieces that can then be processed in parallel. Two key benefits of big data technologies are that they can run queries on vast amounts of data quickly, and they work on both structured and unstructured data.

As mentioned earlier, most HR databases are relational databases, and some of the shortcomings of the big data databases (such as the inability to query one single employee) mean that the intention of big data databases is not to replace these, but to work together with them.

If you are an HR analytics expert or work closely with, or in, an HR MI team, you are likely to already be well aware of the concepts described in this section; indeed the major HR software vendors are investing heavily in analytics platforms, tools and solutions (Bersin, 2021). Indeed, Oracle (including PeopleSoft), SAP and Workday, as well as many other HR solution providers, have introduced analytics products integrated with Hadoop big data technology. Additionally many data analysis tools, including Excel, have interfaces that work with big data technology.

According to a McKinsey report, the introduction of big data is estimated to result in 140,000–150,000 more deep analytical talent positions in the United States (McKinsey Global Institute, 2011). The same report estimates that the US healthcare industry could put a value of $300 billion each year on the increased efficiency and quality improvements that would take place by analysing big data effectively to drive efficiency. Benefits are also estimated in the retail sector to increase operating margin by as much as 60 per cent, and other levers highlighted in government include savings of more than US $100 billion in operational efficiency costs alone using big data. Additionally, the benefits of being able to use big data to reduce fraud, errors and tax gaps between potential and actual revenue have yet to be estimated.

McKinsey warns that organizations need to address many challenges ahead in trying to capture the full potential of big data, and the key, number-one pressing challenge is in having people with deep analytical skills, able to analyse the big data and help organizations to make decisions based on the findings. They identify five ways in which big data will create value in the future:

1 Create transparency.
2 Enable experimentation to discover needs, expose variability and improve performance.
3 Segment populations to customize actions.
4 Support human decision making with automated algorithms.
5 Innovate new business models, products and services.

It is benefit number four where sophisticated analytics such as those outlined in this book can make considerable improvements in decision making and help organizations to minimize risk. Finally, creative use of analytics and big data can uncover valuable insights.

The analytics skills you will use in working through this book, together with a good understanding of the systems you are working with, will make you a valuable commodity in your organization in this information age. Chapter 3 will take you through analysis strategies. We will discuss, in detail, various commonly used statistical tests and strategies and take you through how and when to use them in order to understand what your data is telling you.

References

Bersin, J (2021) HR Technology 2021: The definitive guide, joshbersin.com/wp-content/uploads/2021/04/HR_TechMarket_2021_v7.pdf (archived at https://perma.cc/73NJ-XLLE)

Choi, J H, Hickman, K E, Monahan, A and Schwarcz, D (2023) ChatGPT goes to law school (SSRN Scholarly Paper 4335905), doi.org/10.2139/ssrn.4335905 (archived at https://perma.cc/23GV-8H6M)

Cowen, T and Tabarrok, A (2023). How to learn and teach economics with large language models, including GPT, doi.org/10.2139/ssrn.4391863 (archived at https://perma.cc/2RX3-4842)

Edwards, M R and Edwards, K (2016) *Predictive HR Analytics: Mastering the HR metric*, Kogan Page, London

Edwards, M R and Edwards, K (2019) *Predictive HR Analytics: Mastering the HR metric*, 2nd edn, Kogan Page, London

Gartner (2012) IT glossary: Big data, Gartner, www.gartner.com/en/information-technology/glossary/big-data (archived at https://perma.cc/ZX27-9E3W)

Kane, J (2012) A review of the top five statistical software systems, *Professional Statistical Services*, web.archive.org/web/20161207131051/http://www.prostatservices.com/statistical-consulting/articles-of-interest/a-review-of-the-top-five-statistical-software-systems (archived at https://perma.cc/7DQP-487Z)

Kaur, R (2023) The best statistical software tools, Selecthub, www.selecthub.com/business-intelligence/statistical-software/ (archived at https://perma.cc/FCR6-CQ7L)

McKinsey Global Institute (2011) Big data: The next frontier for innovation, competition and productivity, McKinsey, www.mckinsey.com/~/media/mckinsey/business%20functions/mckinsey%20digital/our%20insights/big%20data%20the%20next%20frontier%20for%20innovation/mgi_big_data_full_report.pdf (archived at https://perma.cc/7TY4-EKK6)

Terwiesch, C (2023) *Would Chat GPT3 Get a Wharton MBA? A prediction based on its performance in the operations management course*, Mack Institute for Innovation Management at the Wharton School, University of Pennsylvania

03

Analysis strategies

In this chapter, we discuss everything you need to get started on predictive HR analytics. You could think of this chapter as your analytic compass. In Chapter 2 we discussed the types of information that you are likely to uncover around your organization, where you are likely to find it, and the type of database it may be stored in. Once you have the data, we now discuss moving from simply producing reports to showing the different analytic techniques that you can use as part of your predictive HR analytics toolkit. Understanding the different techniques will allow you to conduct more meaningful analysis, using statistics to uncover what is really going on and predict what is likely to occur in the future.

Below, we delve into different analytic tests; each of these does something different and can be applied to different data to answer different analytic questions. We discuss specifically which statistical tests to use on which type of variables and when. If you are like most people and do not have a photographic memory, you will find Table 3.4 (Statistical tests by data type, pages 58–61), and Table 3.5 (Case study examples, pages 62–64) to be very useful points of reference.

In Chapter 2 we discussed some common statistical software packages, which may be useful if you are deciding which package to use at your organization or university. In this book we set out our examples using R, so in this chapter we include code examples and libraries for the various analyses.

From descriptive reports to predictive analytics

At present, most HR functions lack the capability to use the available HR data to its full potential, usually because they lack the knowledge or experience, or even the foresight to appreciate the enormous possibilities presented by HR analytic modelling. Indeed the ability to tap into the rich vein of human capital metrics that can be available to organizations will reveal new insights and knowledge about the organization that would have been very difficult to consider up to now.

Descriptive HR reports usually produced by MI teams refer to the illustration of a set of data, a 'snapshot' of what is occurring at that time, presenting the current state of play. Sets of data cut across various parts of an organization; for example: recruitment data such as time to hire, costs to hire per employee, recruiter productivity; workforce demographics such as age, gender, tenure; or headcount data such as percentage turnover and costs per head. For the vast majority of HR functions, this is the limit of the HR analytic capability. With these reports, the most sophisticated statistical techniques that tend to be used are usually calculating a percentage of the population that can be classified in a certain way (e.g. leaver or non-leaver) or an average figure that might represent an indication of how a particular group fares on a particular metric (e.g. average salary or average performance rating); these descriptive reports do not help us fully to understand what is going on in our organization. When running these reports the analysts do not generally interrogate the data fully for other possible explanatory factors (which can help clarify why something might be happening) nor do they tend to test or check the degree to which their data might be robust and valid and whether it might be reasonable to make claims on the basis of any data they may be presenting. In addition, presenting descriptive reports does not in any way help us to try and make predictions about what we might find in the future.

Bersin (2012) outlines the importance of using predictive analytics to help organizations predict or understand the performance of a person or group of people based on historical data. Once sufficient data has been collected over time, it is then possible to analyse patterns and trends based on this historical data. As already mentioned in Chapter 1, Huselid (2014) proposed that: 'Analytics present a tremendous opportunity to help organizations understand what they don't yet know... By identifying trends and patterns, HR professionals and management teams can make better strategic decisions about the workforce challenges that they may soon face.'

There are many examples of predictive analytics in this book. However, to get the ball rolling let's consider that, instead of just having a report showing turnover statistics per region, we are actually able to analyse the turnover percentage against the demographic data over a number of years. Predictive analytics would be able to understand what is likely (i.e. with statistical significance) to cause a low or a high turnover percentage, whether it be a particular region, a certain employee profile or a certain job role.

Once the organization has access to the available data, there really is no limit to the predictive models that could be analysed. Although this is incredibly powerful, it introduces its own challenges, one of the biggest being what, exactly, we should be analysing and what models we should run in the first place. This will be driven by a combination of business need and data availability and will likely evolve as time goes on. We will work through some examples of predictive models in the case study chapters in this book (Chapters 4–9). To give you a further idea, however, we can use predictive modelling to analyse what factors predict turnover of key talent; to investigate the patterns of team diversity across the organization and what this may mean in terms of outcomes; or to assess what factors associated with recruitment, selection and induction predict the retention of new joiners.

Statistical significance

Throughout this book, we discuss and perform various statistical tests. The key aim of the statistical testing is to determine whether the results point to a 'statistically significant' outcome.

The basic idea behind statistical significance is linked to hypotheses testing. This simply involves us developing a 'research hypothesis' and what is called a 'null hypothesis'. To test the research hypothesis we carry out particular statistical analysis on the associated data and obtain a test statistic. The test statistic then tells us whether a particular pattern of results (which may support the research hypothesis) can be relied upon and if it is robust enough for us to make various assumptions about what is going on in our population (e.g. in our organization if we are trying to explore data linked to employees); or whether it is more likely that we came by our particular set of findings by chance alone (in other words, the results we find are not robust).

If there is strong evidence from our data that there is something really meaningful going on, and our test indicates that a finding is unlikely to have occurred by chance alone, we would say that we have grounds to 'reject the null hypothesis' in favour of the 'research hypothesis' (or 'alternate' hypothesis as it is sometimes called). In very simple and loose terms, the 'null hypothesis' suggests that the results are not strong enough for us to draw any firm conclusions about the findings. So for us to be able to draw any conclusions from our data we want to be able to push this 'null hypothesis' to one side in favour of the 'research hypothesis'.

Like many terms in this book, this may be better explained by using an example. Let's say our hypotheses are as follows:

- *Research hypothesis:* attendance at a customer-service training course by sales employees will increase customer satisfaction survey scores.
- *Null hypothesis:* attendance at a customer-service training course by sales employees will have *no* impact on customer satisfaction survey scores.

So, in its simplest form, what we might do in researching this hypothesis (in a particular organization) is to collect and analyse data relating to who went on the customer-service training course and who did not. We could then collect data from the customer satisfaction survey (both before and after the training), making sure to record who the customer was served by. We would then run a statistical test (we will cover later in the book which statistical test we should conduct on what data) to understand whether there was a 'statistically significant' improvement in the customer satisfaction scores for those sales staff who attended the training course.

The statistical test produces a test statistic, from which we could determine whether the result is statistically significant. If the test did indicate 'statistical significance', we would have grounds to reject the 'null hypothesis' that the customer-service training course has no impact on customer satisfaction survey scores.

The criterion used universally for testing significance is 95 per cent confidence. This 95 per cent cut-off for significance is a long-standing convention that has been recognized for almost 100 years (generally since 1925 when Fisher published his book *Statistical Methods for Research Workers*). Statistics is a moving field and the mathematical science underlying statistical analysis is continually being debated. The use of this 95 per cent certainty cut-off and the 'null hypothesis test for significance' is no exception. However, in this book we will follow the 100-year-old convention of using 95 per cent confidence to determine whether a result is significant, and we will use the 95 per cent level of certainty as our target cut-off.

So if we can be at least 95 per cent confident (from statistical tests) that the pattern of data found would be unlikely to occur by chance, we would say that the finding is 'statistically significant'. If we want to be 95 per cent certain about our findings then another way of putting this is that we want to be able to say that there is only a 5 per cent likelihood that our findings might be due to chance alone. The term used to indicate the level of significance in statistical tests is the probability level. A 5 per cent likelihood is presented as a 0.05 probability. This is called a p-value and this is what our statistical tests present: the probability that our findings could be due to chance alone. So with the statistical tests we want our p-values to be 0.05 or lower (commonly indicated as $p<0.05$). We want the likelihood that our findings are due to chance alone to be less than 5 per cent in order for us to be 95 per cent (or more) confident that our findings are meaningful. Thus we want $p<0.05$ (note: 5 per cent is the same as a p-value of 0.05, because it is 0.05×100).

It is important to remember this 0.05 p-value. We always want our statistical tests to indicate a significance level of 0.05 in order for us to say we have a 'statistically significant' finding.

$p<0.05$

$P<0.05$ will be the key to our decision making in interpreting the analysis results for most of the statistical analysis in this book.

Importantly, sometimes our statistical tests indicate that we can be more than 95 per cent confident that our findings are meaningful and not due to chance alone. For example, our statistical test may indicate that we can be 99 per cent confident that our results would not occur by chance and thus the p-value presented here will be $p=0.01$. If the p-value of the result is smaller than 0.01 then we indicate $p<0.01$.

Equally, our test results may indicate that we can be 99.9 per cent confident that our findings would not occur by chance; the associated p-value for this would be 0.001. This in effect would be saying that our findings are so strong that we can be *really* confident that the results are robust. If our p-value is smaller than 0.001 then we would generally present this as p<0.001. This, in effect, says the following: 'The likelihood that the results we find would occur by chance alone is less than 1 in 1,000.' Therefore, the smaller the p-value the more confident we can be with our results.

Importantly, if our p-value is more than 0.05 (p>0.05) we have not reached our desired 95 per cent level of confidence in our results. This means that our findings are not 'statistically significant' and, because our results might be due to chance, we cannot cast aside the null hypothesis.

It is important to remember the p<0.05, cut-off p-value. It will be the key to most of the statistical analysis in this book. As you go through the case study chapters in particular, and also when you carry out your own analysis, you will find yourself eagerly scanning the statistical output tables looking for a p-value of 0.05 or less. Note that p-values are often indicated with an asterisk '*' or two '**' in R output.

We will go through the meaning of statistical significance with each test in more detail as we cover each test later in this chapter.

Examples of key HR analytic metrics/measures often used by analytics teams

Predictive HR analytics experts do not have standard metrics or measures that are always used – each project is likely to have indicators and measures specific to the project. However, there are key metrics that any HR analyst should be familiar with. In each of the case study examples used in this book we use particular metrics that are described in each case. Here are some examples of a range of focal measures (this is not an exhaustive list and there are often many ways to measure each of these depending upon the project at hand).

Recruitment metrics

Common metrics in the recruitment sphere include indices such as 'cost per hire' – loosely this will involve the recruitment budget in a given period divided by the number of employees hired in a given period. Another metric used is 'time to hire' (per-job or for an average job; often measured for each business unit).

Employee flows

The most used turnover measure is 'separation rate', which involves the calculation of 'the number of members who left during period' divided by 'the average number of members during this period'. This will often be presented as a percentage (so multiplied by 100). The organization should be careful to signify (and separate) the type of leaver included in this statistic. For example, the analyst should separate terminations and redundancies from retirees and voluntary leavers.

Turnover cost

An analytics team should spend some time perfecting a metric of turnover costing tailored to their organization. Assumptions will often be made when calculating this; the actual cost of replacing a member of staff may include, for example, the cost per hire. A calculation should be included to incorporate the cost of induction as well as training. More advanced metrics should include costs of lower productivity of the joiner. A specific metric will not be presented here because different organizations could have unique considerations in the way they think about this metric. However, analytic teams should identify a formula that fits their organization.

Revenue metrics

The measures here will vary depending on context; a key metric might involve measures of 'revenue/income over time' (hour/day/week) relating to certain units (e.g. with each employee or average per employee or a total or average per team).

Performance metrics

There are many performance metrics that an analyst might draw on and each might vary depending upon the job. Later in the book we discuss the potential variety in performance-related measures. Most performance indicators associated with individuals have the potential to be aggregated to other unit levels (e.g. groups or teams, given that these are made up of individuals). Example indices can include performance appraisal ratings, competency ratings, peer feedback, sales figures and measures that will be context-specific (e.g. scanning rate, customer feedback, call speed, call numbers). Examples of unit or team performance indices can include team engagement index, team/store customer feedback, staff turnover, customer satisfaction/loyalty.

Productivity oriented metrics

Productivity measures require potential measurable output indices for employees. Important with these is that a measure of output over time (hour/day/week) associated with particular units (e.g. with each employee or as an average with each employee/total or average per unit or team) can be constructed.

Diversity metrics

Possible metrics used to measure diversity include the following examples: 'percentage of women per team/percentage of women in certain senior jobs/percentage of ethnic minorities in each team/percentage of ethnic minorities within senior jobs/ percentage pay gap between females and males'. Importantly, diversity metrics may include combinations of metrics comparing different demographic groups. For example, 'percentage of underrepresented groups' for males versus females. Metrics of diversity will be discussed in more detail later in the book.

Talent/potential metrics

Talent metrics can involve time-to-promotion: 'time (e.g. in months) until promotion relating to particular units' (e.g. total or each employee or as an average per employee/ total or average with each team). Talent management often involves stacking performance ratings against a measure of 'potential' for each employee. For performance potential the nine-box grid is often used. This groups employees into three categories of performance (low/medium/high) and three categories of some indicator of 'potential' (low/medium/high).

Sickness absence

This data is not always collected by organizations and the measurement of this may vary across teams or units within the organization. Where this data is collected, it is likely to include an indication of the number of days sick over a given time (e.g. per week/month/year) relating to identified units (e.g. average per employee/total or average per team). Analytics teams can also use sickness absence rates at the organization level (the percentage of annual days lost to sickness per unit or organization). Analytics teams will often cost the total days lost due to sickness ('total days lost × average cost of a working day in the organization'), which can amount to many millions (£€$) in big organizations.

Engagement metrics

There are many ways to measure engagement (see Chapter 5 for a discussion of engagement measures). Engagement measures are generally tapped at the individual level (usually with survey questionnaires). However, individual scores are rarely analysed at the individual level due to confidentiality issues (though this is possible if permissions have been granted and employees have been linked to answers). An engagement metric might involve an average score per unit (individual/work unit such as a team); this is often presented as the percentage of a work unit that has agreed or strongly agreed to certain engagement measures. The aggregated average of these are often used to benchmark organizational units (or sub-units) against each other. In some organizations the team scores on these are used as a performance indicator of the leader of the team.

Data integrity

It is important to note how critical it is that the data you are analysing is up to date and reliable. It is the practice of many organizations to put on to employees and line managers the ownership of keeping HR and people-management information up to date, and it is critical that the processes surrounding key people-management activities be sufficiently robust to ensure that the information in the database is comprehensive and regularly updated.

Linking data from different sources usually just requires a unique identifier such as an employee ID on which the other information relates. Data can be combined in data warehouses, databases such as Microsoft Access or spreadsheet packages such as Microsoft Excel, and imported into an R environment. Care is needed to ensure the integrity of the information. Indeed a key challenge with developed HR analytics is to understand the complexity of the data available, linking it up, and getting it to a format where it can be swiftly analysed. As mentioned earlier in this chapter, there are many different sources of data in the organization from which HR professionals can mine; however, it may take considerable data manipulation on these files and information sets to get predictive models to run. This can take a considerable amount of time, skill and experience in data handling and statistical analysis to ensure the models that are being run are suitable for the data they are analysing.

The type of data is critical in determining which type of analysis should be carried out. In the next three sections of this chapter, we go through the different types of data and how to recognize them, some common statistical analysis tests that can be carried out on organizational (and indeed other) data, and which statistical tests should be used on which types of data.

Types of data

The data that we collect, or that is collected in an organization, can be grouped into certain types based on what it is measuring and how it behaves. Each data field, whether it is salary, name, gender, or anything else in the data set, is termed a variable. Variables can be classed as either categorical or continuous.

Put simply, variables are things that can vary, or change. It might be, for example, eye colour (which varies from person to person), temperature (which varies from day to day), or performance rating (which varies from employee to employee). This notion of variance is absolutely central in statistical analyses. If we think about any characteristic or data linked to employees (e.g. age, gender, salary, engagement levels, bonuses, competency rating, performance rating, whether they are a leaver or not, etc) in our organization, this characteristic will vary across individuals. Ultimately, it is this variation that we analyse with our statistical tests.

Categorical variable types

A categorical variable is one that is made up of categories. For example, we talk about 'role' level in the diversity case study when analysing the prevalence of women in senior-level roles. The 'role levels' existing within the organization in question are: clerical, administrative, graduate consultant, consultant, senior consultant, principal consultant and partner. Each employee is only one or the other. They may be a graduate consultant, they may be a partner, but they cannot be both a graduate consultant and a partner. There is no overlap. When you think about what this data looks like, there is no immediate quantitative or numerical value. Indeed it is best thought of as a collection of labels or names representing some category within our organization or employee group. And clearly because these types of variables have no numerical value, it is not possible to add, subtract, multiply or divide them, any more than you could add a graduate consultant to a senior consultant and hope to get a partner.

It is worth noting here that categorical variables can use numbers as labels. However, this does not mean they are meaningful numbers with which we can use arithmetic. An example would be if the base country code might be recorded in the HR PeopleSoft system as a number, for example:

01 – Australia

02 – United Kingdom

03 – United States

04 – Hong Kong

05 – Singapore

06 – Canada

So although the system stores country as a number, it is not a numeric value with which we could meaningfully add, subtract, multiply or divide. Clearly you cannot hope to multiply the UK by three and get Canada. Hence the numbers are just labels here too.

There are three different types of categorical variable: binary, nominal and ordinal, as set out below.

Binary variable

Binary variables are categorical variables that are unique in that they name only two distinct entities or ideas. Certainly it is the simplest form of categorical variable. Binary variables are also referred to as binomial or dichotomous. Some examples are:

Employee is leaving organization: leaver/stayer

Attended customer service training: yes/no

Nominal variable

Nominal variables are categorical variables that name three or more distinct entities. They are in no particular order and each value is mutually exclusive. Some examples are below:

Home office location: Australia, United Kingdom, Canada, United States, Singapore, Hong Kong, etc.

Division: sales, legal, HR, finance, etc.

Ordinal variables

Ordinal data takes things a step further. It is essentially categorical data for which there is a meaningful order. So it increases or decreases in order. Importantly, although there may be an order to the variable, and each case in the variable may have a number associated with it representing some kind of order (e.g. in the case of a rank), a characteristic of an ordinal variable is that the meaningful interval between each position or number in the order may not be equal. If you ranked all employees in an organization on the basis of their salary, the rank you give each person would represent an order; however, the actual amount of salary that each person (and thus ranked position) differs by will not necessarily be equal. The person who is paid the most, who is first in the variable, may get £200,000, the second person may get £190,000 and the third person may get £100,000. As such, the meaningful intervals underlying the ordered numbers may not be equal. Aside from this salary ranking, some other examples are presented below:

Role level: 1) graduate, 2) consultant, 3) senior consultant, 4) managing consultant, 5) vice principal

Job satisfaction: 1) very dissatisfied, 2) dissatisfied, 3) neither satisfied nor dissatisfied, 4) satisfied, 5) very satisfied

So, in summary, the values within a categorical data variable are labels, or names. There are three types of categorical data: binary, nominal and ordinal. Binary is when there are only two possible values, nominal is when there are three or more possible values, and ordinal is when the values are in a meaningful order. Because they are names only, we cannot perform any arithmetic on them. For this reason, we cannot quantify the difference between different points on the scale.

Continuous variable types

Continuous variables can take on any numerical value on a measurement scale. There are two key types of continuous variable: interval variables and ratio variables.

Interval variables

Interval data is measured on a numeric scale. The numbers are continuous – so as well as knowing the order, interval data records the exact value. This means that, unlike ordinal data where there is a limited set of responses, with interval data the value could be anything on a scale:

Daily temperature (Celsius): some examples might be 21.4, 37.8, 16.0, 8.5, etc. Although it is likely to be between –50 and +50, it could really take on any value on that temperature scale, including as many decimal points as you care to record.

Start date: some examples might be 6/6/1994, 28/9/2013, 4/5/2015, etc. Whilst we can measure the difference between two dates, we cannot add or multiply this data.

So we have the ability to quantify the difference between each value. So, for example, if you wanted to know the difference in temperature from one day to the next, you could calculate the space in between, or *interval*, by simply subtracting.

Interval data lacks a zero starting point, which makes comparisons of magnitude not possible. Whilst we can say that the difference between 8 and 9 degrees is the same as the difference between 22 and 23 degrees, we cannot say, however, that 20 degrees is twice as hot as 10 degrees in the same way that we could say that 20 apples is twice as many as 10 apples. It is more complex than that because temperature does not start at zero and there is no such thing as having no temperature. There is such a thing as having no apples though.

So you cannot have 'no date' when measuring date or 'no temperature' when measuring temperature. Even a zero temperature is still a tangible temperature and even year zero on our calendar was still an actual year.

Ratio variables

Ratio data is similar to interval data in that it is a continuous numerical value but, unlike interval data, there is a defined zero point. As in the earlier example, if we had a variable 'number of apples on table' it would start at zero and then go up to any number (depending on the size of your table). Some examples in an organizational context are below:

Annual salary (£): Some examples might be 16000, 120000, 564482, 34909, 86269, etc.

Height (cm): 170, 182, 163, 134.5, etc.

Weight (kg): 67, 48, 120.3, 98.4, etc.

Job tenure (years): 0.25, 0.5, 1, 23, 20, etc.

These values are meaningful numerically and can be added, subtracted, divided and multiplied. Ratio data enables you to say things like 'The average annual salary of men in this organization is 2.78 times greater than the average annual salary of women.' Tables 3.1 and 3.2 provide a summary of these five data types.

TABLE 3.1 Categorical variable types – variables divided into distinct categories

Data Type	Description	Examples
Binary	Only two categories	Pregnant or not pregnant; attended training or not; someone who has left versus someone still employed
Nominal	Three or more categories	Division or function (e.g. HR, Risk, Finance, Sales, etc); country (e.g. Canada, Australia, India)
Ordinal	Categories have a meaningful order	Customer satisfaction scale (very dissatisfied, dissatisfied, neutral, satisfied, very satisfied); ranked sales position of employee or team (1st, 2nd, 3rd, etc)

TABLE 3.2 Continuous variable types – variables with a distinct numerical value

Data Type	Description	Examples
Interval	Numerical value. No defined 'zero' starting point.	Temperature in Celcius; year.
Ratio	Continuous numerical data with a defined zero starting point. Ratios of scores on a scale also make sense.	Height; weight; salary; age; job tenure; sales figures (€£$); % linked to an individual object such as individual, team, department (e.g. % of the team who indicated that they were 'engaged' or staff turnover % in each team or division).

With continuous data, the measure of difference between two points is quantifiable and equal intervals on the variable represent equal differences in the item being measured.

Using group/team-level or individual-level data

Depending on the topic and what it is you are trying to achieve, it may be more appropriate to analyse the data at a team level, or at an individual level. Typically, more sensitive information such as employee engagement survey results will, for ethical reasons, only be available at a team level (organizations usually make promises of confidentiality and anonymity with engagement surveys; see Chapter 5). Equally, it may be more appropriate when assessing leadership effectiveness to assess the aggregated performance of the team they are leading. On the other hand, there are examples where it makes more sense to conduct the analysis at an individual level, particularly where we are looking at the attributes of an individual rather than the attributes of a team. Some examples are given in Table 3.3.

Dependent variables and independent variables

As mentioned earlier in this chapter, the type of statistical test to use is reliant on the type of data being analysed. Before we get into this, it is important to understand the difference between dependent variables and independent variables. Why? Because it is actually the data type of your dependent variable (rather than independent variables) or variables that will determine the type of statistical test you need to use. You can only determine this if you actually know the difference between the two! So what is the difference? The answer to the question really lies in what it is you are trying to model or what it is you are trying to explain or account for with your research question or analysis.

TABLE 3.3 Data measurement levels with examples

Level	Example Measures
Team	Employee opinion survey output (such as team engagement index, team leadership index, aggregate % confidence in leadership, composite team scores on work–life balance), store/branch customer feedback, store/branch customer loyalty, team staff turnover %, team size, team leader rating.
Individual	Performance appraisal rating, behavioural rating, sales performance figures, checkout scan rate, individual customer feedback, peer feedback, call rates, call loads, leaver status, length of service, gender.

Dependent variables

The dependent variable (or variables) (DV), also called the 'outcome variable', refers to what it is you are trying to model, predict or account for variation in. In our discussion about statistical significance earlier in this chapter, we outlined the research hypothesis as follows:

> 'Attendance at the customer service training course by the sales team will increase customer satisfaction survey scores.'

In this example, our outcome variable, the one we are trying to model, predict or account for variation in (and change if we can!) is the customer satisfaction survey score. This is our dependent variable. Customer satisfaction is expected to be affected by changes in the customer service training-course attendance, which is our independent variable. Thus we would expect that variation in customer satisfaction scores within our workforce might (to some degree) be dependent upon whether or not someone has been on a training course.

Independent variables

The independent variable (or variables) (IV), also called 'predictor variable', refers to the variable that we think has an effect, cause or influence on the outcome or dependent variable. So, in our example, we can now say the following:

Dependent variable: customer satisfaction survey scores

Independent variable: customer service training-course attendance

This is because we think (or we hypothesize) that there is a possibility that customer service training-course attendance has an impact on customer satisfaction survey scores.

One caution here is that, even when we do find a significant relationship or link between two variables (where we assume that one is an independent variable and the other a dependent variable), it does not necessarily mean that changes in the independent variable 'cause' changes in the dependent variable. It would just mean that there is a relationship between the two where change in one relates to or is associated with changes in another. A classic example of this is the sales of ice cream and the prevalence of skin cancer. It has been found that countries that have high ice cream sales are also likely to have high rates of skin cancer. Does this mean that ice cream causes skin cancer? No. In reality the cause is something else: probably something to do with the sun. In countries where there are higher temperatures, there are higher sales of ice cream and there are also higher rates of skin cancer. So whilst the information is useful, we can only determine relationships (and not causality) in cross-sectional analysis. We will talk more about challenges with inferring causality from analysis later in the book (Chapter 12).

Importantly, dependent variables might be binary, nominal, ordinal, interval or ratio, and independent variables might be binary, nominal, ordinal, interval or ratio. The combination present in the data that we want to analyse will determine which analytic test we can use.

Your toolkit: types of statistical tests

As mentioned earlier in this chapter, the type of statistical test used depends on two main things. First, the nature of the research question that you are hoping to answer, and second, the data types of your independent and dependent variables. Table 3.4 gives a brief summary of what to use (note that the list is confined to the subset of tools we use in the case studies in this book, which we believe would meet the need in 95 per cent of the analyses that HR analytics professionals will need to conduct.).

TABLE 3.4 Statistical tests by data type

Dependent Variable (DV)	Independent Variable (IV)	Analysis Test	Nature of the test: what type of research question is it trying to explore?
Categorical DV (Binary, Nominal, or *Ordinal)	Categorical and only one IV	Chi-square analysis – applied to a crosstabs of frequencies	Chi-square analysis explores whether the frequencies and proportions found across particular categories (e.g. male versus female) might vary or be linked to another category (e.g. part-time versus full-time).
	Continuous or together continuous and categorical	Logistic regression analysis	Logistic regression analysis attempts to predict the likelihood of something in particular occurring (e.g. whether someone leaves the organization versus whether they stay) on the basis of possible characteristics across a range of independent variables (e.g. performance criteria, gender, salary increases, promotion, etc).
		Survival analysis	Survival analysis examines the distribution of time between two events. For example, the time between the start date and end date of an employee's service. Thus we are predicting the 'chances of survival' after, for example, 3 months, 6 months, 12 months based on a range of independent variables.

(continued)

TABLE 3.4 (Continued)

Dependent Variable (DV)	Independent Variable (IV)	Analysis Test	Nature of the test: what type of research question is it trying to explore?
Continuous DV (Interval or Ratio – and sometimes *Ordinal)	Binary IV–Group A versus Group B; Time Based Binary IV–Group A at Time 1 versus Group A at Time 2	Independent samples t-test Paired samples t-test	**Independent samples t-test** explores whether two groups of data differ on some dimension. E.g. are males more stressed than females? Are females more engaged than males? **Paired samples t-test** explores whether two separate times/instances of data collection of the same group differ or are the same across time – has there been a change in some data? Are the leadership team performing better than they were a year ago?
Continuous DV (Interval or Ratio – and sometimes *Ordinal)	Categorical IV with three or more groups; Group A versus Group B versus Groups C etc...	One-way independent ANOVA	**One-way independent ANOVA** explores whether three or more groups of data differ on some continuous dimension, e.g. are the HR function's employees more engaged than those from finance or marketing?
	Time Based IV with three or more time points (e.g. Group A at Time 1 versus Group A at Time 2 versus Group A at Time 3)	One-way repeated measures ANOVA	**One-way repeated measures ANOVA** explores whether three or more separate times/instances of data collection differ or are the same across time – has there been a change in some metric (e.g. team engagement scores) across time?
	Continuous (assumed) DV and only one other continuous IV	**Pearson's correlation**, or **Simple linear regression**	**Pearson's correlation, or Simple linear regression** – if you want to look at the degree to which two continuous variables are related in some way – with correlations you may just be interested in the 'co'-relation between two variables; with simple regression you might be making some assumptions about which variable could be 'caused' or 'predicted' by the other.[†]

(continued)

TABLE 3.4 (Continued)

Dependent Variable (DV)	Independent Variable (IV)	Analysis Test	Nature of the test: what type of research question is it trying to explore?
	Time based categorical IV with two or more time points – Time 1 versus Time 2 (etc) in combination with one or more categorical IVs (e.g. gender)	**Repeated measures ANOVA** (generalized linear model). The DV metric will have been collected on more than two occasions with the same objects (e.g. employees or teams) but the sample can be broken up into one or more other category (e.g. male versus female; received training versus not; HR versus marketing versus finance etc).	**Repeated measures ANOVA** (generalized linear model) explores whether two or more separate times/instances of data collection differ or are the same across time – has there been a change in some metric across time? This approach also enables you to explore whether particular comparator groups vary in the degree to which each differs across time (e.g. male versus female; received training versus not; HR versus marketing versus finance etc).
Continuous DV (Interval or Ratio –and sometimes *Ordinal)	Two or more continuous IVs	**Multiple regression (linear)**	**Multiple regression** analysis – here we are trying to predict and account for variation in a continuous dependent variable (e.g. sales €£$ figures for each individual – importantly we do this by exploring the degree to which this variation can be 'accounted for' by the degree to which two or more other (possible) causal factors/IVs share variance with this DV. For example – might the variation in $ sales that an employee achieves in a week be linked to the number of hours worked in a week and the age of the employee?

(continued)

TABLE 3.4 (Continued)

Dependent Variable (DV)	Independent Variable (IV)	Analysis Test	Nature of the test: what type of research question is it trying to explore?
	Both categorical and continuous IVs	Multiple regression (linear)	Multiple regression analysis: as immediately above – with the difference that some of the IVs included represent memberships of a particular category/group (e.g. male versus female). If the number of categories in a particular IV is above two then dummy variables have to be created. See discussion in Chapter 7.

*Although technically incorrect, in practice, sometimes ordinal data is treated as continuous data for the purpose of analysis. An example is answering multiple-item questions in a survey to give your line manager a score of 1 to 5 (where 1 means very poor and 5 means very good). Technically you cannot select anything other than 1, 2, 3, 4 or 5. Many analysts, though, will treat this data as continuous to perform arithmetic to get findings such as Manager A having a mean of 3.2 versus Manager B having a mean of 3.9.

†Again we caveat this statement by raising the issue that correlation does not imply causality (see Chapter 12).

NOTE There are many different tests available not discussed here. We restrict our test choices to the most straightforward tests with regard to HR analytics.

A note on parametric tests and parametric data

Most of the statistical procedures in Table 3.4 are 'parametric tests'. Statisticians use the word 'parameter' when talking about characteristics of the population that the sample data (that they are analysing) comes from, and parametric tests are making various assumptions about the populations that the data being analysed is drawn from. One of the key assumptions of parametric tests (that enable us to draw conclusions about the wider population) is that distributions linked to the data form a normal distribution. This is when the data is distributed symmetrically around the centre (or mean) and is shaped like a bell curve, which you may have come across before. Characteristically, most of the results will be nearest the mean, and then, as you move away from the mean in either direction, the numbers will get smaller.

Sometimes, however, the data that we analyse might not behave in this way. The distribution curve of the data may lean (be skewed) to the left (+) or the right (–), or it may be bunched up and 'pointy' (*lept*okurtic: the data distribution *leapt* up in the middle) or more spread out and flat (*platy*kurtic: flat like a *plate*) than we would expect for a normal distribution. In this case, we have to be careful when drawing assumptions from the tests; we may need to use other tests that are robust against violations of assumptions of normality.

As we have discussed, it is only continuous data on which we can do arithmetic and calculate means and standard deviations. Hence it is only when we are analysing continuous data that we need to test whether the data meets the assumptions of the parametric test we are using. Further details on how this is done in R are in the case study chapters (Chapters 4–9).

The best way to learn these methods is to use them in an organizational example in context. This is where the case studies in this book are very useful. Table 3.5 provides a summary of the case study examples for each statistical test mentioned.

TABLE 3.5 Case study examples

Test	Case Study Examples
Chi-square analysis	1 Diversity case study (Chapter 4) example 1: gender and job grade analysis using frequency tables and chi-square. Pages 99–111.
	2 Employee turnover case study (Chapter 6) example 1b: exploring differences in individual staff turnover across a number of different countries using cross-tabulation and the chi-square test. Pages 189–192.
	3 Recruitment and selection case study (Chapter 8) examples 1 and 2: diversity analyses looking at potential bias in the recruitment and selection decisions. Pages 99–111.
Logistic regression analysis	1 Employee turnover case study (Chapter 6) example 3: using logistic regression to set up a predictive model for individual turnover. Pages 203–212.
	2 Recruitment and selection case study (Chapter 8) example 2: predicting candidate rejection or shortlisting taking into account graduate gender and ethnicity. Pages 282–292.
	3 Recruitment and selection case study (Chapter 8) example 4: predicting graduate turnover. Pages 302–308.
	4 Predictive modelling case study (Chapter 10) example 3: predictive modelling and obtaining probabilities for the likelihood of employees leaving. Pages 368–372.
	5 Predictive modelling case study (Chapter 10) example 6: using historical patterns to predict the likelihood of new graduate candidates leaving. Pages 385–386.
Survival analysis	1 Employee turnover case study (Chapter 6) example 4: using survival analysis to predict length of service. Pages 212–218.
Independent samples t-test	1 Diversity case study (Chapter 4) example 2b: comparing ethnicity and gender across two functions in an organization using the independent samples t-test. Pages 117–123.
	2 Engagement case study (Chapter 5) example 4: using the independent samples t-test to determine whether engagement levels are significantly different depending on functional grouping and location. Pages 170–175.

(continued)

TABLE 3.5 (Continued)

Test	Case Study Examples
Paired samples t-test	1 Monitoring the impact of interventions case study (Chapter 9) example 1: assessing stress before and after an intervention using a paired samples t-test. Pages 316–320.
One-way independent ANOVA	1 Employee turnover case study (Chapter 6) example 2: exploring team-level turnover by country using the one-way ANOVA test. Pages 194–203.
One-way repeated measures ANOVA	1 Monitoring the impact of interventions case study (Chapter 9) example 3: value change. Exploring staff commitment levels at three different time points in a values change project. Pages 325–330.
Within and between ANOVA: General Linear Model	1 Monitoring the impact of interventions case study (Chapter 9) example 2: testing stress before and after intervention by gender using a repeated measures ANOVA. Pages 320–325. 2 Monitoring the impact of interventions case study (Chapter 9) example 4: value change. Assessing the change in staff commitment over time by department. Pages 331–337. 3 Monitoring the impact of interventions case study (Chapter 9) example 5: measuring the impact of a supermarket checkout training intervention on scan rates over time. Pages 337–343.
Multiple linear regression	1 Diversity case study (Chapter 4) example 3: using multiple linear regression to model and predict ethnic diversity variation across teams from base location, function, group size, team lead gender, and team gender breakdown. Pages 124–132. 2 Engagement case study (Chapter 5) example 5: using multiple linear regression to predict team level engagement. Pages 175–181. 3 Turnover case study (Chapter 6) example 5: using multiple linear regression to predict team level turnover. Pages 218–223. 4 Performance case study (Chapter 7) examples 1a and 1b: using multiple linear regression to predict customer loyalty and reinvestment in a financial services organization. Pages 233–238 and 239–241. 5 Performance case study (Chapter 7) example 2: using multiple linear regression when combining customer survey data with 'pulse' survey to predict customer loyalty in a financial services organization. Pages 242–245. 6 Performance case study (Chapter 7) example 3: using multiple linear regression when combining performance appraisal data, sickness records and pulse survey data to predict individual performance in a manufacturing organization. Pages 246–251. 7 Performance case study (Chapter 7) example 4: using stepwise multiple linear regression to find the best model for predicting performance using combined performance appraisal data, sickness records and pulse survey data in a manufacturing organization. Pages 251–255.

(continued)

TABLE 3.5 (Continued)

Test	Case Study Examples
	8 Performance case study (Chapter 7) example 5: tracking performance over time using stepwise regression with combined performance appraisal data, sickness records and pulse survey data in a manufacturing organization. Pages 255–258.
	9 Performance case study (Chapter 7) example 6: using multiple regression to predict sickness absence using employee attitude scores in a manufacturing organization. Pages 258–261.
	10 Performance case study (Chapter 7) example 7: using multiple regression to explore patterns of performance with employee profile data in a manufacturing organization. Pages 261–266.
	11 Performance case study (Chapter 7) example 8a: using data interrogation techniques and multiple linear regression to predict checkout scan rates from employee profile data in a retail organization. Pages 266–268.
	12 Performance case study (Chapter 7) example 9: using dummy variables in multiple linear regression to determine the presence of high-performing age groups in predicting scan rates in a retail organization. Pages 271–274.
	13 Recruitment and selection case study (Chapter 8) example 3: assessment centre selection technique validation, predicting graduate performance from demographic, assessment centre and onboarding data. Pages 297–302.
	14 Monitoring the impact of interventions case study (Chapter 9) example 6: conditional panel model predicting change in checkout scan rates with supermarket operators. Pages 343–348.
	15 Predictive modelling case study (Chapter 10) example 1: predictive modelling of customer reinvestment intentions. Pages 352–358.
	16 Predictive modelling case study (Chapter 10) example 2: predictive modelling the impact of training on checkout scan rates. Pages 358–367.
	17 Predictive modelling case study (Chapter 10) example 4: predictive modelling the impact of induction day on graduate performance. Pages 376–379.
	18 Predictive modelling case study (Chapter 10) example 5: predicting expected performance of graduate candidates. Pages 379–384.

Other analysis examples used in the book using simple descriptive statistics:

- Diversity case study (Chapter 4). Example 2a: exploring ethnic diversity across teams using descriptive statistics. Pages 111–116.

- Turnover case study (Chapter 6). Example 1a: exploring differences in individual staff turnover across a number of different countries using frequencies tables. Pages 189–192.

- Predictive modelling case study (Chapter 10): obtaining descriptive statistics to enable various predictive models. Page 351.

Statistical tests for categorical data (binary, nominal, ordinal)

Here we outline each test in greater detail. Importantly, in each of the case study chapters we discuss further what the tests are doing in context. So in order to get to grips with each test the reader will also want to read each test in the context of each case study example in subsequent chapters.

Cross-tabulation and the chi-square (χ^2) test

Remembering from earlier in this chapter that the categorical data is all about categories and names on which we cannot do any arithmetic, we can be certain that if adding, subtracting, multiplying and dividing are not possible, then calculating means or standard deviations are out of the question! We can, then, only analyse the number of things that fall into each category, or the frequencies. This limitation determines which analytic test we can use. With categorical data, we can only analyse frequencies. The best way to start is by doing a cross-tabulation of the frequency of occurrence for each category of interest. This is similar to the results that you might get if you produced a pivot table in Excel. Then, we apply the chi-square (or χ^2) test to the cross-tabulated frequencies; in this case we do this in order to analyse the significance of any link or relationships between two or more categorical variables.

A very simple example might be a cross-tabulation showing the results of frequencies of men and women in our organization (of 15,338 employees) and whether they were promoted or not in 2015. It would look something like the results shown in Table 3.6.

TABLE 3.6 Observed gender and promotion values

Gender	2015 Promotions		
	Promoted	Not Promoted	Total
Male	127	6,784	6,911
Female	49	8,378	8,427
Total	176	15,162	15,338

By combining gender and promotions in this way, we end up with four discrete categories:

• male promoted

• male not promoted

• female promoted

• female not promoted

If we wanted to look at this descriptively we would want to calculate some percentages to get a feel for the data. For example, 54.94 per cent of the employees are female and 45.06 per cent are male. Only 1.147 per cent of employees were promoted in 2015. Of those promoted, just over 72 per cent were male; just under 2 per cent of men were promoted but the proportion of women who were promoted was just over 0.5 per cent. We can describe these findings and tell a story; however, we need to check whether there is a significant link between gender and promotion rates in 2015 before making any claims about statistically significant patterns.

If we want to see whether there is a statistically significant relationship between gender and 2015 promotions, we would do the chi-square test. The chi-square test compares the frequencies that you actually observed in particular conditions with the frequencies you would expect to get if there were absolutely no relationship between the two variables. If, in our organization, there is no relationship between gender and promotion rates, our chi-square tests could tell us that a set of frequencies could be gained by chance alone.

So in our example, the chi-squared statistic is obtained by calculating the overall difference between the observed frequency in each of the four categories and the 'expected' frequency in each of the four categories (that we would find if there were no real link between gender and promotions in our organization), and dividing it by the model total.

CHI-SQUARE EXAMPLE (R WILL DO THIS FOR YOU!)

The equation (that R calculates when you run your code) looks like this:

$$\chi^2 = \sum ((\text{observed value} - \text{expected value})^2/\text{expected value})$$

Or the sum of ((observed value – expected value)^2/expected value) for each of the four categories.

Note that there is a slight variation on this equation when we have a 2 × 2 table, as in the example below, which is referred to as a Yates's continuity correction:

$$\chi^2 = \sum ((|\text{observed value} - \text{expected value}| - 0.05)^2/\text{expected value})$$

For simplicity we are going to ignore this version of the equation as it is only used with 2 × 2 tables.

Looking at our crosstabs of gender and 2015 promotion counts, we have the observed values for each category, but what are the 'expected' values that our equation refers to here? These are calculated by using the total values and the general proportions of males versus females found in the organization regardless of promotions.

Another way of putting this with our example is that the 'expected frequency' in each of the promotion versus not-promoted/male versus female condition is what you would expect if you simply translated the proportion of our organization that was promoted in 2015 into our populations of males and females in our organization. For example, if 1.1 per cent of our organization was promoted in 2015, then the 'expected frequency' of promoted versus non-promoted employees would amount to 1.1 per cent versus 98.9 per cent of both our male and female population (if there was no link between gender and promotion rates). But, in reality, it may be the case that more than 1.1 per cent of males were promoted and less than 1.1 per cent of females were promoted... as in this case.

Let's work through the equation for each category:

1 Male promoted:

   Observed value = 127

   Expected value that we would probably have if there was no link between gender and promotions

   = (total # men) × (total # promoted) / total people

   = 6,911 × 176 / 15,338

   = 79.3

   For simplicity, we will round this down to 79; so if gender was not linked to promotions we should have 79 males who were promoted in 2015 – the observed figure is obviously higher than this.

2 Male not promoted:

   Observed value = 6,784

   Expected value

   = (total # men) x (total # not promoted) / total people

   = 6,911 x 15,162 / 15,338

   = 6,831.7

   For simplicity, let's round this to 6,832 – so if gender was not linked to promotions we should have 6,832 males who were not promoted in 2015.

3 Female promoted:

   Observed value = 49

Expected value

= (total # women) x (total # promoted) / total people

= 8,427 x 176 / 15,338

= 96.7

For simplicity, we will round this to 97 – so if gender was not linked to promotions we should have 97 females who were promoted in 2015 – the observed figure is obviously lower than this.

4 Female not promoted:

Observed value = 8,378

Expected value

= (total # women) x (total # not promoted) / total people

= 8,427 x 15,162 / 15,338

= 8,330.3

For simplicity, let's round this to 8,330 – so if gender was not linked to promotions we should have 8,330 females who were not promoted in 2015.

Looking at these figures, we can see that we would expect more women to be promoted and fewer men to be promoted than we actually observed in our organization if there was no link between gender and promotions. But could these numbers have come about by chance anyway, with no particular significant relationship between promotion and gender? Let's work out the chi-square statistic and test it!

So, going back to the formula:

$X^2 = X$ ((observed value – expected value)^2/expected value) = (observed male promoted – expected male promoted)^2/expected male promoted+ (observed male not promoted – expected male not promoted)^2/expected male not promoted + (observed female promoted – expected female promoted)^2/expected female promoted + (observed female not promoted – expected female not promoted)^2/expected female not promoted

= (127 – 79)2/79 + (6,784 – 6,832)^2/6,832 + (49 – 97)^2/97 + (8,378 – 8,330)^2/8,330

= 2,304/79 + 2,304/6,832 + 2,304/97 + 2,304/8,330

= 29.16 + 0.34 + 23.75 + 0.28

= 53.53

This chi-squared (X^2) statistic is then checked against a X^2 distribution with known properties in a table (online or in a stats book) along with the degrees of freedom that, in this case, is calculated as (r–1)(c–1) where r is the number of rows and c is the number of columns. So (2–1)(2–1) = 1 x 1 = 1.

Any statistics book will usually include statistical tables outlining critical values of the chi-square distribution. When you look up what the critical values of a chi-square test for a 2 x 2 table (1 degree of freedom), these amount to the following:

$p < 0.05 = 3.84$

$p < 0.01 = 6.63$

$p < 0.001 = 10.83$

These figures tell us how big the chi-square value needs to get to in order for us to be 95 per cent, 99 per cent or 99.9 per cent confident that our results are not due to chance alone.

Our value of 53.53 is far greater than the chi-square value required for us to be 99.9 per cent confident that our findings are not due to chance. We can confidently say that *as a proportion of males and females in our organization*, males get promoted significantly more frequently than females. Thus there is a link between gender and the likelihood of being promoted in our organization (and there is less than a 1 in 1,000 chance that this result would occur by chance alone).

You will be happy to know that R does all of these calculations for you. All you need to do is have a data set with each employee entered – with an indication of whether they were promoted in 2015 and whether they are male or female. R will provide:

- a table as set out in Table 3.6
- the degrees of freedom
- the X^2 statistic
- the p-value.

We can create a table of values in R and conduct a chi-squared test. Run the code below.

```
# Create the cross tabulation with the counts as given in Table 3.6
# Create a table by combining two sets of numeric values, as in Table 3.6
crosstabs <- as.table(rbind(c(127, 6784), c(49, 8378)))

# Specify the row and column labels for the table we just created;
# Row first then column second
dimnames(crosstabs) = list(gender = c("male", "female"), promoted =
c("promoted", "not promoted"))

# Display the cross tabulation
print(crosstabs)
```

```
# Perform the chi-squared test on the cross tabulation
chisq.test(crosstabs)
```

The results you will get from running the code differs slightly from our hand-calcu-
lated result. This is because of the rounding we did to simplify hand calculations and
because of a correction automatically applied by R for cross tabulations with a small
number of rows and columns.

CHI-SQUARE ANALYSIS CASE STUDY EXAMPLES

- Diversity case study (Chapter 4). Example 1: gender and job grade analysis using
  frequency tables and chi-square. Pages 99–111.
- Employee turnover case study (Chapter 6). Example 1b: exploring differences in
  individual staff turnover across a number of different countries using cross-tabulation and the chi-square test. Pages 192–194.
- Recruitment and selection case study (Chapter 8). Examples 1 and 2. A diversity
  analysis looking at potential bias in the recruitment and selection decisions.
  Pages 279–282 and 282–292.

The chi-square analysis used here covered the situation where we were analysing the
relationship between two categorical variables. If, however, there were three or more
categorical variables, we could set up a chi-square analysis for particular combinations of categorical variables; yet we might prefer to use a technique called loglinear
analysis. This is not a technique covered in this book (indeed, you can also use logistic regression in this situation and we do cover that in a number of chapters);
however, if you would like to learn more about loglinear analysis, see Field (2017).

Logistic regression analysis

If the dependent variable is binary and the independent variables are either categorical or continuous, then you can use logistic regression analysis to model or predict
the dependent variable. To extend the example given previously, we could try to
model what factors can help predict whether someone was promoted in 2015: from
a range of factors that include gender we could include contractual status, education
level, training, job tenure, etc.

Another simple example of when we might use logistic regression in an organizational context might be when we are trying to predict factors that explain why
someone might leave our organization. The data stored in our HR database in relation to this might be something like 'left/leaver' or 'active employee'. This example is
a binary (2 level) categorical: yes or no variable. If we wanted to try to find predictors of whether someone is likely to be a leaver then we may wish to include a
number of possible independent variables such as age (continuous), gender (categorical) and assessment centre scores (continuous), amongst others.

Analysis of historical data using logistical regression analysis will help us to find patterns in the data and create models with which to make some future predictions. In Chapter 10 we use this approach to predict the likelihood that graduate candidates might leave in the first year after they are hired. We use independent variables such as:

- assessment-centre scores (are extroverts more likely to leave; are candidates with higher numerical reasoning scores more likely to stay?)
- gender (are male or female candidates more likely to stay after a year?)
- age (are younger candidates less likely to stay beyond a year?).

Here, with our analysis we are attempting to predict the likelihood of something happening; the likelihood of one particular occurrence of a set of possible occurrences (in this case the likelihood of someone being a 'leaver'). This is different from linear regression (to be discussed next), where the dependent variable is continuous. In linear regression we would be predicting the expected proportion (and direction) of change in a dependent variable that can be attributed to any particular independent variable; or, to put it another way, what makes the dependent variable increase or decrease (such as predicting the sales figures achieved by the new joiner – and what factors account for a particular proportion of change in these figures – what would make these sales higher or lower? Do young women bring in higher figures on average? Does a high assessment-centre score mean high sales figures?).

However, more on linear regression later… To return to logistic regression, we are trying to model or predict the likelihood of the occurrence of a binary categorical variable.

Just as in the chi-square test, there is an equation behind this. The equation will take the data as the input, calculate the estimated statistics/coefficients and 'parameters' (estimated characteristics of our organization) and produce an output of key information. With binary logistic regression this includes (but is not limited to) the following (which are all output in R):

- *Model chi-square*: to test how well the model fits the data using an observed versus expected comparison of the data you would expect if you used only the model logistic regression equation to calculate it versus the actual data.
- *Model chi-square p-value (Sig.)*: uses the model chi-square value to provide a p-value for the overall model (remembering that we need the p-value to be <0.05 for the model to be significant). This tells you whether your model significantly predicts your dependent variable.
- *The Nagelkerke R-square*: this is a 'pseudo R-square' figure that gives an estimate of the percentage variation that we account for in our dependent variable with our proposed model. For example, if this came out as 60 per cent in our example, we could say that 60 per cent of the variance in our data set – that indicated

whether someone left or not after the first year – is accounted for by the model we have created (e.g. using age, gender and assessment-centre scores).

• *P-value (Sig.) for each independent variable*: remembering again that any p-value < 0.05 is significant. Having the p-value for each independent variable will tell us which independent variables potentially significantly 'impact' the dependent variable. In our example, it will tell us if age, gender or assessment-centre scores (or a combination of the three) have a significant impact (or significantly predict) the likelihood of a graduate leaving in the first year.

• *Odds ratios (Exp(B))*: indicates the changes in probability (or 'odds') of the occurrence in the dependent variable incurred by a change in one unit of the independent variable. In our example, it would be the increase (or decrease) in the chances of someone leaving in the first year with every increase (or decrease) in assessment-centre scores.

If you are using a statistical software package such as R, you will not need to understand or work with the background equation for logistic regression. If you are curious, though, and would like to know what it looks like, here you go:

$$P(Y) = 1/(1+e^{-(b_0 + b_1 x_{1i} + b_2 x_{2i} + \ldots + b_n x_{ni})})$$

where 'e' is the base of natural logarithms, i is the instance of the variable, Y is the dependent variable, x(1 to n) are the n independent variables, and b is the degree to which that independent variable impacts the dependent variable in the equation.

Put another way:

$$Ln(p/(1-p)) = b_0 + b_1 x_{1i} + b_2 x_{2i} + b_n x_{ni}$$

where p is the probability that Y=1 and Ln denotes the natural logarithm.

That is quite enough talk of logarithms and equations in this chapter, and indeed the sum total of logarithmic talk. Let's get back to what you need to know to master HR analytics.

When the dependent variable (or outcome variable) has only two options, as it does in this example (yes or no), the analysis is referred to as 'binary logistic regression'. If the dependent variable has more than two options, for example if we were trying to predict the colour of somebody's eyes, the analysis we would carry out is called 'multinomial logistic regression'. Other terms you may hear are 'dichotomous logistic regression' and 'binomial logistic regression' (this is the same as binary logistic regression), or 'polychotomous logistic regression'.

To conduct a binary logistic regression analysis in R, we can use the *glm* program. To illustrate, below is example code you can use as a template, for the purpose of illustration – as it is an example, it will not run if you copy and paste it into R as is:

```
# Logistic regression in R
logit_reg <- glm(dep_var ~ ind_var1 + ind_var2, data = df, family =
"binomial")

summary(logit_reg)
```

In the code above, we use the *glm* program. *glm* stands for generalized linear model, which can estimate a wide variety of models. We specify a dependent variable (*dep_var*), and two independent variables (*ind_var1*, *ind_var2*). The *data = df* component of the code tells R to use the dataframe labelled *df*. The *family = binomial* part of the code tells the *glm* program to use the binomial distribution for the dependent variable, which is how a logistic regression is specified for this program. We put the results of the model estimation into the object *logit_reg*. Finally, the *summary(logit_reg)* line asks R to show us the summary of the model. The code above is just an example that you can use as a template. When conducting these analyses with real data, you will need to ensure to substitute in your own variable and dataframe names.

For worked-through examples of binary logistic regression analyses, including a discussion of the output, see the following examples.

LOGISTIC REGRESSION ANALYSIS CASE STUDY EXAMPLES

- Employee turnover case study (Chapter 6). Example 3: using logistic regression to set up a predictive model for individual turnover (see pages 203–212).
- Recruitment and selection case study (Chapter 8). Example 2: predicting candidate rejection or shortlisting taking into account graduate gender and ethnicity (see pages 282–292).
- Recruitment and selection case study (Chapter 8). Example 4: predicting graduate turnover (see pages 302–308).
- Predictive modelling case study (Chapter 10). Example 3: predictive modelling and obtaining probabilities for the likelihood of employees leaving (see pages 368–372).
- Predictive modelling case study (Chapter 10). Example 6: using historical patterns to predict the likelihood of new graduate candidates leaving (see pages 385–386).

Survival analysis

Also known as event history analysis and duration analysis, survival analysis has possibly the most intuitive name of the methods in this book and it is perhaps one of the most user-friendly when it comes to explaining results to others. We are analysing the expected amount of time until an event occurs. That event might be death (hence the term 'survival' analysis) or it may be something else for which we can practically apply the same methods. Some examples of questions that survival analysis might be used to try to answer are below.

In medicine:

- How long can we expect patients to survive with certain medical conditions?
- What proportion of patients with certain conditions are expected to survive beyond a given time?
- What variables/factors/interventions are likely to increase or decrease their life expectancy?

In engineering:

- For how many hours will certain types of light bulbs operate?
- How long will certain types of concrete remain structurally sound before beginning to crumble or crack?
- How long should we make the manufacturer's warranty period for this washing machine?

In HR analytics:

- What proportion of our graduate intake are expected to last longer than 6 months, 12 months, 2 years?
- What factors will increase or decrease the amount of time they stay with us?
- Can we identify different patterns of 'survival' (how long they tend to stay in the organization) for different groups?

So, in our HR analytics example:

- The event is 'leaving the organization'.
- The duration is 'the length of service before leaving'.
- The dependent variable is 'the probability of leaving'.
- The survival function is 'the probability of *not* leaving until a specific time'.

CENSORED CASES

For some cases, we won't know the time until the event occurred – either because it did not occur during the study or it did not occur at all. For example, during a study:

- some patients will not die
- some light bulbs will still be burning

- some leaders will still be in office

- some employees will not have resigned (one would hope!)

It is also important to consider that not all cases enter and leave the study at the same time, just as not all employees would enter and leave an organization at the same time. Consider the illustration in Figure 3.1 for survival analysis at the organization Hazardcorp.

In this example, the shaded box shows the duration of the study and the arrows represent the start and end dates for each person in the study. In survival analyses of staff turnover, the period of study would be the period for which we actually hold data on people; e.g. we may only have digital records for people that have been employed for the past 10 years. The censored cases are the people for whom the event did not occur within the duration of the study/period of observation. Here, the event is an employee leaving the organization. Thus, in our example, the censored cases are Josephine, Fernando, Douglas, Paul and Mia. For these people we don't know how long they survived because, as far as the study is concerned, they are 'still alive'. It follows that the only people for whom an event did occur within the study are Max and Kievan.

3.1   Survival data for Hazardcorp showing censored cases

HAZARDS

Continuing with this rather dramatic life and death theme, the event in question is often referred to as a 'hazard'. So the hazard would be death, light bulb burning out, washing machine breaking down, or in this case the employee leaving. The following three terms follow:

- Hazard rate – the probability of the hazard occurring at any point in time. For example, new graduates at a particular organization may have 70 per cent chance of leaving in the first 2 years; 50 per cent between years 2 and 3; and 35 per cent between years 3 and 4.

- Hazard function – if we plot the probability of the event occurring against time, the equation that describes this plotted line is the hazard function.

- Hazard ratio – a bit like the odds ratio we covered in logistic regression. It is also called the relative risk.

SURVIVAL ANALYSIS METHODS

There are three key methods when it comes to survival analysis:

- life tables
- Kaplan-Meier
- Cox regression analysis

A very brief description of each is given in Table 3.7.

For worked-through examples of survival analysis using Kaplan-Meier using R, including a discussion output and illustration of a survival curve, see Example 4 in Chapter 6 (pages 212–218) (also outlined in Table 3.5).

To conduct survival analyses in R, we will be using the *Surv* command, see the example code below:

```
# Load the survival package
library(survival)

# Conduct the survival analysis
surv_reg <- survfit(Surv(dep_var, time) ~ 1, data = df)

# Display the results
summary(surv_reg)
```

The *library(survival)* line loads the *survival* package, which is required for the programs needed for the analysis. Remember in Chapter 2 that we mentioned that R has over 20,000 packages available. The *survival* package is one of those. Survival analysis is a complex analysis that goes beyond the basic set of analysis tools built into R. So we must load an appropriate package to conduct the analysis. One thing we will be doing in the book is to identify the packages you will need for a particular analysis, if at all. For example, the chi-square analysis shown earlier does not need additional packages to be loaded.

The next line of code conducts the analyses. We start with the *survfit* program, which fits the survival curve to the data. The next part *Surv(dep_var, time)* creates an object the *survfit* program can analyse. It comprises of *dep_var*, or our name for the dependent variable, which will depend on the specific label you decide for your data.

TABLE 3.7 Key methods in survival analysis

Method	Description	When to Use
Life tables	Subdivides the duration of the study into smaller time periods (e.g. 1 month). The probability of the event occurring during each time period is then estimated.	Used much less than Kaplan-Meier, which is seen as superior; however, life tables were developed first and are still widely used for large samples because they provide a simple summary of a large set of data. Time variable must be continuous. (Event) status variable must be binary or categorical. Factor variable must be categorical. Regardless of when the cases enter the study, they are expected to behave in the same way. There are no systematic differences between cases, whether they are censored or uncensored, and the probability of the event occurring must only depend on time.
Kaplan-Meier	Calculates the nonparametric estimates of survival and the hazard rates. Logrank tests are calculated and provide the parametric and randomization test significance levels.	Can be used when the data is non-parametric, which means the data is not required to fit a normal distribution and no assumption can be made about the shape of the hazard function. There are censored cases in the data set and the hazard function is estimated based on the data, showing changes in the probability of survival over time. Time variable must be continuous. (Event) status variable can be categorical or continuous. Factor variable must be categorical. Stratification variable (if using a stratified sample) must be categorical. Can be used to compare the survival curves by different categorical levels of a factor variable (e.g. gender – male versus female – or different functions) or to produce separate analyses for different groups/levels in a stratified sample. There is an assumption that censored and uncensored cases behave the same way.
Cox regression	Similar to logistic regression analysis. Cox regression models time to the event based on different values of the independent variables. The key statistic is the hazard ratio, Exp(B) (odds ratio in logistic regression). Here it shows the changes in probability of the event occurring over time in relation to a change in one unit of the independent variable.	Use when you have one or more independent variables to predict the status of the event. Time variable must be numeric but can be continuous or discrete/ordinal. (Event) status variable must be binary. Independent/predictor variables can be categorical or continuous. Stratification variable must be categorical.

It should be 1 if the event occurred, such as employee resignation, and 0 if the event has not occurred. The next part, *time*, is a variable that represents the time increments in which the event did or did not occur. The ~ *1* indicates that no independent variables are used in the model. As in previous examples, we define the example dataframe *df* (*data* = *df*). The result of the analysis is stored in the *surv_reg* object, and the line *summary(surv_reg)* shows the results of the analysis.

Statistical tests for continuous/interval-level data

T-tests (two sample)

Two sample t-tests are used to identify whether there is a difference between two samples. The two samples can either be data taken from two completely different groups of objects (e.g. groups of employees or teams) or the two samples could be data taken on two separate occasions from the same group of objects (such as employees or teams). When the dependent variable is continuous (for example '€£$ sales') and there is only one independent variable, which is categorical and binary (for example, group 1 versus group 2 or Time 1 versus Time 2), then you should use a t-test.

There are two types of two-sample t-tests:

- The independent samples t-test is used when comparing two distinct groups on a continuous dependent variable. These groups can consist of different individuals, whether they're people, teams or even animals like bears or pigeons. For instance, you might compare a group of men to a group of women, or examine the difference in sales performance between two teams. The test helps determine whether there is a significant difference between the groups on the measure you're studying.

- The paired samples t-test can be used when you are interested in whether a sample of workers or a sample of teams (that have the same employees over time) changes significantly on some particular continuous dependent variable (e.g. '€£$ sales' or engagement scores) across two different occasions of data collection (thus two repeated samples). For example, you could compare customer satisfaction ratings of 100 employees in June 2014 with the customer satisfaction ratings of the same 100 people in September 2014 after they had all undergone training.

In both types of t-test, we have two samples of data collection and look for differences on a particular continuous dependent variable. We could use descriptive statistics and simply compare the means (either between the two groups that we are comparing at any one time or between the two sets of data collected with the same group across time). If the means are similar, then we might conclude that there is no difference between the two samples of data (or that 'the samples come from the same population'). Unless we test this for significance, however, we will not understand the degree of confidence that we should have in any difference in means (and thus the population that the samples of data represent) that we might find.

We discussed hypothesis testing earlier in this chapter in the section on statistical significance. Here, we might say the following:

- *Research hypothesis*: there is a difference between the samples in the data that we are comparing.
- *Null hypothesis*: there is no difference between the samples in the data that we are comparing.

Using a repeated measures t-test example:

- *Research hypothesis*: there is a significant difference in sales figures when you compare Time 1 (before attendance at a training course) with Time 2 (after attendance at a training course).
- *Null hypothesis*: there is no difference in employees' sales figures when you compare Time 1 (before attendance at a training course) with Time 2 (after attendance at a training course).

Intuitively, the larger the difference between the sample means, the more confident we would be that the research hypothesis was true or, in our example, that the training course did impact the sales figures and we could reject the null hypothesis (cast it aside like a chalice of bitter wine…).

Independent samples t-test

Also known as the 'between-subjects' t-test or the 'independent measures' t-test, the independent samples t-test is for comparing the difference between two groups when we have different people in each group that we compare. An example of using this in an organizational context might be to compare the average engagement levels for staff who work part-time with those who work full-time. We could also have teams as our object of data collection and still use an independent t-test: for example, we could look at the difference in team level engagement scores for finance teams versus sales teams in our organization.

Conceptually, the way the independent t-test works is that it compares the difference between the sample means that we find to the difference between the sample means that we would expect to get if the null hypothesis were true (that there were no real differences between the two samples/populations):

> t = ((observed difference between sample means) – (expected difference between sample means of the samples i.e. 0))/(estimate of the standard error of the difference between two sample means).
>
> The standard error is an estimate of the standard deviation of a sampling distribution where means from multiple samples of the same N have been plotted, so it is an estimated measure of the variability, or spread, of multiple sample means. So if the standard error is small, we would expect most samples to have very similar means.

Put simply, the independent t-test checks whether the difference in the means between groups is big enough for us to say that the likelihood that we would randomly find two groups that had such large differences in means is so slim that we have a meaningful, statistically significant difference.

Importantly, there are three things that will influence whether a difference between means of two groups of employees (or any object of study such as teams, etc) is likely to yield a significant (and thus meaningful) difference. The first of these is how big the observed differences are between the two groups; the second is how many cases (e.g. employees or teams) we have in each sample that we are comparing; and the third is how much variation we tend to have on our measures within each of our sample groups.

To conduct an independent t-test with R, we will be using the *t.test* command – see the example code below:

```
# Conduct an independent samples t-test
t.test(df$dep_var ~ df$group)
```

In the code above, we use the *t.test* program, then specify the dependent variable (the *dep_var* variable in the dataframe *df*), as well as the grouping variable (the *group* variable in the dataframe *df*).

For worked-through examples of the independent samples t-test using R, including a discussion of the output, see the following examples (these are also outlined in Table 3.5).

INDEPENDENT SAMPLES T-TEST CASE STUDY EXAMPLES

- Diversity case study (Chapter 4). Example 2b: comparing ethnicity and gender across two functions in an organization using the independent samples t-test (see pages 117–123).
- Engagement case study (Chapter 5). Example 4: using the independent samples t-test to determine whether engagement levels are significantly different in two locations (see pages 170–175).

Paired samples t-test

Also known as the 'dependent t-test', the 'related t-test', the 'matched-pairs t-test' or the 'repeated t-test', the paired samples t-test compares the difference between two groups of data when we have the same people in each group. An example of using this is the one referred to previously where group 1 is the sales team before the training course and group 2 is the sales team after the training course. The dependent variable we are measuring in each group is the sales revenue data.

Conceptually, the way that a paired samples t-test works is that it compares the means of differences found between the individual cases (e.g. employees) when comparing Time 1 with Time 2, with the mean of differences that we would expect if there were no change over time (thus 0) or the mean of differences over time that we would expect if the null hypothesis were true. Then this is divided by an estimate of the standard error of means of differences (estimated to represent the standard deviation of a sampling distribution of means of differences):

t = ((observed mean of differences in individual cases between samples) – (expected mean of differences between cases across the sample, i.e. 0)) / (estimate of the standard error of the means of differences between two sample means of a given N).

Luckily, R can calculate this for us. To conduct a paired t-test with R, we will be using the *t.test* command again – see the example code below:

```
# Conduct a paired samples t-test
t.test(df$time1, df$time2, paired = T)
```

In the code above, we use the *t.test* program, then specify the time 1 and time 2 variables (the *time1* and *time2* variables in the dataframe *df*), then specify the paired t-test by adding the *paired = T* option. Note that unlike the independent samples t-test, we separate the variables with a comma instead of a tilde.

PAIRED SAMPLES T-TEST CASE STUDY EXAMPLE

- Monitoring the impact of interventions case study (Chapter 9). Example 1: assessing stress before and after an intervention using a paired samples t-test (see pages 316–320).

One-way independent analysis of variance test

Similar to the independent samples t-test, the one-way analysis of variance (ANOVA) test is used when the dependent variable is continuous, the independent variables are categorical, and when there are different participants (or entities) in each category. Again we are comparing the means of groups. The difference with the one-way ANOVA is that we have more than two groups to compare.

So the one-way ANOVA test is a powerful method for testing the significance of the difference between sample means where more than two conditions are used. It effectively tests the null hypothesis that all the samples are drawn from the same population and that there is no difference between them. Because there are more than two groups, if the test suggests there is a difference, then further testing (called 'post-hoc testing') is needed in order to determine specifically which samples are different and by how much (Coolican, 2009).

To conduct the one-way ANOVAs in R, we can use the *anova_test* program in the *rstatix* package.

```
# Conduct the one-way ANOVA test

library(rstatix)
mod_1 <- anova_test(data = df, dep_var ~ conditions)
get_anova_table(mod_1)
```

In the code above, we use the *anova_test* program to specify a data source (data = df), then a formula, where the dependent variable is placed ahead of the independent variable (*dep_var ~ conditions*). We then put the results of the model into an object called *mod_1* (short for model 1). We then ask for the summary of the model with the next line: *get_anova_table(mod_1)*.

For worked-through examples of the one-way independent ANOVA, including post-hoc analysis and a full explanation of the output that R produces, see the following example.

ONE-WAY ANOVA CASE STUDY EXAMPLE

- Employee turnover case study (Chapter 6). Example 2: exploring team-level turnover by country using the one-way ANOVA test (see pages 194–203).

Post-hoc tests

The ANOVA tests can only tell us whether the samples differ or not, but this is only half of the story. If the ANOVA test comes back indicating there is a significant difference (three or more) between the samples/groups of workers, surely the next question would be 'Which groups are different from each other?' followed closely by 'And how different is it?'

TABLE 3.8 Post-hoc tests

Situation	Test	Benefit
If the group variances are not equal.	Games-Howell	A good idea to select this in all analysis alongside the other tests because we don't know until after the ANOVA has run whether the group variances are equal or not (until we look at Levene's test). That way, it will be there if you need it without having to run the ANOVA again. If you don't need it, you can ignore it.
Equal sample sizes and population variances are similar.	Tukey-Kramer	Good statistical sensitivity to correctly reject the null hypothesis (that there is no difference between the group means).
	Bonferroni	More conservative than Tukey (so less chance of getting a significant result) but good to use if you want guaranteed control that you will not make a Type I error (i.e. that you will not incorrectly reject the null hypothesis that the group means are the same).
Sample sizes are slightly different.	Gabriel's procedure	Good statistical sensitivity to correctly reject the null hypothesis in this situation.
Sample sizes are very different.	Tukey-Kramer	Tukey-Kramer also takes into account differences in group sizes.

The post-hoc tests will answer this for us. There are many different types of post-hoc tests available and it can be a bit confusing when deciding which one to use. If you are interested in further reading on these tests, we recommend Field (2017). Table 3.8 provides an overview of the procedures you can use in R. Please be aware that this table is very simplified and only a subset of the information available on this topic. It should, however, get you through most situations that you are likely to come across in HR analytics.

To conduct the post-hoc tests in R, we will use a variety of packages. We will use the *rstatix* package to conduct the Games-Howell test:

```
# Conduct the Games-Howell post-hoc test
library(rstatix)

games_howell_test(df, dep_var ~ conditions)
```

The code above calls the *games_howell_test* program, specifies the *df* dataframe. We further specify the dependent variable *dep_var* and the independent variable *conditions*.

To conduct the Tukey-Kramer test, we can revisit the code used to conduct the one-way ANOVA and add an extra line:

```
# Conduct the one-way ANOVA test
mod_1 <- aov(dep_var ~ conditions, data = df)
summary(mod_1)

# Conduct the Tukey test
TukeyHSD(mod_1)
```

The code above calls the *TukeyHSD* program. The *TukeyHSD* program just needs the ANOVA model specified.

To conduct a Bonferroni adjustment, we can use the *PostHocTest* program in the *DescTools* package:

```
# Conduct a Bonferroni adjustment
library(DescTools)
PostHocTest(mod_1, method = c("bonferroni"))
```

The code above calls the *PostHocTest* program in the *DescTools* package. The *PostHocTest* program needs the ANOVA model specified, followed by the method of p-value adjustment, which is 'bonferroni' in this case.

To conduct Gabriel's test, we can use the *rgabriel* program in the *rgabriel* package:

```
# Conduct Gabriel's test

library(rgabriel)
rgabriel(df$dep_var, df$condition)
```

The code above calls the *rgabriel* program in the *rgabriel* package. The *rgabriel* program needs the dependent variable *df$dep_var* specified first, followed by the independent variable *df$condition*.

One observation to make is that the decentralized nature of R means that we sometimes need to use different packages to conduct tests we need. That is one of the reasons why R can be tricky to learn. One of the aims of this book is to help navigate the maze of packages so you can focus on conducting the analyses you need to do. We recognize that, in due course, some of the programs and libraries we mention will be updated or new programs and libraries may come along that are more convenient to use. That is the nature of an evolving programming language, and our hope is that things will become easier for beginners to use. In one of the authors' experience, programs have become much easier and more powerful to use over time.

One-way repeated measures analysis of variance (ANOVA)

Just as the one-way independent ANOVA can be compared to the independent samples t-test, the one-way repeated measures ANOVA can be compared to the paired samples t-test. In both cases, the dependent variable is continuous and we are comparing samples that have been collected at different time points and the same participants/cases (e.g. employees or teams) are found at each time point. The key difference is that we use the paired samples t-test for two different sets of samples collected (e.g. two time points of data), and the one-way repeated measures ANOVA for more than two groups.

So the one-way repeated measures ANOVA compares the means of differences with three or more groups where each group has the same participants/cases – e.g. employees or teams. In HR analytics, examples of this might be comparing the engagement levels of the same group of people at three or more time points in a corporate merger, or perhaps if the same function may have experienced a fundamentally changing work environment over an extended period of time and the HR director was keen to track stress levels every six months over a two-year period.

To conduct the one-way repeated measures ANOVA in R, we can use the *anova_test* program in the *rstatix* package.

```
# Conduct one-way repeated measures ANOVA

library(rstatix)
mod_2 <- anova_test(data = df, dv = dep_var, wid = id, within = time)
get_anova_table(mod_2)
```

The code above calls the *anova_test* program in the *rstatix* package. The *anova_test* program needs the dataframe (*data = df*) specified first, followed by the dependent variable (*dv = dep_var*), a variable to identify each individual or team (*wid = id*), and the name of the within-subjects factor (*within = time*). We then put the results of the model into an object called *mod_2* (short for model 2). We then ask for the summary of the model with the next line: *get_anova_table(mod_2)*.

REPEATED MEASURES ANOVA CASE STUDY EXAMPLE

- Monitoring the impact of interventions case study (Chapter 9). Example 3: value change. Exploring staff commitment levels at three different time points in a values change project (see pages 325–330).

Within and between ANOVA – general linear model

A further variation on the repeated measures ANOVA and the one-way ANOVA mentioned here is the 'within and between' ANOVA – general linear model variation. We will not go into too much detail about this type of analytic model here, as we walk through some examples (including the output) in Chapter 9 and the various combinations of this model can get very complicated. However, it is in effect an extension of our repeated measures one-way ANOVAs, but it can take into account any change or differences (across two or more time points); importantly between two or more different groups.

If we wanted to run such a test then we would again use the *anova_test* program in the *rstatix* package.

```
# Conduct within and between ANOVA

library(rstatix)
mod_3 <- anova_test(data = df, dv = dep_var, wid = id, between =
condition, within = time, type = 3)
get_anova_table(mod_3)
```

The code above calls the *anova_test* program in the *rstatix* package. The command is nearly identical to the one-way repeated ANOVA. Two differences are that we are specifying a between subjects factor *condition*, and Type 3 sums of squares *type = 3*. We then ask for the summary of the model with the next line: *get_anova_table(mod_3)*.

We discuss this form of analysis more in Chapter 9. We will examine a case which involves testing for a change in employee stress levels across two time points (before and after a work–life balance intervention) and this change is compared with males versus females.

WITHIN AND BETWEEN ANOVA CASE STUDY EXAMPLES

- Monitoring the impact of interventions case study (Chapter 9). Example 2: testing stress before and after intervention by gender using a repeated measures ANOVA (see pages 320–325).
- Monitoring the impact of interventions case study (Chapter 9). Example 4: value change; assessing the change in staff commitment over time by department (see pages 331–337).
- Monitoring the impact of interventions case study (Chapter 9). Example 5: measuring the impact of a supermarket checkout training intervention on scan rates over time (see pages 337–343).

Pearson's (product-moment/zero-order) correlation

Determining whether two continuous variables are correlated or not is a key activity in predictive HR analytics and the Pearson's test of correlations is the key tool used. Whilst the use of a Pearson's correlation is to some extent determined by the nature of the variables involved (e.g. it is not appropriate to use a categorical variable with a Pearson's correlation test). The Pearson's test of correlation gives the analyst an indication of the extent to which there is a significant linear relationship between two variables. When conducting the Pearson's test with R a correlations coefficient ('r') is produced, which gives a considerable amount of information. It tells us the direction of any relationship (e.g. a positive or negative relationship between two variables) and the magnitude of the relationship (whether the relationship is strong, weak or non-existent). The Pearson's test will also indicate the significance of the relationship: is our linear relationship significant?

The correlation coefficient ranges from –1, through 0 to +1. Where two variables are not in any way correlated you will have an r=0.00 (this very rarely happens). Where two variables are completely correlated we will have an r=1 or –1.

The sign in front of the correlation coefficient indicates a positive versus a negative relationship. A positive (+) relationship indicates that you tend to find an increase in one variable in tandem (to some degree) with an increase in the other. Average ice-cream sales per person and average temperature of the country is a good example of this. The country is the object of analysis, average temperature in each country is one variable and the average consumption (in kilogrammes) of ice cream per person each year is another variable. You would expect a positive relationship between these two variables. A negative correlation (–) is obviously the reverse; as one variable goes up the other tends to go down. The size of the absolute value of the coefficient (between 0 and 1) indicates the magnitude of the relationship. A medium to strong correlation might have an 'r' of somewhere between 0.5 to 1.0 or –0.5 to –1.0. A medium correlation would be somewhere between 0.3 to 0.5 or –0.3 to –0.5. A weak or low correlation would be somewhere between 0.1 to 0.3 or –0.1 to –0.3. Importantly, the Pearson's correlation coefficient test will tell you how significant any relationship is, as well as the magnitude and direction of its linear relationship.

With R you can obtain correlation coefficients using the *cor.test* program.

```
# Obtain a Pearson's correlation coefficient

cor.test(df$var1, df$var1)
```

The code above calls the *cor.test* program. The command is similar to how we conducted the paired t-test, and so we need to specify the two variables we want to find correlations for *df$var1, df$var2*. Executing this command will show the extent of correlation between the two variables as well as the p-value.

It is very important to recognize that, whilst sometimes an analyst might make some assumptions that a significant correlation may suggest evidence of causality between an X and a Y variable (e.g. engagement as an X and performance as a Y), a Pearson's correlation coefficient merely shows the extent to which two variables co-relate. A correlation does not imply causality; any inferences relating to causality that an analyst makes are based on analyst-imposed or inferred assumptions. Just looking at the ice-cream sales and skin cancer rates example mentioned previously can help demonstrate the danger of making assumptions of causality from correlations. There may be a correlation between ice-cream consumption and skin cancer rates across countries, but eating an ice cream is unlikely to be the causal factor here – a third variable of exposure to hot sun may indeed be the causal factor. The Pearson's correlation test therefore has limitations in that the test only looks at the shared linear relationship between two variables; whilst not without its problems, for a better understanding of possible causal factors at play in influencing variation in certain dependent variables, multiple regression analysis is a much more powerful analytic tool.

Multiple linear regression analysis

Despite the long-winded name, multiple linear regression analysis is a straightforward procedure by which we collect data about our dependent variable (which must be continuous) and our independent variables (which can be either continuous or categorical). We then analyse the data to obtain evidence for which of the independent variables could be having a significant impact on the dependent variable, as well as the size and direction of that impact.

The theory behind the scenes comes down to a straight line on a graph: plotting a number of data points on a graph to see if they form into some sort of straight line, the line of best fit for those data points, and the equation for that straight line. You may (or may not) remember equations for straight lines from secondary-school mathematics as something along the lines of y = mx + c. Regardless of whether you remember or not, you can rest assured that multiple linear regression analysis is based on clever algebra associated with straight lines and the equations and calculations for which are all done for you by R. In its simple form (a simple linear regression) a line of best fit (solid line) through a notional scatter graph is plotted with an assumed independent variable on the x-axis and an assumed dependent variable on the y-axis, as shown in Figure 3.2. On this graph we also plot an alternative possible 'line of best fit'.

3.2   Simple linear algebra

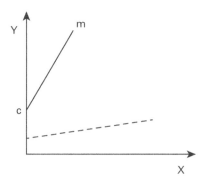

In the example shown in Figure 3.2, the value of c is simply the point where the line touches the y-axis, and the value of m is the gradient. So on the solid line, the gradient would be much higher (steeper) than the dotted line. This means that for every unit increase in x on the solid line, it will result in a much bigger change in the value of y than an increase in the value of x on the dotted line, because the gradient is much less steep. As it were, if the solid and the dotted lines were two different sides of a mountain and the y-axis represented the altitude and the x-axis represented the number of steps taken, one step forward on the solid line will get you to a much higher altitude than will one step forward on the dotted line. In this example, c would be the altitude of your starting point at the bottom of the mountain (which is rarely zero). So the greater the gradient, the greater a change in the value of x will have on the value of y.

Instead of y = mx + c, we expand this out to enable us to include many variables in our 'model'. Importantly, in regression analysis, we use an 'a' to represent the point at which the line intercepts the y-axis and a 'b' (to represent a gradient coefficient) instead of c and m. So 'y= mx + c' becomes: 'y= a + bx'. When we have multiple independent variables in our model the equation becomes more complex and longer:

$$y = a + b_1x_1 + b_2x_2 + b_3x_3 \text{ (and so on)}$$

where y is the dependent variable, x is the independent variable(s), a is the constant value and b is the gradient for each of the independent variables.

So if we use our mountain analogy and add 'length of legs of climber' as another variable, our model might look something like:

Altitude = a + b_1(number of steps) + b_2(leg length)

We would run a different model for each route (both the dotted and the solid).

If we plugged in the data for, say, 1,000 climbers over the two routes, R would then generate for us something that looked like this:

Route 1 (solid):
Altitude = 300m + 3 (number of steps) + 5 (leg length)

Route 2 (dotted):
Altitude = 240m + 1 (number of steps) + 5 (leg length)

You can see from this that one step on route 1 will get you three times higher than one step on route 2.

Applying this to HR analytics and using the data available to us through many of the sources described early in this chapter, we might say, for example:

Job satisfaction score = 3 + 0.05 (size of bonus in $1,000) + 0.2 (managerial level) + 0.4 (performance rating)

In its simplest form of interpretation, we might say that if the average job satisfaction level (on a 1 to 7 scale) in our organization was 3 for non-managers, getting a thousand-dollar bonus should increase this by 0.05 (to 3.05) and then being at the first step of a managerial level should increase the expected level of satisfaction by 0.2 (to 3.25) and getting an increase in a notional performance rating of 1 should again increase this job satisfaction level by another 0.4 (to 3.65). Thus Bob (a non-manager with no bonus and an average performance rating of 3) should have a satisfaction level (perhaps) of 3; importantly 0.65 lower than Sally (a level one manager, who received a $1,000 bonus and a performance rating of 4).

When we run a multiple regression analysis, we are looking for a number of key things (in terms of the statistical output of interest):

1 Multiple R^2: the multiple R^2 is very important in our multiple regression analysis. It is an indicator of the total amount of variance in our dependent variable that can be accounted for by its shared relationship with all independent variables in the model (whilst taking into account the shared relationships amongst the independent variables and the dependent variables). This is a value between 0 and 1; 1 being 100 per cent of the variance in our dependent variable and 0 being 0 per cent. The closer the value of R^2 is to 1, the better our model is at accounting for variation in our dependent variable of interest.

2 Model parameters: R will calculate the model parameters, which are the F-statistic (the regression ANOVA statistic) and the model degrees of freedom. Simply put, in multiple linear regression, these two parameters are then used to calculate the statistical significance of the regression model. The degrees of freedom figures are directly related to the sample size and the number of variables that we have included in our model. The F-statistic is calculated on the basis of ratios of the variation in our dependent variable (sum of squares) that our model accounts for versus what remains unaccounted for (this statistic is therefore linked to the R^2). The F-test is the 'test-statistic' and we can refer to statistical tables to find out what value of f we need to reach before we can be 95 per cent, 99 per cent or 99.9 per cent confident that our model accounts for variation in our dependent variable. In the days before statistical software packages, statisticians would calculate these parameters by hand, and then reference a table to look up the level of significance resulting from the given parameters. Like other software packages, though, R will calculate the statistical significance value at the same time (which, you may argue, removes the need to manually calculate the model parameters). It is good practice, though, to always report the model parameters along with the statistical significance.

3 Statistical significance: from the statistical significance section earlier in this chapter, we know that we are looking for a p-value of 0.05 or less in order for the result to be significant. In multiple linear regression, R will give us a p-value for the model.

4   Finally, the coefficients for each assumed independent variable that we include in our model. These are our '*b*' values – or our line gradients for each independent variable in the model. For each independent variable, R will provide the *b* value for the equation as well as the significance of that independent variable in the model. As well as the *b* value, R can also calculate the 'Beta' value, which is linked to the *b* value but is unique and important in its own right. The Beta value is an indication of the importance of a particular independent variable (IV) in the prediction (accounting of variance) of the dependent variable (DV) and it also gives an indication of the direction of the unique linear relationship that exists between the IV and the DV, whilst taking into account the interrelationships between all IVs (and the DV) in the model. Importantly it gives information about the '*unique* contribution of each variable to the prediction of the y[DV]' (Howell, 2002).

To conduct multiple linear regression analysis in R, we can use the *lm* program:

```
# Conduct a multiple linear regression

mod_4 <- (dep_var ~ var1 + var2 + var3, data = df)
summary(mod_4)
```

The code above calls the *lm* program. We first specify the dependent variable *dep_var*, and use the tilde ~ to indicate that it is going to be predicted by the variables to follow: *var1*, *var2*, and *var3*. With *data = df*, we specify the dataframe the variables are in. We then put the results of the model into an object called *mod_4* (short for model 4). We then ask for the summary of the model with the next line: *summary(mod_4)*.

Because multiple regression analysis is such an important analytic tool for the predictive HR analyst, there are many worked-through examples of multiple linear regression, including discussions of the output, in the case study chapters (in almost every case Pearson's correlation coefficients are also provided). The examples that we work through are listed below.

MULTIPLE LINEAR REGRESSION CASE STUDY EXAMPLES

- Diversity case study (Chapter 4). Example 3: using multiple linear regression to model and predict ethnic diversity variation across teams from base location, function, group size, team lead gender and team gender breakdown (see pages 124–132).
- Engagement case study (Chapter 5). Example 5: using multiple linear regression to predict team-level engagement (see pages 175–181).
- Turnover case study (Chapter 6). Example 5: using multiple linear regression to predict team-level turnover (see pages 218–223).

- Performance case study (Chapter 7). Examples 1a and 1b: using multiple linear regression to predict customer loyalty and reinvestment in a financial services organization (see pages 233–238 and 239–241).

- Performance case study (Chapter 7). Example 2: using multiple linear regression when combining customer survey data with 'pulse' survey to predict customer loyalty in a financial services organization (see pages 242–245).

- Performance case study (Chapter 7). Example 3: using multiple linear regression when combining performance appraisal data, sickness records and pulse survey data to predict individual performance in a manufacturing organization (see pages 246–251).

- Performance case study (Chapter 7). Example 4: using stepwise multiple linear regression to find the best model for predicting performance using combined performance appraisal data, sickness records and pulse survey data in a manufacturing organization (see pages 251–255).

- Performance case study (Chapter 7). Example 5: tracking performance over time using stepwise regression with combined performance appraisal data, sickness records and pulse survey data in a manufacturing organization (see pages 255–258).

- Performance case study (Chapter 7). Example 6: using multiple regression to predict sickness absence using employee attitude scores in a manufacturing organization (see pages 258–261).

- Performance case study (Chapter 7). Example 7: using multiple regression to explore patterns of performance with employee profile data in a manufacturing organization (see pages 261–266).

- Performance case study (Chapter 7). Example 8a: using data interrogation techniques and multiple linear regression to predict checkout scan rates from employee profile data in a retail organization (see pages 266–268).

- Performance case study (Chapter 7). Example 9: using dummy variables in multiple linear regression to determine the presence of high-performing age groups in predicting scan rates in a retail organization (see pages 271–274).

- Recruitment and selection case study (Chapter 8). Example 3: assessment-centre selection technique validation, predicting graduate performance from demographic, assessment centre and onboarding data (see pages 297–302).

- Monitoring the impact of interventions case study (Chapter 9). Example 6: conditional panel model predicting change in checkout scan rates with supermarket operators (see pages 343–348).

- Predictive modelling case study (Chapter 10). Example 1: predictive modelling of customer reinvestment intentions (see pages 352–358).

- Predictive modelling case study (Chapter 10). Example 2: predictive modelling the impact of training on checkout scan rates (see pages 358–367).

- Predictive modelling case study (Chapter 10). Example 4: predictive modelling the impact of induction day on graduate performance (see pages 376–379).

- Predictive modelling case study (Chapter 10) Example 5: predicting expected performance of graduate candidates (see pages 379–384).

Factor analysis and reliability analysis

In human resources, it is very common for us to try to measure something that cannot easily be measured, such as 'engagement', 'leadership' or 'job satisfaction'. Unfortunately, we cannot take out our ruler and set square, go up to an employee and measure their level of engagement – 'Ah, 4.2 this time, great news, Josephine.' Instead, we need to look at what we can measure directly, such as answers to a survey question, and then measure how closely we think those direct measures actually reflect what it is that we are trying to measure. The latter is sometimes termed the 'latent variable' or 'latent construct'.

Factor analysis

What factor analysis will do for us is to take a number of different indices (such as a number of different survey questions) and analyse whether the responses appear to be measuring an expected variable (or variables). It helps tell us whether multiple indices are tapping the same variable of interest. In essence it can help tell us which indices we should and should not use to represent and tap any particular (latent) variable or measure (e.g. engagement or job satisfaction). This is very useful in survey design to identify which questions are most useful in measuring our particular variable and which are not; it can help us to simplify or reduce the size of the data set that we are analysing to a more manageable level (by helping us to remove the least useful measures). A more extensive discussion of factor analysis can be found in Chapter 5, linked to the measurement of engagement.

To conduct a factor analysis in R, we can use the *fa* program in the *psych* package.

```
# Conduct an exploratory factor analysis

library(psych)
fa(df[, c("var1", "var2", "var3")], 2)
```

The code above calls the *fa* program in the *psych* package. We first specify the dataframe *df*, and the set of variables we wish to select for the analysis. The braces *[]* enclose the set of variables *c('var1', 'var2', 'var3')* we wish to select. Finally, we specify two factors to explore. As with all of the other code shown in this chapter, this is just an example, so there is no particular reason for choosing three variables or two factors. We will delve into greater details in the worked-through examples in later chapters:

- Engagement case study (Chapter 5). Example 1: two constructs: exploratory factor analysis (see pages 149–157).

- Engagement case study (Chapter 5). Example 3: analysing group-level engagement data (see pages 162–167).

Reliability analysis

As outlined in the engagement case study (Chapter 5), even if you are using factor analysis to validate a survey questionnaire it is a good idea to use reliability analysis to check if the measures consistently reflect or tap the construct or latent variable that they are expected to measure. So if we asked the same person the same question again and again, we would expect to consistently get much the same answer, if it was a reliable measure. Put another way, we can test the degree to which results/responses to the different measures we are using (to measure a particular construct or latent variable) follow a similar pattern. As we discuss in more depth in Chapter 5, with specific examples, we would expect responses to follow a consistent pattern across items with a scale when it is measuring a single construct – because the idea, trait, attitude or perception in the person's head that we are trying to measure should end up causing them to respond in a similar way across all of the items designed to measure this idea (assuming the items measure this single idea). For example, if someone is very extraverted then this level of extraversion should influence how they respond to a set of questionnaire items designed to measure extraversion; and highly extraverted people are likely to follow a certain pattern of responding across a multiple-item extraversion scale (and introverts are likely to follow a different but consistent pattern across a multiple-item extraversion scale). See Chapter 5 for a more in-depth discussion of reliability analysis.

We can use R to conduct a reliability analysis and output something called 'Cronbach's alpha' for each of the variables. The Cronbach's alpha statistic gives an indication of how much variation exists (and is shared) in the responses given. The Cronbach's alpha ranges from 0 to 1. If there is no internal consistency in the results, we would expect the value to be 0, while an accepted rule of thumb for the Cronbach's alpha to be considered to reflect a 'good' or 'acceptable' level of shared variance, indicating the measures are internally consistent, is 0.7.

To conduct a reliability analysis in R, we can use the *alpha* program in the *psych* package.

```
# Obtain a Cronbach's alpha

library(psych)
alpha(df[, c("var1", "var2", "var3")])
```

The code above calls the *alpha* program in the *psych* package. This program requires similar input to the *fa* program. We first specify the dataframe *df*, and the set of variables we wish to select for the analysis. The braces *[]* enclose the set of variables *c('var1', 'var2', 'var3')* we wish to select. Executing this command should show us the Cronbach's alpha for these three variables. A worked example is in Chapter 5:

- Engagement case study (Chapter 5). Example 2: reliability analysis on a four-item engagement scale (see pages 159–162).

Summary

As mentioned previously, this chapter can be considered a reference section that you can return to when considering which type of analysis might be most appropriate for your modelling needs. This should put you in a good position to start to work through the case studies in the following chapters. Once you do start to work through these and see the application in a real-world sense, the theory, analysis and tests described in this chapter should become clearer, as will the benefits of using statistical analysis in HR data.

References

Bersin, J (2012) The HR measurement framework, Bersin and Associates Research Report, November

Coolican, H (2009) *Research Methods and Statistics in Psychology*, Hodder Education, Abingdon

Field, A (2017) *Discovering Statistics Using IBM SPSS Statistics*, 5th edn, Sage Publications, London

Fisher, R A (1925) *Statistical Methods for Research Workers*, Oliver and Boyd, Edinburgh

Howell, D C (2002) *Statistical Methods for Psychology*, 5th edn, Duxbury, Belmont CA

Huselid, M (2014) The corporate mirror, D'Amore-McKim School of Business, web.archive.org/web/20160329115926/http://www.damoremckimleadersatworkblog.com/corporate-mirror-looking-big-data-analytics-workforce-management/#sthash.4qx5y7F3.dpuf (archived at https://perma.cc/KU43-XXZL)

04

Case study 1

Diversity analytics

No doubt you will have come across diversity and inclusion (D&I) at some point in your career or studies up to this point. Effective D&I practices should be integrated throughout an employee's entire journey, from recruitment and onboarding to development, performance management, promotions, and exit. Conversely, poor D&I management can manifest in workplace bias, unfair treatment, increased turnover of valuable employees, and a lack of innovation and customer empathy in corporate strategies.

In this chapter, we cover the following:

- Equality, diversity and inclusion.
- Approaches to measuring and managing D&I.
- Example 1: gender and job grade analysis using frequency tables and chi-square.
- Example 2a: exploring ethnic diversity across teams using descriptive statistics.
- Example 2b: comparing ethnicity and gender across two functions in an organization using the independent samples t-test.
- Example 3: using multiple linear regression to model and predict ethnic diversity variation across teams from base location, function, group size, team lead gender, and team gender breakdown.
- Testing the impact of diversity: interacting diversity categories in predictive modelling.

Equality, diversity and inclusion

Many countries, including Australia, Belgium, Bolivia, France, Germany, Hong Kong, Italy, the Netherlands and the UK, have equality legislation in place. The countries mentioned here have, at the time of writing, updated their legislative frameworks in the last ten to fifteen years. In many cases governments require regulated reporting of data from organizations to show that there is no unfair treatment on the basis of protected characteristics such as gender, ethnicity, age and disability. Inclusion and the management of diversity focus on the positive benefits to the organization of managing this well; predictive analytics are key to determining where problems and opportunities may exist in the organization, and where resources should be concentrated to improve the working environment.

According to Gartner (2023), workforce diversity is the collective mixture of employees' differences and similarities, including individual characteristics, values, beliefs, experiences, backgrounds, preferences and behaviours; and inclusion means to 'foster a work environment in which all employees feel respected, accepted, supported and valued'.

Why focus on diversity and inclusion?

Organizations are increasingly raising the priority of D&I through efforts such as inclusiveness and unconscious bias training; leadership programmes; sponsorship programmes for talented young female or underrepresented groups (UG) staff; and through large-scale culture change programmes where all people processes in the firm are scrutinized and updated to ensure that no bias is occurring. Why? There are two key arguments for wanting to successfully manage diversity and inclusion. The first is the social case for diversity, whereby employers have a moral obligation to treat employees with fairness and dignity and should ensure that decisions are made without resorting to prejudice and stereotypes. The challenge here is that moral obligations and social justice are not the prime concern of organizations. By nature organizations are driven by profit and efficiency, and indeed a business plan guided by social justice would be detrimental to the bottom line (Noon, 2010).

The other key argument is the diversity business case. Some of the key benefits cited by researchers and academics include the ability to maximize people potential, better understand customers, draw from a wider candidate pool, develop a more positive company image, engender greater discretionary effort from employees, increase employee engagement and improve retention, innovation and team performance (Kandola and Fullerton, 1998). A particular challenge highlighted in the literature for the business case for diversity, however, is that it is difficult to quantify, and that it can take a long time to realize the benefits. The analytics presented in this chapter break down some of the data and demystify the link between a diverse organization and some of the benefits that can be realized.

Approaches to measuring and managing D&I

Diversity dashboards

As discussed in previous chapters, when analysing their workforce, current HR functions tend to stop at simply describing the characteristics of the workforce within their organization. In our diversity example this would be the equivalent of saying 'Did you know that 12 per cent of our senior managers are Black or Asian ethnicity and 20 per cent of our senior managers are women?' To which a response might be: 'So what?' or 'I'll look at this later.' Why? Because there is no context. Is 12 per cent what we should expect, or should it be more like 30 per cent? What is the likelihood that we would get 20 per cent women completely by chance anyway? And does this proportion actually reflect a male-weighted gender ratio in our organization? How do we know if this is due to bias, discrimination or some identifiable factor inhibiting inclusion?

Descriptive reports, often produced at quarterly or monthly intervals, aside from being rather uninteresting reading can very quickly become 'check-box' exercises, produced to fulfil a requirement, but rarely reviewed closely unless external pressures (either external to the organization or the HR function) are applied. Examples of these external pressures in D&I may be regulatory reports as required in the financial and public sectors, or particular requests for information if the organization is taking part in a benchmarking exercise.

Diversity benchmarking

For organizations, knowing their diversity statistics engenders a key benefit in that it can enable them to conduct benchmarking activities with regard to D&I. A number of organizations such as Stonewall, The Business Disability Forum, *The Times* (Top 50 Places for Women to Work report), Saratoga Human Capital Measurement and Benchmarking, etc, collect and analyse information on organizational D&I data and advertise the best organizations on the basis of their D&I statistics. The reports can often produce gap analyses to help organizations understand where they may fall short on particular demographic membership linked to diversity (compared to industry averages). A note of caution with external benchmarking activities is that it is important to be careful interpreting any differences that might be found when comparing one's own organization with others in relation to diversity statistics. Even in the same industry, jobs and functions are usually structured differently, so the same role may be classified as a 'senior manager' in one firm and a 'middle manager' in another firm.

Just looking at the numbers and comparing them against others, however, is not particularly helpful unless you fully understand what it means for your organization. What we need to know is what the numbers are telling us and how we should use this information to make sound decisions about the future of the business. This is where predictive analysis using simple statistical tools bridges the gap.

Ultimately, descriptive D&I reports tend to be current 'state of play' descriptive snapshots of the organization. Examples of these types of reports may include female representation by seniority level, promotion data by age and gender, representation of ethnic minorities among employees who joined the firm in the past three years, performance ratings given to staff with/without disabilities, etc.

Moving towards predictive models

D&I reports are a great example of the kind of descriptive reports that the HR function (or sometimes a separate MI function working closely in collaboration with HR) often produces. To what extent, however, can we rely on descriptive reports to provide us insights into D&I issues within the organization? With a few simple steps the level of interrogation that can be applied to the data can fundamentally increase the rigour of the analysis presented and its importance in defining corporate strategy. The examples throughout the remainder of this chapter will demonstrate how the incorporation of predictive statistical methods can be used to enhance the analysis of diversity data.

Example 1: gender and job grade analysis using frequency tables and chi-square

In showing how HR functions can take a step forward and interrogate their descriptive data in more detail, we can use a simple diversity analysis that explores whether or not women tend to be underrepresented in senior roles within the organization. From a commercial perspective, the organization may be interested in having a greater diversity of thought in senior, strategic discussions; and from a people perspective, the organization may want to understand the degree to which there is a gender balance of positive role models for younger employees. The analysis required here is to check for possible discrimination or (for example) unconscious bias within the organization. To check for this, what an HR analyst may do is simply to look at how many women versus men work in different job grades.

With our diversity case study example 1 (named *Ch4_diversity.xlsx*), we have a management consulting firm, SlidesRUs, with 1,493 employees. Of these, 746 are female, 745 are male and two didn't declare their gender. On first look, this seems to represent an organization with an even gender balance of 50 per cent male and 50 per cent female. There are eight different job grades in the organization and these are listed with their numbers in Table 4.1.

If there was no evidence of any kind of glass ceiling or discrimination/unconscious bias within this organization then we would expect there to be an equal proportion (approximately) of men and women in each of the eight grades shown in Table 4.1.

The actual gender ratios in this current organization, however, are far from an even split of gender in each of the grades. Figure 4.1 shows the proportions of male and female in each of the grades in graphical form. In the graph, we can see how men and women are spread across the organization. We can see that over one-third of women are in the administrator/assistant role, and then the number of women gradually decreases as the role becomes more senior. We can see that the most prevalent roles for men (where the male and female ratio leans more towards the male side) are the managing consultant and senior consultant roles.

At the moment, this is generally the kind of analysis that HR functions can and do provide in relation to HR diversity – such graphs can easily be produced with Excel. The bar graphs represent the proportion of the gender groups in each of the grades. Because the proportions of men and women in this organization are even, this bar chart is visually meaningful and is easy to interpret. One can see just from casting an eye over this graph that men dominate the more senior roles on the right-hand side and women dominate the more junior roles on the left-hand side. The data can also be presented in a different form, with the bars representing the proportion of each grade that is made up of women versus men (see Figure 4.2). The graph looks quite different but presents the same general message: that women are more prevalent in the junior grades.

TABLE 4.1 SlidesRUs employee numbers breakdown by role

Grade	Role	Number of People Currently in Role
1	Clerical/Officer	39
2	Administrator/Assistant	343
3	Graduate/Trainee Consultant	263
4	Consultant	243
5	Senior Consultant	250
6	Managing Consultant	239
7	Principal Consultant	81
8	Partner	33

4.1   Graphical representation (description) of % of the male/female groups across the eight grades within the organization

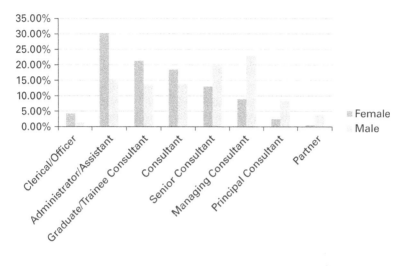

What the graph in Figure 4.2 tells us is that, looking at all of the clerical/officer roles, almost 80 per cent of them are held by women and just over 20 per cent are held by men; conversely, looking at all the partner roles, almost 90 per cent are held by men and just over 10 per cent are held by women.

4.2   Graphical representation (description) of the male/female % within each grade

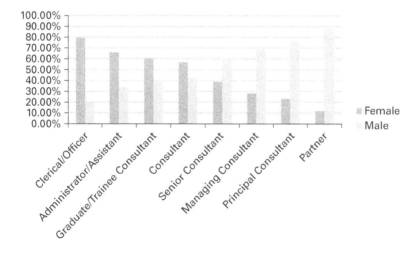

Interrogating the description

One of the main problems with this kind of analysis is that the data has generally not been subject to any kind of interrogation. To a degree, the data speaks for itself and seems to show a very strong pattern. However, even with such a pattern, it is not possible to say that there is a D&I problem with any degree of certainty. Were an HR professional to stand in front of a board of directors or an executive committee to argue for a case that there may be a glass ceiling or bias/discrimination problem within the organization, the graphs in Figure 4.1 and Figure 4.2 do not hold up under scrutiny and could be passed off as coincidence or circumstance.

Imagine if you or your team spent a month putting this report together as part of a D&I proposition, only for it to be pulled apart with questions that the report cannot answer or suggestions that the data is just a coincidence. Or worse, if you embarked on an expensive programme based on the data when, in actual fact, there was no robust evidence to suggest there was a D&I problem at this organization – and the proportion of women in senior roles could indeed be explained by chance.

It is essential that an HR analyst has interrogated this data to ensure that there is a statistically significant pattern (see Chapter 3, page 46–48 for our discussion on significance).

The chi-square test

The chi-square is a simple test that we can use to interrogate the patterns presented in the graphs shown in Figures 4.1 and 4.2. This test will immediately tell the analyst how certain they can be that the pattern is statistically meaningful. It will tell the HR analyst whether such a pattern could actually be a fluke or due to chance alone. Or, putting it another way, it will tell the HR analyst (and therefore any decision maker that they are trying to persuade) that it is *not* a fluke and is *not* due to chance alone, and is therefore something that should not be ignored.

The test follows a very simple idea. It checks whether the data pattern found (e.g. in Figure 4.2) is what we would expect to find if there was no link (or association) between gender and seniority in our organization. In other words, it tells the reader whether there is evidence that a gender bias might exist.

Looking at this from a purely statistical perspective (with all other factors being equal), if there were no gender bias or discrimination, we would expect the male:female ratio to be very close to 50:50 in any job grade because this is the gender ratio across our organization as a whole. So it would look something like Table 4.2.

For simplicity, where the number of people currently in role is an odd number, the extra person added is a woman for the first four grades and a man for the last four grades. For comparison, the *actual* number of men and women in the organization is illustrated in Table 4.3.

A chi-square test enables us to check the actual frequencies of males and females in each job grade within our organization against what we would expect to have if there were no bias (or link between gender and job level).

Simply put, the bigger the bias, the bigger the chi-square statistic will be. What does 'the bigger the bias' mean in this case? Well, as we have roughly 50:50 males and females in this particular organization, a 'no bias' scenario would be one where each job level is made up of about half males and half females, as illustrated in Table 4.2. This pattern should be maintained as the roles get more senior.

However, the more we find that men dominate the senior roles, the greater 'evidence' that some kind of bias exists. The calculations going on behind the chi-square test calculation involve a check of what we actually have in terms of gender proportions compared to what we would have if there were no evidence of any bias. The greater the difference between the gender patterns in each grade (that we actually *observe* in our organization) and what we would *expect* (if no bias existed), the more our chi-square test will start to tell us that something is really going on that we cannot ignore (i.e. the chi-square statistic shows that statistical significance is found).

Our statistical software package (see Chapter 2 for our discussion of statistical software packages) then applies this information and calculates for us the statistical likelihood of finding our gender distribution by chance alone (if there was no link between gender and job grade). In other words, it tells us whether there is a meaningful and unexpected pattern of gender variation across the job grades.

TABLE 4.2 SlidesRUs expected gender breakdown of employee numbers by role

Grade	Role	Expected Number of Men in Role	Expected Number of Women in Role	Number of People Currently in Role
1	Clerical/Officer	19	20	39
2	Administrator/Assistant	171	172	343
3	Graduate/Trainee Consultant	131	132	263
4	Consultant	121	122	243
5	Senior Consultant	125	125	250
6	Managing Consultant	120	119	239
7	Principal Consultant	41	40	81
8	Partner	17	16	33

TABLE 4.3 SlidesRUs observed gender breakdown of employee numbers by role

Grade	Role	Observed Number of Men in Role	Observed Number of Women in Role	Number of People Currently in Role
1	Clerical/Officer	8	31	39
2	Administrator/Assistant	116	227	343
3	Graduate/Trainee Consultant	103	160	263
4	Consultant	104	139	243
5	Senior Consultant	152	98	250
6	Managing Consultant	171	68	239
7	Principal Consultant	62	19	81
8	Partner	29	4	33

Let's take a closer look at the data that our chi-square analysis produces.

Before we conduct a chi-square analysis in R, we can generate a table to observe how women and men are distributed across job types. We will first load the file *Ch4_diversity.xlsx*, which you can find at www.koganpage.com/urhra.

As a reminder, we can load the Excel file by going to the clicking on the *Import Dataset* button on the Environment pane, top right of the RStudio interface, as in Figure 4.3:

4.3

Click the *From Excel…* option, and you can navigate to the directory where you downloaded the data and R files, by using the *Browse* button on the top right-hand side as in Figure 4.4.

4.4

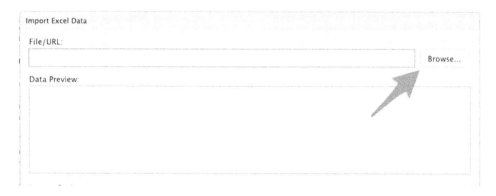

Once you have found the folder containing the data file, you should be able to see it listed, as in Figure 4.5:

4.5

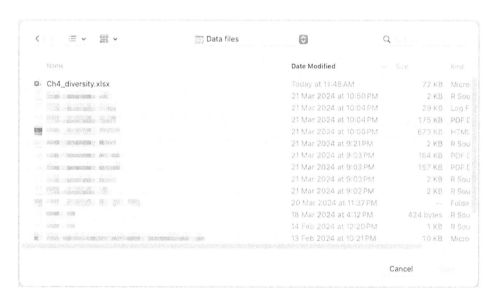

Next, we load the file into the R environment. Click on the file and you will see a preview of the file, as shown in Figure 4.6. This shows various options for importing the file, as well as a preview. You can click 'Import' to load the file in R, as the default options don't need changing. Note that on the bottom right, RStudio gives you the code you would need to run to achieve the same result.

Now the data set should be available as *Ch4_diversity* in the R environment, ready to be called and used. One thing to note about the data from looking at the

4.6

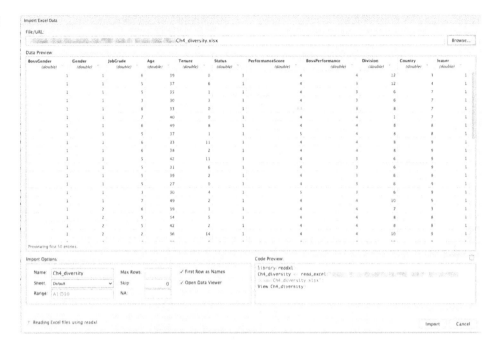

preview in Figure 4.5 is that it is entirely numeric. You should keep good records of how you coded every variable, but to make the data more interpretable, let's recode the *Gender* variable. To do this, we'll need to load some libraries, as certain functions beyond the base capabilities of R can make this easy. The code you are about to see is in the file *Ch4_example_1.R*.

```
if (!require("pacman")) install.packages("pacman")
pacman::p_load(dplyr, descr)
Ch4_diversity$Gender_text <- case_match(Ch4_diversity$Gender, 1 ~
"Women", 2 ~ "Men")
CrossTable(Ch4_diversity$JobGrade, Ch4_diversity$Gender_text, prop.t =
FALSE, prop.chisq = FALSE, expected = TRUE)
chisq.test(Ch4_diversity$JobGrade, Ch4_diversity$Gender_text)
```

The first line installs the *pacman* package. It first asks R if the package is installed, and if not, it installs it. If you have a fresh installation of R, then you probably won't have many packages installed. The *pacman* package (portmanteau of package manage-ment) saves a lot of hassle when dealing with packages. Specifically, the *p_load* function helps you to load packages by: 1) checking to see if you have the package installed; 2) automatically downloading and installing any packages you do not have; and 3) loading that package for you so you can use it. It performs all three functions in one go, which simplifies things considerably. If you do not have the packages installed already, you will need an internet connection for the *p_load* program to get

4.7

them. You will need those packages before you can progress. The first time you run this code, it may take a few minutes to download all of the required packages.

You might at this point ask: How do I actually run lines of code? There are two ways. One is to highlight the code with your mouse or keyboard – this should highlight the code in blue. Then: 1) click the *Run* button on the top right, as indicated in Figure 4.7; or 2) use this key combination: *Control + Enter* (Windows and Linux) / *Command + Return* (MacOS). For the second method, highlight the code you wish to run, then hold down Control / Command then press Enter. With either method, you must highlight the entire line, not just a part of it. R will attempt to run just the highlighted portion of the code.

The second line loads the two libraries we need to use, namely *dplyr* and *descr*. The *dplyr* package contains programs that help you load and manipulate data, while the *descr* package contains tools to generate descriptive statistics, in our case a cross-tabulation. The line of code first asks R to look in the *pacman* library and to use the *p_load* function. Then you can list the libraries you need, separated by a comma. It's a good idea only to load the libraries you need, because loading some large libraries can take some time.

SNAPSHOT HIDDEN GEM

You can find out more about a package by putting a question mark in front of an installed package name. For example, try running the following code, after the *dplyr* package has been installed:

```
?dplyr
```

Running that code will reveal a short description of the package in the Help pane in the bottom right of the screen. Often, this help page will contain links to the package website, which may contain tutorials to show you the various functionalities of the package.

In the third and fourth lines, we create the *Gender_text* variable. We use the *case_match* function in the *dplyr* library. The *case_match* program switches one given value for another. In our case, we specify the variable *Gender* in the *Ch4_diversity* dataframe, and we then specify that every '1' should be converted to the value

4.8

```
Cell Contents
|-------------------------|
|                      N  |
|             Expected N  |
|          N / Row Total  |
|          N / Col Total  |
|-------------------------|
```

```
=================================================================
                                   Ch4_diversity$Gender_text
Ch4_                          Men          Women          Total
diversity$JobGrade
-----------------------------------------------------------------

1                               8             31             39
                             19.5           19.5
                            0.205          0.795          0.026
                            0.011          0.042
-----------------------------------------------------------------
2                             116            227            343
                            171.4          171.6
                            0.338          0.662          0.230
                            0.156          0.304
-----------------------------------------------------------------
3                             103            160            263
                            131.4          131.6
                            0.392          0.608          0.176
                            0.138          0.214
-----------------------------------------------------------------
4                             104            139            243
                            121.4          121.6
                            0.428          0.572          0.163
                            0.140          0.186
-----------------------------------------------------------------
5                             152             98            250
                            124.9          125.1
                            0.608          0.392          0.168
                            0.204          0.131
-----------------------------------------------------------------
6                             171             68            239
                            119.4          119.6
                            0.715          0.285          0.160
                            0.230          0.091
-----------------------------------------------------------------
7                              62             19             81
                             40.5           40.5
                            0.765          0.235          0.054
                            0.083          0.025
-----------------------------------------------------------------
8                              29              4             33
                             16.5           16.5
                            0.879          0.121          0.022
                            0.039          0.005
-----------------------------------------------------------------
Total                         745            746           1491
                              0.5            0.5
=================================================================
```

'Woman', and every '2' should be converted to the value 'Man'. The result of this transformation is written into a new variable called *Gender_text* so that the original values are retained in the original variable, and we can use this recoded variable for descriptive interpretation. Having both numeric and textual representation of the same variable can be useful.

In the fifth and sixth lines of code, we ask for a cross tabulation. We use the *CrossTable* program in the *descr* library. We specify our two variables, and some options for what data we want to see in the table (you can see the full list of the possible options by running this command: *?descr::CrossTable*). Running the code results in the table below (Figure 4.8), which replicates Table 4.3.

The output presented in Figure 4.8 gives us a considerable amount of information. Aside from the rich amount of information that is provided with regard to descriptive statistics on our organization [e.g. the proportions of male/female within each job grade (N / Row Total, or the third set of numbers in each job grade), the proportion of the gender groups that each grade makes up (N / Col Total, or the fourth set of numbers in each job grade)], it also provides the expected count of males and females in each grade that should be found in the organization if there were no bias in any way [(Expected N, or the second set of numbers in each job grade)]. This is a useful target for HR to present as an internal gender ratio benchmark comparison that each job grade *should* have.

The final line conducts the chi-square test. The results are shown in Figure 4.9:

4.9

```
Pearson's Chi-squared test

data: Ch4_diversity$JobGrade and Ch4_diversity$Gender_text
X-squared = 164.7, df = 7, p-value < 2.2e-16
```

The key statistics of interest are the Pearson's chi-square statistic of 164.7 and the p-value of '<2.2e-16'. That strange number should be interpreted as a p-value of zero. R is trying to be accurate here and to say the p-value is the smallest number it can plausibly compute, which is 0.00000000000000022 when written out. In practical terms, this number is close enough to zero to call it zero.

This tells us that there is a pattern in our gender proportions that is meaningful. Indeed this tells us that we have a statistically significant link (or 'association' in this case) between gender and grade. As our descriptive statistics show that females are underrepresented in the senior grades and over-represented in the junior grades, this significance figure is saying that we can be certain that this finding is meaningful to a very high level of certainty (see Chapter 3 for our discussion of significance). Or, put differently, there is almost zero chance that this gender proportion could happen by coincidence, hence we know that some other factor has influenced it (this other factor could be some form of discrimination, but we will not know this without further exploration).

> SNAPSHOT HIDDEN GEM
>
> In this organization women are underrepresented in senior roles (to a level of certainty that means it pretty much could never happen by chance alone), and no one could try to deny it, due to the overwhelming evidence.

Statistical interpretation caveat: it is of course one thing to say that women are under-represented in senior roles in an organization and another thing to say that there is some form of discrimination or bias going on. A highly competent HR analytics expert would be very careful not to state that the analysis says more than it actually does. The statistical result needs to be carefully combined with a rational and considered set of arguments as to why the very strong pattern of female underrepresentation may be occurring. It would also be sensible to develop a plan for further research within the organization in order to try to explore why these patterns exist.

The analysis produced in Figures 4.8 and 4.9 is ready for the HR analytics master to use in persuasive arguments to get the senior management to take D&I seriously in the organization.

So, instead of the discussion around the executive committee table going like this:

Scenario one – descriptive data only:

ExCo member: 'Well, the gender proportions across the grades vary quite a bit so that data could easily be a coincidence.'

HR analyst: 'The pattern looks very strong and has done for a number of years...'

ExCo member: 'Well, could you please produce this same report every month for six months so we can keep an eye on it.'

ExCo member (unspoken): 'I've seen this pattern over a number of years but we will never actually prioritize this because we don't believe this is a problem.'

With the chi-square analysis, it would go something like this:

Scenario two – using some statistical analysis:

ExCo member: 'Well, the gender proportions vary quite a bit so that data could easily be a coincidence.'

HR analyst: 'It is no coincidence. If you look at this chi-square test checking for statistical significance, you can see that the chance of this being a coincidence is less than 1 per cent, in fact close to zero. We have a real problem and, with some further analysis into what the contributing factors may be, my team has some suggestions for how to address it.'

ExCo member: 'I'm very impressed with your technical competency and I am grateful you have brought this to our attention. Thank you. Let's arrange a separate meeting to discuss possible causes and go through some of these suggestions.'

If you have ever seen the movie *Groundhog Day* whereby Bill Murray relives the same day again and again, you will understand what life will be like for the HR professional in scenario one. They will be producing the same descriptive report each month, having the same conversation with the executive committee (or probably someone lower down) again and again until they are reassigned to do analysis on something else and start a new cycle of conversations again.

Scenario two presents a far stronger argument and really helps the executive to see what is happening in the business. It also provides greater credibility to the data and has a good chance of really making a difference in the business where it counts.

But D&I is not just about gender. Let's expand on our analysis using information we have about ethnicity and employee engagement.

Example 2a: exploring ethnic diversity across teams using descriptive statistics

There are many arguments for why organizations should make every effort to ensure that their workforce is ethnically diverse. These include general arguments for the utility of having a diverse set of perspectives, which should help ensure innovation because of the range of different perspectives and competencies (Kandola and Fullerton, 1998). But there are also other key business-case arguments presented, linked to the idea that as consumer markets are diverse, having representation from diverse groups as an employee group helps organizations to better understand their customers' needs.

When operating in an ethnically diverse country (such as the UK), the HR analytics expert needs to be very aware of the possible importance that ethnic origin might have for employees in the workplace. It is well documented that some industries tend to find it harder to demonstrate a good level of underrepresented groups (e.g. First Nations, Black, Asian or Latina/o) employees than others. This difficulty in ensuring a good level of representation may be for a number of reasons. For example, a Business in the Community report (2021) shows that underrepresented groups (UG) rely on recruitment agencies to a greater extent, which may limit access to specific professions and industries. Organizations need to understand why this is the case, look at what is happening in their own organization and develop a plan to address underrepresentation.

Exploring diversity in teams within a large organization

In understanding patterns of ethnic diversity within our organization, one possible set of analysis that can be conducted would be to analyse patterns of team diversity in order to investigate whether specific ethnic groups are clustered together – and, also, if there are variations in the level of underrepresented groups in teams within our organization, might we be able to identify patterns that could help explain this?

Following on from the previous discussion about UG candidates feeling as though some industries are not open to them, or that they feel excluded in certain industries, it would be useful to identify whether any bias is occurring at a more micro level in the organization. Are some teams more welcoming to UG staff? Do some teams attract, develop and retain UG individuals more effectively than others? If we found, for example, that a certain type of team had few people from underrepresented groups, can we identify what factors might be influencing this? Might we be able to find some evidence within the organization that certain factors could be associated with low levels of UG in teams? If we can find such evidence we can then identify possible levers with which to try to increase representation.

If we assume that the organization is interested in ensuring levels of diversity in teams, and there are a large number of teams that can be analysed meaningfully, then there are a number of interesting predictive models that can be run to identify patterns of team diversity (or lack of diversity).

Here, we will talk about 'predicting' diversity. By this, we mean identifying patterns that might exist, which show that people from underrepresented groups are found in some professions or job types but not others. We could say that we 'predict' levels of UG representation by identifying the particular job type found in certain teams and exploring its relationship with UG levels. If there were a high representation of UG in certain job types, this might mean that UG individuals actually feel more welcome in such jobs (either at recruitment or once they have joined). Similarly, analysis of teams may show that more people from underrepresented groups are found in a certain type of team (e.g. sales-based teams) but they are not found in other types of team (e.g. admin-based teams). Depending on the statistical significance, we could say that we 'predict' variation in UG representation at the team level on the basis of the job type that we tend to find in the team. This allows the organization to look at which teams might be better at attracting, developing and retaining UG employees.

An assumption with predictive analysis is that factors can be identified that predict (and potentially influence or cause variation in) a dependent factor. So this can be easily applied here to see which team factors (department, team size, gender split, etc) influence or cause variation in the proportion of UG staff.

In addition to this, there may be lots of information available at the team level that would be quite useful information in a D&I analysis that is not available at the individual employee level; in particular, scores from an employee attitude or employee engagement survey. As discussed in Chapter 5, many organizations receive engagement survey information at the team level but not at the individual level. This allows us to easily link team-level UG statistics with team-level scores produced by the engagement survey.

Team diversity case study example

In this second diversity example we have branch/departmental/team-level data from two functions within a (very large) financial organization.

First a few important points on ethnicity data:

1 Ethnicity data is often collected on a diversity form completed by employees on joining the organization, and is sometimes updated in subsequent exercises whereby the analytics team may ask staff to review this.

2 Ethnicity data is rarely mandatory, so it is reasonable to expect some blank data in the report. R will help to identify complete records and use the appropriate test.

3 The term 'underrepresented group' is now the primary term used to describe people who do not come from the majority group. One might expect different definitions of 'underrepresented group' in different countries. For example, if your analysis was in China, 'Asian' would not be in the minority. It is also important to look at the data closely before grouping underrepresented people together, particularly if you are in a multinational institution. In the United States, you might see terms such as 'visible minorities' and an emphasis on analysing Hispanic/Latino ethnicities. Indeed, it is important to consider these differences in the data capture process as well.

Now, back to our financial institution.

There are 29,976 employees in these two functions across the UK and these employees are organized into 928 teams or employee units. These are sometimes branches, sometimes departments and sometimes teams within larger work settings. The data from the employee engagement survey is organized into these 928 units for analysis. It is also important to note that they have been organized with a 'work unit' key that was used by the engagement survey provider in order to supply engagement survey data in aggregate form (to protect identities in this anonymous survey, no unit here is identified if it has fewer than 10 employees). The data set that we are working with, therefore, is average/aggregate data at the work team level and there are rows of data in the data set entitled *Ch4_div_group.xlsx*. The variables in the data set include the information in Table 4.4.

TABLE 4.4 Employee engagement survey variables for diversity analysis

Variable Label	Description
DepartmentGroupNumber	Team/unit key identifier
GroupSize	Number of employees in the unit
PercentMale	Percentage of the unit made up of males
UG	Percentage of the unit made up of people from underrepresented groups (e.g. Black, Asian)
NumberTeamLeads	Number of team leaders in the unit (in general this organization has a team leader for every seven or so employees)
NumberFeMaleTeamLeads	Number of team leads in the unit who are female

(continued)

TABLE 4.4 (Continued)

Variable Label	Description
Location	Geographical location: 1 = Central London, 2 = Greater London, 3 = Rest of UK
LondonorNot	Geographical location recoded to 1 = Central London or Greater London and 2 = Rest of UK
Function	Function 1 = Sales staff (customer-facing people) or 2 = Professional Service (non-customer-facing people)
EMPsurvEngage_1 – EMPsurvEngage_9	Proportion of the unit who answered favourably (with either 'agree' or 'strongly agree' on a 1 to 5 'strongly disagree' to 'strongly agree' response scale) to each of nine employee engagement questions:
	I work with full intensity in my job; I try my hardest to perform as well as I can in my work; I concentrate hard in my job; My mind is always focused on my job; I strive very hard to complete my work well; I would recommend this organization as a place to work; My job inspires me; Time flies at work; I am proud of the work I do
EMPsurvEngagement	Average unit/team score for the nine engagement questions
EMPorgIntegrity1 – EMPorgIntegrity5	Proportion of the unit who answered favourably (with either 'agree' or 'strongly agree' on a 1 to 5 'strongly disagree' to 'strongly agree' response scale) to each of five employee 'organizational integrity' questions:
	My organization listens to staff; My organization does the right thing; My organization treats external stakeholders with respect; My organization encourages staff to point out questionable practices; We all do the right thing in this organization
EmpSurvOrgIntegrity	Average unit/team score for the five organizational integrity questions
EMPsurvSUP1 – EMPsurvSUP4	Proportion of the unit who answered favourably (with either 'agree' or 'strongly agree' on a 1 to 5 'strongly disagree' to 'strongly agree' response scale) to each of four 'supportive supervisor' questions:
	My supervisor listens to me; My supervisor cares about my well-being; My supervisor helps ensure we get things done; My supervisor is there when he/she is needed
EmpSurvSupervisor	Average unit/team score for the four 'supportive supervisor' questions

There are a number of ways that we could analyse the data set provided, which would give us information about potential predictors of variation in underrepresented group prevalence across the teams.

First, let's look at basic descriptive information linked to gender and UG prevalence across the teams. We can easily produce averages and range information with R. We will also try a different way of loading data into R, which is quicker than using the point and click options. First, put the data file for this example (*Ch4_example_2a.R*) in the same directory as the data file we will be using (*Ch4_diversity.xls*). It can be any directory you find convenient. Then open the R file. The file will have comments describing each line as well as the lines of code below:

```
if (!require("pacman")) install.packages("pacman")
pacman::p_load(readxl, modelsummary, this.path, huxtable)
setwd(this.path::here())
Ch4_div_group <- read_excel("Ch4_div_group.xlsx")
datasummary(PercentMale + UG ~ N + Mean + SD + Min + Max, data = Ch4_
div_group, output = "huxtable")
```

The first line asks R to look for the *pacman* package. If it is not on your computer, it will install it.

The second line uses the *p_load* program to load the packages we need: *readxl*, *modelsummary*, *this.path*, and *huxtable*. The *readxl* package allows you to open Excel files and the *modelsummary* package allows you to generate summaries of data efficiently. The *this.path* package simplifies setting the working directory and the *huxtable* package will help generate well-formatted tables.

The third line tells R to set its working directory, or the location where R will look for files, to the directory where this file currently is. Whatever that location, R will find it. The third line tells R to set its working directory, or the location where R will look for files, to the directory where this file currently is. The fourth line loads the data in R by using the *read_excel* program.

The fourth line uses the *read_excel* program in the *readxl* package to open the Excel file. The content of the Excel file is stored in the *Ch4_div_group* dataframe.

The fifth and sixth lines use the *datasummary* program in the *modelsummary* package. It tells the program to select two variables to look at, the percentage of males in a work group *PercentMale* and the percentage of underrepresented group individuals in a work group *UG*. It then specifies we need the count of cases in each variable (N), the mean (Mean), standard deviation (SD), minimum (Min), and maximum (Max). It also tells the program to look specifically in the *Ch4_div_group* dataframe. Once you run the code, you should see the output in the Console pane below the Source pane, as in Figure 4.10.

*.10

	N	Mean	SD	Min	Max
PercentMale	927	58.95	22.27	1.00	100.00
UG	746	0.12	0.11	0.00	0.45

Looking at Figure 4.10, we can see that 927 groups (or teams) reported the percentage of the team that are male, whilst only 746 teams reported the percentage of UG individuals in the group. This reflects the discussion earlier about ethnicity data – because it is rarely mandatory, we should expect to find some gaps in the data. Breaking down the information in Figure 4.10, let's look at the figure showing the percentage of team members who are male.

We have 927 teams who were able to report the percentage male. The smallest/minimum male percentage was a team who had 1 per cent men, while the maximum shows that at least one team had 100 per cent men. The mean/average percentage of men in the teams was 58.95 per cent, and the standard deviation was 22.27 per cent, meaning that there was quite a wide variation in the percentage of males in the teams across our organization. Remember that standard deviation is a measure to quantify the amount of dispersion or variation across the data and, in a normal distribution such as this one, we would expect 95 per cent of the data to be within two standard deviations (plus or minus) from the mean, and 68 per cent of the data to be within one standard deviation. So, using this knowledge, we can say that in approximately two-thirds of teams the percentage of men is between 36.68 per cent (or 58.95 per cent minus 22.27 per cent) and 81.22 per cent (58.95 plus 22.27 per cent). This indicates that there is quite a wide variation of male percentages across teams.

The UG data represented needs to be multiplied by 100 to make it a percentage. The HR analyst needs to be on the lookout for percentage data that is presented as a decimal and needs to be multiplied by 100, or when it is stored as an actual percentage. First, we can see that 746 teams have reported the percentage of UG. The smallest was .00, or 0 per cent, and the largest was .45, or 45 per cent, showing that one or more teams have 45 per cent UG members. The mean is .12, or 12 per cent, and the standard deviation is .11, or 11 per cent. From what we know about normal distributions, we can deduce that approximately two-thirds of the teams have their percentage of UG between one standard deviation below or above the mean; here 1 per cent (12 minus 11) and 23 per cent (12 plus 11).

Now we can look at these statistics across the two functions that we have in the data set to really investigate what is happening in this organization with regard to ethnicity.

The financial institution can be split at a very high level between those on the front line who are customer facing (called 'sales' in our data set) and those who support the front-line staff in roles such as product development, marketing, HR, finance, etc (this group are called 'professional service' in our data set).

So what we want to do here is compare two functions in the organization (or two samples), namely customer facing (sales) and non-customer facing (professional service), on UG.

For this we will use a test that looks at differences between two independent (different) samples on a variable we are really interested in: this is the independent samples t-test.

Example 2b: comparing ethnicity and gender across two functions in an organization using the independent samples t-test

The independent samples t-test is simple and practical. Used in certain situations, it will give you greater confidence in the group comparisons you are making. Essentially we should use the independent samples t-test when we have one grouping (independent) variable (e.g. two functions: sales or professional service in our example, which determines which group people belong to) and one variable that we want to compare the two groups on – the dependent variable (team level UG in our example).

We want to test whether there is a significant difference *between the means* of UG prevalence in teams from the two functional groups. The rationale for this terminology is that, potentially, the UG prevalence across the teams may to some extent be dependent upon the type of teams (i.e. the function).

Why are we doing this again? For both commercial reasons and for employee engagement and well-being reasons our organization would like to ensure there is a good representation of UG individuals to enhance the diversity of our organization. Research has indicated that UG individuals are often clustered into particular professions because they may feel that others are closed-off to them and potentially some professions may not make UG individuals very welcome. Business in the Community (2021) suggests that UG individuals rely much more on recruitment agencies. This could result in limited access to professions and industries that do not often use this method of recruitment.

We want to test whether there may be instances of this in our organization by first testing whether there is a difference in the proportion of UG individuals in 'sales' (customer-facing banking roles, which are usually more highly paid) than in 'professional service' (non-customer-facing professions such as HR, finance, risk assessment, etc). This will help us to identify whether this problem exists in our organization and then carefully diagnose and recommend a D&I strategy that is specific to the needs of this organization.

So is there a difference in the prevalence of UG in sales versus professional service? Let's test it.

In fact, it seems like such a good idea, let's do the test for percentage of males too. The R code for this example is in the same file as the previous example (*Ch4_example_2b.R*) and follows from it. Open the R file. The first four lines of code will be very similar to the previous example:

```
if (!require("pacman")) install.packages("pacman")
pacman::p_load(readxl, modelsummary, dplyr, car, this.path, huxtable)
setwd(this.path::here())
Ch4_div_group <- read_excel("Ch4_div_group.xlsx")
```

As in Example 2a, the first line asks R to look for the *pacman* package. If it is not on your computer, it will install it. The second line uses the *p_load* program to load the three packages we need: *readxl, modelsummary, dplyr, car, this.path,* and *huxtable*.

The third line tells R to set its working directory, or the location where R will look for files, to the directory where this file currently is. The fourth line loads the data in R by using the *read_excel* program.

Next, we will recode the *Function* variable to be more interpretable. The *Function* variable represents the sales role as *1*, and professional service as *2*. We will use similar code to Example 1 to recode the variable. The next lines of code are:

```
Ch4_div_group$Function_text <- case_match(Ch4_div_group$Function, 1 ~
"Sales", 2 ~ "Professional service")
```

The code below ensures that this new variable is treated as a grouping variable (i.e. a *factor* variable, in R jargon), instead of merely text:

```
Ch4_div_group$Function_text <- as.factor(Ch4_div_group$Function_text)
```

In the next set of lines, we examine the average percentage of male and UG for each type of function. We use the *datasummary* program as before, but specify that we want to see the *PercentMale* and *UG* variables, grouped by *Function_text*, and that the statistics we want to see are the number of cases, mean and standard deviation.

```
datasummary((PercentMale + UG) * Function_text ~ (N + Mean + SD), data =
Ch4_div_group, output = "huxtable")
```

Running the line above should produce output in the Console pane, as in Figure 4.11:

4.11

	Function_text	N	Mean	SD
PercentMale	Professional service	425	44.40	19.45
	Sales	502	71.26	16.27
UG	Professional service	342	0.14	0.12
	Sales	404	0.10	0.10

We can see whether the differences in averages are statistically significant, using the code below. First, we examine whether the percentage UG differs across *Function_text*:

```
t.test(Ch4_div_group$UG ~ Ch4_div_group$Function_text)
```

Note that the numeric values go first, followed by the grouping variable, separated by a tilde ~. Figure 4.12 shows the output:

4.12

```
        Welch Two Sample t-test

data: Ch4_div_group$UG by Ch4_div_group$Function_text
t = 5.6553, df = 640.61, p-value = 2.345e-08
alternative hypothesis: true difference in means between group
Professional service and group Sales is not equal to 0
95 percent confidence interval:
0.03069866 0.06335727
sample estimates:
mean in group Professional service    mean in group Sales
                0.14385965                    0.09683168
```

Analysis of the percentage of UG in teams

So, remembering what we said earlier about completion rates for ethnicity data collection initiatives, we can see that we have 404 teams within the sales function who have reported the percentage UG, and we have 342 teams within the professional service function who have reported the percentage UG. This shows that we are comparing two groups of different size, so behind the scenes R will account for this in the calculations.

We can also see that the mean value for the percentage of UG in the sales function is .0968, or 9.7 per cent, compared to the mean value for the percentage of UG in the professional service function, which is .1439, or 14.39 per cent. The standard deviation of the UG in the sales and professional service functions is 10 per cent and 12 per cent respectively, as can be seen in Figure 4.11.

Levene's test

One last thing we need to consider when comparing the two groups is whether they have a similar spread of values. For example, imagine if all the percentage UG for the sales function were clustered around the mean, i.e. all the teams in the sales function actually reported a very similar prevalence of UG (which would involve a small variation or spread in the data), yet within the professional service functions some teams had almost 100 per cent UG, while others had only 1–2 per cent, or even zero (which would involve a large variation or spread in the data). We need to consider this difference in spread or variance patterns in the UG prevalence in teams when comparing the two groups, because it will represent an important difference between the two.

Professor Howard Levene came up with a test that would clearly tell us whether the two groups were similar enough that we could assume 'equal variance'. If Levene's F-test statistic produces a significance value of greater than 0.05, then we can assume that the functional groups have similar patterns of spread or variance in team UG prevalence, or they have 'equal variance' (that they are not significantly different in their patterns of variance). However, if Levene's F-test statistic produces a significance value of less than 0.05 ($p<0.05$), then the functional groups that we are comparing can be considered to have very different variation in team UG prevalence; the functional groups do not have 'equal variance'.

We can test for this in R, using the *leveneTest* program in the *car* library, which is the next line of code:

```
leveneTest(UG ~ Function_text, Ch4_div_group)
```

This produces Figure 4.13:

4.13

```
Levene's Test for Homogeneity of Variance (center = median)
            Df F  value     Pr(>F)
group        1    8.7285 0.003232 **
           744
```

Looking at our result, Levene's test shows a significance value (denoted by *Pr(>F)*) of 0.003, so we cannot assume equal variance patterns in UG across our two functional groupings as $p<0.05$. Just to be clear, Levene's test does not tell us whether the means of UG prevalence are significantly different in their levels, but it does tell us that the variance of UG prevalence is different when we compare the two groups. By variance, we mean how far the data points are spread from the middle point of the data. It is possible to have two groups that have the same average, but one group to have greater spread around that average (i.e. have the same average but differ in variance). In terms of our example, the spread of UG prevalence is higher in professional services and sales, given the higher standard deviation in Figure 4.11 (standard deviation is a measure of variance). We routinely examine the variance of data because many statistical procedures rely on equal variance across groups. In contrast, the t-test tells us whether the average levels of UG differ significantly when we compare the professional service function with front-line sales function.

Luckily, the default program used in R to conduct t-tests does not require equality in variances, so we can rely on the result we obtain in Figure 4.11. But we do need to be aware that variances across these two groups differ, and to report that you used a t-test procedure that is robust to unequal variances.

How do we report these results? We can see in Figure 4.11 that the t-value for UG is -5.655; the degrees of freedom are 640.61, and the significance (known as the p-value) is 2.345e-08 (or 0.00000002345). For convenience, we can simplify the p-value as $p<0.001$. The degrees of freedom is a statistical parameter that is used to determine the significant p-value. It refers to the number of values in the calculation of a statistic that are free to vary.

If we were all students in Levene's class, before the days of statistical software we would have worked out this t-value and degrees of freedom with a pen and paper, and then looked up the corresponding p-value in a table to ascertain how significantly different the two groups are (if at all). However, R gives this information to us and we just need to be able to interpret the output. So, to follow formal conventions for reporting these statistics, you would say something like: 'The t-test was significant: $t(640.61) = -5.655$, $p<0.001$. There is a significant difference in percentage UG between the two functions. Sales (mean=.10, SD=.10) have a lower percentage UG in their teams than professional service (mean=.14, SD=.12). The variance in percentage of UG varied across the sales and professional service roles so Welch's t-test was used.'

The p-value means that the probability of this happening by chance alone is much less than 1 in 1,000 – so there must be something else (other than random fluctuations) at play (we don't know what or why these functions differ – but we now know that this is an issue in our organization that needs to be addressed).

The format of the above write-up is recommended so that you can use it to compare with other, similar tests. When you are presenting this to senior executives, though, the best way to present this might be just to keep it simple and say something like:

SNAPSHOT HIDDEN GEM

In comparing the sales and the professional service functions, the proportion of male staff is significantly higher in sales than in professional service groups within our organization. The average percentage of male staff in teams within sales is 71.26 per cent, and by comparison the average proportion of male staff in teams within the professional service function is 44.4 per cent. Deeper analysis shows the chance of this difference occurring randomly is less than 1 in 1,000, suggesting that we have a clear issue of male dominance within our sales function; this potentially needs attention if we want gender proportions to be similar across our organization.

As HR professionals, the next step might be to recommend interviewing UG individuals in the sales teams about their experiences. Depending on the outcome and assuming that you find some evidence of a potential bias, you might recommend interventions such as reviewing approaches for recruitment, retention and development of UG individuals in the sales function, or diversity training such as unconscious bias and inclusive leadership.

A quick note on negative t-values as we had in this example: in all cases, the bigger the absolute t-value, the more there are differences *between* the two groups than *within* the two groups. Given that the important thing is the absolute value, or size of the t-value, rather than whether it is negative or not, feel free to ignore the negative sign here because it is only negative because we (fairly arbitrarily) coded our first group 'sales' as 1 and our second group 'professional service' as 2, which has a higher mean than the first group. If we coded the groups the other way around we would not have a negative t-value. So a negative t-value is a function of which group you put into the analysis first (to compare with another group). Importantly, the value of the mean for each group tells us the important information and the t-test is just testing whether the groups are significantly different.

Analysis of the percentage of men in teams

We will also need to test whether there is a difference between sales and professional service functional groups with regard to the proportion of teams that are male. So with the next line of R code, we test this:

```
t.test(Ch4_div_group$PercentMale ~ Ch4_div_group$Function_text)
```

This produces this output in Figure 4.14:

4.14
```
     Welch Two Sample t-test

data: Ch4_div_group$PercentMale by Ch4_div_group$Function_text
t = -22.557, df = 828.77, p-value < 2.2e-16
alternative hypothesis: true difference in means between group
Professional service and group Sales is not equal to 0
95 percent confidence interval:
-29.19569 -24.52151
sample estimates:
mean in group Professional service    mean in group Sales
                  44.40235                  71.26096
```

We will also conduct Levene's test:

```
leveneTest(PercentMale ~ Function_text, Ch4_div_group)
```

Which produces Figure 4.15:

4.15
```
Levene's Test for Homogeneity of Variance (center = median)
          Df F value     Pr(>F)
group      1  28.923 9.544e-08 ***
         925
```

So, in interpreting our output for this we can see that again in Figure 4.15 our Levene's statistic has a small p-value (shown in the figure as *Pr(>F)*) associated with it that is below 0.05. We would follow conventions and write up the statistics in the following way: 'The t-test was significant: t(828.77)=-22.557, p<0.001. There is a significant difference in the percentage of men between the two functions. Sales have a higher percentage of men (mean=71.26, SD=16.27) in their teams than professional service (mean=44.40, SD=19.45). The variance in percentage of males varied across the sales and professional service roles so Welch's t-test was used.'

But of course this actually means:

SNAPSHOT HIDDEN GEM

In comparing the sales and the professional service functions, the proportion of UG staff is significantly lower in sales than in professional service. The average proportion of UG staff in teams within sales is 10 per cent, and by comparison the average proportion of UG staff in teams within professional service is 14 per cent. Deeper analysis shows that the likelihood of this difference occurring by chance alone is less than 1 in 1,000, suggesting we have an issue that needs attention within the sales function.

As with the UG example, it suggests there is also a potential gender issue in the sales team. The t-value is far higher in the second example, suggesting that the gender issue is greater than the ethnicity issue.

So the independent samples t-test has helped us to identify that the prevalence of women and of UG employees is significantly lower in the sales function compared to the professional service function. Because the dependent variables (percentage of the team who are UG, and percentage of team who are men) are continuous variables (i.e. a meaningful number rather than a category) and because there are only two groups (sales versus professional service), the independent samples t-test was the most appropriate choice here. For more information around which test to use in which situation, see Chapter 3, page 58–64). Another good example of when to use an independent samples t-test in diversity may be to test the difference between male and female average salary. Gender would be the independent variable and the dependent (continuous) variable would be salary.

So we now know that our organization faces some challenges in UG, particularly in the sales function. This opens things up for us now to delve deeper into what might be the possible reasons for this. Multiple regression will help us explore to a greater extent what factors might be at play or are associated with variations in diversity across our teams. Here we can use multiple regression to predict diversity statistics in teams; in particular we can try to predict the UG proportions in teams using a number of possible internal factors that we have available.

First, let's recap on multiple regression and why we might use it.

Example 3: using multiple linear regression to model and predict ethnic diversity variation across teams

Multiple linear regression

To be clear, the term 'regression' here has nothing to do with age regression, past-life regression or some form of Freudian psychoanalytic regression therapy. Rather, it refers to the attempt to model the relationship between two or more independent (or 'explanatory') variables and a dependent (or 'response') variable by analysing many observations. That model could then be used to predict and inform future behaviours with a degree of statistical confidence.

So, as interesting as the exercise might have been, we will not be accessing any childhood or past life memories (not even once, let alone multiple times – unless of course you were a statistician in your past life, which may explain why you were drawn to this book). To simplify things, let's use an example and talk about factors that influence whether an individual might be satisfied in their job.

In a simple example, an employee pulse survey (see Chapter 5 for a discussion of pulse surveys) might ask people to report satisfaction in their job on a scale of 1 to 7, where 1 is 'very dissatisfied' (and 4 is 'neutral', etc); and another question might be to ask them whether they think the level of pay they receive is fair compared to the effort they put in, by putting the answer on a scale of 1 to 5, where 1 is 'very unfair' and 5 is 'very fair' (with 3 as neutral). Initial analysis may find a relationship between these two variables, and conducting analyses in R may tell us that the correlation between job satisfaction and pay fairness is r=0.4. Then an extremely rough regression formula might look like this:

Job satisfaction = 4 (neither satisfied nor dissatisfied) + 0.4 * (perceived fairness)

So if pay fairness was the main driver of job satisfaction and you did something at work that increased a sense of fairness (e.g. paid people a merit bonus), which increased a person's judgement of fairness by a response scale increase of 1 (for example representing a fairness increase from a 4 to a 5 on the response scale), then this should lead to a boost of their satisfaction levels by 0.40.

Now, if we take into account that having supportive co-workers (on a scale of 1 = 'very unsupportive' to 5 = 'very supportive'; with 3 as neutral) might be correlated with job satisfaction in a unique way and add that to the model in R with pay fairness and job satisfaction, and the resultant correlation value is 0.3, we could add this to the equation as follows:

Job satisfaction = 4 (neither satisfied nor dissatisfied) + 0.4 * (perceived fairness) + 0.3 * (perceived co-worker support)

What this means is that the level of job satisfaction that someone feels increases by 0.4 for every one-point increase in perceived fairness, and increases by a further 0.3 for every one-point increase in perceived co-worker support.

So here we can start to build up a model that can help predict people's expected levels of job satisfaction, given the observed unique relationships that we find between perceived pay fairness, co-worker support and the general average levels of satisfaction in our organization. If we have the necessary data and we have identified predictive models from our analysis we can add other factors that are found to be important predictors of job satisfaction such as perceived organizational support, job autonomy and job variety. The same logic can be applied to a model that tries to predict the prevalence of UG in our teams across our organization.

In our HR analytics example, we want to use multiple regression to determine what factors appear to predict a low prevalence of UG individuals in teams. What is especially useful about multiple regression is that it can help you to establish the relationship between the dependent variable (UG percentage in this case) and multiple possible predictor variables, in this case: base location, function, group size, team lead gender and team gender breakdown.

But that is not all. It will also help you to examine just how much each predictor variable has an impact on the dependent variable on its own (for example, after taking function and percentage 'male' into account, we may wish to know the extent to which team location, on its own, predicts the prevalence of UG). And, finally, it will help show which of the predictor variables has the greatest impact on the dependent variable; this will give us the key information we need to identify where the problem areas are, and then to define a bespoke solution for the organization.

Next let's look at whether we can find predictors of UG using multiple regression.

UG is our dependent variable, or the variable we want to find predictors for. Thus, UG is our dependent variable. We also have a number of candidate variables that could predict UG prevalence. They are:

- LondonorNot (whether the team is located in London);
- Function (which function – sales or professional service);
- GroupSize (the number of employees in the team);
- NumberFeMaleTeamLeads (number of team leads in the team who were female);
- PercentMale (percentage of the team made up of males).

So these are our independent variables.

Let's open the next R file (*Ch4_example_3*.R). We again put this file in the same directory as the data file we used before (*Ch4_div_group.xlsx*). The next lines of code should be familiar:

```
if (!require("pacman")) install.packages("pacman")
pacman::p_load(readxl, modelsummary, this.path, huxtable)
setwd(this.path::here())
```

```
Ch4_div_group <- read_excel("Ch4_div_group.xlsx")
mod_1 <- lm(UG ~ LondonorNot + Function + GroupSize +
NumberFeMaleTeamLeads + PercentMale, data = Ch4_div_group)
summary(mod_1)
```

The fourth and fifth lines of code uses the *lm* program to estimate the linear regression. We predict *UG*, using the variables *LondonorNot*, *Function*, *GroupSize*, *NumberFeMaleTeamLeads*, and *PercentMale*. Note that the dependent variable is on the far left, and separated from the independent variables by the ~ symbol. The independent variables are separated with a + sign and we need to tell R that we are working in the Ch4_div_group dataframe. We store the results of the model in an object called *mod_1*.

The last line of code uses the '*summary*' program to get the results of estimating this model, which results in Figure 4.16.

4.16

```
Call:

lm(formula = UG ~ LondonorNot + Function + GroupSize +
NumberFeMaleTeamLeads + PercentMale, data = Ch4_div_group)

Residuals:
      Min             1Q       Median           3Q         Max
  -0.18001       -0.07915     -0.02669      0.06482     0.36599

Coefficients:
                         Estimate    Std.Error    t value    Pr(>|t|)
(Intercept)             0.1992030    0.0280904      7.091    3.16e-12 ***
LondonorNot            -0.0851266    0.0079754    -10.674     < 2e-16 ***
Function                0.0376668    0.0095606      3.940    8.94e-05 ***
GroupSize              -0.0001020    0.0002389     -0.427       0.669
NumberFeMaleTeamLeads  -0.0004358    0.0036879     -0.118       0.906
PercentMale            -0.0002739    0.0002237     -1.225       0.221
---
Signif. codes: 0 '***' 0.001 '**' 0.01 '*' 0.05 '.' 0.1 ' ' 1

Residual standard error: 0.1033 on 724 degrees of freedom
    (198 observations deleted due to missingness)
Multiple R-squared: 0.174, Adjusted R-squared: 0.1682
F-statistic: 30.49 on 5 and 724 DF, p-value: < 2.2e-16
```

The results in Figure 4.16 tell us that the R-squared (Multiple R-squared) is .174. The R-squared is the variance in the dependent variable that is accounted for by the model. If we multiply this number by 100 that will give us the percentage of variance. This means that 17.4 per cent of the variance in UG prevalence across the teams (the 700+ that we have UG data for) in our organization is accounted for by its shared relationship with the independent variables (i.e. whether they are in London or another location, whether they are sales staff or professional services staff, the number of employees in the work unit, the number of female team leads in the work unit, and the percentage of the overall work unit that are male) outlined above (whilst taking into account the degree to which the independent variables are amongst themselves related).

The F-statistic tests whether the model that includes our five independent variables significantly predicts the prevalence of UG. We say that the model 'accounts for variance in UG' because, in theory, if the variables in the model change then the prevalence of UG will change; so variation in our independent variables can account for a significant degree of variance in our dependent variable. The F-value here is in effect a figure that is highly linked to the R-squared value, but it is the statistic that R uses to obtain the level of significance that our model has, in terms of how good it is at predicting variation on UG (greater than you might get if you were predicting variation in UG prevalence across teams by random factors). R gives us a significance value for our regression model with an F-value of 30.492, as being close to zero, or we could say p<0.001, which means there is less than 1 in 1,000 chance that we would get this result by chance alone, so the model is significant – we should use it!

But how do we know which variables had an impact on UG? And, for that matter, which variables have the most impact?

There is a lot of information on this table, but to pull out the pieces that are of most use, and getting to grips with the fact that we are comfortable with R calculating the significance level for us and that we trust it, let's look down the significance column *Pr(>|t|)* on the far right column.

Here, we can see that the following two variables individually have a significant impact: 1) London or other location; 2) sales staff or professional services. The other independent variables are not contributing to the prediction of variation in UG across teams in our organization in a meaningful way (these are factors that seem to be unrelated to UG prevalence in our organization). So we can consider removing them from our model (though if our sample is big enough it is sometimes worthwhile leaving these factors in to make sure that any residual relationship they have with our other independent variables is factored out). Just looking at points 1) and 2) above, to what extent and in what way do they contribute? To decide, we can take a less cluttered look at the coefficients. Fortunately, the *modelsummary* program can help us create a neat table, using the next two lines:

```
modelsummary(mod_1, stars = TRUE, statistic = NULL, title =
"Unstandardized coefficients", output = "huxtable")
```

This results in Figure 4.16, which should be shown in the Source pane.

4.17

	Unstandardised coefficients
	(1)
(Intercept)	0.199***
LondonorNot	-0.085***
Function	0.038***
GroupSize	0.000
NumberFeMaleTeamLeads	0.000
PercentMale	0.000
Num.Obs.	730
R2	0.174
R2 Adj.	0.168
AIC	-1234.6
BIC	-1202.5
Log.Lik.	624.317
F	30.492
RMSE	0.10
+ p < 0.1, * p < 0.05, ** p < 0.01, *** p < 0.001	

Note that the R-squared and F-values are identical. The coefficients are identical to Figure 4.15. But these do not quite tell us how important each variable is. For that, we will need the standardized coefficients. We can also obtain them with the next lines:

```
modelsummary(mod_1, stars = TRUE, statistic = NULL, standardize =
"basic", title = "Standardized coefficients", output = "huxtable")
```

This results in Figure 4.18, which should be shown in the Viewer pane:

4.18

| | Standardised coefficients |
	(1)
(Intercept)	0.000***
LondonorNot	-0.361***
Function	0.166***
GroupSize	-0.015
NumberFeMaleTeamLeads	-0.004
PercentMale	-0.052
Num.Obs.	730
R2	0.174
R2 Adj.	0.168
AIC	-1234.6
BIC	-1202.5
Log.Lik.	624.317
F	30.492
RMSE	0.10

+ p < 0.1, * p < 0.05, ** p < 0.01, *** p < 0.001

In Figure 4.18, R shows the standardized coefficients (sometimes called 'Beta' values), which give us this information. The greater the standardized coefficient (positive or negative), the greater the potential impact that it has on the dependent variable.

So, looking at the standardized coefficient for our two significant variables, we can see the following:

1 Standardized coefficient for the 'London or other location' variable is Beta = −0.361.

2 Standardized coefficient for the 'sales staff or professional services' variable is Beta = 0.166.

This says that teams in London have a higher UG prevalence when taking the functional differences and other variables into account. This is because the variable *LondonorNot* is coded 1 if it is in London, and 2 if elsewhere. So as the value of *LondonorNot* increases from 1 to 2 (i.e. changes from London to elsewhere), UG prevalence decreases. Analogously, those in the professional service function have higher UG prevalence compared to the sales function. This is because the function variable is coded 1 if in sales and 2 if in professional service. So as the value of the function variable increases (i.e. changes from sales to professional service), UG prevalence also increases.

There is one last thing we can do. You may have noticed that the results in the source pane are temporary – when there is new output, it will be moved above, until, eventually, you cannot scroll up to see it. How do you save the results from your analyses? There is a button we have not discussed yet that can save the results to either an HTML, PDF, or Microsoft Word document. Figure 4.19 shows a button with a picture of a notebook you can click. You can achieve the same result if you go through the menu options: *File >> Compile Report…*

4.19

Pressing that button does a couple of things. It will first ask you which kind of file you want to save, as in Figure 4.20:

4.20

It will then run all of the code in your R file in order. It will put the results of the analysis into a file – saved in the working directory. We recommend the HTML option. Software to open HTML files is ubiquitous and often free, and once results are saved to a HTML, it is relatively difficult to alter them, as is possible with Microsoft Word files. You can still copy and paste results from the report or clip sections, such as graphs, if needed.

A useful exercise at this point is to group similar analyses together in one file, so that you have one document for several analyses that tell a coherent story. We leave it to you to attempt this, by combining the code found in example files 2a, 2b, and 3.

SNAPSHOT HIDDEN GEM

We have a significantly higher proportion of UG in our teams within the 'professional service' functions as compared to 'sales' teams even when we take into account that the diversity levels tend to be much higher in our London teams than our outside London teams. This is potentially very useful information given the fact that there tend to be rather large differences in the general population prevalence of UG across different geographical locations.

The census map shown in Figure 4.21, on the Office for National Statistics website, shows the percentage of various ethnicities across different parts of the UK. Not only can you inspect the map, you can also download the data as well. These figures should be taken into account when assessing predictors of UG in our organization across the teams.

Using the interactive map in Figure 4.21, we can compute the percentage of UG for each region, if we assume that the White population is the majority. Specifically, from a total of 100 per cent, we can subtract the percentage of White people to estimate the percentage UG within each region. You can see that in the City of London, for example, the percentage of UG residents is about 30 per cent, whilst in Northumberland it is only 2.4 per cent. So if all things were equal and our UG representation in teams represented that of the local population then we might expect to find this pattern. Importantly, however, when we take the geographical differences into account across our organization we still find a big tendency for a lesser prevalence of UG in our 'sales' function compared to 'professional service'.

4.21   Ethnicity of people in the UK

SOURCE Office for National Statistics: www.ons.gov.uk/census/maps/choropleth/identity/ethnic-group/ethnic-group-tb-6a/asian-asian-british-or-asian-welsh

Testing the impact of diversity: interacting diversity categories in predictive modelling

One of the key things that an HR analytics master will consider doing with regard to D&I is to see whether variation in important HR-related outcomes such as engagement, turnover, sickness absence and performance might be 'predicted' by particular categories/groups of interest to the D&I specialist, and also whether certain predictive models work in the same way for particular categories. Because in these analyses diversity is being used as a predictor of these important HR-related business outcomes, the predictive models for these will be outlined in other case study chapters within this book, and we discuss conducting analysis with interactions in Chapter 11. We also focus on additional diversity analyses in our case study in Chapter 8 (recruitment and selection).

A final note

Throughout this chapter we have discussed common approaches to measuring and managing D&I and worked through two examples covering ethnicity and gender. It is important to note here that this is just the tip of the iceberg when it comes to what can and should be measured as part of a comprehensive D&I programme. Many easily observed indices of diversity include gender and ethnicity as well as disabilities, age, marital status and sexual orientation. The management of diversity reaches far more broadly than exploring these primary characteristics; secondary characteristics include factors such as parental status, social status, nationality, language, accent, communication style, appearance, location, hobbies, educational background, religion – and even the department a person works in the organization itself can lead to bias. We differ in many ways that might make us favour one person over another in the workplace that have nothing to do with the individual's ability to do the job. This is where we can also consider measuring inclusion. Many organizations endeavour to measure how inclusive their culture is through a series of survey questions; either as part of a wider employee attitude survey or on its own. The resulting metric is often referred to an 'inclusion index', in much the same way as organizations often refer to the aggregation of engagement questions as an 'engagement index'. For more information on surveys, see Chapter 5 on employee attitude surveys – engagement and workforce perceptions.

As mentioned at the beginning of this chapter, the ability to quantify the benefits of having a diverse and inclusive organization is the number-one key challenge in the diversity business case. In this chapter, we have used frequency tables, chi-square analysis, independent samples t-tests and multiple linear regression to model, predict and investigate diversity data. These methods can be applied to any diversity characteristics for which there is data available and, as we discuss in Chapter 11, can be used in a business case.

References

Business in the Community (2021) The scorecard report: Race at work 2021, www.bitc.org.uk/wp-content/uploads/2021/10/bitc-race-report-raceatwork2021scorecardreport-oct2021.pdf (archived at https://perma.cc/6VEL-WEW4)

Gartner (2023) Workforce diversity, Gartner. www.gartner.com/en/human-resources/glossary/workforce-diversity (archived at https://perma.cc/MDC5-5BWJ)

Kandola, B and Fullerton, J (1998) *Diversity in Action: Managing the mosaic*, Chartered Institute of Personnel and Development, London

Noon, M (2010) Managing equality and diversity, in *Human Resource Management: A contemporary approach*, ed J Beardwell and T Claydon, FT Prentice Hall, Edinburgh

Office for National Statistics (2023) Census maps, www.ons.gov.uk/census/maps/choropleth/identity/ethnic-group/ethnic-group-tb-6a/asian-asian-british-or-asian-welsh (archived at https://perma.cc/4YVY-AJAF)

05

Case study 2

*Employee attitude surveys – engagement
and workforce perceptions*

Over the last decade or so, the idea of employee engagement has become one of the key people issues discussed at executive and senior manager level. Having engaged employees can be seen as one of the key objectives for which HR functions are expected to strive. With an enormous amount of literature written about, it including a UK government-sponsored research report (MacLeod and Clarke, 2009), and vast amounts of money being spent on it, from an HR analytics point of view employee engagement is something that HR professionals, people managers and students of HR or management need to be highly knowledgeable about.

In order to access levels of engagement within their organizations, many large corporates will use external research companies such as Willis Towers Watson, Glint, CultureAmp, Medallia and Qualtrics, to name just a few, whilst others design and run their own employee engagement surveys. Regarding the former, this chapter will talk through how to get the most out of working with these external providers, understanding what they are doing for the organization, and asking the right questions to get meaningful results and outcomes. After reading this chapter you will understand their methods, which will make for a far more productive working relationship. Regarding the latter, this chapter will help you if you want to design your own in-house employee engagement survey; it will help you to ensure that the questions that you are measuring are tapping what you want them to measure using validity and reliability testing, and how to interpret the results when you run models to predict employee engagement. Ultimately, this chapter will help you to get the outcome you want for your organization.

You may choose to use a combination of the above. For example, your organization may use an external research company for the larger employee engagement survey and then you may use the methods below to structure ongoing 'pulse' surveys on a subset of the population, such as one division that had particularly low engagement scores.

In this chapter, we cover the following:

- What is employee engagement?
- How is it measured?
- Interrogating the measures.
- Results, analysis and outcomes.
- Actions and business context.

What is employee engagement?

There is, quite simply, no agreed definition of employee engagement. MacLeod and Clarke (2009) quote David Guest, Professor of Organizational Psychology and Human Resource Management at King's College London, as pointing out that 'much of the discussion of engagement tends to get muddled as to whether it is an attitude, a behaviour or an outcome or, indeed, all three', and that 'the concept of employee engagement needs to be more clearly defined… or it needs to be abandoned'. The research report then goes on to say that 'there is too much momentum and indeed excellent work being done under the banner of employee engagement to abandon the term'. Undeniably, academics and HR professionals (including professional survey companies that make a business out of employee engagement) have very different ideas about what engagement is.

Within the world of academic research, two main definitions of engagement are used. One of the first was a measure of 'behavioural work engagement' by Kahn, which was defined as 'the simultaneous employment and expression of a person's "preferred self" in task behaviours that promote connections to work and to others, personal presence (physical, cognitive, and emotional) and active, full performances' (1990: 700). An example of a scale used to measure this (Rich et al, 2010) includes survey questions based on physical, emotional and cognitive engagement.

A second measure used in academia is 'work engagement', referred to as the Utrecht Work Engagement Scale (UWES) and defined as 'a positive, fulfilling work-related state of mind that is characterized by vigour, dedication and absorption' (Schaufeli and Bakker, 2003). The full questionnaire scale items used to measure this can be found in Schaufeli and Bakker (2010) and on the following web page: www.wilmarschaufeli.nl/publications/Schaufeli/Tests/UWES_GB_17.pdf.

In the world of HR professionals and consultancies a number of different definitions also exist, for example:

From consultancies:

- CultureAmp (2023) define employee engagement as a metric that represents the levels of enthusiasm employees feel toward their organization. It captures more than just job satisfaction or feeling happy at work – it's a measure of how motivated people are to put in extra effort for their organization, and a sign of how committed they are to staying there.
- Mercer (2011) defines employee engagement as 'A psychological state in which employees feel a vested interest in the company's success and are both willing and motivated to perform to levels that exceed the stated job requirements.'
- Korn Ferry's Engaged Performance Framework defines employee engagement as a function of commitment and discretionary effort (Finnemore, 2018).
- Willis Towers Watson (2021) defines employee engagement as 'the intensity of the employee relationship with an employer, marked by three elements: (i) committed effort to achieve goals ("engaged"), (ii) in an environment that enables work ("enabled"), and (iii) energizes performance ("energized")'.

From businesses:

- 'Employee engagement is when the business values the employee and the employee values the business' (MacLeod and Clarke, 2009).

And even:

- 'You sort of smell it, don't you, that engagement of people as people. What goes on in meetings, how people talk to each other. You get the sense of energy, engagement, commitment, belief in what the organization stands for' (Lord Currie, cited in MacLeod and Clarke, 2009).

So, enough said. From the definitions, it seems that engagement is somewhere between being in the zone, feeling positive, enjoying work, feeling proud of it, having commitment to organizational success, going the extra mile, having a bit of energy around it all and feeling valued – or a combination of some or all of those things – depending on who you talk to.

In support of some of the extremely bold claims often found in the practitioner literature, a considerable amount of research has been carried out to explore the importance of engagement; this research seems to show a consistent pattern in that engagement tends to be positively correlated with both task and contextual performance, well-being measures and negatively related to intention to quit (see Table 5.1). To recap on correlation, it shows the relationship between two variables. Because the p-value is <0.001 for all outcomes, we know that the relationship is significant. Looking at each variable in turn and remembering with correlations that the magnitude of correlation ranges from 0 to 1 with 1 the highest, we can see that task

TABLE 5.1 Summary of research findings exploring the outcomes of engagement

Outcomes	Corrected Correlations	Source
Task performance	0.43	Study 1 (k = 14, N = 4562)
Contextual performance	0.34	Study 1 (k = 10, N = 3654)
Health	0.20	Study 2 (k = 17, N = 11593)
Turnover intention	−0.26	Study 2 (k = 4, N = 1893)

SOURCE Peccei (2013)
NOTE k = number of unique samples; N = total sample size. For all correlations p< 0.001

performance and contextual performance have a moderate positive relationship with engagement. So we might *infer* from this (remembering that correlation does not *imply* causality) that when engagement goes up, task performance (performance on work activities) and contextual performance (performance on social workplace behaviours) goes up a moderate amount. Health has a weaker, but significant positive relationship with engagement; so when engagement goes up, health and well-being go up by a small amount. Finally, voluntary turnover intention (the measurement of whether employees plan to leave their position) has a weak, but significant, negative relationship with intention to leave; so when engagement goes down, intentions to leave the organization go up by a small degree.

How do we measure employee engagement?

Employee engagement is not a tangible idea, so it cannot be measured as easily as, say, salary, sales performance figures or attendance at leadership training.

The only way to gather information about how engaged an individual might be is to ask them. Rather than just having a one-question survey with the question 'How engaged are you?', to which the answer would be as variable as each individual's own definition of employee engagement, thus rendering the survey useless, we can ask a range of questions that will indicate to us how engaged that person is, based on the definitions we choose. Asking someone 'How engaged are you?' could lead to a wide variety of responses depending upon what the respondent had in their head when thinking about engagement. Some people, for example, might answer the question in the context of how long they had been engaged to their future marriage partner. Asking a range of questions specifically designed to measure a range of aspects associated with what we mean by 'engagement' ensures that the researcher has some control over the measurement of engagement and can (to some extent) ensure that the idea of engagement in the employees' heads is as defined. This means that we can compare across the organization in a controlled and measured way and that we find out what we need to. We will discuss later in this chapter how to choose questions in order to be sure we are measuring what we want to measure.

As an example of a range of questions that we could use, let's look at one of the academic definitions of employee engagement mentioned previously: behavioural work engagement and the associated Rich et al (2010) set of questions. These questions are fully tested and validated measures of engagement. The full set of 17 questions can be found in Rich et al (2010), but to give you a quick view, the following is a sample:

Employees answer questions on a five-point response scale ranging from 1 'strongly disagree' to 5 'strongly agree', with the statements:

- 'I exert my full effort to my job' [measuring physical engagement].
- 'I am proud of my job' [measuring emotional engagement].
- 'At work, my mind is focused on my job' [measuring cognitive engagement].

The other academic engagement example presented above, the UWES (Schaufeli and Bakker, 2003), also uses 17 questions. The full set of questions can be found in Schaufeli and Bakker (2010), but to give you a quick view, below is a sample (again on a response scale from 'strongly disagree' to 'strongly agree'):

- 'When I get up in the morning, I feel like going to work' [vigour].
- 'My job inspires me' [dedication].
- 'Time flies when I'm working' [absorption].

Interestingly, professional measures of engagement used by consultancies and survey companies tend to be quite different from those used in academic research. Examples of some of the main measures used include the Q12 measure used by Gallup and an employee engagement measure used by Willis Towers Watson.

The Q12 measure, although often mistaken for a measure of employee engagement, does not actually measure engagement; according to Gallup it measures: 'the actionable issues for management – those predictive of attitudinal outcomes such as satisfaction, loyalty, pride and so on'. Unfortunately the items cannot be presented here as a scale because Gallup has a copyright associated with their 12 questions (although, as mentioned, examples of similar individual items can be found in freely available measures presented by academic researchers over a number of decades), but the Gallup questions can be found relatively easily with a simple internet search of 'Gallup Q12 questions'. Also, interested readers should read the chapter by Schaufeli and Bakker (2010) where these researchers set out both the Q12 and the UWES scales, along with a discussion of the psychometric properties of these measures.

A brief examination of the Q12 items shows that the 12 true/false questions measure a wide scope of issues (e.g. having a good friend in the workplace; whether resources are made available; whether there are opportunities for development and growth, etc). Importantly, the Q12 is not an engagement measure as such but more of a measure that aims to tap a range of issues associated with employee engagement. Gallup presents some meta-analysis results that also, similar to the research conducted by academics, show a consistently positive relationship with the Q12 measure and performance (Gallup, 2008).

One other example of professional survey companies' measures of employee engagement is a scale by Willis Towers Watson (2021), whose conceptualization of engagement includes employees having a belief in company goals and objectives, an emotional connection with the organization and a willingness to make extra effort to support success. A definition such as this will have a number of links with traditional measures of organizational commitment, which has been heavily researched in the academic field for many decades.

Below is an example of some questions taken from one validated organizational commitment scale (Allen and Meyer, 1990), measured on a five-point scale ranging from 'strongly disagree' to 'strongly agree':

- 'I would not recommend a close friend to join this organization.'

- 'I am extremely glad that I chose this organization to work for, over others I was considering at the time I joined.'

- 'I really feel as if this organization's problems are my own.'

So, whether you are designing your own survey questionnaire or partnering with a consultancy to run an employee survey (so as to benchmark measures), you need to be sure that the questions included in your employee survey are good indicators of what you are trying to measure (and that they are reliable). How can you be sure about this?

Before answering this we shall make the following assumptions:

- You want to survey your employee base to find out what people are thinking, feeling and doing.

- You want to ensure you measure the attitudes and perceptions that you *think* you are measuring.

- You presumably want to conduct a survey in order to take prescriptive action based on meaningful findings.

- You do not want to waste everyone's time with unreliable measures or meaningless results.

- You do not want to waste money on expensive interventions carried out based on recommendations from meaningless survey results.

In short, it is absolutely worth the time and effort to understand how to interrogate the measures.

Interrogating the measures

Interrogating measures of engagement and associated constructs used in surveys

Put simply, a good measure of a concept (such as engagement) is one that accurately and consistently taps the degree to which employees vary or differ on that concept. So a good measure of engagement will accurately and consistently identify when employees vary in engagement.

To fully understand what makes a good measure, we need to refer to a few central ideas linked to survey measurement theory. Yes, we are referring to 'theory'. When an academic starts talking about theory, practitioners often roll their eyes because there is a danger that it will not have any practical relevance. However, here the words of Kurt Lewin apply: 'there is nothing more practical than a good theory' (1952: 169). Measurement theory argues (amongst a range of things) that a measure has two key ideas linked to it: a 'construct' and an 'indicator'. The construct is the idea that the measure is trying to tap into. In the example above, the construct is 'engagement' and an example indicator could be the statement 'I am proud of my job', which leads to a 1–5 response. To ensure rigorous measurement, one indicator is not enough on its own. Just as you would look at many indicators when trying to assess whether a potential candidate is likely to be a good new hire (such as CV, online profile, performance at interview, assessment-centre results, references and recommendations, etc), it is necessary to look at many indicators when trying to ascertain the levels of engagement.

When presenting a measure of a construct a survey provider/consultancy should be able to clearly explain exactly what that construct entails: they should be able to present a clear definition of exactly what they are attempting to measure, and the indicators they are using to do so. If, as with engagement, this construct refers to a state or trait expected to be inside an employee, then a construct is referring to a state in someone's head (or maybe even somewhere else in their body… but let's not get drawn into some abstract Cartesian dualistic debate about whether 'my body is my mind' and 'my mind is my body'). Importantly, a measure of engagement should tap into how engaged someone is, or their state of engagement. Hence the construct is what we are trying to measure.

The measure will have an indicator; an indicator is what is used to gauge the construct in employees' heads. A question, or a range of questions, in a survey will be the 'indicator' or 'indicators'; importantly, the questions are used to *indicate* the level of the construct in the employees' heads (this is quite an important point in measurement theory).

So if, for example, we have a question in a questionnaire that requires employees to answer on a 1–5 'strongly disagree' to 'strongly agree' response scale with the statement 'I am fully engaged', then the idea is that the number an employee chooses – 1, 2, 3, 4 or 5 – will 'indicate' the degree of engagement that the employee feels (in their heads... or heart, depending upon how one conceptualizes engagement). So in our organization, employees will vary in their answers to this question: some will say 1, some 2, some 3, some 4 and some 5. A good measure of engagement, with precise indicators, will produce 'accurate' variation in the numbers recorded in the survey. If, for example, the wording of the question was complex or confusing, the results across employees may vary depending on how well the person understands the question. This would be an imprecise measure of engagement and hence the results will be quite inaccurate. So, by accurate here we mean that engagement levels vary in employees' heads, and the variation that our survey records indicate will correspond closely to the variation in employees' heads.

Of course, it is unlikely that any indicator will indicate or gauge engagement in employees' heads perfectly. This is where classical test theory comes in and has a very practical relevance to HR analytics.

Classical test theory and construct measurement

Classical test theory can be used to further understand the mechanics of measurement testing. Before proceeding, it is worth adding that we should also consider things that might influence how someone will respond to survey questions that are outside the survey questions themselves. For example, did the person just have a particularly bad commute? Were they just involved in a meeting where they found out their project had been cancelled? Did they just receive news that they have been nominated for promotion? Or perhaps their partner had recently left them because they had been spending too much time at work? There is a strong possibility that provocations like this could influence their answer to the question.

Classical test theory considers all the types of influences discussed. It can be represented as follows:

$$X = t + e$$

Where each set of survey results contain a true component and an error component:

X = set of survey results – the degree to which the numbers produced in our survey records vary (i.e. the engagement survey results).

t = true component: an indication of true variation in levels of engagement in employees' heads.

e = error component: measurement error.

So the numbers produced in the survey and the degree to which these numbers vary in our survey records will be made up of two things: 1) some indication of true variation in feelings (or states) of engagement in employees' heads; and 2) measurement error.

Or, put another way:

Variation in employee answers to survey questions = variation in actual true engagement levels + some error.

If an indicator is a bad measure of a construct, then the error will be large. Variation will exist in the numbers recorded in our survey records that does not correspond with actual true variation in engagement amongst our employees. This variation can be considered 'measurement error'. So with $X=t+e$, variation from our indicator is made up of true variation in our construct plus error in our measure; a very simple notion really. Despite the theory, this is a very practical idea, as it raises the issue that a company's engagement survey may produce engagement results that have some degree of error in the measurement of engagement…

The main aim of measurement testing is to try to tease out, separate and identify e from t in order to establish whether X is a good measure of our construct.

What is a good (valid) measure?

A good measure is one that has indicators that accurately tap the construct under investigation. Importantly, the first thing that is needed to ensure a good measure is a clear definition of what the construct actually is. Only if we have this can we hope to understand whether an associated measure is good. By good, we mean valid. Validity refers to whether the measure accurately represents the construct intended, for example, whether the survey questions intended to ascertain whether an employee is engaged actually do measure whether an employee is engaged. In measurement model testing there are a number of different types of validity, as set out below.

FACE VALIDITY

Face validity is more art than science. It is not measured in any sophisticated statistical way, rather it relies on an experienced professional who knows and understands the construct to cast their steely eye over the indicators, consider them carefully, and say something like, 'Yes, on the face of it, these indicators seem to be good measures of the construct.' The notion of face validity revolves around the idea that the indicators actually look as if they should measure the construct at hand. When factor and reliability analyses are conducted, the results can often tell us whether any particular questions might be problematic (see below). When this happens, we can carefully read the items and make a sensible judgement about whether they might be tapping another construct instead of the one we are trying to measure.

CONSTRUCT VALIDITY

Construct validity is when the indicators do actually measure the construct at hand, and we know this because they behave analytically in a way that we would expect them to behave. We will cover below how to determine this and what it looks like. In our example, we would want our measure of engagement to show good factor analysis structure, good reliability statistics and tend to correlate with other measures (e.g. performance scores and supervisor ratings of motivation) in a way that we would expect. We will cover these later in this chapter.

DISCRIMINANT VALIDITY

The notion of discriminant validity revolves around the idea that the measures actually demonstrate that they are *not* measuring some other construct. We could determine this by using factor analysis, or by analysing a correlation matrix of all measures in a data set, both of which will tell us the relationships that the measure has with other variables.

For example, if one of our measures of engagement is a question about having pride in the organization, we would expect it to correlate highly with other engagement measures, but not quite so highly with non-engagement measures such as performance scores, 360-degree feedback ratings or answers to other questions about leadership effectiveness.

CRITERION VALIDITY

After performing statistical tests, do the measures demonstrate the appropriate degree of statistical robustness that tells us they are measuring the construct?

Measure contamination

Measure contamination is when the measures are actually sharing variance with other constructs due to imprecise measurement, measurement error and inaccurate indicators.

Conceptual explanation of factor analysis

The basic idea behind factor analysis in relation to survey research is actually very simple. It is a form of analysis that helps check that questionnaire items in a survey are actually measuring the construct that they are supposed to be measuring, rather than other constructs. Well, that is the simple explanation, though in reality it is a little more complicated. The analysis examines the pattern of respondents' answers to a set of questionnaire items to see if responses follow a particular pattern. If responses to a certain set of questions (specifically designed to measure a particular construct) tend to group together then this provides some evidence that the items are measuring this construct. The example below should help to make this clearer as to why this is the case. Conceptually, you would expect all the questions about the same construct to yield a similar answer – a perhaps overly simple example might be:

Employee questionnaire:

1 Do you feel your line manager guides you in your career?

2 Do you feel your line manager cares about your development?

3 Do you feel your line manager does all he/she can to help you be successful?

4 Is your working environment hygienically clean?

5 Do you feel you need a shower after you leave the office?

6 Are there unexplained odours near your workstation?

Here, you would expect the responses to questions 1 to 3 to be similar because they seem to be all about measuring line manager support. Questions 4, 5 and 6, however, appear to be measuring something entirely different (office cleanliness?). So here you would expect items 1–3 to share variance (i.e. go up and down at the same time, probably depending on whether the line manager is supportive); and items 4–6 to share variance (i.e. go up and down at the same time, probably based on what sort of office environment people have), but you would not expect 1–3 to share variance with 4–6 (although, having said this, if the employees' line manager regularly spilled a Thai curry lunch over his or her subordinates, there might be some shared variance across the items; presumably this would be rare, so the amount of shared variance in the data set across these two sets of items would still be limited). It is clear here that the questions are not all tapping into the same construct.

The next example is more similar to what you would see in an employee engagement survey. Note that this is *not* a recognized engagement scale and the authors have created items loosely based on questions used by various researchers to present as an example here.

So let's say that a survey provider has a questionnaire with the following nine questions that are supposed to measure employees' 'engagement'. The response scale ranges from 1 to 5 where 1 = strongly disagree and 5 = strongly disagree:

1 I work with full intensity in my job [intensity].

2 I try my hardest to perform as well as I can in my work [performance].

3 I concentrate really hard in my job [concentration].

4 My mind is always totally focused on my job [focus].

5 I strive very hard to complete my work as well as I can [quality].

6 Time flies at work [absorption].

7 I would recommend this organization as a place to work [recommend].

8 I feel a sense of belonging with my organization [belonging].

9 I am proud of the work I do [pride].

If this is a good and valid multi-item measure of engagement then we would expect respondents to answer all questions in a similar way (i.e. to give a similar point on the 1 to 5 scale for all nine items). If people had very low levels of engagement, we might expect them to answer 1 or 2 on most of these items, and people who are highly engaged to answer 4 or 5 on most of these. The important point is that if the items truly gauge the state of engagement in the employee's head, their individual responses should not vary too much across all these items. We would expect some variation, but the pattern of responses should be reasonably consistent across the items for each person if it is tapping into a single construct of engagement.

See Figure 5.1, which is a diagrammatic representation of a construct of engagement where employees' responses to the nine items above are generally consistent across the nine items because they neatly tap the state of engagement in their heads.

5.1   The engagement construct

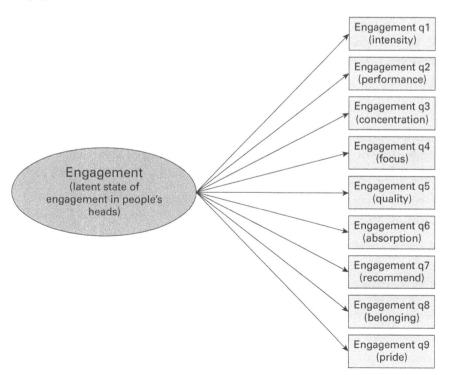

Factor analysis will enable us to examine the extent to which people respond in a consistent pattern across the nine questions. It will then confirm one of four outcomes:

1 The question responses show a consistent pattern (and indeed form a good measure of engagement).

2 The question responses do not show a consistent pattern (and hence the questions are not a good measure of engagement).

3 The question responses show a consistent pattern across some of the items but not all (this could suggest that some of the items form a good measure of engagement but some do not).

4 The question responses show a consistent pattern across two or more sets of items (this might suggest that our measure actually taps more than one construct).

If the items used here actually measure more than one construct then the factor analysis will tell you this. It might be the case that some of the questions were badly designed and these badly designed items actually measured something other than engagement. This would be evident in analysing the pattern of responses, as you will see in the example below.

The analysis may indicate that there were two sets of responses found, suggesting that the scale was measuring two separate constructs rather than one single construct of engagement. If a two-construct pattern was found then it may also be the case that the designer of the survey actually defined engagement with two separate notions, i.e. with some items designed to measure one notion or element of engagement and other items measuring another notion or element of engagement.

So if we defined 'engagement' as a combination of 'organizational engagement' and 'psychological job engagement', we might actually design some items to gauge the psychological job engagement (e.g. mental focus) and design others to tap the organizational engagement aspect (e.g. organizational commitment). This may then lead to a two-factor structure being identified in the pattern of responses rather than a single factor. The analysis would be picking up the fact that we are measuring two sub-constructs of engagement or two slightly different forms of engagement. Figure 5.2 is a conceptual/diagrammatic representation of such a scenario.

5.2 Two-'sub-factor' engagement structure

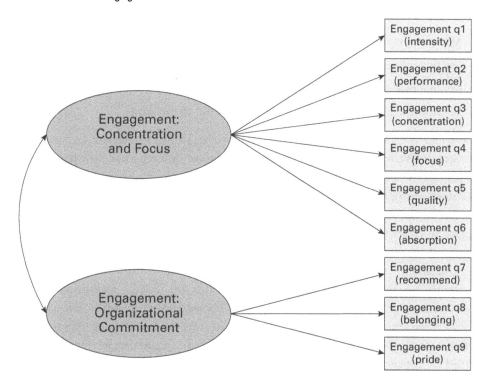

The state of engagement that the survey provider is working with in the case of Figure 5.2 (see questionnaire items listed previously) is made up of two slightly different ideas: mental concentration in people's heads when they engage in their job, and the degree to which these employees feel a sense of engagement with their organization or 'organizational commitment'. If the engagement scale has three items that ask questions more around organizational engagement and six items that focus on mental engagement linked to concentration, people's answers on these two subsets are likely to be slightly different – factor analysis can pick this up and identify that there are two sub-factors to our engagement scale.

So if a multi-item measure is actually measuring more than one construct, factor analysis will identify this. Factor analysis can also be used to check that different measures, designed to gauge different constructs, actually do seem to be measuring different constructs. For example, we could have nine items designed to measure engagement in a questionnaire (above) and four items designed to measure whether employees feel that their line manager is supportive, by asking the following four questions on the same scale:

1 My line manager supports me [support].

2 My line manager helps me out when I am faced with difficulties [help].

3 My line manager gives me good guidance when I really need it [guidance].

4 My line manager knows how to get the best out of me [best].

We could use factor analysis to ensure that the 13 items measure two separate constructs. We would expect that there may be some differences in how people tend to respond to the four 'manager' items as compared to the nine engagement items. If our items are measuring these two constructs then this should happen (see Figure 5.3).

One of the things that an HR analytics expert needs to be able to assess, with regard to either their own in-house engagement survey or with engagement surveys provided by external providers, is the degree to which items grouped together to form a single combined composite measure are actually measuring the unified construct (i.e. the degree to which these questions are actually measuring engagement of a range of different mental states). The composite measure that a survey provider presents is likely to be an aggregate average score for engagement derived from responses to the range of questions intended to measure engagement, perhaps called an 'engagement index'.

Putting our above definitions of validity into practice, the items should have *face validity*, in that they look like the kind of questions that would measure 'engagement' in accordance with the definition used. However, the construct also needs to demonstrate *criterion validity* in that the factor analysis statistics (calculated using R in the two-construct example below) demonstrate that the items do indeed 'load' together to measure a single factor. Also, the *criterion validity* should demonstrate that the engagement scale separates from other measures used and, finally, when combined as a composite should demonstrate different magnitudes of correlations with other constructs compared to any other scale, showing that the scale demonstrates *discriminant validity*.

5.3   Two-factor structure: engagement and manager support

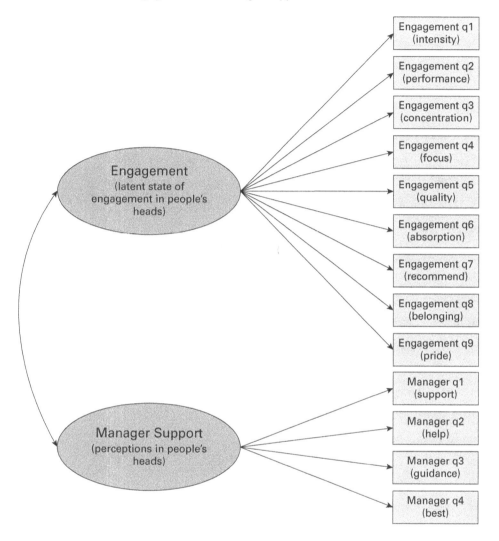

Example 1: two constructs – exploratory factor analysis

In this section we will be using the Excel file named *Ch5_RAW_Survey_Results.xlsx*. In this file you will see 34 different variables that hold individual survey responses of 832 employees. The first five variables hold data linked to employees' demographic profiles and the remaining variables (6–34) are employee responses on a 1 'strongly disagree' to 5 'strongly agree' response scale for a range of specific questions (these are indicated). The variables are as follows:

1   Sex (gender).
2   jbstatus (job status).
3   age (age category).
4   tenure (years in job).
5   ethnicity (ethnicity category).
6   ManMot1 – My manager motivates me.
7   ManMot2 – My manager knows how to get the most out of me.
8   ManMot3 – My manager encourages me to do my best.
9   ManMot4 – My manager is great.
10 ocb1 – I work harder than my job requires.
11 ocb2 – I put a huge amount of effort into my job.
12 ocb3 – I help out my teammates.
13 ocb4 – I go the extra mile.
14 aut1 – I have the freedom to choose how I work.
15 aut2 – I can decide how to work during the day.
16 aut3 – I am given enough leeway to get the job done.
17 Justice1 – Procedures are fair here.
18 Justice2 – Procedures are applied fairly.
19 Justice3 – Procedures are the same for all.
20 JobSat1 – I am satisfied in my job.
21 JobSat2 – My job is good.
22 Quit1 – I am thinking of leaving.
23 Quit2 – I am ready to look for other work.
24 Quit3 – I have looked for employment elsewhere in the last week.
25 Man1 – Management help workers out when they experience difficulties.
26 Man2 – Management supports employees who are faced with discrimination.
27 Man3 – Management acts decisively.
28 Eng1 – I share the values of this organization.
29 Eng2 – I am proud of this organization.
30 Eng3 – This organization is a big part of who I am.
31 Eng4 – I would recommend this organization as a place to work.

32 pos1 – This organization cares about my well-being.

33 pos2 – This organization is interested in my contribution.

34 pos3 – This organization is there for me when I need help.

In this analytic example, we use exploratory factor analysis to assess construct structure and criterion validity in a survey that has seven questions.

The survey includes the following seven questions, in which respondents are asked to answer on a scale of 1 to 5 where 1 = strongly agree and 5 = strongly disagree (a word summary is given in brackets afterwards for reference purposes later). These questions are the final seven columns of the data set:

1 I share the values of this organization [values].

2 I am proud of this organization [pride].

3 This organization is a big part of who I am [who I am].

4 I would recommend this organization as a place to work [recommend].

5 This organization cares about my well-being [cares].

6 This organization is interested in my contribution [interested].

7 This organization is there for me when I need help [helps].

Before we proceed, it is useful at this point to review the questions and reflect, based on your knowledge of this topic, whether you believe the questions look as though they might fall into two categories. We will come back to this point later.

The R code for this example is in file *Ch5_example_1.R*. The first line of code checks to see if the *pacman* package is installed, and installs it if it is not. The second line loads the required packages for the example. The third line sets the working directory to be the same as the directory that the example file is in (where the Excel file should also be!). The fourth line loads the data and stores it in the *Ch5_exp_fa* dataframe. You can run each line of code by highlighting it and clicking the *Run* button, or through the keyboard shortcut *Control* + *Enter* (Windows and Linux) / *Command* + *Return* (MacOS). The first time you run this code, you will need to be connected to the internet and it may take a few minutes to download all of the required packages.

```
if (!require("pacman")) install.packages("pacman")
pacman::p_load(readxl, psych, dplyr, GPArotation, this.path)
setwd(this.path::here())
Ch5_exp_fa <- read_excel("Ch5_RAW_Survey_Results.xlsx")
```

To conduct factor analysis on the data, we will first create a smaller data set containing only the variables we need: *Eng1, Eng2, Eng3, Eng4, pos1, pos2* and *pos3*. We store this smaller set of variables in a new dataframe called *fa_analysis*.

```
fa_analysis <- Ch5_exp_fa %>% select(Eng1, Eng2, Eng3, Eng4, pos1, pos2,
pos3)
```

Next, we remove any rows that contain missing variables, as this interferes with the analysis:

```
fa_analysis <- na.omit(fa_analysis)
```

We can then get a visual sense of how the variables might be structured by examining a correlation table that has been coloured in, with different colours representing the size of the correlation (shown in Figure 5.4 using grey rather than coloured shading):

```
corPlot(fa_analysis)
```

Running this line results in the output in Figure 5.4:

5.4   Correlation plot from data

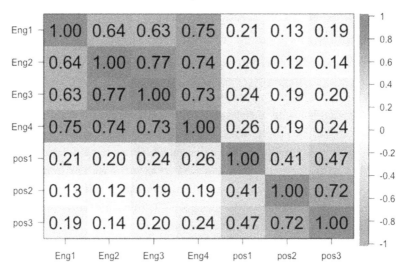

Correlation plot from data

We can see two groups of variables that are more strongly within them than across them. Beyond such visual inspection, we can have R compute various groupings of questions to give us an optimal number for the number of underlying constructs we should look for in the data – i.e. determine the number of factors we should look for. One method is parallel analysis, which tries this by comparing the outcome of two processes. The first task is to examine the number of coherent possible groupings (also called 'factors') that explain as much systematic variance as possible, given the data. The second task is to generate a completely random data set that has the same number of columns and rows as our data set. Using the same procedure as in the first task, we try to look for factors in this second, random set of data. We then compare the amount of variance explained by the factors generated in the real data and in the random data. The number of factors we generate with the real data should explain greater variance than factors generated using totally random data – this is the rule we use to ensure that we extract a number of factors that would be expected at a greater-than-chance level. The next line of code conducts the parallel analysis:

```
fa.parallel(fa_analysis)
```

It also produces Figure 5.5 in the Console pane, and Figure 5.6 in the Plots panel:

5.5

```
> fa.parallel(fa_analysis)
Parallel analysis suggests that the number of factors = 2 and the
number of components = 2
```

5.6

Parallel Analysis Scree Plots

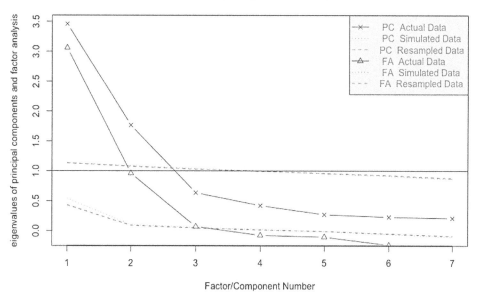

Generating the scree plot in Figure 5.6 will replace the previously generated plot (the correlation plot in Figure 5.4). Once a figure is generated, you can save it as an image file by clicking the *Export* button just above the plot area. You can save the plot in a size of your choosing and in multiple formats in the menus that appear after you click that button.

If we compare the 'FA Actual Data' line ('FA' stands for factor analysis, whereas 'PC' stands for principal component analysis, which we will discuss later), it is convincingly higher than the 'FA Simulated Data' (i.e. the randomly generated data) until it gets to three factors. The program concurs with this, suggesting that the optimal number of factors is two. Remember, we are trying to find a solution that is superior than what can be found in a random shuffling of our data, so the number of factors indicated in the 'FA Actual Data' line should be higher than the number of factors in the 'FA Simulated Data' line.

The next step is to identify which items (questions) load together into which factors. The next line of code conducts the factor analysis, with the instruction to create two factors the items can correlate with:

```
fa(fa_analysis, nfactors = 2, rotate = "oblimin")
```

This produces Figure 5.7 in the Console pane:

5.7

```
> fa(fa_analysis, nfactors = 2, rotate = "oblimin")
Factor Analysis using method = minres
Call: fa(r = fa_analysis, nfactors = 2, rotate = "oblimin")
Standardized loadings (pattern matrix) based upon correlation matrix
                        MR1       MR2        h2        u2     com
Eng1                   0.78      0.00      0.61      0.39     1.0
Eng2                   0.87     -0.06      0.74      0.26     1.0
Eng3                   0.83      0.03      0.71      0.29     1.0
Eng4                   0.89      0.03      0.80      0.20     1.0
pos1                   0.15      0.48      0.29      0.71     1.2
pos2                  -0.02      0.79      0.62      0.38     1.0
pos3                  -0.01      0.92      0.83      0.17     1.0

                        MR1       MR2
SS loadings            2.89      1.71
Proportion Var         0.41      0.24
Cumulative Var         0.41      0.66
Proportion Explained   0.63      0.37
Cumulative Proportion  0.63      1.00


  With factor correlations of
                        MR1       MR2
MR1                    1.00      0.26
MR2                    0.26      1.00


Mean item complexity = 1
Test of the hypothesis that 2 factors are sufficient.

df null model = 21 with the objective function = 3.83 with Chi
Square = 2948.92
df of the model are 8 and the objective function was 0.1

The root mean square of the residuals (RMSR) is 0.02
The df corrected root mean square of the residuals is 0.03

The harmonic n.obs is 775 with the empirical chi square 13.73 with
prob < 0.089
The total n.obs was 775 with Likelihood Chi Square = 77.7 with prob
< 1.4e-13
```

```
Tucker Lewis Index of factoring reliability = 0.937
RMSEA index = 0.106 and the 90 % confidence intervals are 0.085 0.128
BIC = 24.48
Fit based upon off diagonal values = 1
Measures of factor score adequacy
                                                    MR1         MR2
Correlation of (regression) scores with factors     0.96        0.94
Multiple R square of scores with factors            0.92        0.88
Minimum correlation of possible factor scores       0.83        0.75
```

One thing to note about the code is that we selected a rotation method, which helps us improve the interpretability and utility of the dimension reduction solution. This idea of rotation is a little complex to explain (see Tabachnick and Fidell, 2018 for further discussion) and there is a danger that the explanation may cause the less statistically minded reader to close the book; so let's just imagine, in this case, someone looking at a glass jar full of pink and white marshmallows from different angles – we can rotate the jar so that more of the pink marshmallows appear on one side and more of the white marshmallows appear on the other. We will choose the *oblimin* method because it allows the factors to be correlated. This method is generally recommended as the most versatile and helps us to identify different factors where they exist.

Let's examine the output produced in Figure 5.7. The first line tells us the method used in the factor analysis is the minimum residual (*minres*) method. It uses a logic similar to multiple regression. The next line tells us exactly what command was used to generate the numbers that follow. The next few lines show us the pattern matrix, or how much each question correlates with the factors, after they have been rotated. We see that the first four questions have high (above 0.6) factor loadings on *MR1* (or, the first factor – the MR stands for the method used, which is minimum residual), and two of the bottom three questions have high factor loadings (above 0.6) on *MR2* (or the second factor), along with a lower but reasonably high factor loading (about 0.5) on this second factor. Because one of the loadings on MR2 is lower than 0.6 it is important to consider the cross-loading of this item onto factor 1. This item, 'This organization cares about my well-being' has a loading of 0.15 on the first factor. This is definitely a low loading (<0.3). As the loading of this item on factor 2 is about 0.5 and the difference between the loading for this item on factor 2 and its loading on factor 1 is substantive (0.48 minus 0.15 = 0.33), we can be confident that this item can be considered to be a meaningful part of factor 2. Thus the first four items load onto factor 1 and the last three items load onto factor 2. The column labelled *h2* is the communality, or what you get if you squared the loading. The higher this number, the greater the overlap between this question and the underlying construct. The column labelled *u2* is the uniqueness, or 1 minus communality. The final column, *com*, is the item complexity. It equals one if the question loads well on one factor, equals two if the question has equal loadings on two factors, and so on.

The output also includes some rows that inform us of the total variance explained (*Proportion Var / Cumulative Var*). *Proportion Var* informs us that the first factor explains 41 per cent of total variance, while MR2 explains 24 per cent of total variance. The line below it, *Cumulative Var*, is a tally adding up all of the variance explained by the factors – the two factors together account for 66 per cent of variance (not quite 41% + 24% = 65%, due to rounding). *Proportion Explained* tells us how much variability the factor explains, among all of the variability that can be explained. *MR1* explains 63 per cent, *MR2* explains what is left over, or 37 per cent. The remainder of the output is additional diagnostic information.

Reviewing our questions, is this what you thought might happen? Looking at the first four questions, they do appear to be asking something a little bit similar to each other, but a little bit different to the bottom three questions.

In actual fact, the first four questions appear to be asking questions that could be about organizational engagement, whilst the final three questions appear to be asking questions about perceived organizational support (see Eisenberger et al (1986) for their full perceived organizational support (POS) measure).

In diagrammatic form, it would look like Figure 5.8. Note that we replaced *MR1* and *MR2* with names that represent the underlying idea, in this case, engagement and perceived organizational support.

5.8   Two-factor structure: engagement and perceived organizational support

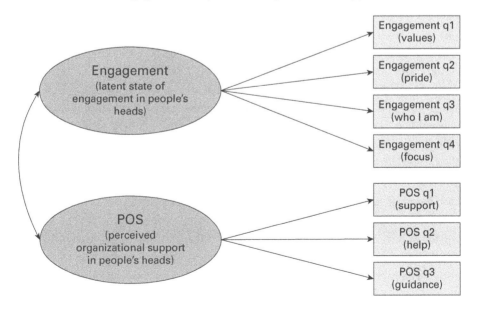

> SNAPSHOT HIDDEN GEM
>
> Our questions are measuring two latent variables: engagement and perceived organizational support.

The results of the survey can give the overall picture on these constructs as well as point towards areas/teams/regions that are doing well or not so well on these measures. And, although both constructs are related, and indeed low POS may contribute to low engagement, this information will be critical to decision making for taking action on specific areas to improve the overall level of engagement in the organization.

Reliability analysis

Reliability analysis (internal consistency reliability in particular) shares a number of common ideas with factor analysis as a questionnaire testing technique in that it enables us to establish the degree to which respondents' answers to a specific set of survey items (e.g. the nine items from the engagement scale presented at the start of this chapter) tend to follow a similar pattern.

We would expect employee responses to follow a similar pattern across items with a scale when it is measuring a single construct – because the level of an idea, trait, attitude or perception in the person's head that we are trying to measure should end up causing them to respond in a similar way across all of the items designed to measure this idea (assuming the items measure this single idea).

If, as we suggested above, a person's engagement level or the degree of engagement that they 'have' is actually something in their heads, then this degree of engagement will compel them to answer a set of engagement items in a similar way. Therefore, although there will be some variation in how any individual responds to the set of nine items (above), there should be a good deal of internal consistency in responses if the scale measures the same construct. Another way of putting this is that the variance in the items will be 'shared' if they tap the same construct.

Reliability analysis assesses this internal consistency or this 'shared variation'. It actually gives us an indication of how much a scale has internal consistency or shared variation by providing us with a figure of *how much variation* in the scale items is shared (the extent of average covariance between multiple items). This particular statistic is called *Cronbach's alpha* and ranges from 0.0 to 1.0.

If there is no internal consistency in respondents' answers across a particular set of items, then our Cronbach's alpha figure could be 0. If every individual in our survey sample gave the same answer for every item (e.g. a disengaged employee answered 1,1,1,1,1,1,1,1,1 to all nine questions and a highly engaged employee gave 5,5,5,5,5,5,5,5,5 to all nine questions) – then we would have perfect-shared variance, perfect internal consistency and our alpha would be equal to 1. In reality, scales will tend to fall between 0 and 1. The level of shared variance within our set of items that is considered a 'good' or 'acceptable' level of variance in a scale that is supposed to be measuring the same construct is 0.70. So any scale that has an alpha figure greater than 0.70 is considered to be a decent measure with decent levels of internal consistency. Note that a scale that has a Cronbach's alpha value of 0.70 still has some variation in how people responded across the multiple items that is not shared across the items. In the case of our nine-item scale, as soon as individuals do not give the same response to all nine items we will have some 'unshared' variance in responses. Note that we are suggesting that if people give exactly the same response to a set of questionnaire items, this indicates a reliable measure. However, the analytics expert needs to be aware of insufficient effort responding patterns (IER) (see Meade and Craig, 2012) that can plague workplace engagement surveys – this is where people tick the same response without attending to the content of the question.

Reliability testing

So, in summary, a measure is reliable when the scale measures a construct with a limited amount of measurement error, i.e. a minimal amount of variation in how people tend to respond across a set of items.

Reliability can only be tested with multiple items, and reliability analysis checks whether the items seem to produce variance that is consistent with scales across respondents. Importantly, the testing compares the item responses with other item responses in order to check whether the items/indicators might be measuring the same construct.

An example of an unreliable measure is a questionnaire scale that has items that could be interpreted differently by different people. With low reliability, more variance will occur in responses that do not represent variance in the actual construct in the heads of respondents. Measurement error is therefore occurring.

Necessity of multiple item indicators

Many professional survey providers use single-item measures to measure a construct, i.e. just one question to determine whether someone is engaged. Whilst this is a very efficient method of measuring constructs in a survey (as you only need to ask a limited number of questions to measure a variety of constructs), single-item measures suffer from a key problem in terms of measurement testing in that they cannot be tested for reliability.

With a single-item question we cannot be sure that variation in responses is not due to some problem with the question: for example, is there measurement error due to ambiguous wording of the question, or are there meaningful variations in respondents' heads? When we measure constructs with multiple indicators, we can and should consider how they operate together and hence we need multiple indicators to model validity and reliability of a measure.

Example 2: reliability analysis on a four-item engagement scale

Scale reliability can be determined in a fairly straightforward manner using R.

In this example, we test a four-item scale that is testing discretionary effort – or organizational citizenship behaviour (OCB) – using the following questions:

- I work harder than my job requires.
- I put a huge amount of effort into my job.
- I help out my teammates.
- I go the extra mile.

These questions are associated with a response scale of 1 to 5 where: 1 = I always do this; 2 = I frequently do this; 3 = I sometimes do this; 4 = I occasionally do this; 5 = I never do this.

Employee responses to a survey that included this set of questions can be found in the data file we used before: *Chapter_5_RAW_Survey_Results.xlsx*. Remember that in total 832 employees completed this survey.

The R code for this example is in file *Ch5_example_2.R*. The first line of code checks to see whether the *pacman* package is installed, and installs it if it is not. The second line loads the required packages for the example. The third line sets the working directory to be the same as the directory that the example file is in. The fourth line loads the data and stores it in the *Ch5_exp_fa* dataframe:

```
if (!require("pacman")) install.packages("pacman")
pacman::p_load(readxl, psych, dplyr, this.path)
setwd(this.path::here())
Ch5_exp_fa <- read_excel("Ch5_RAW_Survey_Results.xlsx")
```

To compute Cronbach's alpha, run the fourth and fifth lines of code:

```
ca_analysis <- Ch5_exp_fa %>% select(ocb1, ocb2, ocb3, ocb4)
alpha(ca_analysis)
```

The fourth line selects the subset of variables we will need for the analysis, and stores it in a new dataframe. The fifth line conducts the analysis, using the *alpha* program in the *psych* package.

It will produce the output in the Console pane, as in Figure 5.9:

5.9

```
> alpha(ca_analysis)

Reliability analysis
Call: alpha(x = ca_analysis)

   raw_alpha std.alpha G6(smc) average_r   S/N    ase  mean    sd median_r
        0.68      0.73     0.7       0.4   2.7  0.019   2.3  0.77     0.38

   95% confidence boundaries
                lower    alpha    upper
Feldt            0.64     0.68     0.72
Duhachek         0.64     0.68     0.72

Reliability if an item is dropped:
      raw_alpha std.alpha G6(smc) average_r   S/N  alpha     se  var.r   med.r
ocb1                 0.60    0.65      0.62  0.39    1.9  0.025  0.065    0.25
ocb2                 0.56    0.61      0.53  0.34    1.6  0.026  0.017    0.28
ocb3                 0.53    0.59      0.51  0.32    1.4  0.027  0.017    0.28
ocb4                 0.78    0.78      0.72  0.55    3.6  0.013  0.013    0.49

Item statistics
           n   raw.r   std.r  r.cor  r.drop   mean    sd
ocb1     797    0.71    0.76   0.62    0.53    1.8  0.82
ocb2     791    0.75    0.80   0.75    0.57    2.2  0.91
ocb3     791    0.79    0.82   0.78    0.59    2.4  1.03
ocb4     792    0.69    0.59   0.35    0.30    3.0  1.42

Non missing response frequency for each item
            1       2       3      4       5   miss
ocb1     0.44    0.39    0.14   0.03    0.00   0.04
ocb2     0.24    0.43    0.26   0.05    0.02   0.05
ocb3     0.22    0.36    0.31   0.08    0.04   0.05
ocb4     0.20    0.20    0.20   0.20    0.21   0.05
```

The output here tells us that the reliability of this set of questions in measuring discretionary effort is 0.68. This is below 0.70, which could be better. In the *Reliability if an item is dropped* section in Figure 5.9 the first column gives the Cronbach's alpha value if that item was dropped from the scale. Looking through these values, it shows that the Cronbach's alpha would be much higher (0.78) if the last question, 'I go the extra mile', was deleted from the responses. Hence this item has a lot of measurement error and is causing a lack of reliability, possibly because it is slightly ambiguous and may be interpreted differently by different people. Although from a face validity point of view 'I go the extra mile' might be a reasonable question to ask if one wants to measure 'going the extra mile', and this might be valid to a degree, because it could have a number of interpretations it could lead to low reliability and high measurement error. Without this item the remaining three items show a good Cronbach's alpha of 0.78. Thus:

SNAPSHOT HIDDEN GEM

The three items of 'I work harder than my job requires', 'I put a huge amount of effort into my job', and 'I help out my teammates' form a coherent scale and can be interpreted as being a reliable measure of organizational citizenship behaviour.

Example 3: Principal component analysis with group-level engagement data

Whilst factor analysis and reliability analysis should really be conducted on individual-level responses, this information is generally not available where the services of an external survey provider have been paid for; survey companies tend to hold the data due to confidentiality issues (see Chapter 12). Therefore, if the survey data is not available, the above discussion gives some idea of what questions to ask the survey provider.

Below are some other questions you might want to ask your survey provider:

- Why are we only using one-item scales (if that is the case)?
- How have you assessed whether the single item is valid and reliable?
- Do any multi-item indicators separate into sub-factors?
- Do items measuring different constructs separate into different factors?
- What levels of reliability are you getting with your multi-item scales?
- What are the Cronbach's alpha coefficients of the multi-item composite measures?
- Has the survey provider tested for a problem of insufficient effortful responding?
- What sort of discriminant validity tests have you conducted with your measures?

When the survey providers produce reports, they do not (for good reasons linked to the need for anonymity in surveys) present individual survey responses. What they often provide, however, are group-level statistics, for example the proportion of each team that has a positive response (e.g. 'Agree' or 'Strongly Agree' to an engagement item). If the organization is large enough and if there are enough teams, we can actually conduct factor analyses and reliability analysis at a team level with this data. Whilst this analysis might not be as sensitive as with data at individual level, it provides some data with which to test the measurement integrity of scales used by survey providers. Because the data is aggregated data already combined at a group level, the organization is unlikely to want to carefully explore how the individual items may combine to latent factors that will be representing employees' potential cognitive schema explaining how they perceive (and feel about) the work environment. Thus, the factor analyses approach conducted in the above sections may not be appropriate with already aggregated data. The organization, however, may want to check whether a range of items separate into different components and understand how best to combine elements of the aggregate data and engineer the data set to produce a reduced number of features to use in analyses. For this the organization can use the principal component analysis approach in dimension reduction activities.

The data set *Ch5_SURVEY_PROVIDER_ENGAGEMENT_DATA_TEAM_LEVEL.xlsx* measures the percentage of team members who answered positively on nine engagement measures in 212 teams. The nine engagement measures represent an engagement measure used by Engagement Survey Inc. The nine question items are as follows:

1 I feel a sense of pride with my organization.

2 I would recommend this employer to a friend.

3 I am really engaged.

4 I can manage my workload.

5 My work does not interfere with my home life.

6 I have good work–life balance.

7 My organization is socially responsible.

8 My organization makes sure that no one gets hurt in the workplace.

9 My organization is ethical.

These items are answered on a scale of 1 to 5 where 1 = strongly disagree and 5 = strongly agree. Ideally, we would want to conduct analyses on this data at the individual level to be able to conduct careful reliability and factor analyses on the scales, but we do not have this, we only have data linked to the proportion of employees in each group who answered either 'agree' or 'strongly agree' to the questions.

One of the reasons why an organization may want to analyse group-level survey responses is that it can potentially correlate group level features of the survey data with other workforce data (e.g. group level staff turnover data). If an organization wants to do this kind of analyses, then it is likely that they will want to identify and create a reduced number of variables that represent discrete survey components. For example, they may want to create a variable that represents a feature of the employment experience, such as employees' level of 'engagement with the organization' or 'work–life balance' experiences in the organization. If the aim is to engineer group-level engagement data down to its simplest number of components to conduct additional analyses, the organization will want to check how the data can be combined into its simplest form (or discrete employment experience features). This is where principal component analysis will be useful. As we did with the individual examples, here we will perform dimension reduction analysis to determine which items can be combined into unique components. We will be taking similar steps to what we did in Example 1. The R code for this example is in the file *Ch5_example_3.R*. The first lines should look familiar, with a new package now being loaded, and a different data set specified:

```
if (!require("pacman")) install.packages("pacman")
pacman::p_load(readxl, psych, scatterplot3d, this.path)
setwd(this.path::here())
Ch5_tld <- read_excel("Ch5_SURVEY_PROVIDER_ENGAGEMENT_DATA_TEAM_LEVEL.
xlsx")
```

The next few lines remove rows with missing data, and we repeat the visual inspection of the correlation table and conduct parallel analysis:

```
pc_analysis <- na.omit(Ch5_tld)
corPlot(pc_analysis)
fa.parallel(pc_analysis)
```

The correlation table (Figure 5.10) shows a likely three-component solution:

5.10

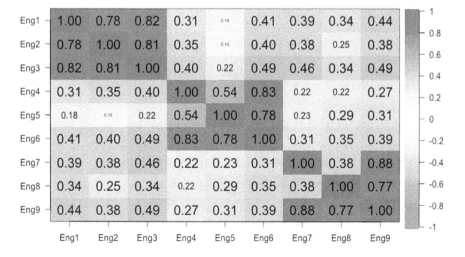

Correlation plot from data

	Eng1	Eng2	Eng3	Eng4	Eng5	Eng6	Eng7	Eng8	Eng9
Eng1	1.00	0.78	0.82	0.31	0.18	0.41	0.39	0.34	0.44
Eng2	0.78	1.00	0.81	0.35	0.16	0.40	0.38	0.25	0.38
Eng3	0.82	0.81	1.00	0.40	0.22	0.49	0.46	0.34	0.49
Eng4	0.31	0.35	0.40	1.00	0.54	0.83	0.22	0.22	0.27
Eng5	0.18	0.16	0.22	0.54	1.00	0.78	0.23	0.29	0.31
Eng6	0.41	0.40	0.49	0.83	0.78	1.00	0.31	0.35	0.39
Eng7	0.39	0.38	0.46	0.22	0.23	0.31	1.00	0.38	0.88
Eng8	0.34	0.25	0.34	0.22	0.29	0.35	0.38	1.00	0.77
Eng9	0.44	0.38	0.49	0.27	0.31	0.39	0.88	0.77	1.00

Which is supported by the parallel analysis (Figure 5.11):

5.11

```
> fa.parallel(pc_analysis)
Parallel analysis suggests that the number of factors = 3 and the
number of components = 3
```

Although the program gives us a warning after this in the R console pane, it is not a serious challenge to our results. So we will ask for a three-factor principal component analysis with the next line. We will ask for Varimax rotation, which is appropriate for this analysis. We will store the results in *pca_result* and then ask R to show it to us:

```
pca_result <- principal(pc_analysis, nfactors = 3, rotate = "varimax")
pca_result
```

The results are shown in Figure 5.12:

5.12

```
> pca_result

Principal Components Analysis
Call: principal(r = pc_analysis, nfactors = 3, rotate = "varimax")
Standardized loadings (pattern matrix) based upon correlation matrix
```

	RC1	RC2	RC3	h2	u2	com
Eng1	0.88	0.13	0.23	0.85	0.1495	1.2
Eng2	0.91	0.15	0.15	0.87	0.1335	1.1
Eng3	0.88	0.21	0.26	0.88	0.1161	1.3
Eng4	0.26	0.84	0.05	0.78	0.2240	1.2
Eng5	-0.03	0.86	0.21	0.78	0.2172	1.1
Eng6	0.28	0.91	0.19	0.94	0.0562	1.3
Eng7	0.28	0.08	0.81	0.73	0.2688	1.3
Eng8	0.10	0.19	0.79	0.67	0.3347	1.2
Eng9	0.24	0.16	0.95	0.99	0.0063	1.2

	RC1	RC2	RC3
SS loadings	2.67	2.42	2.40
Proportion Var	0.30	0.27	0.27
Cumulative Var	0.30	0.57	0.83
Proportion Explained	0.36	0.32	0.32
Cumulative Proportion	0.36	0.68	1.00

```
Mean item complexity = 1.2
Test of the hypothesis that 3 components are sufficient.

The root mean square of the residuals (RMSR) is 0.07
  with the empirical chi square 64.71 with prob < 3.1e-09

Fit based upon off diagonal values = 0.98
```

In the output in Figure 5.12, we see output similar to what we saw with the exploratory factor analysis. Instead of *MR1*, etc... we see *RC1*, *RC2*, and *RC3*, with RC standing for rotated component. For each item, we see loadings on each of the components, communalities (*h2*), uniquenesses (*u2*), and complexity (*com*). As the output shows, even with this team-level data (rather than individual responses) using percentage of team responses that are positive, this engagement scale shows evidence of being made up of three separate constructs.

This tells us that the responses to the nine-item scale seem to be clustering into three possible separate components. In considering the component loadings in Figure 5.12, we can see that each of the columns tend to have three items that load together onto each of the components with loadings that are greater than 0.70. This provides us with information about what items tend to load together into a particular component.

SNAPSHOT HIDDEN GEM

Our data suggests that if the survey provider created a composite measure comprised of all nine survey questions and used it as an indicator of team-level engagement, they would be misrepresenting the survey data and ignoring the fact that the nine questions (as shown in Figure 5.12) seem to be clustering into three separate components. Looking at the face validity of the questions, the first three appear to be about engagement, questions 4–6 are similar and appear to be about work–life balance, whilst the last three are more about perception of the organization's ethics.

Figure 5.13 presents a very stylish three-dimensional graph that shows how these items plot in 3D rotated space (Figure 5.12 is really the one that we look at to get proper indication of loadings and cross-loadings – but this 3D graph is rather interesting... let's face it, who wouldn't want this on their report?). We can generate the graph using some R code, as in the final lines on the example R file:

```
plot_df <- as.data.frame(unclass(pca_result$loadings))
s3d <- scatterplot3d(plot_df, angle = 200, pch = 16)
text(s3d$xyz.convert(plot_df[, 1:3]), labels = rownames(plot_df), cex =
1, adj = 1.5)
```

5.13   A 3D figure to represent factor loadings

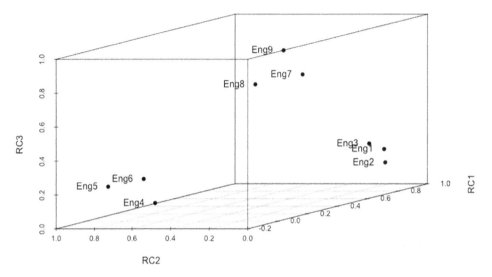

So, separating these three constructs would result in a more in-depth picture of what is going on in relation to the group level responses to different features of the employee survey in this organization. It would enable us to identify how best to organize these sets of items into a reduced number of different measures (in this case three different measures) for further HR analytic activities. We could use the combined items across the three constructs as separate dimensions, analyse their relationships with other HR data features (e.g. employee turnover) and consider taking prescriptive action around organizational engagement, well-being and ethics that would be far more useful than if we had bundled all the information together into one 'engagement' measure. Indeed, the three separated organizational engagement questions (1–3), when combined into a single variable and included in analyses with other HR data features, might show quite a different result on their own than if we assumed the nine items could be merged together into one component. In addition, it is likely to be the case that a three-item combined component linked to work–life balance (which our analyses identified) would feature differently (e.g. in terms of its correlation) in analyses linked to other HR data (e.g. group turnover) than either a measure that combined all nine variables or a more discrete three-item engagement measure that combined the first three items above.

Analysis and outcomes

Current trends in survey practices

There are pros and cons of using survey consultancies/research companies to run employee surveys and some of these have already been explored in this chapter. A summary of what survey companies usually provide is given below:

- A ready-made measure of engagement used by hundreds of organizations.

- Benchmark norms of 'employee engagement' scores that the organization can compare itself to, for example across peers in the same industry, and to compare against 'high performing' or 'top quartile' organizations.

- Interactive reports where the organization can obtain bespoke scores cut across organizational functions, teams and demographic groups.

- A team and subordinate group average 'engagement score' (that is often used as a performance indicator for supervisor/leader).

- A breakdown of data to show which teams, regions, etc are more engaged/feel they have a better leader.

Whether you are designing the survey yourself or using the skills gleaned in this chapter to interrogate your survey provider to ensure you are getting meaningful results, the next step is an analysis of what else you can do with your engagement survey data. Perhaps some of the survey output data could be combined with some of the HR MI data that already exists about teams in order to really probe into what might be influencing engagement.

Analysing and predicting employee engagement with MI/demographic data – engagement analysis example

Given that engagement is such a key behaviour for organizations to want to develop, it is important to know whether there are any team-level factors that might 'predict' engagement. The following data set includes a combination of team-level HR metrics, employee demographic data and engagement survey data. There are 29,976 employees in these functions across the UK and these employees are organized into 928 teams or employee units. These are sometimes branches, sometimes departments and sometimes teams within larger work nestings. They have, however, been organized with a 'work unit' key that was used by the engagement survey provider in order to supply engagement survey data in aggregate form (to ethically protect identities in this anonymous survey, no unit here is identified if it has fewer than 10 employees). The data set that we are working with, therefore, is average/aggregate data at the work-team level and there are 928 objects or units of analysis in the data set; this data is stored in 29 variables (note our discussion on team analyses, pages 400–01). The data set can be found in the Excel file *Ch5_Engagement_CASE_Group_level_data_2023.xlsx*.

The variables in the data set include those listed in Table 5.2.

TABLE 5.2 Employee engagement survey variables

Variable Label	Description
DepartmentGroupNumber	Team/unit key identifier
GroupSize	Number of employees in the unit
PercentMale	Percentage of the unit made up of males
UG	Percentage of the unit made up of underrepresented groups (e.g. Black, Asian)
NumberTeamLeads	Number of team leaders in the unit (in general this organization has a team leader for every seven or so employees
NumberFeMaleTeamLeads	Number of team leads in the unit who are female
Location	Geographical location: 1 = Central London, 2 = Greater London, 3 = Rest of UK
LondonorNot	Geographical location recoded to 1 = Central London or Greater London and 2 = Rest of UK
Function	Function drawn from: 1 = Sales staff (customer-facing people) or 2 = Professional Service (non-customer-facing people)
EMPsurvEngage_1 – EMPsurvEngage_9	Proportion of the unit who answered favourably (with either 'agree' or 'strongly agree' on a 1 to 5 'strongly disagree' to 'strongly agree' response scale) to each of nine employee engagement questions:
	I work with full intensity in my job; I try my hardest to perform as well as I can in my work; I concentrate hard in my job; My mind is always focused on my job; I strive very hard to complete my work well; Time flies at work; I would recommend this organization as a place to work; I feel a sense of belonging with my organization; I am proud of the work I do
EMPsurvEngagement	Average unit/team score for the nine engagement questions
EMPorgIntegrity1 – EMPorgIntegrity4	Proportion of the unit who answered favourably (with either 'agree' or 'strongly agree' on a 1 to 5 'strongly disagree' to 'strongly agree' response scale) to each of five employee 'organizational integrity' questions:
	My organization listens to staff; My organization does the right thing; My organization treats external stakeholders with respect; My organization encourages staff to point out questionable practices

(continued)

TABLE 5.2 (Continued)

Variable Label	Description
EmpSurvOrgIntegrity	Average unit/team score for the four organizational integrity questions
EMPsurvSUP1 – EMPsurvSUP4	Proportion of the unit who answered favourably (with either 'agree' or 'strongly agree' on a 1 to 5 'strongly disagree' to 'strongly agree' response scale) to each of four 'supportive supervisor' questions:
	My supervisor listens to me; My supervisor cares about my well-being; My supervisor helps ensure we get things done; My supervisor is there when he/she is needed
EmpSurvSupervisor	Average unit/team score for the four 'supportive supervisor' questions

Example 4: using the independent samples t-test to determine differences in engagement levels

The independent samples t-test

The first thing we can do is to run a t-test with the team-level engagement results as the dependent variable.

So what we want to do here is to compare two regional and geographical groupings in the organization (or two samples), namely 'London' or 'Not London', on their engagement survey results. This is testing the strongly held belief (held by senior management at the organization) that people in regional offices are less engaged than those based in the 'dynamic' London branches. The independent samples t-test is used when we have one independent variable with two groups (the location in our example), which determines which group people belong to, and one dependent variable (team engagement in our example). We want to test whether there is a significant difference between the team means of the two groups on the dependent variable. The example code for this example is in *Ch5_example_4.R*. The first few lines load needed packages, set the working directory, and load the data:

```
if (!require("pacman")) install.packages("pacman")
pacman::p_load(readxl, dplyr, car, modelsummary, this.path)
setwd(this.path::here())
```

```
Ch5_ttest <- read_excel("Ch5_Engagement_CASE_Group_level_data_2023.
xlsx")
```

Next, we will look at the mean, standard deviation, minimum, maximum and number of cases of engagement, across the two locations. We have set up the *LondonorNot* variable in the data file as follows:

1 = London

2 = Other Location

To make it easier to read, and to generate a grouping variable, we will recode the *LondonorNot* variable with the next lines of code:

```
Ch5_ttest$LondonorNot_text <- case_match(Ch5_ttest$LondonorNot, 1 ~
"London", 2 ~ "Other Location")
Ch5_ttest$LondonorNot_text <- as.factor(Ch5_ttest$LondonorNot_text)
```

Now we are ready to create a descriptive statistics table. The next lines produce a table in the Source pane:

```
datasummary((EMPsurvEngagement) * LondonorNot_text ~ N + Mean + SD + Min +
Max, data = Ch5_ttest, output = "huxtable")
```

We see the table generated in Figure 5.14. In the table, we can see that our 533 London teams are on average (mean positive engagement answers for all London teams = 81.55) slightly more engaged than our 394 non-London teams (mean positive engagement answers for all non-London teams = 80.67).

Before we move on, we might want to reflect on what these means represent. The engagement index for each team is an average of nine indices for each team linked to the nine questions. So, for each of these nine questions, the team members will have ticked a 1-to-5 scale and the indicator for the team associated with each question is the proportion of the team who ticked either 4 or 5 for each question. The engagement index is therefore a team average of proportions of positive responses for each of the nine questions. The 81.55 mean figure (London teams) represents the average of 533 team averages of the nine indices (which are the percentage of the teams who answered 4 or 5 on each of the nine engagement questions). The 80.67 mean figure (non-London teams) represents the average of 394 team averages of the nine indices (which are the percentage of the teams who answered 4 or 5 on each of the nine engagement questions).

Here, the non-London averages are slightly lower than the London averages. This kind of finding is a good example of a situation where a statistical test such as the t-test is very useful. We could make an assumption that our non-London and London teams differ and that London employees are more engaged. However, could this difference be due to random fluctuation of engagement levels across teams in our organization? Teams vary in levels of engagement and some of this variation will be random variation (teams will never, for purely random reasons, all have exactly the same engagement scores) and we should not take some degree of variation seriously. To see if these geographical locations differ significantly in a meaningful way we need to carry out the t-test. You will also recall from our earlier discussion of t-tests

5.14

	LondonorNot_text	N	Mean	SD	Min	Max
EMPsurvEngagement	London	533	81.55	10.11	42.00	99.00
	Other Location	394	80.67	9.89	39.00	99.00

(Chapter 4) that a pre-test checking for assumption violations should be carried out. Our next line of code conducts the test:

```
leveneTest(EMPsurvEngagement ~ LondonorNot_text, Ch5_ttest)
```

It produces Figure 5.15:
The Levene's test output shows that the Levene's here has a very low F-value (2e-04, or *0.0002*) and this is not significant (p > 0.05), suggesting that the patterns of vari-

5.15

```
> leveneTest(EMPsurvEngagement ~ LondonorNot_text, Ch5_ttest)
Levene's Test for Homogeneity of Variance (center = median)
       Df  F value Pr(>F)
group   1   2e-04 0.9879
       925
---
Signif. codes:  0 '***' 0.001 '**' 0.01 '*' 0.05 '.' 0.1 ' ' 1
```

ation in team engagement means across the two locations are similar – the pattern of variance is not significantly different. We can conduct the independent samples t-test with the next line of code:

```
t.test(Ch5_ttest$EMPsurvEngagement ~ Ch5_ttest$LondonorNot_text)
```

Which gives us the following output (Figure 5.16):
Here our t-test is p>0.05, which means we do not have a significant difference in engagement scores when we compare London teams with non-London teams.

5.16

```
> t.test(Ch5_ttest$EMPsurvEngagement ~ Ch5_ttest$LondonorNot_text)

        Welch Two Sample t-test

data: Ch5_ttest$EMPsurvEngagement by Ch5_ttest$LondonorNot_text
t = 1.3201, df = 856.94, p-value = 0.1872
alternative hypothesis: true difference in means between group London and
group Other Location is not equal to 0
95 percent confidence interval:
 -0.4260878 2.1765949
sample estimates:

      mean in group London mean in group Other Location
            81.54784                     80.67259
```

Without doing this test, if an engagement provider tells us that there is a difference in engagement scores when you compare London with non-London, all you could

---

SNAPSHOT HIDDEN GEM

The difference in engagement means of 81.55 for London compared to 80.67 for other locations should not be taken seriously as it could easily have occurred by random chance fluctuations in team engagement levels.

---

do is nod and say: 'okay'. You might even take action on the back of this, when actually it may not be the best option for your organization.

In a formal write-up convention, we would write: 'The t-test was not significant: $t(856.94) = 1.320, p > 0.1$. There is no significant difference in engagement between teams based in London and those that are based in non-London locations; 'London' (mean = 81.55, SD = 10.11) is not significantly different to 'other location' (mean = 80.67, SD = 9.89).'

So, on this example, we would not want to recommend any specific action or any adjustment to the organization's engagement strategy with regards to the importance of location. Next, let's do the exact same test, but with function as the independent variable (and keeping the dependent variable as engagement).

We will need to recode the function variable so that it reflects the following schema: 1 = sales: 2 = professional service. The code is on the following lines:

```
Ch5_ttest$Function_text <- case_match(Ch5_ttest$Function, 1 ~ "Sales",
2 ~ "Professional service")
Ch5_ttest$Function_text <- as.factor(Ch5_ttest$Function_text)
```

We can generate a descriptive statistics table with the following lines of code:

```
datasummary((EMPsurvEngagement) * Function_text ~ N + Mean + SD + Min +
Max, data = Ch5_ttest, output = "huxtable")
```

The table generated (Figure 5.17) shows professional service employees to have higher engagement than sales employees:

5.17

	Function_text	N	Mean	SD	Min	Max
EMPsurvEngagement	Professional service	425	83.57	9.11	46.00	99.00
	Sales	502	79.15	10.30	39.00	99.00

The next line conducts Levene's test:

```
leveneTest(EMPsurvEngagement ~ Function_text, Ch5_ttest)
```

Which results in the following output (Figure 5.18):

5.18
```
> leveneTest(EMPsurvEngagement ~ Function_text, Ch5_ttest)

Levene's Test for Homogeneity of Variance (center = median)
       Df    F value     Pr(>F)
group  1     3.7604      0.05278 .
       vv925
---
Signif. codes: 0 '***' 0.001 '**' 0.01 '*' 0.05 '.' 0.1 ' ' 1
```

We can see from the results that our Levene's test is not significant, so patterns of variation in team engagement means across the two functions do not vary. We can perform the t-test as in the next line of code:

```
t.test(Ch5_ttest$EMPsurvEngagement ~ Ch5_ttest$Function_text)
```

Which results in the following output (Figure 5.19):

5.19
```
> t.test(Ch5_ttest$EMPsurvEngagement ~ Ch5_ttest$Function_text)

        Welch Two Sample t-test

data: Ch5_ttest$EMPsurvEngagement by Ch5_ttest$Function_text
t = 6.9432, df = 923.21, p-value = 7.22e-12
alternative hypothesis: true difference in means between group
Professional service and group Sales is not equal to 0
95 percent confidence interval:
 3.176910 5.680489
sample estimates:
mean in group Professional service       mean in group Sales
               83.57412                           79.14542
```

Immediately, we can see from Figure 5.19 that the average engagement scores for our sales team functions (with a mean of 79.15) are a bit lower than teams from the professional service function (mean of 83.57). Whilst there is a difference here, it is not that big; our t-test will, however, inform us whether we should interpret this difference as meaningful or whether it could again be due to random fluctuation that we tend to find in team engagement levels across the organization.

SNAPSHOT HIDDEN GEM

Team engagement scores are significantly different across the functions. We can actually say with 99.9 per cent confidence that there is a significant difference in engagement results between people who work in the sales function (customer facing) and people who work in the professional service function (non-customer facing). Professional service teams are significantly more engaged than those in the sales function. Given that it is people in the sales function who deal directly with customers, this highlights a key challenge to be addressed in any engagement strategy.

In formal write-up convention, we would say: 'The t-test was significant: $t(923.21) = 6.943$, $p < 0.001$. There is a significant difference in engagement scores of teams where employees work in the sales function compared to teams from professional services. Sales teams (mean = 79.15, SD = 10.30) are significantly less engaged than teams from professional services (mean = 83.57, SD = 9.11).'

Example 5: using multiple regression to predict team-level engagement

In the following example, we conduct an ordinary least squares (OLS) multiple linear regression model to predict team-level engagement scores with a number of other team-level survey measures provided by our external survey company; we also use some team demographic information (obtained from MI data) as possible predictors of team-level engagement. Some of this information includes diversity-based information such as team gender proportions and the proportion of team members who are made up of underrepresented groups (UG; a more detailed discussion on diversity demographics can be found in Chapter 4). So we are still using the same data set (*Ch5_Engagement_CASE_Group_level_data_2023.xlsx*) as with the t-tests but we are going to utilize more of this data set – integrating more varied metrics from different data sets. So here we are going to predict team-level engagement (*EMPsurvEngagement*) from unit demographics and other survey composites.

As discussed in Chapter 3, multiple regression can be used to predict variation in a dependent variable by using two or more independent variables, using a model in the form of:

$$Y_i = (b_0 + b_1 X_{i1} + b_2 X_{i2} + \ldots + b_n X_n) + \varepsilon_i$$

where Y_i is the value of the dependent variable for the i'th participant (where 'i' could be 1, 2, 3, etc and refers to the specific case/employee in the sample), b_0 is the constant, b_1 is the coefficient of the first independent variable (X_1), b_2 is the coefficient of the second independent variable (X_2), and b_n is the coefficient of the n'th independent variable (X_n) (where 'n' is the number of independent variables), and ε_i is the error in prediction (Field, 2009).

In this example, Y is equal to team-level engagement, and the values of X are the other variables.

So in this model team-level engagement index (EMPsurvEngagement) is the dependent variable and the following variables are independent variables:

- Team survey composite – supervisor aggregate score.
- Team survey composite – integrity aggregate score.
- How many employees in the team.
- Percentage of males in the team.
- Percentage of UG in the team.
- London versus other location.
- Sales versus professional service function.

So, replacing the Ys and Xs with the values in our example, our model will look something like:

Team Engagement =
$a + b_1$ (supervisor score) $+ b_2$ (integrity score) $+ b_3$ (work unit size) $+ b_4$ (% male) $+ b_5$ (% UG) $+ b_6$ (London or other) $+ b_7$ (Sales or Prof services)

Basically, we are suggesting (and testing) that team-level engagement might be (to a significant extent) a function of the type of work that people do in the teams, where the teams are based, the ethnic diversity in the team, the gender mix in the team, how big the team is, their general judgements of the organization's moral integrity and how good the supervisor is. Just from looking at this list, it is possible that any of these factors might actually influence a team's engagement score. As such, it is important to take into account as many possible meaningful factors as we can in trying to predict engagement levels.

The R code for this example is in the file *Ch5_example_5.R*. The first few lines should be familiar, except this time we name the dataframe *Ch5_mreg*.

```
if (!require("pacman")) install.packages("pacman")
pacman::p_load(readxl, dplyr, modelsummary, this.path, huxtable)
setwd(this.path::here())
Ch5_mreg <- read_excel("Ch5_Engagement_CASE_Group_level_data_2023.xlsx")
```

Then, as in the previous example, we recode the *LondonorNot* and *Function* variables, for ease of interpretation.

```
Ch5_mreg$LondonorNot_text <- case_match(Ch5_mreg$LondonorNot, 1 ~
"London", 2 ~ "Other Location")
Ch5_mreg$LondonorNot_text <- as.factor(Ch5_mreg$LondonorNot_text)
Ch5_mreg$Function_text <- case_match(Ch5_mreg$Function, 1 ~ "Sales", 2 ~
"Professional service")
Ch5_mreg$Function_text <- as.factor(Ch5_mreg$Function_text)
```

As an aside, it is entirely possible that you copy and paste the code from the previous example and continue to work with the dataframe name *Ch5_ttest*. You can give a dataframe any convenient name. Ensure that it is relatively short, to lessen the amount of typing you do. Coming out of our digression, we can conduct the linear regression with the following code:

```
engage_mod <- lm(EMPsurvEngagement ~ EmpSurvSupervisor +
EmployeeSurvOrgIntegrity + GroupSize + PercentMale + UG +
LondonorNot_text + Function_text, data = Ch5_mreg)
```

You may notice that the regression command is spread over multiple lines. That is okay in R. In fact, you do not want lines to be too long, lest they get cut off in the output. For readability, you should end the line with some kind of punctuation (e.g. comma) or function (e.g. + or -) symbol. We have conducted the regression, and stored the results in the *engage_mod* object. We can see the summary with the next line.

```
summary(engage_mod)
```

This results in the following output (Figure 5.20):

5.20

```
> summary(engage_mod)

Call:
lm(formula = EMPsurvEngagement ~ EmpSurvSupervisor + EmployeeSurvOrgIntegrity +
    GroupSize + PercentMale + UG + LondonorNot_text + Function_text, data = Ch5_
    mreg)

Residuals:
    Min                     1Q      Median          3Q          Max
-30.7690                -3.8568      0.2736      4.2352      21.0466

Coefficients:
                                Estimate   Std. Error   t value   Pr(>|t|)
(Intercept)                     22.61239      2.92323     7.735   3.39e-14 ***
EmpSurvSupervisor                0.14689      0.03206     4.582   5.40e-06 ***
EmployeeSurvOrgIntegrity         0.62226      0.03646    17.067   < 2e-16 ***
GroupSize                        0.02122      0.01561     1.359     0.1745
PercentMale                     -0.09576      0.01460    -6.560   1.01e-10 ***
UG                               0.61687      2.41258     0.256     0.7983
LondonorNot_textOther Location  -0.79329      0.55649    -1.426     0.1544
Function_textSales               1.17516      0.63181     1.860     0.0633 .
---
Signif. codes:  0 '***' 0.001 '**' 0.01 '*' 0.05 '.' 0.1 ' ' 1

Residual standard error: 6.78 on 738 degrees of freedom
   (181 observations deleted due to missingness)
Multiple R-squared: 0.5541,   Adjusted R-squared: 0.5499
F-statistic: 131 on 7 and 738 DF, p-value: < 2.2e-16
```

The model summary table in Figure 5.20 tells us that the R-square is 0.554. Multiplying this by 100 gives the percentage of variance in the dependent variable that is accounted for by the model. This means that 55.4 per cent of the variance in the average team engagement index (the average of proportions of the team who answered 4 or 5 to the nine engagement survey items) can be accounted for when modelling the variance found in the independent variables (or predictor variables). Importantly, this is the variance of engagement that can be accounted for when modelling and identifying its variance shared with all of the independent variables at the same time (whilst considering the interrelationships amongst the independent variables).

The F-statistic in Figure 5.20 tests the significance of how well the model predicts variations in the team-engagement index and is linked to the R2 figure. Here the regression ANOVA F-value is 131, with associated degrees of freedom of 7 (for the regression) plus 738 (for the residual). The results show the statistical significance of the regression ANOVA as being close to zero, or we would say p<0.001, which means there is less than 1 in 1,000 chance that we would find this pattern of shared variance (between our team engagement index scores and our seven independent variables) randomly by chance alone, so the model is significant.

We can also generate a neat table of unstandardized and standardized coefficients.

```
modelsummary(engage_mod, stars = TRUE, statistic = NULL, title =
"Unstandardized coefficients", output = "huxtable")
modelsummary(engage_mod, stars = TRUE, statistic = NULL, standardize =
"basic", title = "Standardized coefficients",
output = "huxtable")
```

Which results in the following tables (Figures 5.21 and 5.22):

5.21

Unstandardised coefficients	
	(1)
(Intercept)	22.612***
EmpSurvSupervisor	0.147***
EmployeeSurvOrgIntegrity	0.622***
GroupSize	0.021
PercentMale	-0.096***
UG	0.617
LondonorNot_textOther Location	-0.793
Function_textSales	1.175+
Num.Obs.	746
R2	0.554
R2 Adj.	0.550
AIC	4982.7
BIC	5024.3
Log.Lik.	-2482.372
F	131.029
RMSE	6.74
+ p < 0.1, * p < 0.05, ** p < 0.01, *** p < 0.001	

5.22

Standardised coefficients	
	(1)
(Intercept)	0.000***
EmpSurvSupervisor	0.148***
EmployeeSurvOrgIntegrity	0.571***
GroupSize	0.034
PercentMale	-0.209***
UG	0.007
LondonorNot_textOther Location	-0.038
Function_textSales	0.058+
Num.Obs.	746
R2	0.554
R2 Adj.	0.550
AIC	4982.7
BIC	5024.3
Log.Lik.	-2482.372
F	131.029
RMSE	6.74
+ p < 0.1, * p < 0.05, ** p < 0.01, *** p < 0.001	

Now we need to look at the coefficients table to assess which of our independent variables potentially have an impact on engagement and the degree to which they uniquely contribute to the prediction of variation in team engagement (and in what way or what direction they seem to be related to variation in team engagement).

The coefficients table in Figure 5.21 and Figure 5.22 tell us that of the seven possible drivers of engagement only three seem to come out as significantly predicting variation in levels of team engagement. These significant predictors can be identified as the following:

1 Supervisor aggregate (with a significant standardized coefficient = +0.148, $p < 0.001$).

2 Integrity aggregate (with a significant standardized coefficient = +0.571, $p < 0.001$).

3 Percentage of the work unit who are male (with a significant standardized coefficient = -0.209, $p < 0.001$).

SNAPSHOT HIDDEN GEM

Team perception of the integrity credentials of the organization is the most important driver of team engagement – the more that employees in a team perceive that their organization has integrity, the more likely they are to report positively to engagement questions (at the team level). In addition, how supportive their supervisors are is also an important potential driver of team engagement. The better the team tends to rate their supervisor then the higher the team's level of engagement. Importantly, gender diversity is also found to be a key potential driver of engagement. The higher the proportion of males that are found in the teams, the less engaged the teams tend to be. Team size is not important as a predictor of engagement, however sales staff versus professional service (which showed a significant t-test) loses its importance when we take into account the range of other factors.

A potential interpretation of why the functional groups no longer come out as being significant may be because of variations in gender mix, levels of supervisory support and perceptions of organizational integrity across the two functional groups; these factors may be possible causes of the earlier differences that we found in team engagement across sales versus professional service. These interesting results show us the greater diagnostic possibilities of using more complex predictive statistics in our analysis than we would have if we just had descriptive means to work with. If we had not conducted this regression analysis, we might have mistakenly diagnosed the type of job as the possible cause of variations in fluctuations in engagement, when in fact the potential causal factor may well be something that is associated with the different jobs, such as gender-mix differences across the jobs, whether people in the different jobs perceived the organizational integrity differently and potential differences in supervisory style that we tend to find across the two functional groups.

Survey comments analysis

Although this book focuses on quantitative analysis, it would be remiss to have a chapter about employee engagement surveys and not talk about comments. Most of the off-the-shelf survey tools come with the ability for the survey respondent to add an open-ended comment; either in addition to the quantitative response given on the survey scale, or as a response to an entirely new question, such as, 'If you could change one thing about this organization, what would it be?'

The ability to analyse survey comments has come a long way in the last decade with tools such as large language models (LLMs) and generative AI hitting the scene more recently. Even so, some of the challenges and benefits of taking the time to understand qualitative data still hold true. Key challenges with qualitative data include a decreased ability to control the theory and hypotheses behind the data, less structure in the approach and responses and lower ability to generalize and categorize responses to the survey population (Bell et al, 2003). The benefits, however, include an enriched, deeper point of view of the survey respondent and a greater understanding of the organizational context. Indeed, themes and meanings are likely to emerge that were never considered by the survey team.

The use of generative AI and LLMs by in-house data science teams and also by vendors is still very new. At this stage there are no experts with deep experience and we are all learning from each other. Depending on the size of the organization, there can be tens of thousands, if not hundreds of thousands of survey comments to read through and some methods have emerged to unlock insights from comments that may otherwise be time consuming and highly manual to interpret. Gartner (2023) outlined some key methods over the last decade to include:

- Natural language processing (NLP). This aims to understand the meaning of words in a sentence, how the words relate to each other and the context in which they appear. This is then used to predict their topic and meaning.

- Sentiment analysis. This analyses text to determine the overall sentiment or emotion on a given topic.

- LLMs and generative AI such as ChatGPT. LLMs are trained on many hundreds to billions of pieces of language. They can be used to build a customized model that can identify when a comment is talking about something bespoke to the organization such as a particular initiative, value or theme. Generative AI allows for a conversational interaction with the model through human-like language and prompting, with the model generating a conversational response.

For more about machine learning and AI, refer to Chapter 11.

Actions and business context

The analysis outlined in the previous section provides a wealth of information that will help the organization determine where to focus engagement activities. Recommendations may now be focused on supervisor training as well as the diversity training across the organization as a whole. Analysis of diversity data has also been addressed in Chapter 4.

This analysis highlights the importance of thoroughly understanding and diagnosing the current organizational behaviours before rolling out any engagement interventions. Depending on the outcome of a set of analyses (such as those discussed in this chapter), interventions, which are typically found on the engagement agenda in organizations, may include increased communication, town halls, more access to senior leaders, career development, recognition schemes, better onboarding for new staff, mentoring and informal social events.

A final note on employee engagement surveys: individuals give up their time and often put a lot of thought into their answers to employee opinion surveys (as you would want them to do!). This care and thought needs to be repaid by timely publishing of the survey results across the organization along with a plan of what changes will take place as a result of the answers in an attempt to address the survey results, and what that means for each individual. Attitudes and behaviours change with the environment, and if you take too long over the results, analysis and action from the survey then there is an increased likelihood that the survey will lose credibility; even worse, the prescriptive action will not be as relevant, particularly if you are working in a dynamic environment where outside influences such as business restructures, press attention or competitor success may impact people's engagement levels.

We talk about ethics and data sensitivity in Chapter 12; however, it should go without saying that employee opinion surveys are a key area where these must be considered. If people are completing a survey with the understanding that it is anonymous, under no circumstances should that individual-level data be shared.

References

Allen, N J and Meyer, J P (1990) The measurement and antecedents of affective, continuance, and normative commitment to the organization, *Journal of Occupational Psychology*, 63, pp 1–18

Bell, E, Bryman, A and Harley, B (2003) *Business Research Methods*, Oxford University Press, Oxford

CultureAmp (2023) HR's complete guide to employee engagement, www.cultureamp.com/blog/employee-engagement-guide (archived at https://perma.cc/L8VP-MX7H)

Eisenberger, R, Huntington, R, Hutchison, S and Sowa, D (1986) Perceived organizational support, *Journal of Applied Psychology*, 71, pp 500–07

Field, A (2009) *Discovering Statistics Using SPSS*, Sage, London

Finnemore, R (2018) Don't settle for satisfied: Discover what really powers performance. focus.kornferry.com/dont-settle-for-satisfied-discover-what-really-powers-performance (archived at https://perma.cc/N7N7-Z5X9)

Gallup (2008) Meta analysis research, www.gallup.com/workplace/321725/gallup-q12-meta-analysis-report.aspx (archived at https://perma.cc/5ZUB-BL3A)

Gallup (2024) Q12 meta-analysis, www.gallup.com/workplace/321725/gallup-q12-meta-analysis-report.aspx (archived at https://perma.cc/U3NY-6NJK)

Gartner (2023) Gartner experts answer the top Generative AI questions for your enterprise: Generative AI isn't just a technology or a business case – it is a key part of a society in which people and machines work together, www.gartner.com/en/topics/generative-ai (archived at https://perma.cc/RK93-2K84)

Kahn, W (1990) Psychological conditions of personal engagement and disengagement at work, *Academy of Management Journal*, December, p 33

Lewin, K (1952) *Field Theory in Social Science: Selected theoretical papers by Kurt Lewin*, Tavistock, London

MacLeod, D and Clarke, N (2009) Engaging for Success, https://engageforsuccess.org/
engaging-for-success/ (archived at https://perma.cc/5YSR-WNCM)

Meade, A W and Craig, S B (2012) Identifying careless responses in survey data,
Psychological Methods, 17 (3), pp 437–55

Mercer (2011) Engaging employees to drive global business success, http://mgt2210.
pbworks.com/w/file/fetch/57707963/Mercer_Whats%20Working_final.pdf (archived at
https://perma.cc/34FX-PL88)

Peccei, R (2013) Employee engagement: An evidence-based review, in *Managing Human
Resources: Human resource management in transition*, 5th edn, ed S Bach and
M R Edwards, John Wiley, New York

Rich, B L, LePine, J A and Crawford, E R (2010) Job engagement: Antecedents and effects
on job performance, *Academy of Management Journal*, 53, pp 617–35

Schaufeli, W B and Bakker, A B (2003) *Utrecht Work Engagement Scale: Preliminary
manual*, Department of Psychology, Utrecht University, Netherlands

Schaufeli, W B and Bakker, A B (2010) Defining and measuring work engagement: Bringing
clarity to the concept, in *Work Engagement: A handbook of essential theory and
research*, ed A B Bakker and M P Leiter, Psychology Press, New York

Tabachnick, B G and Fidell, L S (2018) *Using Multivariate Statistics*, 7th edn, Pearson,
New York

Willis Towers Watson (2021) What is employee engagement? www.wtwco.com/en-au/
insights/2021/04/what-is-employee-engagement (archived at https://perma.cc/6P5V-
LLC3)

06

Case study 3

Predicting employee turnover

Employee turnover and why it is such an important part of HR management information

Employee turnover usually refers to all leavers of an organization, including those who resign, are made redundant, take retirement, or exit the organization for any other reason. In this chapter, however, we are only concerned with voluntary turn over and its possible causes.

In this chapter, we cover:

- Descriptive turnover analysis as a day-to-day activity.
- How to measure turnover at individual and team levels.
- Exploring differences in turnover between different countries at both individual and team levels using two practical examples from a multinational organization.
- Predicting turnover at both individual and team levels using survey and profile data using two practical examples from a multinational organization.
- Modelling the costs of turnover and the business case for action.

The cost of employee turnover can be substantial and has been projected at 93–200 per cent of each single leaver's salary depending on his or her skill, level of responsibility and how difficult it is to replace them (Griffeth and Hom, 2001). When this is accumulated across all leavers in an organization, the cost is substantial and it is hence a key area where sound analysis into causes and problem diagnosis can make an enormously valuable contribution to the organization's bottom line. Putting a figure on the cost of employee turnover is valuable because it can help the business case to justify programmes and interventions to address the problem. Costs of voluntary turnover will vary depending on the organization and type of role. Griffeth and Hom (2001) break down some of these costs as separation costs, replacement costs and training costs. Table 6.1 provides further detail.

TABLE 6.1 Cost of employee turnover

Separation Costs	Replacement Costs	Training Costs
• Exit interviews	• Job advertisements	• Formal orientation
• Administrative costs	• Recruitment	• Formal job training
• Separation benefits such as unused vacation time paid out	• Administrative processing	• Offsite training
	• Entrance interviews	• On-the-job training
• Lost revenues due to vacancy	• Applicant selection	• Productivity inefficiency
	• Assessment centres/testing	
• Productivity declines	• Travelling and relocation expenses	
• Overtime costs for extra labour during job vacancy	• Pre-employment screening	
• Hiring temporary personnel during job vacancy	• Medical examination (if applicable)	
• Client reassignment costs (if a customer-facing role)		

In some roles it can take up to 12 months for the new joiner to be brought up to speed, build internal networks, gain client trust, etc, to the level of competence and productivity experienced by the predecessor, and organizations are looking at efficient onboarding methods in order to reduce this time to productivity (Watkins, 2013).

As this book is about predictive HR modelling and analytics, we will not cover how to calculate the costs of employee turnover; however, if you are interested in exploring this further then Griffeth and Hom (2001) cover this in detail.

As mentioned, we are only looking at voluntary turnover. It is worth noting here that, whilst we would like to reduce the costs involved in voluntary turnover, and as an organization it is invaluable to understand why people leave, it can be argued that some voluntary turnover is potentially desirable and the goal is not necessarily to have 0 per cent voluntary turnover. Some voluntary turnover is potentially functional, for example a poor performer who is deeply unhappy with their career choice and realizes that the job is not for them; it may be best for such a person to seek employment elsewhere, and/or resign voluntarily in favour of a different career. However, as a general rule, one can consider low voluntary turnover to indicate that the organization is doing something right in terms of how it manages the people-management environment.

One of the most common activities that an HR information or MI function will conduct is the regular reporting of turnover statistics. This is partly because of the potentially massive costs associated with replacing people who leave, including recruiting and then getting new joiners up to the same level of productivity (as well as the importance of having people in the right place at the right time doing the right things).

Descriptive turnover analysis as a day-to-day activity

Most organizations will view turnover reports in a spreadsheet showing the percentage of people in a team, function or division who have left over a given period, but very little analysis will be conducted to explore why this might be. There may be some graphs on a spreadsheet showing which countries or teams have the highest turnover rates, but little modelling or controlling for other explanatory factors will be carried out. The result is often unfounded speculation about possible causes, such as 'The culture is different in Asia and people are more likely to move jobs' or 'The nature of sales is to chase the money so turnover will naturally be higher in that team', etc. This potentially leads to overgeneralized assumptions and a likely misdiagnosis of organizational problems, masking the real issues, which may run far deeper. The real causes of the problem, or predictors, can potentially be found with inferential statistical testing across a number of data sources taking into account a variety of possible causes of turnover simultaneously.

Without proper analysis, causes may be misdiagnosed and interventions may be misdirected. An example might be if the MI report shows that the 'sales' team in Australia seems to have particularly high turnover compared to other countries, so the leadership team decide to introduce a 'retention bonus' in Australia whereby anyone who resigns to go to a competitor is offered a bonus to stay. Whilst this might decrease the turnover numbers to a degree, it does not address the root cause; further analysis using inferential statistics in this particular case may have revealed a much more specific root issue that needed to be addressed (such as poor leadership, a gender bias that favours men over women for promotion or even a lack of training to enable staff to do the job they need to do on a particular technical skill). Having this kind of knowledge would have enabled the organization to direct their resources towards more specific, impactful interventions.

Measuring turnover at individual or team level

Organizational turnover is often presented as a percentage of all employees on a monthly or yearly basis. For example, the UK's Chartered Institute of Personnel and Development (CIPD) recommends the following formula:

$$\frac{\text{Total number of leavers over the period}}{\text{Average total number of employees over the period}} \times 100$$

The measures of employee flows, as set out below, have all been seen in organizations. Note that item number 1 is the same as the CIPD recommendation and the one that we will be using in our example.

Measures of employee flows

Note, these are usually presented as a percentage ($\times$ 100):

$$1 \text{ Separation rate} = \frac{\text{Number of members who left during period}}{\text{Average number of members during period}}$$

$$2 \text{ Accession rate} = \frac{\text{Number of new members added during the period}}{\text{Average number of members during period}}$$

$$3 \text{ Stability rate} = \frac{\text{Number of new joiners who stayed during a period}}{\text{Number of members at the beginning of a period}}$$

$$4 \text{ Instability rate} = \frac{\text{Number of new joiners who leave during a period}}{\text{Number of members at the beginning of a period}}$$

$$5 \text{ Survival rate} = \frac{\text{Number of new joiners who remain during period}}{\text{Number of new joiners during period}}$$

$$6 \text{ Wastage rate} = \frac{\text{Number of new joiners who leave during a period}}{\text{Number of new joiners during period}}$$

According to the CIPD, separation rate is a common measure of employee turnover at organizational or unit level, and hence is the measure that we will use in this chapter. Individual turnover is more simple to measure – either a person has left or they have not – however, it is not quite so simple to model and predict.

Exploring differences in both individual and team-level turnover

As mentioned, an activity that to some extent is the 'bread and butter' of MI and HR information professionals is regular reporting on staff turnover. Indeed, a very common report that HR people have to produce is staff turnover levels across difference 'cuts' or sub-samples of the organization. However, it is not always the case (as explained in Chapter 3) that much of the analysis that HR functions carry out is tested for any kind of significance. Thus the analysis most often presented is one that has been produced without the analyst checking whether any pattern found could easily have been due to random fluctuations (one needs to recognize that some voluntary turnover might have absolutely nothing to do with the organization – it may just be that some random factor led certain employees to leave their jobs). As individual turnover is a dichotomous event (leaver versus non-leaver) this restricts (or determines) the type of analysis that we can do to check for significance. For example, it would not necessarily make sense to explore linear relationships with a dichotomous variable, mainly because such data is not numerically meaningful (you cannot, for example, have 'more' gender, or have 'more' stayer/leaver). We deal with this issue in greater depth later in this chapter (though see Chapter 3 for a discussion of this issue).

One aspect of the analysis that we do here ('crosstabs') is the kind of analysis that the HR function might naturally do; however, we add a level of statistical interrogation to the data. We explore and interrogate differences in individual staff turnover patterns across a number of different countries. For this we use a crosstab analysis (cross-tabulation, similar to the diversity analysis we conduct in Chapter 4, example 1) and we apply a chi-square test to the results to check for significance.

Example 1a: using frequency tables to explore regional differences in staff turnover

The data set we use for this analysis is called: *Ch6_Individual_Turnover.xlsx* and includes data on 1,653 employees within a financial services organization across 10 countries.

The following variables are in this data set:

1   BossGender (gender of line manager/direct boss: 0 = female, 1 = male).

2   Gender (gender of individual: 0 = female, 1 = male).

3   Age (actual number).

4   LengthOfService (number of completed years).

5   AppraisalRating (performance appraisal rating on a scale of 1 to 5, with 5 being the highest).

6   Country (1 = Belgium; 2 = Sweden; 3 = Italy; 4 = France; 5 = Poland; 6 = Mexico; 7 = Spain; 8 = UK; 9 = United States; 10 = Australia).

7   LeaverStatus (whether or not the individual has left the organization: 0 = stayer; 1 = leaver).

First let's explore the data set in terms of how many people left over the last year and how many people are based in the different countries, by using a frequencies table.

The example code for this exercise is in the file *Ch6_example_1.R*. The first line of code checks to see if the *pacman* package is installed, and installs it if it is not. The second line loads the required packages for the example. The third line sets the working directory to be the same as the directory that the example file is in (where the Excel file should also be!). The fourth line loads the data and stores it in the *Ch6_it* dataframe. You can run each line of code by highlighting it and clicking the *Run* button, or through the keyboard shortcut *Control + Enter* (Windows and Linux) / *Command + Return* (MacOS). The first time you run this code, you may need an internet connection to download the required packages.

```
if (!require("pacman")) install.packages("pacman")
pacman::p_load(readxl, dplyr, modelsummary, this.path, huxtable)
setwd(this.path::here())
Ch6_it <- read_excel("Ch6_Individual_Turnover.xlsx")
```

The next set of lines recode the *Country* and *LeaverStatus* variable so they are more easily read – in their original form, the various countries and statuses are indicated only with numbers.

```
Ch6_it$Country_text <- case_match(Ch6_it$Country, 1 ~ "Belgium",
                2 ~ "Sweden",
                3 ~ "Italy",
                4 ~ "France",
                5 ~ "Poland",
                6 ~ "Mexico",
                7 ~ "Spain",
                8 ~ "UK",
                9 ~ "United States",
                10 ~ "Australia")

Ch6_it$LeaverStatus_text <- case_match(Ch6_it$LeaverStatus,
0 ~ "Stayer", 1 ~ "Leaver")
```

We can now use the *CrossTable* program to generate the table shown in Figure 6.1:

```
CrossTable(Ch6_it$Country_text, Ch6_it$LeaverStatus_text,
prop.t = FALSE, prop.chisq = FALSE, expected = TRUE)
```

6.1

```
> CrossTable(Ch6_it$Country_text, Ch6_it$LeaverStatus_text, prop.
t = FALSE, prop.chisq = FALSE, expected = TRUE)
   Cell Contents
|-------------------------|
|                       N |
|              Expected N |
|           N / Row Total |
|           N / Col Total |
|-------------------------|
============================================================================

                                              Ch6_it$LeaverStatus_text
Ch6_it$Country_text           Leaver              Stayer              Total
- - - - - - - - - - - - - - - - - - - - - - - - - - - - - - - - - - - - - -
Australia                        8                  39                 47
                                6.0                41.0
                              0.170               0.830              0.028
                              0.038               0.027
- - - - - - - - - - - - - - - - - - - - - - - - - - - - - - - - - - - - - -
Belgium                          7                  33                 40
                                5.1                34.9
                              0.175               0.825              0.024
                              0.033               0.023
```

```
- - - - - - - - - - - - - - - - - - - - - - - - - - - - - - - - - - - - - - - - - - - - -
France                            6                    31                   37
                                4.7                  32.3
                              0.162                 0.838                0.022
                              0.028                 0.022
- - - - - - - - - - - - - - - - - - - - - - - - - - - - - - - - - - - - - - - - - - - - -
Italy                            15                    55                   70
                                8.9                  61.1
                              0.214                 0.786                0.042
                              0.071                 0.038
- - - - - - - - - - - - - - - - - - - - - - - - - - - - - - - - - - - - - - - - - - - - -
Mexico                            7                    39                   46
                                5.9                  40.1
                              0.152                 0.848                0.028
                              0.033                 0.027
- - - - - - - - - - - - - - - - - - - - - - - - - - - - - - - - - - - - - - - - - - - - -
Poland                            5                    35                   40
                                5.1                  34.9
                              0.125                 0.875                0.024
                              0.024                 0.024
- - - - - - - - - - - - - - - - - - - - - - - - - - - - - - - - - - - - - - - - - - - - -
Spain                            12                    64                   76
                                9.7                  66.3
                              0.158                 0.842                0.046
                              0.057                 0.044
- - - - - - - - - - - - - - - - - - - - - - - - - - - - - - - - - - - - - - - - - - - - -
Sweden                            8                    28                   36
                                4.6                  31.4
                              0.222                 0.778                0.022
                              0.038                 0.019
- - - - - - - - - - - - - - - - - - - - - - - - - - - - - - - - - - - - - - - - - - - - -
UK                               28                   168                  196
                               25.0                 171.0
                              0.143                 0.857                0.119
                              0.133                 0.117
- - - - - - - - - - - - - - - - - - - - - - - - - - - - - - - - - - - - - - - - - - - - -
United States                   115                   949                 1064
                              135.9                 928.1
                              0.108                 0.892                0.644
                              0.545                 0.659
- - - - - - - - - - - - - - - - - - - - - - - - - - - - - - - - - - - - - - - - - - - - -
Total                           211                  1441                 1652
                              0.128                 0.872
=========================================================================
```

So we have data for 1,653 employees in this small financial services organization and the second-last row in Figure 6.1 tells us that there is only one employee for whom we do not know whether they are a stayer or a leaver, because the data is missing for that person – the row total is 1,652 instead of 1,653.

Looking at the table in Figure 6.1, we can see that the United States is (by far) the country with the most employees, while some other countries have very small populations (and we know from our research into the organization that they are start-up offices). If we were doing any analysis that might be sensitive in terms of dealing with confidential private information for employees (e.g. analysing survey responses) we would need to carefully consider whether or not to include some of those countries because it might expose the individuals (see our discussion on this in Chapter 12 – ethical considerations).

However, as we are just analysing fairly generic 'HR produced' data here we can consider these small populations not to be at any risk from the analysis. Ideally, chi-square requires subgroups to have more than five cases in each cell (i.e. data for five people in each country), and if any fall below this we might want to consider removing some of the countries from analysis.

Looking at the *Leaver* column, we can see that there were 211 voluntary leavers over the past year. We can see that the crude snapshot (just calculated from the data we have here) separation rate is 211/1,653 = 12.8 per cent. This figure is shown just below the total number of leavers.

We can assume that this indicates a separation rate of 12.8 per cent. To provide a reference for this, Mercer (2023) gives an account of the 2023 average voluntary turnover rates by industry. The average for banking and finance is 8.3 per cent. So it appears that this financial services organization has higher than the industry average turnover figure. A quick note on benchmarks, though – just because it is better than or the same as the industry average does not mean it is good.

It would be interesting at this point to investigate how the turnover patterns compare across the 10 different country locations. We can do this by a simple cross-tabulation. Additionally, we can also conduct a chi-square test to ascertain whether there is a significant difference between what we would expect the separation rate to be in each country and what we observe it to be.

Example 1b: using chi-square analysis to explore regional differences in individual staff turnover

Chi-square analyses

The next lines of code in the example file (*Ch6_example_1.R*) and follows from the example above. The line below conducts the chi-square analysis.

```
chisq.test(Ch6_it$Country_text, Ch6_it$LeaverStatus_text)
```

Running the line above produces the following output (Figure 6.2):

6.2

```
> chisq.test(Ch6_it$Country_text, Ch6_it$LeaverStatus_text)

        Pearson's Chi-squared test

data: Ch6_it$Country_text and Ch6_it$LeaverStatus_text
X-squared = 14.509, df = 9, p-value = 0.1053

Warning message:
In chisq.test(Ch6_it$Country_text, Ch6_it$LeaverStatus_text) :
  Chi-squared approximation may be incorrect
```

As we can see from the main crosstabs table in Figure 6.2 (which is the kind of data that MI functions produce all of the time using Excel and pivot tables), the pattern clearly shows some differences in terms of percentages of staff turnover across the different countries. In Australia, 17 per cent of staff (eight employees) left in 2014, whereas 22.2 per cent of staff left in Sweden in 2014 (eight employees). The country with the most amount of leavers was the United States with 115 leavers, though this was only 10.8 per cent of the country population; only five people left in Poland, but this was 12.5 per cent of the 40 employees. The variations in these leaver percentages are the sort of variations that may cause some concern when presented in a report. It would be easy to think that a country with a 22.2 per cent turnover rate is a real problem, especially when you compare it with the turnover rate of 10.8 per cent in another country.

However, random factors across the globe may influence whether someone has left their job, so you would expect some variation across countries; we can only tell if these variations might be statistically meaningful (in that there might be something about the countries that 'causes' or 'explains' variation in turnover rates in our company) by conducting an inferential test.

The chi-square inferential test in Figure 6.2 shows a Pearson chi-square test parameter value of 14.509 with 9 degrees of freedom, giving a p-value (significance value) of 0.105. Using our rule of thumb that $p < 0.05$ is the point at which we determine significance, we would say that there is no significant difference between what we would expect the country turnover figures to be, and what we observe the country turnover figures to be, suggesting that, although the variations in country turnover rates look like a big problem, these are more likely to be due to chance alone.

We also see that R has given a warning about the result, in red text (*Warning message: In chisq.test...*). The message suggests the results could be incorrect. This stems from a limitation of the data – the expected value for some of the *Country / LeaverStatus* combinations is low, for example the number of expected leavers in France and Sweden is less than five. Ideally, the smallest expected number in any combination should be five. Given we are so close to five for the minimum values, we will continue with the analysis.

Note that in the data set used here, the leaver status is categorical, i.e. 1 = stayer, 2 = leaver; and the country variable is also categorical (i.e. 1 = Belgium, 2 = Sweden, 3 = Italy, etc). Since both the independent and dependent variables are categorical, and we are looking at the association between these variables, the most suitable test is the chi-square test. This conclusion is supported by Table 3.4 in Chapter 3, which guides the selection of statistical tests.

In the next example, we look at a different type of data – team data. In this data set, the dependent variable is a continuous number, showing the team separation rate (i.e. the number of team members that left during the period/average number of members during the period). So here, while we are still looking at the association between two variables, the difference is that the dependent variable is continuous. As the country variable is still a categorical variable, the best test for us to use is the one-way ANOVA test (see Table 3.4 in Chapter 3).

Example 2: using one-way ANOVA to analyse team-level turnover by country

As a reminder, the one-way ANOVA test is a powerful method for testing the significance of the difference between sample means (i.e. between the means of country samples) where more than two categorical conditions/groups are compared. It effectively tests the null hypothesis that all the samples are drawn from the same population and that there is no difference between them. If the test suggests there is a difference, then further testing (called 'post-hoc testing') is needed to determine which samples are different and by how much (Coolican, 2009).

The data set used is *Ch6_Turnover_Team_Data.xlsx* and the data variables look like this:

1 Team identifier (unique team number).

2 Team size (number of people in the team).

3 TeamSeparation (separation rate between 0 and 1).

4 Country (1 = UK; 2 = United States; 3 = Canada; 4 = Spain).

5 SURVEY: ENGAGEMENT items COMBO (composite engagement percentage across the team).

6 SURVEY: TeamLeader Rating (composite team leader percentage across the team).

7 SURVEY: CSR rating (composite corporate social responsibility percentage across the team).

8 SURVEY: Drive for Performance (composite percentage team score on perceived 'Drive for performance' percentage).

9 SURVEY: Performance, Development and Reward (composite percentage team score on perceived fairness of performance, development and reward across the team).

10 SURVEY: Work–Life Balance (composite percentage team score on perceived work–life balance across the team).

11 UK dummy variable (0 = not UK; 1 = UK).

12 USA dummy variable (0 = not United States; 1 = United States).

13 Canada dummy variable (0 = not Canada; 1 = Canada).

14 Spain dummy variable (0 = not Spain; 1 = Spain).

Here we are going to explore the turnover differences between the four countries in the data set (the UK, United States, Canada and Spain). Here we have 2,910 employees employed across four countries organized in 212 teams. We have team-level engagement survey data provided by our external survey company; for each team we have an average positive response score from a 2013 engagement survey that measured scales of engagement, team leader rating, organizational corporate social responsibility (CSR) rating, perceived culture of 'drive for performance' (the organization's motto), fairness of performance development and reward, and perceived work–life balance (WLB). We also have an indicator of which country the team is based in along with the 2013–14 staff turnover percentage for each team.

First, let's generate a table of frequencies to take a closer look at the data. The R code for this example is in the file *Ch6_example_2.R*. The first few lines install required packages, set the working directory, and load the data.

```
if (!require("pacman")) install.packages("pacman")
pacman::p_load(readxl, dplyr, car, modelsummary, rstatix, ggplot2,
this.path, huxtable)
setwd(this.path::here())
Ch6_av <- read_excel("Ch6_Turnover_Team_Data.xlsx")
```

We will recode the Country variable to be more interpretable, since it is only represented by numbers.

```
Ch6_av$Country_text <- case_match(Ch6_av$Country, 1 ~ "UK",
                   2 ~ "United States",
                   3 ~ "Canada",
                   4 ~ "Spain")
```

We then convert the *Country_text* variable to be a factor type, so that we can analyse it as an independent variable later on.

```
Ch6_av$Country_text <- as.factor(Ch6_av$Country_text)
```

We can then generate a table of frequencies with the next line.

```
datasummary_skim(Ch6_av, type = "categorical", output = 'huxtable')
```

The following output is produced (Figure 6.3):

6.3

Country_text	N	%
Canada	32	15.1
Spain	55	25.9
UK	52	24.5
United States	73	34.4

It shows that we have data for 212 teams and the that the teams are not evenly distributed across the countries.

A question we want to answer is: are there country differences in team engagement and turnover? Because our turnover variable in this case is a ratio scale of percentage turnover for each team and not split into categories (like the 'leaver' or 'stayer' categories in the last example) we do not use a crosstabs to ascertain country differences. Here we have to use a test that compares average differences in percentage turnover for the teams across our multiple countries. For this, we need to conduct a particular type of statistical test called a one-way ANOVA.

First, we should look at some descriptive statistics for this variable.

Descriptive statistics

We can generate a table of descriptive statistics with the next line of code:

```
datasummary((Engagement) * Country_text ~ N + Mean + SD + Min + Max,
    data = Ch6_av, output = 'huxtable')
```

This produces Figure 6.4:

6.4

	Country_text	N	Mean	SD	Min	Max
Engagement	Canada	32	81.69	17.74	34.00	99.00
	Spain	55	69.49	10.46	34.00	79.00
	UK	52	82.69	8.44	44.00	99.00
	United States	73	86.62	10.57	44.00	99.00

What is this showing us? We describe each column below.

- **N:** the number of employees measured in each country. We can see that the United States has the largest number of employees measured (73 employees) and Canada has the smallest (32 employees).

- **Mean:** the average calculated engagement score for each country. We can see here that the United States has the highest engagement score and Spain the lowest.

- **SD (standard deviation):** showing the standard deviation of the engagement score for each country. We can see that Canadian teams show a far greater degree of variation in engagement responses than other countries, and the UK much less variation.

- **Min (minimum) and Max (maximum):** showing the highest and lowest team value for each country on the survey engagement score. So, for example, the minimum average team engagement score for the UK is 44, while the maximum average team engagement score for the UK is 99.

Test of homogeneity of variances

As with independent samples t-tests, we should check the equality of variances within each country. As a reminder, Levene's test will test whether the variance patterns of the particular statistic analysed (team average engagement scores) across the groups (countries) are the same. Put another way, it tests the null hypothesis that the variance patterns of the groups are the same. If the test comes out as significant (i.e. with $p < 0.05$) then we could say that the variance patterns across the groups are significantly different (see Chapter 3 'Significance'). We conduct the test with the next line of code:

```
levene_test(data = Ch6_av, Engagement ~ Country_text)
```

This will generate the following output (Figure 6.5):

6.5
```
> levene_test(data = Ch6_av, Engagement ~ Country_text)
# A tibble: 1 × 4
                    df1           df2         statistic              p
                  <int>         <int>             <dbl>          <dbl>
1                     3           208              10.8     0.00000125
```

The reason this is important is that one of the assumptions of ANOVA is that the variance patterns of data in groups should be the same. In our example, Figure 6.4 shows a significance level of the Levene's test of less than 0.001. In practice, what this means is that we need to compute Welch's F-statistic rather than the F-statistic given in the ANOVA table. This is done using the *welch_anova_test* program. If Levene's test were not significant (i.e. with a p-value > = 0.05) then we would use a different program to conduct the ANOVA test: *anova_test*.

Robust test of equality of means

The next lines conduct the Welch one-way test:

```
mod_6_1 <- welch_anova_test(data = Ch6_av, Engagement ~ Country_text)
get_anova_table(mod_6_1)
```

This will generate the following output (Figure 6.6):

6.6
```
> get_anova_table(mod_6_1)
# A tibble: 1 × 7
  .y.            n statistic    DFn    DFd          p method
* <chr>      <int>     <dbl>  <dbl>  <dbl>      <dbl>      <chr>
1 Engagement   212      29.3      3   93.5   1.99e-13  Welch ANOVA
```

The results tells us that there is a significant difference in level of engagement across the four countries. The p-value associated with the F statistic (*statistic*) is a very small number, much smaller than p < 0.05.

Now that we can see a significant difference in levels of engagement in teams across countries, we need to further investigate those differences.

Post-hoc tests

After any ANOVA, you need to undertake further analysis to determine *which* groups differ. In our situation, we know from the Welch's F-statistic that *Country_ text* has a significant impact on both the average level of team engagement.

Given that variances are not equal across groups, the most suitable post-hoc test is the Games-Howell. We can conduct this test with the next line of code:

```
games_howell_test(Ch6_av, Engagement ~ Country_text))
```

The results are shown in Figure 6.7:

6.7

```
> games_howell_test(Ch6_av, Engagement ~ Country_text)
# A tibble: 6 × 8
  .y.                  group1  group2   estimate conf.low conf.high     p.adj p.adj.
                                                                              signif
* <chr>                <chr>   <chr>       <dbl>    <dbl>    <dbl>      <dbl> <chr>
1 Engagement Canada    Spain              -12.2    -21.4    -3.01  5   e- 3  **
2 Engagement Canada    UK                  1.00    -7.97     9.98 9.9 e- 1  ns
3 Engagement Canada    United              4.93    -4.10    14.0  4.69e- 1  ns
                       States
4 Engagement Spain     UK                 13.2      8.42    18.0  6.08e-10  ****
5 Engagement Spain     United             17.1     12.2     22.0  4.55e-14  ****
                       States
6 Engagement UK        United              3.92    -0.511    8.36 1.03e- 1  ns
                       States
```

Note that there are many different types of post-hoc tests, which can be confusing when deciding which one to use. If you are interested in further reading on these tests, we recommend reading Field (2017). For the purposes of this book, though, Table 3.8 may help.

Please be aware that Table 3.8 is very simplified and only a subset of what is available. It should, though, get you through most situations that you come across in HR analytics.

Because we have no specific hypothesis about the effect that country may have on the average team engagement score, then we carry out this post-hoc test to compare all countries with each other.

In Figure 6.6 the difference between country means is shown in the *estimate* column. For example, looking at the first line in Figure 6.6, we see that mean difference in team engagement between Spain and Canada is –12.2. If we were to calculate this manually, we would look back to the descriptives table (Figure 6.5) and calculate it as follows:

Spain mean – Canada mean

= 69.49 – 81.69

= –12.2

Then it compares each pairs of countries in a similar way.

Moving to the right, we can see the 95 per cent confidence interval (*conf.low* and *conf.high*), the Games-Howell adjusted p-value, and significance indicators. An asterisk is shown if the p-value is significant at the 0.05 level, and more asterisks are shown with lower p-values.

Looking down the *p.adj* and *p.adj.signif* columns, we see some significant differences ($p < 0.05$):

- Canada and Spain ($p = 0.005$, $p < 0.01$)
- Canada and UK ($p = 0.990$, $p > 0.05$)
- Canada and USA ($p = 0.469$, $p > 0.05$)
- Spain and UK ($p = 0.000$, $p < 0.001$)
- Spain and USA ($p = 0.000$, $p < 0.001$)
- UK and USA ($p = 0.103$, $p > 0.05$)

We can now repeat the analyses for the TeamSeparation variable, which represents the average percentage of turnover within a team. First, we examine the descriptive statistics. Running the following line gives us the N, mean, standard deviation, minimum and maximums for each country.

```
datasummary((TeamSeparation) * Country_text ~ N + Mean + SD + Min + Max,
    data = Ch6_av, output = 'huxtable')
```

Which shows Figure 6.8:

6.8

	Country_text	N	Mean	SD	Min	Max
TeamSeparation	Canada	32	0.19	0.13	0.00	0.60
	Spain	55	0.27	0.22	0.00	0.70
	UK	52	0.16	0.20	0.00	0.70
	United States	73	0.16	0.14	0.00	0.70

We next check for equality of variances with Levene's test:

```
levene_test(data = Ch6_av, TeamSeparation ~ Country_text)
```

Which results in the following output (Figure 6.9):

6.9

```
> levene_test(data = Ch6_av, TeamSeparation ~ Country_text)
# A tibble: 1 × 4
           df1          df2       statistic               p
         <int>        <int>           <dbl>           <dbl>
  1          3          208            5.37         0.00140
```

Because Levene's test is significant and variances differ across countries for *TeamSeparation*, we need to conduct a test for Welch's F-statistic, as before:

```
mod_6_2 <- welch_anova_test(data = Ch6_av, TeamSeparation ~ Country_text)
get_anova_table(mod_6_2)
```

Running the lines above shows the following result (Figure 6.10):

6.10
```
> get_anova_table(mod_6_2)
# A tibble: 1 × 7
  .y.                 n statistic    DFn    DFd        p method
* <chr>           <int>    <dbl>  <dbl>  <dbl>    <dbl>  <chr>
1 TeamSeparation    212     3.45      3   98.8     0.02  Welch ANOVA
```

The output above shows a significant result, as the p-value is less than 0.05. We can now conduct the post-hoc test. As before, Games-Howell is most appropriate, since variances are not equal. The next line performs the test:

```
games_howell_test(Ch6_av, TeamSeparation ~ Country_text)
```

Which results in Figure 6.11:

6.11
```
> games_howell_test(Ch6_av, TeamSeparation ~ Country_text)
# A tibble: 6 × 8
  .y.              group1  group2  estimate  conf.   conf.high p.adj p.adj.
                                             low                     signif
* <chr>            <chr>   <chr>     <dbl>    <dbl>     <dbl> <dbl> <chr>
1 TeamSeparation Canada  Spain    0.0775  -0.0216    0.177    0.178 ns
2 TeamSeparation Canada  UK      -0.0304  -0.125     0.0646   0.835 ns
3 TeamSeparation Canada  United  -0.0289  -0.102     0.0442   0.725 ns
                         States
4 TeamSeparation Spain   UK      -0.108   -0.216     0.000101 0.05  *
5 TeamSeparation Spain   United  -0.106   -0.196    -0.0168   0.013 *
                         States
6 TeamSeparation UK      United   0.00148 -0.0835    0.0865   1     ns
                         States
```

Looking down the *p.adj* and *p.adj.signif* columns, we see some significant differences (p<0.05):

- Canada and Spain (p = 0.178, p > 0.05)
- Canada and UK (p = 0.835, p > 0.05)
- Canada and USA (p = 0.725, p > 0.05)
- Spain and UK (p = 0.05, p = 0.05)
- Spain and USA (p = 0.013, p < 0.05)
- UK and USA (p = 1.00, p > 0.05)

The last comparison is no surprise as mean of team turnover for both the UK and United States is much the same at 16 per cent. Recommendations that may come from the above would be to investigate possible causes of the low engagement in

Spain (see Chapter 5, engagement case study, for more details about analysis linked to engagement). Now that we can be certain that Spain has a significantly higher turnover than both the UK and the United States, a recommendation can be made to direct resources into investigating why this is – using predictive models such as the regression analysis later in this chapter. It may be a combination of things, including market conditions (such as local competition for talented employees), employee engagement and desire to leave (as the results here seem to hint) or other factors such as length of service or appraisal rating. Regardless, we can be confident in recommending that resources be directed towards Spain to more closely diagnose the turnover situation and prescribe action. To generate a graphical representation of the differences we can create a plot using this code:

```
ggplot(Ch6_av, aes(x = Country_text, y = TeamSeparation)) +
geom_bar(stat = "summary", fun = "mean")
```

Figure 6.12 shows the resulting plot of team average turnover rate by country.

6.12

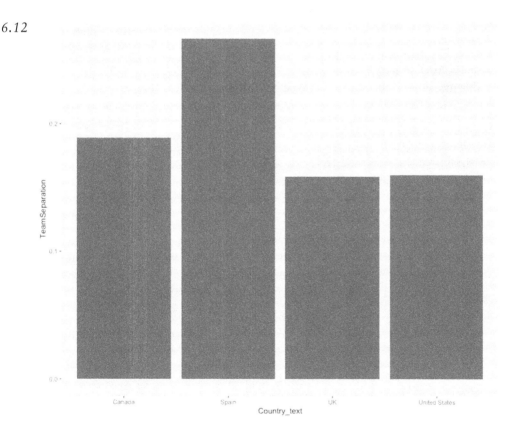

In the two examples below, we use regression modelling to predict turnover. In the first example, we look at individual turnover. Now, because individual turnover is a binary event – i.e. there are only two outcomes – we will use logistic regression; and because team turnover is a continuous variable – a percentage that could take on any value between 1 and 100 on a linear scale – we use multiple linear regression to predict it.

Example 3: predicting individual turnover

The data set that we used in this example is *Ch6_Individual_Turnover.xlsx*; the predictive models use binary/dichotomous data as the logistic regression.

Logistic regression

We discuss logistic regression in more detail in Chapters 3 and 4; here is a quick recap. We see in Chapter 5 (engagement case study) – and in other chapters to follow – that we can use ordinary least squares (OLS) multiple linear regression to model and predict performance based on recorded/historical data. Some dependent variable measures are ideal for this type of regression because they are often continuous variables. What is a continuous variable? It is one that could be measured along a continuum and has a numerical value: for example, the average scan rate (how many items) per minute for each checkout operator; the higher the average scan rate then the faster the operator tends to scan products (thus this suggested 'better' performance on this indicator).

Not all dependent variables are continuous, and some variables, such as individual turnover, are categorical variables. Categorical variables are discrete, or nominal. They do not have a meaningful numeric value: for example, the office country location or whether someone is male or female. For this type of variable (if we want to account for variation in this categorical variable), the regression modelling we need to undertake is called logistic regression. In logistic regression, the predictor variables (independent variables) may be categorical or continuous.

So, as discussed in Chapter 3, the nature of the data included in our variable will dictate which type of statistical analysis we use. And while team turnover in the example above is a continuous number (i.e. the percentage of people who left in a specific time period within each team), individual turnover is a binary event: either someone has left or they have not.

As a reminder, the data in this file is linked to 1,653 employees and looks like this:

1 BossGender (gender of line manager: 0 = female, 1 = male).

2 Gender (gender of individual: 0 = female, 1 = male).

3 Age (actual number).

4 LengthofService (number of completed years).

5 AppraisalRating (performance appraisal rating on a scale of 1 to 5, with 5 being the highest).

6 Country (1 = Belgium; 2 = Sweden; 3 = Italy; 4 = France; 5 = Poland; 6 = Mexico; 7 = Spain; 8 = UK; 9 = United States; 10 = Australia).

7 LeaverStatus (whether or not the individual has left the organization: 0 = stayer; 1 = leaver).

We are going to predict leaver status with the other variables in the data set. Code for this example is in the file *Ch6_example_3_4.R*. The first few lines install and load required packages, set the working directory, and loads the data:

```
if (!require("pacman")) install.packages("pacman")
pacman::p_load(readxl, modelsummary, dplyr, rcompanion, this.path,
huxtable)
setwd(this.path::here())
Ch6_it <- read_excel("Ch6_Individual_Turnover.xlsx")
```

As before, we recode the Country variable to be more legible:

```
Ch6_it$Country_text <- case_match(Ch6_it$Country, 1 ~ "Belgium",
                  2 ~ "Sweden",
                  3 ~ "Italy",
                  4 ~ "France",
                  5 ~ "Poland",
                  6 ~ "Mexico",
                  7 ~ "Spain",
                  8 ~ "UK",
                  9 ~ "United States",
                  10 ~ "Australia")
```

This is an important process because we cannot use the *Country* variable (coded from 1 to 10). Using the *Country* variable as is would result in R treating the 1–10 country coding as a numerical variable and the analysis would assume that this was a single numerical scale – it would check to see whether 'the *more* country a person works in, are they *more* likely to be a leaver'. This of course makes no sense. You cannot have *more country*. The next line tells R to treat this new variable like a categorical variable:

```
Ch6_it$Country_text <- as.factor(Ch6_it$Country_text)
```

We have seen this procedure done before (applied the *as.factor* program to a variable), but mostly out of convenience in interpreting what the various codes mean. But in more complex analyses, this procedure tells R that the variable is a categorical one and to treat it as such. Most of the time, character variables are automatically treated like factor variables, but this procedure ensures we communicate to R what we intend.

We then define the logistic regression model in the next lines. We will predict leaver status with the combination of the leader's status (*BossGender*), the employee's gender (*Gender*) and age (*Age*), the amount of time they worked in the company (*LengthOfService*), their appraisal rating (*AppraisalRating*) and the country they work in (*Country_text*). This estimates the model and puts the results in *logit_reg*:

```
logit_reg <- glm(LeaverStatus ~ BossGender + Gender + Age +
LengthOfService + AppraisalRating + Country_text,
data = Ch6_it, family = "binomial")
```

Omnibus tests of model coefficients

We can check how well our model is accounting for turnover across our organization. We can do this by comparing the fit of our model with all of our predictors against the fit of a model with no predictors. This procedure is called the likelihood ratio test and we can conduct this test with the next line of code:

```
nagelkerke(logit_reg, restrictNobs = TRUE)
```

Which produces the following output (Figure 6.13):

6.13

```
> nagelkerke(logit_reg, null = NULL, restrictNobs = TRUE)
$Models

Model: "glm, LeaverStatus ~ BossGender + Gender + Age + LengthOfService +
AppraisalRating + Country_text, binomial, Ch6_it"
Null: "glm, LeaverStatus ~ 1, binomial, fit$model"

$Pseudo.R.squared.for.model.vs.null
                                  Pseudo.R.squared
McFadden                                0.0397124
Cox and Snell (ML)                      0.0297306
Nagelkerke (Cragg and Uhler)            0.0558494

$Likelihood.ratio.test
Df.diff  LogLik.diff   Chisq     p.value
   -14        -24.9   49.799   6.5971e-06

$Number.of.observations

Model:1650
Null: 1650

$Messages
[1] "Note: For models fit with REML, these statistics are based on
refitting with ML"

$Warnings
[1] "None"
```

If you look in the '*$Likelihood ratio test*' section of the output, we see that the chi-squared difference between our model and a model with no predictors is 49.799 and this is deemed to be significant (p = 0.0000065971). Thus, importantly in this case, our five independent variables plus our country categories significantly account for variation in the leaver versus stayer variable in our data set. In other words, we can identify features that may well account for whether or not people have left.

Model summary

Figure 6.12 also has estimations of R-square statistics. As we have discussed in previous sections, our R-square figure is an indication of the degree of variation in our dependent variable that is accounted for by the variation in our predictor variables. In the output it is under the heading of *$Pseudo.R.squared.for.model.vs.null*. Don't let the *Pseudo* label put you off. It is an analogy to R-square we have seen with multiple regression, but because it is not calculated in the exact same way, statisticians are hesitant to call it by the same label. They function in a similar way, however, by giving us an estimate of how much variability our model explains. The Nagelkerke R-square is a figure that most closely equates with the multiple R-square figure in multiple linear regression (that we have used in previous chapters). So on the assumption that this works the same as an R-square statistic produced with linear multiple regression, here this indicates that just from looking at these six variables in our data set, we can account for 5.6 per cent of turnover across our organization. Whilst this may seem like a small percentage, we need to consider all of the possible causes of people leaving an organization and be impressed that these few predictors actually account for a not-insubstantial amount of variation.

Variables in the equation

We can generate a table to see which variables explain significant variance. We can run the following line of code:

```
summary(logit_reg)
```

The output is shown in Figure 6.14:

6.14

```
> summary(logit_reg)

Call:
glm(formula = LeaverStatus ~ BossGender + Gender + Age + LengthOfService +
    AppraisalRating + Country_text, family = "binomial", data = Ch6_it)

Coefficients:
                           Estimate   Std. Error  z value         Pr(>|z|)
(Intercept)                0.168371     0.656593    0.256         0.797618
BossGender                -0.183855     0.163275   -1.126         0.260147
Gender                    -0.608303     0.161704   -3.762         0.000169 ***
Age                       -0.001347     0.009392   -0.143         0.885962
LengthOfService           -0.017194     0.010900   -1.577         0.114683
AppraisalRating           -0.248002     0.097284   -2.549         0.010795 *
Country_textBelgium       -0.249247     0.603715   -0.413         0.679712
Country_textFrance        -0.455198     0.624276   -0.729         0.465903
Country_textItaly         -0.058845     0.516308   -0.114         0.909259
Country_textMexico        -0.415403     0.596774   -0.696         0.486379
Country_textPoland        -0.734433     0.648954   -1.132         0.257753
Country_textSpain         -0.571556     0.535051   -1.068         0.285418
Country_textSweden         0.001673     0.593760    0.003         0.997752
Country_textUK            -0.505547     0.470520   -1.074         0.282624
Country_textUnited States -0.698382     0.433822   -1.610         0.107433
---
Signif. codes: 0 '***' 0.001 '**' 0.01 '*' 0.05 '.' 0.1 ' ' 1

(Dispersion parameter for binomial family taken to be 1)

    Null deviance:     1254.0    on 1649    degrees of freedom
Residual deviance:     1204.2    on 1635    degrees of freedom
    (3 observations deleted due to missingness)
AIC: 1234.2

Number of Fisher Scoring iterations: 5
```

There is a lot in this table, so we will generate a nicer looking table for the purposes of interpretation. The following lines produce a more readable table:

```
mod = list("Log Odds" = logit_reg, "Odds Ratio" = logit_reg)
modelsummary(mod, exponentiate = c(FALSE, TRUE), statistic = NULL,
stars = TRUE, output = 'huxtable')
```

The first line defines two models, one that should be labelled *Log Odds*, and another *Odds Ratio*. The second line uses the *modelsummary* program to generate a table, which can be seen in Figure 6.15:

6.15

	Log Odds	Odds Ratio
(Intercept)	0.168	1.183
BossGender	-0.184	0.832
Gender	-0.608***	0.544***
Age	-0.001	0.999
LengthOfService	-0.017	0.983
AppraisalRating	-0.248*	0.780*
Country_textBelgium	-0.249	0.779
Country_textFrance	-0.455	0.634
Country_textItaly	-0.059	0.943
Country_textMexico	-0.415	0.660
Country_textPoland	-0.734	0.480
Country_textSpain	-0.572	0.565
Country_textSweden	0.002	1.002
Country_textUK	-0.506	0.603
Country_textUnited States -0.698	0.497	
Num.Obs.	1650	1650
AIC	1234.2	1234.2
BIC	1315.3	1315.3
Log.Lik.	-602.101	-602.101
F	3.498	3.498
RMSE	0.33	0.33

+ p < 0.1, * p < 0.05, ** p < 0.01, *** p < 0.001

See Chapter 3 for our more detailed explanation of logistic regression; however, it is clear from the analysis that gender and appraisal ratings are the two factors (that we have looked at here) that significantly account for individual staff turnover. The stars next to the numbers for those variables indicate p-values below 0.05 ($p < 0.05$). Gender has a significance level of $p < 0.001$ and appraisal rating is 0.011, $p < 0.05$. To interpret what this means, we need to what is in the column labelled 'Odds ratio'.

Odds ratios

At this point it might be useful to take a step back and explain odds ratios.

The most well-known use of odds in everyday life is betting on horse racing or other sports. At the time of writing this chapter (early 2024), the odds of England winning the 2024 UEFA EURO football tournament were 3/1, or '3 to 1'. In this way, the bookmaker believed that the odds of England winning were 3/1. These are relatively good odds, and anyone who follows football (soccer) will know that England is a strong football nation (although England has never won the EURO tournament; in early 2024 hopes were high…). By comparison, other countries such as Romania and Georgia had higher odds because there was less chance of them winning. At the time of writing these odds were 200/1 and 500/1 respectively. Indeed, the table of the odds at one of the leading sports networks looked like this:

England 3/1	Serbia 80/1
France 3.4/1	Austria 80/1
Germany 6/1	Scotland 80/1
Spain 7/1	Hungary 80/1
Portugal 8/1	Ukraine 100/1
Belgium 14/1	Poland 100/1
Italy 16/1	Czech Republic 150/1
Netherlands 16/1	Romania 200/1
Denmark 35/1	Slovenia 200/1
Croatia 40/1	Albania 250/1
Turkey 50/1	Georgia 500/1
Switzerland 65/1	Slovakia 500/1

Talking about money for a moment, if you put £10 down on England to win, you would win £30 if they did indeed win. If, however, you put £10 down for Romania to win and they surprised everyone and came through to win the cup, you would win £2,000. You would be taking a bigger risk, but the payout would be higher. The bookmakers calculate these odds to ensure that the big payouts are unlikely. How do they know who is more likely to win? Bookmakers are known to use logistic regression to determine this by modelling independent variables such as past performance, stadium size and the distance that the team has to travel. Indeed Paddy Power, a UK bookmaker, famously employed Professor Stephen Hawking to determine the optimum conditions of England to succeed in the football World Cup, as well as how the team could triumph in a penalty shootout.

Which method did Stephen Hawking use? Logistic regression, of course! He used it to find what they could do to maximize the odds of winning. This was referenced in many newspaper articles and blogs; however, Moore-Bridger and Lynch (2014) in the *London Evening Standard* wrote that Hawking, using logistic regression, found that the four conditions (independent variables) that account for the probability of winning a penalty shootout (dependent variable) are:

- Have a run-up of more than three steps.
- Use the side foot rather than laces.
- Put the ball in the top left or right corners.
- Choose a fair-haired player, because statistically they are more likely to score.

Odds ratios are calculated and interpreted in a similar way.

So, while OLS multiple linear regression uses ordinary least squares to find a best-fitting line and comes up with coefficients that predict the change in the dependent variable for one unit change in the independent variable, logistic regression estimates the probability of an event occurring. So what we want to predict is not a precise numerical value of a dependent variable (because it is a binary variable, not a continuous variable), but rather the probability (p) that the value of it is (1) 'leaver' rather than (0) not-leaver – or 'stayer' (much as we were predicting the probability of a team winning the UEFA EURO tournament (1) versus not winning the tournament (0)).

In our example, logistic regression estimates the probability of an individual leaving the organization. Logistic regression allows us to calculate odds ratios, which are the ratio of the odds of the event occurring to it not occurring.

Say England progresses to the final and the probability of winning the tournament has now increased to 0.8. Therefore p = 0.8. Then the probability of not winning would be 0.2 (calculated as 1 – p). It may be helpful to think of it as an 80 per cent chance of winning and 20 per cent chance of not winning.

The odds of winning are then defined as p / (1 – p), or 0.8 / 0.2. We would say that the odds of winning are 4 to 1 on. The odds of not winning would be 0.2 / 0.8, or 1 to 4, or '1 to 4' against.

In our turnover example, the odds ratio is the likelihood or odds of Y = 1 (rather than 0) if the value of x is increased by one unit. In our example using leaver status and the continuous variable tenure it would be:

Odds Ratio = ratio of the probability that Leaver Status
(Y) = Leaver (1) / Leaver Status (Y) = 0 (stayer)
if the value of Tenure (x) is increased by one unit.

So if the odds ratio for tenure was 2.00, we could say that odds of an individual being a 'leaver' compared to being a 'stayer' doubles for every additional year of service. Another way of looking at this is that you are twice as likely to be a leaver as a stayer for every one year you stay with the organization.

If we include a categorical variable such as country, R will automatically create the 'dummy' variables for you. R will order the levels of the categorical variable in alphabetical order. It will make the first level of the categorical variable the reference category and this is why Australia is not shown in Figures 6.13 and 6.14. Every other level of the categorical variable is compared to the reference category.

This means the number next to each country is a comparison against Australia. To be concrete, let's unpack the meaning of the coefficients linked to each level of the categorical variable in Figures 6.13 and 6.14:

Country_textBelgium	(1 = Belgium; 0 = Australia)
Country_textFrance	(1 = France; 0 = Australia)
Country_textItaly	(1 = Italy; 0 = Australia)
Country_textMexico	(1 = Mexico; 0 = Australia)
Country_textPoland	(1 = Poland; 0 = Australia)
Country_textSpain	(1 = Spain; 0 = Australia)
Country_textSweden	(1 = Sweden; 0 = Australia)
Country_textUK	(1 = UK; 0 = Australia)
Country_textUnited States	(1 = United States; 0 = Australia)

So an odds ratio for *Country_textUnited States* of .497 would mean that after controlling for all other factors, if an individual were based in the United States, they would be nearly half as likely to be a leaver than if they were based in Australia (our reference country category in this case).

The logistic regression model equation does look very similar to the linear regression equation, except that it looks at the probability of y instead of the value y. In the equation below, p refers to the probability that y = 1, and Ln is the natural logarithm (that makes it all work). For more information on natural logarithms see Field (2017).

The odds ratio for each independent variable is in the 'Odds ratio' column of Figure 6.14. So remember that 1 is a leaver and 0 is a stayer. With 'Gender' in Figure 6.14, we have an odds ratio of 0.544. This means that the probability of leaving/probability of staying = 0.544 if the gender = 1 (rather than 0) i.e. men, rather than women.

Because the odds ratio here is less than 1, we know that the probability of staying is greater than the probability of leaving if the individual is male. So women are more likely to leave. We could present this in a number of ways:

- The odds of men leaving the organization are 0.544 to 1 on.

Or we could flip it and say:

- The odds of men leaving the organization are (1 / 0.544 =) 1.8382 to 1 against.
- The odds of men staying are 1.8382 to 1.

Or:

- Women are 1.8382 times more likely to leave than men.

As a reminder, an odds ratio of 1.0 would mean that men are no more likely to stay or leave than women.

If we look at our other significant finding, which is the previous year's performance appraisal rating, we can see that the odds ratio (Exp(B)) is 0.780. So the probability of staying/probability of leaving ratio is 0.78 if the performance rating goes up one point.

This means that the lower the appraisal rating the year before, then the more likely the individual is to have left. Again it might be easier to convert the odds ratio here and do the sum 1 / 0.780 = 1.282. This means that a person who got a particular rating (e.g. 3 in a 1–5 scale) in their appraisal would be 28.2 per cent more likely to stay the following year than a person who got a lower appraisal rating of 2. Lower rating = more likely to leave. For example:

- individuals who get a '3' performance rating are 1.282 times more likely to stay than individuals who get a '2' performance rating; or

- individuals who get a '4' performance rating are 28.2 per cent more likely to stay the following year than individuals who get a '3' performance rating.

As we can see from the results, country differences do not come out as significant in accounting for turnover.

Example 4: comparing expected length of service for men vs women using the Kaplan-Meier survival analysis technique

In this example we use the same data set as Example 3, *Ch6_Individual_Turnover.xlsx*.

Survival analysis using Kaplan-Meier

Survival analysis is extremely helpful when really trying to dig underneath the surface and understand general patterns and trends of employee turnover. In the last example we carried out analysis to try to predict the likelihood of employee turnover. Here, we break it down and try to predict the patterns of length of service before leaving and how this is different for men vs women in our example organization.

What does this add? While predicting turnover is extremely helpful in identifying which employees are more likely to leave than others, being able to predict the amount of time employees are likely to be with the organization before leaving (i.e. how long they 'survive') helps us identify useful things that might lead us to understand the process of leaving. For example, if our analysis found that employees were twice as likely to leave in the first three months than at any other time, then we would invest in our onboarding processes. Alternatively, if our analysis found that people were most likely to leave at the two year mark, we may decide to conduct some further analysis to help us determine why this might be the case.

Kaplan-Meier survival analysis enables us to include a categorical factor with which we can make comparison of survival patterns, and for this example we will use gender.

Code for this example is in the file *Ch6_example_3_4.R*. Because we are following on from the last example, we will not repeat the code that sets the working directory or loads the data file. We will however need to load some additional packages to conduct survival analysis:

```
pacman::p_load(survival, survminer, gtsummary)
```

We will also create a factor variable for gender for ease of interpretation:

```
Ch6_it$Gender_text <- case_match(Ch6_it$Gender, 0 ~ "Female", 1 ~
"Male")
Ch6_it$Gender_text <- as.factor(Ch6_it$Gender_text)
```

Cross tabulation summary

Next, a cross tabulation may reveal some interesting patterns. When we run this code, keeping in mind that stayers are coded as 0 and leavers are coded as 1:

```
CrossTable(Ch6_it$Gender_text, Ch6_it$LeaverStatus, prop.t = FALSE,
prop.c = FALSE, prop.chisq = FALSE)
```

We see Figure 6.16:

6.16

```
> CrossTable(Ch6_it$Gender_text, Ch6_it$LeaverStatus, prop.t = FALSE,
  prop.c = FALSE, prop.chisq = FALSE)
   Cell Contents
|-------------------------|
|                       N |
|             N / Row Total |
|-------------------------|


===================================================
                        Ch6_it$LeaverStatus
Ch6_it$Gender_text          0          1    Total
-------------------------------------------------
Female                    696        136      832
                        0.837      0.163    0.504
-------------------------------------------------
Male                      745         73      818
                        0.911      0.089    0.496
-------------------------------------------------
Total                    1441        209     1650
===================================================
```

This cross-tabulation tells us immediately that, of the 832 women in the sample, 136 were leavers and 696 (or 83.7 per cent) did not leave during the study period when we took the data. It also tells us that, of the 818 men in the sample, 73 were leavers and 745 (or 91.1 per cent) were stayers in the same period.

Next we conduct the Kaplan- Meier analysis with the following line:

```
km_analysis <- survfit(Surv(LengthOfService, LeaverStatus) ~ Gender_text,
data = Ch6_it)
```

The line above tells R about two variables critical for survival analysis – the length of time an employee has worked (*LengthOfService*) and an indication of an event occurring, in this case leaving (*LeaverStatus*). This is fundamental to our query – how long does someone stay in the organization until they leave? We also predict this using a factor variable, namely *Gender_text* to discern if there could be differences between women and men. The results are stored in the object *km_analysis*.

Survival table

With the analysis conducted, we can ask R to show us a table of how the genders behave over time. When we run the following line:

```
summary(km_analysis)
```

We obtain Figure 6.17:

6.17

```
> summary(km_analysis)
Call: survfit(formula = Surv(LengthOfService, LeaverStatus) ~ Gender_text,
    data = Ch6_it)
```

3 observations deleted due to missingness

Gender_text=Female

time	n.risk	n.event	survival	std.err	lower 95% CI	upper 95% CI
0	832	25	0.970	0.00592	0.9584	0.982
1	726	12	0.954	0.00741	0.9395	0.969
2	669	13	0.935	0.00887	0.9182	0.953
3	602	6	0.926	0.00957	0.9075	0.945
4	572	7	0.915	0.01036	0.8946	0.935
5	537	18	0.884	0.01228	0.8603	0.908
6	467	5	0.875	0.01286	0.8498	0.900
7	417	4	0.866	0.01340	0.8403	0.893
8	381	3	0.859	0.01386	0.8326	0.887
9	344	2	0.854	0.01423	0.8270	0.883
10	313	3	0.846	0.01485	0.8176	0.876
11	295	5	0.832	0.01593	0.8012	0.864
12	249	1	0.829	0.01621	0.7974	0.861
13	220	4	0.813	0.01758	0.7797	0.849
14	198	1	0.809	0.01796	0.7749	0.845
16	165	1	0.804	0.01851	0.7690	0.842
17	157	1	0.799	0.01909	0.7628	0.838
19	144	3	0.783	0.02097	0.7426	0.825
22	131	1	0.777	0.02165	0.7354	0.820
23	120	2	0.764	0.02314	0.7197	0.810
24	108	3	0.743	0.02554	0.6941	0.794
25	91	2	0.726	0.02746	0.6743	0.782
26	75	3	0.697	0.03106	0.6389	0.761
27	62	2	0.675	0.03389	0.6114	0.744
28	51	3	0.635	0.03888	0.5632	0.716
32	28	1	0.612	0.04360	0.5325	0.704
33	20	1	0.582	0.05105	0.4898	0.691
36	7	2	0.415	0.10581	0.2522	0.684
37	3	2	0.138	0.11846	0.0259	0.740

Gender_text=Male

time	n.risk	n.event	survival	std.err	lower 95% CI	upper 95% CI
0	818	24	0.971	0.00590	0.959	0.982
1	699	2	0.968	0.00620	0.956	0.980
2	632	5	0.960	0.00703	0.947	0.974
3	574	3	0.955	0.00757	0.940	0.970
4	546	7	0.943	0.00878	0.926	0.960
5	499	3	0.937	0.00931	0.919	0.956
6	450	4	0.929	0.01012	0.909	0.949
7	409	2	0.924	0.01057	0.904	0.945
8	379	2	0.920	0.01106	0.898	0.941
9	345	2	0.914	0.01162	0.892	0.937
10	325	3	0.906	0.01249	0.882	0.931
11	309	2	0.900	0.01308	0.875	0.926

12	274	3	0.890	0.01412	0.863	0.918
13	253	1	0.887	0.01450	0.859	0.915
14	237	2	0.879	0.01531	0.850	0.910
15	217	2	0.871	0.01621	0.840	0.903
17	178	1	0.866	0.01684	0.834	0.900
22	157	1	0.861	0.01761	0.827	0.896
24	127	1	0.854	0.01873	0.818	0.891
25	116	1	0.846	0.01996	0.808	0.886
36	10	2	0.677	0.10825	0.495	0.926

The survival table for women (as indicated by *Gender_text=Female*) shows very useful data. Remember that *LengthOfService* is measured in years and this is the data represented in the column labelled *time*. At *LengthOfService* = 0, there are 832 total people at risk of leaving (*n.risk*), and 25 actually leave (*n.event*), this means a 97 per cent survival rate (*survival*; multiply figures here by 100 to obtain a percentage). The table also shows us the standard error (*std.err*) and the associated 95 per cent confidence interval (CI) boundaries (*lower 95% CI; upper 95% CI*). Looking into the next line, we could say that 37 out of 832 females leave within the first two years, or that the chance of survival after two years is 95.4 per cent.

Let's move on towards the bottom of the table now, where we get to the end of the list of women. Here, we can see that the survival rate of women is 13.8 per cent for women who had tenure below 38 years (between 0.000 and 37 years of tenure).

The table then moves on to analyse the male employees in a similar way. For comparison, if we look towards the end of the male survival table, we see that out of the 818 males in the organization, the survival rate is 67.7 per cent for those between 0 and 36 years of tenure.

Means and medians for survival time

To obtain means and medians for survival time, we run the following code:

```
print(km_analysis, print.rmean = TRUE)
```

Which shows Figure 6.18:

6.18

```
> print(km_analysis, print.rmean = TRUE)
Call: survfit(formula = Surv(LengthOfService, LeaverStatus) ~ Gender_text,
    data = Ch6_it)

   3 observations deleted due to missingness
                       n  events  rmean*  se(rmean)  median  0.95LCL  0.95UCL
Gender_text=Female  832     136    29.1      0.934      36       33       NA
Gender_text=Male    818      73    35.9      0.857      NA       36       NA
    * restricted mean with upper limit = 42
```

Looking at the output, we can see that the mean value for female survival completed years of service is 29.1 and the mean value for male survival time is higher at 35.9 completed years of service before leaving. Looking at the median values, we can see that the median survival period for females is 36 years; however, this is *NA*, or not a number for males because the R calculates medians returns no value if the chance of survival is over 50 per cent for all cases in the sample.

This indicates for us that there is a difference between the two groups. Is the difference statistically significant though? The answer lies in the overall comparisons table (Figure 6.19).

Overall comparisons

We compute the overall comparisons with the next line of code:

```
survdiff(Surv(LengthOfService, LeaverStatus) ~ Gender_text, data = Ch6_it)
```

Which produces Figure 6.19:

6.19

```
> survdiff(Surv(LengthOfService, LeaverStatus) ~ Gender_text, data = Ch6_it)
Call:
survdiff(formula = Surv(LengthOfService, LeaverStatus) ~ Gender_text,
    data = Ch6_it)

n=1650, 3 observations deleted due to missingness.

                      N  Observed  Expected  (O-E)^2/E  (O-E)^2/V
Gender_text=Female  832       136       103       10.7       21.6
Gender_text=Male    818        73       106       10.4       21.6
Chisq= 21.6 on 1 degrees of freedom, p= 3e-06
```

The chi-squared test is significant with the p-value much smaller than $p < 0.05$, and hence the result is statistically significant. Women are less likely to stay with the organization over time compared to men.

Survival function

Finally, we may want to see the result graphically. The next line takes the information in the km_analysis object and plots it:

```
ggsurvfit(km_analysis) + labs(x = "Years", y = "Survival probability")
```

Which produces Figure 6.20:

6.20

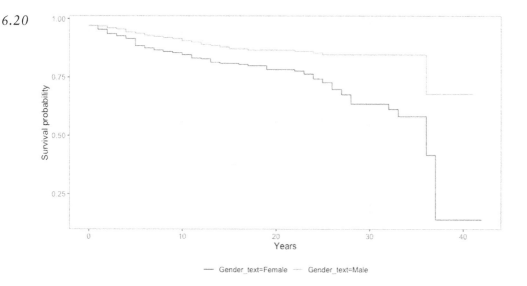

The plot shows us that the males and females start at a similar rate of survival. However, the difference between the groups expands as tenure increases. Just after the 20-year service mark, it is evident that the survival rate for females drops considerably while the male survival rate tends to level out. As we get towards 33 to 35 years of service, we can see that the chance of survival decreases greatly for both males and females, but to a greater degree for females. Finally, it is interesting to note that the chance of survival for males is greater than females at every point in tenure.

Having now completed both a logistic regression analysis on individual turnover and a Kaplan-Meier survival analysis on length of service for this data set, we are beginning to gather more information about stayers and leavers in this organization.

If we were to dig even further, we might consider:

- conducting a Cox Regression survival analysis to better understand the impact of age and country on length of service;
- gathering further information so we can separate employees who leave due to retirement, resignation or other termination from the analysis.

Example 5: predicting team turnover

Here, we predict team-level turnover using a linear regression model that includes six employee attitude/engagement survey measures (or composite – an average of responses to six survey questions), controlling for team size and including country as a measure.

We use the same team-level data set as above: *Ch6_Turnover_Team_Data.xlsx*. The data looks like this:

1 Team identifier (unique team number).

2 Team size (number of people in the team).

3 Team turnover 2014 (separation rate between 0 and 1).

4 Country (1 = UK; 2 = United States; 3 = Canada; 4 = Spain).

5 SURVEY: ENGAGEMENT items COMBO (composite engagement percentage across the team).

6 SURVEY: TeamLeader Rating (composite team leader percentage across the team).

7 SURVEY: CSR rating (composite corporate social responsibility percentage across the team).

8 SURVEY: Drive for Performance (composite percentage team score on perceived 'Drive for performance' percentage).

9 SURVEY: Performance, Development and Reward (composite percentage team score on perceived fairness of performance, development and reward across the team).

10 SURVEY: Work–Life Balance (composite percentage team score on perceived work–life balance across the team).

11 UK dummy variable (0 = not UK; 1 = UK).

12 USA dummy variable (0 = not United States; 1 = United States).

13 Canada dummy variable (0 = not Canada; 1 = Canada).

14 Spain dummy variable (0 = not Spain; 1 = Spain).

Because the team turnover variable is a continuous variable, we will use OLS multiple linear regression. It is important to remember that, at any point, if you are unsure which method to use, refer back to Table 3.4 in Chapter 3.

As the country variable is a categorical variable and because we are using linear regression we need to include the pre-prepared dummy variables in the analysis. You will see above that the last four variables indicate whether the countries are UK, United States, Canada or Spain; in each of these country columns a 1 indicates that the team is from that country and a 0 indicates that the team is from another country. In our regression model, we will include three country dummy variables but exclude a reference category. Thus when a country dummy coefficient is presented in the output it is comparing that country with whatever reference country category we chose (by excluding it from the analysis). In the following model we will enter United States, UK and Spain dummy variables – remember that the exclusion of the Canada dummy variable makes this location the 'reference' category that the other countries are compared to.

Our model then looks like this:

Team Turnover =
$b_0 + b_1$(engagement) + b_2(teamleader) + b_3(CSR) +
b_4(Drive for performance) + b_5(PDR) + b_6(WLB) +
b_7(USA) + b_8(UK) + b_9(Spain)

To reiterate, we are using OLS multiple linear regression rather than binary logistic regression because our team-level turnover dependent variable is not a leaver versus stayer dichotomous variable, it is an interval-level measure that involves a percentage of team members who have left in the last year. Thus we can meaningfully explore linear relationships with this variable and use a multiple linear regression.

The code for this example is in the file *Ch6_example_5.R*. The first four lines load packages, set the working directory, and load the data.

```
if (!require("pacman")) install.packages("pacman")
pacman::p_load(readxl, dplyr, modelsummary, this.path, huxtable)
setwd(this.path::here())
Ch6_mreg <- read_excel("Ch6_Turnover_Team_Data.xlsx")
```

Next we estimate the regression model:

```
mod_6_5 <- lm(TeamSeparation ~ Engagement + TeamLeader +
SociallyResponsible +DriveForPerformance + PerfDevReward +
WLB + USAdummy + UKdummy + SpainDummy, data = Ch6_mreg)
```

And show the model summary:

```
summary(mod_6_5)
```

Which produces Figure 6.21:

6.21

```
> summary(mod_6_5)

Call:
lm(formula = TeamSeparation ~ Engagement + TeamLeader +
SociallyResponsible +
    DriveForPerformance + PerfDevReward + WLB + USAdummy + UKdummy +
    SpainDummy, data = Ch6_mreg)

Residuals:
      Min                1Q        Median            3Q            Max
  -0.29403          -0.11092      -0.01540       0.09768        0.52136

Coefficients:
                        Estimate    Std. Error    t value    Pr(>|t|)
(Intercept)             0.3949701    0.1464107      2.698     0.00757 **
Engagement             -0.0062110    0.0011424     -5.437     1.55e-07 ***
TeamLeader             -0.0005596    0.0010944     -0.511     0.60967
SociallyResponsible     0.0014334    0.0016452      0.871     0.38466
DriveForPerformance     0.0019808    0.0007626      2.597     0.01008 *
PerfDevReward           0.0014074    0.0017107      0.823     0.41163
WLB                    -0.0001195    0.0010594     -0.113     0.91027
USAdummy               -0.0452858    0.0401899     -1.127     0.26117
UKdummy                -0.0545554    0.0412445     -1.323     0.18742
SpainDummy             -0.0262757    0.0446710     -0.588     0.55705
---
Signif. codes:  0 '***' 0.001 '**' 0.01 '*' 0.05 '.' 0.1 ' ' 1

Residual standard error: 0.1608 on 202 degrees of freedom
Multiple R-squared: 0.2653,        Adjusted R-squared: 0.2326
F-statistic: 8.106 on 9 and 202 DF, p-value: 3.043e-10
```

Looking at the model summary above, we can see that the (Multiple) R-square is 0.265, meaning that 26.5 per cent of the variance in team turnover is accounted for by its shared relationship with all of the independent variables in the model.

Looking at the regression F-statistic which tests the significance of how well the model predicts variation in team turnover, we can see that the regression ANOVA F-value is 8.105, with associated degrees of freedom of 9 and 202. These parameters give a significance level of p < 0.001. So we would say it is less than 0.001, which means there is much less than 1 in 1,000 chance that we would find this pattern of shared variance (between the team turnover and the independent variables) by chance alone. Hence the model is significant.

We will examine the independent variables more closely when we put the unstand-ardized and standardized coefficients in a table with the following lines of code:

```
mod1 <- modelsummary(mod_6_5, output = "modelsummary_list")
mod2 <- modelsummary(mod_6_5, output = "modelsummary_list", standardize
= "basic")
```

```
models <- list(
    "Unstandardized" = mod1,
    "Standardized" = mod2)

modelsummary(models, stars = TRUE, statistic = NULL, output =
'huxtable')
```

In the first line, we define *mod1*. For each, we ask the *modelsummary* program to obtain the summary of the model we estimated, namely *mod_6_5*. This will result in *mod1* having the unstandardized coefficients, just like in Figure 6.20. In the second line, we define *mod2*. It is almost identical, but we ask the *modelsummary* program to obtain the standardized coefficients. In the next lines, we put the two summaries (unstandardized and standardized) in a list, and give them names *Unstandardized* or *Standardized*. In the last set of lines, we ask the *modelsummary* program to show *mod1* and *mod2* side-by-side in a table. This results in Figure 6.22:

6.22

	Unstandardized	Standardized
(Intercept)	0.395**	0.000**
Engagement	-0.006***	-0.448***
TeamLeader	-0.001	-0.049
SociallyResponsible	0.001	0.080
DriveForPerformance	0.002*	0.192*
PerfDevReward	0.001	0.090
WLB	0.000	-0.010
USAdummy	-0.045	-0.118
UKdummy	-0.055	-0.128
SpainDummy	-0.026	-0.063
Num.Obs.	212	212
R2	0.265	0.265
R2 Adj.	0.233	0.233
AIC	-161.5	-161.5
BIC	-124.6	-124.6
Log.Lik.	91.774	91.774
F	8.106	8.106
RMSE	0.16	0.16

+ p < 0.1, * p < 0.05, ** p < 0.01, *** p < 0.001

Now, looking at the significance value of the coefficients, we can see that the *Engagement* variable is significant at $p < 0.001$; and that *DriveForPerformance* is significant at $p < 0.05$. Teams with higher engagement have lower turnover and those with higher perception of a drive for performance have higher turnover.

Further investigation would be needed here to explore whether having too high an emphasis on a 'drive for performance' culture could foster team norms and behaviours that could end up making people want to leave.

Modelling the costs of turnover and the business case for action

In our logistic regression example presented above, we realized that gender plays a role in accounting for turnover across our global organization. In that model, when we included lots of our controls (in the form of additional independent variables) we managed to account for 5.6 per cent of turnover across our organization. You will recall that the turnover rate in the organization is 12.8 per cent. If we wanted to translate this into some numbers that executives may pay attention to, we could work out what is the average cost of replacing individuals who leave, work out the total cost of turnover in our organization and then make a rough estimate in £ or $ of how much we are accounting for with 12.8 per cent. Then, we could go further and isolate the monetary cost of any particular factor that we find to be important. For example, if we find that gender accounts for 2.4 per cent of variation in our turnover statistics, we can work out in monetary terms what the gender effect on turnover equates to in staff replacement costs.

We carry out more complex modelling activities in Chapter 10; however, in a simple analysis we can look at variables in isolation (that have been found to be significant in our model, such as gender) and conduct a simple logistic regression to get a general idea of the *potential* percentage of variance in turnover that each might loosely account for. For example, we could use 'gender' as the only independent variable and 'stayer or leaver' as the dependent variable; this will give us a rough idea of the total amount of variance in individual turnover that this particular factor could potentially account for.

For this example we will use the *Ch6_Individual_Turnover.xlsx* file, and continue the code below from the same example file. We will need to also load a new package.

```
Ch6_it <- read_excel("Ch6_Individual_Turnover.xlsx")
pacman::p_load(rcompanion)
```

We will also recode the gender variable to be more interpretable:

```
Ch6_it$Gender_text <- case_match(Ch6_it$Gender, 0 ~ "Female", 1 ~ "Male")
Ch6_it$Gender_text <- as.factor(Ch6_it$Gender_text)
```

We can then specify and estimate the logistic regression, specifying gender as the only independent variable:

```
logit_reg <- glm(LeaverStatus ~ Gender_text, data = Ch6_it,
family = "binomial")
```

Omnibus tests of model coefficients

We can examine the overall fit of the model with the next line of code:

```
nagelkerke(logit_reg, restrictNobs = TRUE)
```

Which produces Figure 6.23:

6.23
```
> nagelkerke(logit_reg, restrictNobs = TRUE)
$Models

Model: "glm, LeaverStatus ~ Gender_text, binomial, Ch6_it"
 Null: "glm, LeaverStatus ~ 1, binomial, fit$model"

$Pseudo.R.squared.for.model.vs.null
                             Pseudo.R.squared
McFadden                            0.0166162
Cox and Snell (ML)                  0.0125489
Nagelkerke (Cragg and Uhler)        0.0235734

$Likelihood.ratio.test
 Df.diff                LogLik.diff        Chisq         p.value
      -1                    -10.418       20.837      5.0014e-06

$Number.of.observations

Model:1650
Null: 1650

$Messages
[1] "Note: For models fit with REML, these statistics are based on
refitting with ML"

$Warnings
[1] "None"
```

We have an index of how good our model is at accounting for turnover across our organization. Here we see that our model chi square is 20.837 and this is deemed to be significant (p < 0.001). This shows us that the logistic regression model fits the data well enough to be considered significant.

Model summary

Figure 6.22 also shows R-square statistics. As we have discussed in previous sections, our R-square figure is an indication of the degree of variation in our dependent variable that is accounted for by the variation in our predictor variables. The Nagelkerke

R-square (referred to as a pseudo R-square) is a figure that most closely equates with the R-square figure in linear regression and this shows that, by just looking at gender, we can account for 2.4 per cent of turnover across our organization.

Variables in the equation

With the next line of code, we show the model results:

```
summary(logit_reg)
```

This results in Figure 6.24:

6.24

```
> summary(logit_reg)

Call:
glm(formula = LeaverStatus ~ Gender_text, family = "binomial",
    data = Ch6_it)

Coefficients:
                  Estimate  Std. Error  z value     Pr(>|z|)
(Intercept)       -1.63269     0.09375  -17.415     < 2e-16 ***
Gender_textMale   -0.69023     0.15437   -4.471     7.78e-06 ***
---
Signif. codes:  0 '***' 0.001 '**' 0.01 '*' 0.05 '.' 0.1 ' ' 1

(Dispersion parameter for binomial family taken to be 1)

    Null deviance: 1254.0   on 1649   degrees of freedom
Residual deviance: 1233.2   on 1648   degrees of freedom
  (3 observations deleted due to missingness)
AIC: 1237.2

Number of Fisher Scoring iterations: 5
```

And we can also show the log odds coefficients and odds ratios in a table:

```
mod = list("Log Odds" = logit_reg, "Odds Ratio" = logit_reg)
modelsummary(mod, exponentiate = c(FALSE, TRUE), statistic = NULL, stars
= TRUE, output = 'huxtable')
```

Which generates the table in Figure 6.25:

6.25

	Log Odds	Odds Ratio
(Intercept)	-1.633***	0.195***
Gender_textMale	-0.690***	0.501***
Num.Obs.	1650	1650
AIC	1237.2	1237.2
BIC	1248.0	1248.0
Log.Lik.	-616.583	-616.583
F	19.992	19.992
RMSE	0.33	0.33

+ p < 0.1, * p < 0.05, ** p < 0.01, *** p < 0.001

This table tells us that gender has a significant impact (p<0.001) on turnover and the odds ratio on the probability that the individual is a leaver versus a stayer, which is 0.501.

The important item to pull out of this analysis, though (and probably the one that everyone will understand), is that gender may well have as much as a 2.4 per cent impact on individual turnover – and if someone (someone like you?) were to recommend an intervention that would remove the gender portion of turnover and retain women at least as well as the organization can retain men, then the organization could potentially reduce turnover by 2.4 per cent.

Just looking at this statistic, let's say that our total cost of turnover is something like £4 million including all of the separation, replacement and training costs (as outlined at the beginning of this chapter). If we could reduce this by 2.4 per cent then this would save £96,000. With this knowledge, we could potentially use this information to build a business case for making some investment into trying to understand and deal with the factors that may be leading women across the globe to be more likely to leave than men. As a caveat to this, from the above analysis, in exploring these factors it is likely that we will need to consider whether there are gender differences in performance ratings that tend to be given to men versus women. The reason this would be important is that performance appraisal ratings are also found to be an important predictor of individual turnover (see above) and therefore there may be some key link between gender, performance ratings and voluntary turnover.

More robust modelling

Strictly speaking, if we wanted to be much more robust in modelling the potential cost savings from our turnover driver analysis, we should explore the percentage of variance in turnover that each factor might account for: e.g. how much variance in turnover does gender account for after controlling for performance appraisal ratings? To do this we would just find the Nagelkerke R-square figure when performance appraisal rating is set as a predictor of individual turnover (coincidently also 0.024) and then we see how much this figure increases when we include gender as a predictor. When we do this the Nagelkerke R-square figure increases to 0.039, thus gender uniquely accounts for 1.5 per cent of individual turnover (0.039–0.024= 0.015). Using these techniques we can identify and attempt to partition the potential variance (and cost) in turnover that can be isolated with each factor when taking into account other possible causes of turnover. With this information we can then potentially translate this information into £ (or $, €, etc) potential cost savings that dealing with these factors could bring.

One further caveat here. In Chapter 11 we discuss more complex forms of analysis and address the importance of testing for interactions in our models. As well as running a turnover model that includes both gender and performance in predicting turnover, we might want to see whether there is an interaction between performance ratings and gender in predicting turnover. For example, is a 1 grade differential in a performance appraisal rating more or less important in accounting for leaver status with women compared to men? We discuss interactions further in Chapter 11.

Summary

You can see that, by using the methods outlined in this chapter, it is possible to determine predictors of both individual and team turnover. Importantly, from our analysis we can then use this information to identify factors that could reduce turnover costs; at the same time our analysis could also eliminate factors (such as country differences in our example) that on the surface could otherwise be considered as being important. When we have information about or potential drivers of turnover we can isolate the unique variance that each factor might play in accounting for turnover and translate this into a potential cost saving (assuming we have an estimate of our current staff turnover costs) that focusing on these 'levers' could result in. This information can be used to build a business case for a turnover intervention programme that could make a real difference to the organization's bottom line. For further examples of possible ways to carry out modelling with regression analysis, especially in predicting actual and potential turnover probabilities, see Chapter 10 on business applications.

References

CIPD (2024) Employee turnover and retention, www.cipd.org/uk/knowledge/factsheets/turnover-retention-factsheet/ (archived at https://perma.cc/2PJH-4AQS)
Coolican, H (2009) *Research Methods and Statistics in Psychology*, Hodder Education, Abingdon

Field, A (2017) *Discovering Statistics Using IBM SPSS Statistics*, 5th edn, Sage, London

Griffeth, R W and Hom, P W (2001) *Retaining Valued Employees*, Sage, London

Mercer (2023) How much turnover is too much? www.imercer.com/articleinsights/workforce-turnover-trends (archived at https://perma.cc/338K-E9W7)

Moore-Bridger, B and Lynch, R (2014) The formula for England World Cup success, according to Professor Stephen Hawking, *London Evening Standard*, www.standard.co.uk/news/uk/stephen-hawking-suarez-england-world-cup-win-9444698.html (archived at https://perma.cc/3MZY-KC2P)

Watkins, M (2013) *The First 90 Days: Strategies for getting up to speed faster and smarter*, Harvard Business Review Press, Boston

07

Case study 4

Predicting employee performance

In response to volatile markets and heightened economic uncertainty, organizations have placed increased emphasis on individual, team and organizational performance (Bach, 2012). Indeed, one could consider the HR analytic ability to predict future performance as the holy grail of HR analytics. The ability to identify, predict, understand and potentially influence high levels of employee or team performance can be considered critical to improving organizational performance and driving people strategy.

Performance management in organizations has evolved over the last 20 years from a stand-alone performance appraisal process to a more integrated system of measures and processes, including customer feedback, sales figures, team productivity and 360-degree feedback, to name just a few. The trend has also been to move responsibility for performance management away from the HR function towards line managers. Although this move has given line managers the opportunity to take more responsibility for the development and performance of their team members, it has introduced greater variation in the employee experience, thus placing greater emphasis on the strength of the performance management system and line managers' competence in and attitude to their people-management responsibilities (Brown and Hirsh, 2011; Armstrong and Baron, 2005).

The downside of this decentralized process is that it is often difficult to get one single view of the performance of all teams and individuals across the organization and across all of the indicators of performance. Indeed, how do senior leaders know who is doing well across all of these, what they are doing right and where they should invest their, often limited, learning and development funds to ensure the greatest return? How do we use this information to make the biggest difference to the bottom line?

In this chapter, we cover:

- What can we measure to indicate performance?
- What methods might we use?
- Practical examples from issues in real organizations.
- Ethical considerations in performance data.

What can we measure to indicate performance?

One of the key challenges with conducting analyses of performance with HR data is deciding what sort of performance to try to predict. One might assume that the annual or biannual performance appraisal rating should be something we focus on trying to predict. However, while there might be good reasons why this is something we could try to do, there are other types of performance indices that can also provide some extremely useful information. What is important here is to remember that we need to not only measure performance, but to think about what measure we might have that may be a predictor of performance. Table 7.1 gives some indication of the types of measures we could be considering.

TABLE 7.1 Team and individual performance measures

Level	Example measures of performance	Example measures of what might influence performance
Team	Employee opinion survey output (team engagement index, team leadership index), store/branch customer feedback, customer loyalty, customer reinvestment/repeat business, staff turnover.	Team function, team leader competence; composite measures of individual team member attitude/engagement survey measures.
Individual	Performance appraisal rating, behavioural rating, sales performance figures, checkout scan rate, individual customer feedback, peer feedback, call rates, call loads.	Gender, age, tenure, job strain, sickness absence, pulse survey data (see Chapter 9 for a discussion of pulse surveys), hours worked, job satisfaction, person-organization fit, perceived organization support, perceptions of justice, salary, base country.

With the move away from manufacturing industries to the service sector, customer satisfaction has become a major measure that we could focus on as a performance measure. In the service sector customer satisfaction, customer loyalty and the likelihood that customers reinvest could be considered very strong indicators of performance, because these factors ultimately impact the bottom line. Many organizations routinely collect customer satisfaction data; however, it is rare that these organizations have the HR analytic capability to be able to fully understand and explore what factors might predict these key performance outcomes.

Whilst measures such as sickness absence, staff turnover and engagement scores may not obviously be performance indices in a traditional sense, these indices are all performance measures of a kind. High sickness-absence rates, high staff turnover and low engagement will all be associated with a detrimental change in the organization's bottom line and are all things that a successful HR function will want to avoid. Therefore they can all be considered to be performance indices that we might want to try to analytically predict. We touch on sickness absence below, and we dealt with engagement in Chapter 5 and turnover in Chapter 6.

As we have discussed in previous chapters, sometimes information that we would want to include in our analytic model is not available at the individual level. As we discuss in Chapter 5 on engagement, individual engagement scores may not always be available due to the confidential nature of most employee opinion surveys. Also, with performance, it may not always be appropriate to judge performance at an individual level, especially when there may be teams involved in the work process. As such we might want to focus on team-level performance of some kind. The actual type of analysis and models that we can run will be dependent upon the availability of the data that we have, and organizations will differ fundamentally in this. For example, an organization that involves some form of selling could focus on getting new customers and the amount of revenue generated directly from sales. A call centre, for example, would focus on call rates, call loads and call duration.

What methods might we use?

In analysing performance, the keys thing we are looking for are relationships and predictors. We might want to answer questions along the lines of:

- What are the characteristics of a high-performing individual or team?
- Where can we invest money that is likely to show an increase in customer loyalty?
- What are the key employee characteristics, capabilities and attributes that make a high performer?

The methods we will use in this chapter are as follows:

- Multiple linear regression: this allows us to analyse a number of independent variables (for example, gender, age, team leader, country location) to see what, if any, impact they have on allowing us to predict a dependent variable (for example, performance rating) by forming a 'best fit' model. The multiple linear regression will tell us the proportion of variance in the dependent variable that is accounted for by all the independent variables collectively, which independent variables have a significant impact on the dependent variable, and the relative 'weighting' of each dependent variable.

- Stepwise multiple linear regression: this will allow us to undertake a number of iterative steps to try to find the most economical (and parsimonious) model that best fits the data we have, by successively adding and removing important independent variables.

- Tracking over time using multiple linear regression: tracking the values of a dependent variable over time allows us to better establish patterns of behaviour in the data. For example: rather than predicting high or low performance ratings, we can predict what causes an *increase* or a *decrease* in performance ratings over time. This can be far more powerful when determining which interventions may be more effective in improving organizational performance.

- Using dummy variables in multiple linear regression: using dummy variables is a way of manipulating the data to enable us to indicate either the absence or presence of a particular characteristic or trait. For example, in the nominal level variable 'contractual status', which might have four categories, instead of having 1 = 'full-time permanent', 2 = 'full-time fixed-term contract', 3 = 'part-time permanent' and 4 = 'part-time temporary' as the values, we might have 'full-time permanent' as one dichotomous variable (i.e. one that has only two categories or values) and record the value as either a 0 or 1 (where full-time permanent is 1). This is a dummy variable. We might set up another 'full-time fixed-term contract' variable and record the value as either a 0 or 1, another for 'part-time permanent' and record the value as either a 0 or 1 and the fourth as 'part-time temporary' and record the value as either a 0 or 1. Importantly, these four dummy variables should cover the whole data set. Having these dummy variables greatly increases our options for data analysis.

Practical examples using multiple linear regression to predict performance

The nine examples below are all laid out in a similar manner. They use data sets based on real data from organizations in the financial services, manufacturing and retail sectors:

- Example 1: uses multiple linear regression to predict customer loyalty and reinvestment in a financial services organization.

- Example 2: uses multiple linear regression and combines customer survey data and pulse survey data to predict customer loyalty in a financial services organization.

- Example 3: uses multiple linear regression and combines performance appraisal data, sickness records and pulse survey data to predict individual performance in a manufacturing organization.

- Example 4: uses stepwise multiple linear regression to find the best model for predicting performance using combined performance appraisal data, sickness records and pulse survey data in a manufacturing organization.

- Example 5: tracks performance over time using stepwise regression and combined performance appraisal data, sickness records and pulse survey data in a manufacturing organization.

- Example 6: uses multiple linear regression to predict sickness absence using employee attitude scores in a manufacturing organization.

- Example 7: uses multiple regression to explore patterns of performance with employee profile data in a manufacturing organization.

- Example 8: uses data interrogation techniques and multiple linear regression to predict checkout scan rates from employee profile data in a retail organization.

- Example 9: uses dummy variables in multiple linear regression to determine the presence of high-performing age groups in predicting scan rates in a retail organization.

The examples listed focus on using multiple linear regression. This is because this is the best method for this type of analysis, where we are trying to predict a particular outcome – in our case, high performance. Because of this, some of the examples and methods may seem repetitive; however, we hope they provide a broad scope of what is possible with all the data available in the organization, and that they may provide inspiration for what you may do with the data in your organization.

Example 1a: using multiple linear regression to predict customer loyalty in a financial services organization

As we have seen in previous chapters, multiple regression can be used to model an independent variable and predict patterns of behaviour. In the example below, we will analyse customer input to try to understand what factors are most important in influencing customer satisfaction and customer loyalty. In this example, we have a data set based on the results of a customer satisfaction survey, which was sent out to customers who have been in contact with a sales person in a financial services organization.

Each customer was sent a survey that included seven questions, four of which specifically related to key sales-person competency elements:

1 The sales person understanding your needs (Sat1).

2 The sales person seems confident (Sat2).

3 The sales person has a recommendation (Sat3).

4 The sales person is knowledgeable (Sat4).

Here, customers were asked to grade the sales person on a scale of 1 to 5, where 1 was 'very dissatisfied' and 5 was 'very satisfied'.

The next two questions relate to loyalty and asked customers to put themselves on a scale of 1 to 5 where:

5 Likelihood of reinvesting (Custloyalty):

   – 1 = Definitely going to go elsewhere with my investments.

   – 2 = Thinking about going elsewhere with my money.

   – 3 = Not sure about where I will place my future investments.

   – 4 = Thinking about investing here again.

   – 5 = Definitely will invest here again.

6 How much they may or may not reinvest (InvestMore):

   – 1 = Definitely will not invest more than now here.

   – 2 = Unlikely to invest more than now here.

   – 3 = Planning to invest 0–50 per cent more than now in this organization.

   – 4 = Planning to invest 50–100 per cent more in this organization.

   – 5 = Going to double my investment or more in this organization.

The final question was about the gender of the sales person:

7 Sex of sales person: 1 = female; 2 = male.

The data set used includes responses from 2,507 customer surveys: *Ch7_customer_satisfaction.xlsx*.

So here we have two dependent variables, or desired outcomes, and we would like to understand whether there is anything we can do as an organization to improve those. The two dependent variables are: customer loyalty and reinvestment.

Using the same approach as in the engagement case study (Chapter 5), we would expect the model to look something like:

Customer Loyalty =

$a + b_1$ (understanding customer needs) + b_2 (sales confidence) +

b_3 (giving a recommendation) + b_4 (product knowledge) + b_5 (gender)

So we want to test whether customer loyalty is a function of any or a combination of the above five factors. Our model will also tell us which factors are the most important. Intuitively, it makes sense that if a customer felt as though a sales person understood their needs, was very confident, was able to provide a recommendation and had a high level of knowledge about their products then they would be more likely to feel a sense of loyalty. But which elements are most important? Which aspects should the organization invest in to maximize customer loyalty? And what part does gender play?

Our model should help us to answer these questions and help us to predict customer loyalty. The code for this example is in the file *Ch7_example_1a_1b.R*. We first load packages, set the working directory, and load the data by running the code below. You can run each line of code by highlighting it and clicking the *Run* button, or through the keyboard shortcut *Control + Enter* (Windows and Linux) / *Command + Return* (MacOS). The first time you run this code, it may take a few minutes to download all of the required packages from the internet.

```
if (!require("pacman")) install.packages("pacman")
setwd(dirname(rstudioapi::getActiveDocumentContext()$path))
pacman::p_load(readxl, dplyr, modelsummary, kableExtra)
Ch7_ex1 <- read_excel("Ch7_customer_satisfaction.xlsx")
```

We then define a multiple regression model with *Custloyalty* as the dependent variable and the five independent variables (sales person understanding your needs, sales person seems confident, sales person has a recommendation, sales person is knowledgeable, sex of sales person). To do this, run the code below:

```
mod_1_a <- lm(Custloyalty ~ Sat1 + Sat2 + Sat3 + Sat4 +
SexOfSalesperson, data = Ch7_ex1)
summary(mod_1_a)
```

This produces the following output (Figure 7.1):

7.1

```
> summary(mod_1_a)

Call:
lm(formula = Custloyalty ~ Sat1 + Sat2 + Sat3 + Sat4 + SexOfSalesperson,
    data = Ch7_ex1)

Residuals:
     Min      1Q  Median      3Q     Max
 -3.8954 -0.5381  0.1046  0.5954  2.6188

Coefficients:
                  Estimate   Std. Error   t value   Pr(>|t|)
(Intercept)        1.85346      0.13022    14.233   <2e-16 ***
Sat1               0.32431      0.03577     9.067   <2e-16 ***
Sat2              -0.03400      0.03339    -1.018   0.3087
Sat3               0.28810      0.02965     9.716   <2e-16 ***
Sat4               0.05275      0.03170     1.664   0.0963 .
SexOfSalesperson  -0.11381      0.05080    -2.240   0.0252 *
---
Signif. codes:  0 '***' 0.001 '**' 0.01 '*' 0.05 '.' 0.1 ' ' 1

Residual standard error: 0.8889 on 1830 degrees of freedom
  (671 observations deleted due to missingness)
Multiple R-squared: 0.3257, Adjusted R-squared: 0.3238
F-statistic: 176.7 on 5 and 1830 DF, p-value: < 2.2e-16
```

Figure 7.1 tells us that the R-square is 0.3257. You may recall from our discussion on multiple regression in Chapter 3 that the R-square is the square of the multiple regression coefficient. Simply put, R shows the coefficient between the dependent variable and all the predictor variables together. So, the greater the R-square, the more the predictor variables are jointly predictive of the dependent variable. If you multiply it by 100, it tells you the percentage of variance in the dependent variable that is accounted for by the other variables. More technically, it is the percentage of variance accounted for in our dependent variable when taking into account its shared linear relationship with our independent variables (whilst taking into account the interrelationships between the independent variables). So, in this case, the R-square is 0.3257, so we can say that 32.57 per cent, or almost one-third, of the variance in expressions of customer loyalty is accounted for by the particular combination of predictor variables used here.

The regression F-statistic in Figure 7.1 is 176.7, with associated degrees of freedom of 5 and 1830. As mentioned in other chapters, these figures provide the parameters for us to determine the statistical significance in a statistical table such as those found in most textbooks. R has calculated the statistical significance for us to be close to zero. So we could say that our significance level reached has a p-value of 0.001, which means there is less than 1 in 1,000 chance that we would find this pattern of shared variance (between the customer loyalty scores and the other survey questions) by chance alone. Hence the model is significant.

Now we are aware that the model is significant, we need to review the coefficients table to ascertain which of our independent variables have an impact on customer loyalty, to what extent and also in what direction (i.e. some may potentially improve customer loyalty while others may decrease customer loyalty). We can produce a nice-looking table of coefficients with the following lines of code:

```
mod1 <- modelsummary(mod_1_a, output = "modelsummary_list")
mod2 <- modelsummary(mod_1_a, output = "modelsummary_list", standardize
= "basic")
models <- list(
"Unstandardized" = mod1,
"Standardized" = mod2)
modelsummary(models, stars = TRUE, statistic = NULL, output =
'huxtable')
```

We've seen almost exactly the same code in Chapter 6, and it's no surprise that once we find code to be useful, we can copy and paste it, and use it for a different application by changing out model or variable names. The code above produces the following table (Figure 7.2):

7.2

	Unstandardized	Standardized
(Intercept)	1.853***	0.000***
Sat1	0.324***	0.307***
Sat2	-0.034	-0.030
Sat3	0.288***	0.290***
Sat4	0.053+	0.048+
SexOfSalesperson	-0.114*	-0.043*
Num.Obs.	1836	1836
R2	0.326	0.326
R2 Adj.	0.324	0.324
AIC	4785.7	4785.7
BIC	4824.3	4824.3
Log.Lik.	-2385.851	-2385.851
RMSE	0.89	0.89

+ p < 0.1, * p < 0.05, ** p < 0.01, *** p < 0.001

Using our knowledge of levels of significance and looking down the list of coefficients, it appears that three of the five predictor variables significantly predict customer loyalty; most important are *Sat1* (sales person understanding your needs) and *Sat3* (sales person has a recommendation). *Sat2* (sales person confidence) and *Sat3* (sales person knowledge) have no significant impact.

From this example, it would be reasonable to make the recommendation to invest in helping sales people to better understand customer needs by, for example, listening and making the customer feel as though they have been listened to, asking questions and keeping appropriate records. Also, training sales people in how to be confident in making the right recommendations would be likely to result in a positive return on investment. Because the data shows the sales person ID, it is possible to go back to the raw data to identify who is skilled at making recommendations and making the customer feel as though they have been understood, and share those skills with others in the team.

Although the result for *SexOfSalesperson* was less significant with a Beta = -0.043, $p < 0.05$, or p is less than 5 in 100, we can say that there is more than a 95 out of 100 chance that the variance in customer loyalty is linked to the gender of the sales person. Because the Beta coefficient is negative, and because we used the following in the data set:

1 = female; 2 = male.

then we can say that the higher this number, the lower the customer loyalty, or that customers with a female sales person are more likely to be loyal than customers of a male sales person.

We can also rewrite our model raw regression formula with the *b* values:

Customer loyalty =
1.853 + 0.324 (understanding customer needs) –
0.034 (sales confidence) + 0.288 (giving a recommendation) +
0.053 (product knowledge) – 0.114 (gender)

SNAPSHOT HIDDEN GEM

Understanding customer needs and having a recommendation are the two key drivers of customer loyalty indices – interestingly, women sales advisers keep their customers more than men do.

Example 1b: using multiple linear regression to predict customer reinvestment in a financial services organization

Using the same data set, let's see if there is anything we can glean to try to understand what might help to increase the level of reinvestment for our customers:

Customer reinvestment =

a + b_1 (understanding customer needs) + b_2 (sales confidence) +

b_3 (giving a recommendation) + b_4 (product knowledge) + b_5 (gender)

Given the similarity in the task, we can make minor adjustments of the code above to complete this task. The following code follows on from above in the file *Ch7_example_1a_1b.R*.

```
mod_1_b <- lm(INvestMore ~ Sat1 + Sat2 + Sat3 + Sat4 + SexOfSalesperson,
data = Ch7_ex1)
summary(mod_1_b)
mod3 <- modelsummary(mod_1_b, output = "modelsummary_list")
mod4 <- modelsummary(mod_1_b, output = "modelsummary_list", standardize
= "basic")
models <- list(
  "Unstandardized" = mod3,
  "Standardized" = mod4)
modelsummary(models, stars = TRUE, statistic = NULL, output =
'huxtable')
```

In the code above, we have changed the name of the dependent variable (*INvestMore*) and created a distinct object to store the multiple regression results (*mod_1_b*). We also stored the coefficients in objects with a distinct name compared to the example above, (*mod3*, *mod4*), which is good practice to keep things organized. Of course, you are free to come up with more descriptive names for objects than *mod_1_b*, *mod3*, and *mod4*.

The summary of the multiple regression model produces Figure 7.3:

7.3

```
> summary(mod_1_b)

Call:
lm(formula = INvestMore ~ Sat1 + Sat2 + Sat3 + Sat4 + SexOfSalesperson,
    data = Ch7_ex1)

Residuals:
      Min       1Q    Median       3Q      Max
  -2.50480  -0.39996  0.01152  0.36830  2.59131
Coefficients:
                    Estimate   Std. Error  t value    Pr(>|t|)
(Intercept)          1.74047      0.11096   15.685    < 2e-16 ***
Sat1                 0.17566      0.03035    5.789    8.37e-09 ***
Sat2                 0.02952      0.02853    1.035    0.301
Sat3                 0.13995      0.02526    5.540    3.48e-08 ***
Sat4                 0.01164      0.02713    0.429    0.668
SexOfSalesperson    -0.01958      0.04326   -0.453    0.651
---
Signif. codes: 0 '***' 0.001 '**' 0.01 '*' 0.05 '.' 0.1 ' ' 1

Residual standard error: 0.746 on 1766 degrees of freedom
   (735 observations deleted due to missingness)
Multiple R-squared: 0.1704, Adjusted R-squared: 0.168
F-statistic: 72.53 on 5 and 1766 DF, p-value: < 2.2e-16
```

Figure 7.3 shows that the R-square = 0.17, or that 17 per cent, approximately one-sixth, of the variance in customer reinvestment is accounted for by the predictor variables used here.

Looking at the F-statistic, its value is 72.53, with associated degrees of freedom of 5 and 1766 and the significance level of close to zero. So we could say that $p < 0.001$, which means there is less than 1 in 1,000 chance that we would find this pattern of shared variance (between the customer reinvestment scores and the other survey questions) by chance alone. Hence the model is significant.

So, while the model only accounts for one-sixth of the output (customer reinvestment), it is significant and hence we can be confident that recommendations we make on the basis of this model should impact the customer reinvestment intentions (but it is important to set the expectations in such a way that the impact will be conservative; see Chapter 10, page 356).

Knowing that the model is significant, as in the customer loyalty example, we can now look at the coefficients to ascertain which predictor variables have the most potential impact. When we use the *modelsummary* program to produce a table, we obtain Figure 7.4:

7.4

	Unstandardized	Standardized
(Intercept)	1.740***	0.000***
Sat1	0.176***	0.219***
Sat2	0.030	0.034
Sat3	0.140***	0.186***
Sat4	0.012	0.014
SexOfSalesperson	-0.020	-0.010
Num.Obs.	1772	1772
R2	0.170	0.170
R2 Adj.	0.168	0.168
AIC	3998.1	3998.1
BIC	4036.4	4036.4
Log.Lik.	-1992.030	-1992.030
RMSE	0.74	0.74

+ p < 0.1, * p < 0.05, ** p < 0.01, *** p < 0.001

Looking down the list of coefficients, we can see that the same two satisfaction variables seem to have an impact, i.e. the sales person understanding your needs (*Sat1*) and the sales person having a recommendation (*Sat3*). The model then looks like this:

Customer reinvestment =
1.740 + 0.176 (understanding customer needs) +
0.030 (sales confidence) + 0.140 (giving a recommendation) +
0.012 (product knowledge) – 0.020 (gender)

Interestingly, gender does not have a significant impact here, so although customers of female sales people are more likely to express loyalty and indicate an intention to stay with the financial organization (thus continue investment), it does not necessarily mean that they will invest more money on top of what they already have there.

So the key findings here can be updated as follows:

SNAPSHOT HIDDEN GEM

Understanding customer needs and having a recommendation are the two key drivers of customer reinvestment indices.

Example 2: using multiple linear regression to predict customer loyalty

In this example we use the same multiple regression analysis technique, but we link data from three sources: the customer survey data used in the above example, including details of which sales person was linked to which respondent; HR employee data found in the employee database; and results of a small employee engagement 'pulse' survey, which did actually track employees in their responses. This enables us to explore whether engaged employees might have greater sales success and also whether any employee profile details have any impact.

It is important to note in the example here that the organization is using a limited engagement survey because it represents data included in a company 'health check'. In this case it actually identifies employees when asking survey questions (though this is not a comprehensive engagement survey) and only limited engagement information is available; however, being able to identify individuals in engagement questions provides particularly useful opportunities to link data sets. Here we have aggregated customer loyalty data at the individual sales-person level – meaning that we have averaged any customer loyalty responses for each sales person (where more than one customer answered a survey for each sales adviser, multiple responses were answered). Often when we combine data sets and choose to analyse data at a particular level, we may have to aggregate data linked to this particular level if there are multiple data points associated with one single variable. Here the employee is the 'level' that we are interested in and we can have multiple customer survey responses from multiple customers for each employee; thus we need to aggregate these multiple customer responses to get one customer score per employee (this actually has the potential to be a 'multi-level' data set-up, which we discuss further in Chapter 11).

The data set used in this example is *Ch7_aggregate_sales_customer_loyalty.xlsx*.

Predicting aggregated customer loyalty scores for each sales adviser

We use the following three survey questions, for which employees were asked to answer on a scale of 1 to 5 (where 1 = strongly agree and 5 = strongly disagree):

1 My manager gives me useful feedback (*q*Man1).

2 I would recommend this organization as a place to work (*q*Eng1).

3 I am really engaged in my work (*q*Eng2).

We also have HR data linked to each employee included in the model as follows:

4 Sex (1 = female, 2 = male).

5 Manager status (0 = non-manager, 1 = manager).

6 Age (actual number).

7 Talent 2014 (0 = not key talent, 1 = key talent).

So, in this multiple regression example, the dependent variable is aggregate customer loyalty scores and the multiple regression model would look something like this:

Customer Loyalty Mean =

$a + b_1$ (Key Talent) + b_2 (Sex) + b_3 (Engaged in my work) +

b_4 (Age) + b_5 (Manager {or not}) + b_6 (Manager gives useful feedback) +

b_7 (recommend this organization)

The example code for this analysis is in the file *Ch7_example_2.R*. We will set the working directory, and load required packages and data.

```
if (!require("pacman")) install.packages("pacman")
pacman::p_load(readxl, dplyr, modelsummary, this.path, huxtable)
setwd(this.path::here())
Ch7_ex2 <- read_excel("Ch7_aggregate_sales_customer_loyalty.xlsx")
```

Next, we'll define and estimate the multiple regression model:

```
mod_2 <- lm(Custloyalty_mean ~ Talent2014 + Sex + qEng2 + Age + Manager +
qMan1 + qEng1, data = Ch7_ex2)
```

We will next look at the model summary:

```
summary(mod_2)
```

This generates Figure 7.5:

7.5

```
> summary(mod_2)

Call:
lm(formula = Custloyalty_mean ~ Talent2014 + Sex + qEng2 + Age +
    Manager + qMan1 + qEng1, data = Ch7_ex2)

Residuals:
     Min       1Q   Median       3Q      Max
  -2.8052  -0.4353   0.0461   0.5086   1.5346

Coefficients:
              Estimate  Std. Error   t value   Pr(>|t|)
(Intercept)   3.794133    0.369719    10.262   < 2e-16  ***
Talent2014    0.007077    0.136212     0.052    0.95860
Sex          -0.046750    0.112210    -0.417    0.67725
qEng2         0.141283    0.050783     2.782    0.00575  **
Age          -0.003753    0.005972    -0.628    0.53021
Manager       0.195245    0.128852     1.515    0.13077
qMan1        -0.048283    0.043760    -1.103    0.27077
qEng1        -0.010786    0.050732    -0.213    0.83178
---
Signif. codes:  0 '***' 0.001 '**' 0.01 '*' 0.05 '.' 0.1 ' ' 1

Residual standard error: 0.7291 on 297 degrees of freedom
  (269 observations deleted due to missingness)
Multiple R-squared: 0.04274,  Adjusted R-squared: 0.02018
F-statistic: 1.894 on 7 and 297 DF, p-value: 0.07013
```

In Figure 7.5 we can see that the multiple R-square = 0.043, or that 4.3 per cent of the variance in customer loyalty is accounted for by the predictor variables used here. Looking at the F-statistic, which tests the significance of how well the model predicts variation in customer loyalty, there are some important indicators to pull out. First, its value is 1.894, with associated degrees of freedom of 7 and 297 and a significance level of 0.070. As discussed in Chapter 3, in statistical analysis, we look for something to have a significance level of less than 0.05 ($p < 0.05$) in order to determine whether it is significant. This is not the case here, so we do not recommend you use this model to make recommendations.

It is important to be aware that models will not always be significant. A possible reason for this result not to be significant is that the number of cases is much smaller than in other examples. This is because we could only analyse rows or cases for which we had information on all three areas, i.e. customer survey, employee pulse survey and complete HR system data. As the pulse surveys (see page 313) are often only sent to a small random sample of employees, this is the most likely cause for the greatly reduced number of rows (or cases) that are included in the analysis.

Another reason may be that there is simply no relationship here, which can be disappointing at the end of an analysis. However, this is still a result and it still means something. It tells us that this is not the right model to use to predict customer loyalty. We can look at the coefficients on their own by examining the *modelsummary* output:

```
mod1 <- modelsummary(mod_2, output = "modelsummary_list")
mod2 <- modelsummary(mod_2, output = "modelsummary_list", standardize =
"basic")
models <- list(
"Unstandardized" = mod1,
"Standardized" = mod2)
modelsummary(models, stars = TRUE, statistic = NULL, output =
'huxtable')
```

This produces Figure 7.6:

7.6

	Unstandardized	Standardized
(Intercept)	3.794***	0.000***
Talent2014	0.007	0.003
Sex	-0.047	-0.024
qEng2	0.141**	0.196**
Age	-0.004	-0.037
Manager	0.195	0.090
qMan1	-0.048	-0.065
qEng1	-0.011	-0.015
Num.Obs.	305	305
R2	0.043	0.043
R2 Adj.	0.020	0.020
AIC	682.7	682.7
BIC	716.2	716.2
Log.Lik.	-332.363	-332.363
RMSE	0.72	0.72

+ p < 0.1, * p < 0.05, ** p < 0.01, *** p < 0.001

Looking at the list of coefficients, the variable *qEng2* (I am really engaged in my work) appears to correlate with customer loyalty because the significance value is less than $p < 0.05$, so that is something worth exploring further in other models.

SNAPSHOT HIDDEN GEM

Not all results are significant. Even when they are not, the data is still telling us something. In some cases it will suggest what we might want to investigate further.

Example 3: using multiple linear regression to predict individual performance

In this example, we use a data set of 626 employees containing their performance appraisal ratings, sickness absence records and scores from the annual employee attitude survey from a manufacturing organization. The data, taken over a period of two years, includes the following:

- Employee attitude survey data collected in November 2014.
- Performance appraisal data collected in January 2014.
- Performance appraisal data collected in January 2015.
- Number of days' sickness absence taken per employee during 2014.

Here, the HR analyst has linked data from the two sources and constructed composite survey measurements (average measures derived from multiple questionnaire items) using the unique employee ID.

We introduce some new terms here and a brief description for each is given below (for more information on engagement survey questions and their validity, see Chapter 5):

- *Perceived organizational support (POS)*: this is the degree to which employees believe that their organization values their contributions, cares about their well-being and fulfils socio-emotional needs (Eisenberger et al, 1986).

- *Distributive justice perceptions*: this is fostered where rewards and outcomes are perceived to be consistent with implicit norms for allocation, such as equity or equality (Colquitt, 2001).

- *Procedural justice perceptions*: this is fostered through voice during a decision-making process or influence over the outcome or by adherence to fair process criteria such as consistency, lack of bias, correctability, representation, accuracy and ethicality (Colquitt, 2001).

- *Job satisfaction*: this is defined as 'a pleasurable or positive emotional state resulting from the appraisal of one's job or job experiences' (Locke, 1976). It is said to have emotional, cognitive and behavioural components where the emotional component refers to feelings regarding the job such as boredom, anxiety or excitement; the cognitive component of job satisfaction refers to beliefs regarding one's job, such as feeling that one's job is mentally demanding and challenging; and finally the behavioural component includes people's actions in relation to their work, which may include being tardy, staying late or pretending to be ill in order to avoid work (Bernstein and Nash, 2008).

- *Person–organization fit*: this refers to the compatibility between an employee and their organization. It can lead to increased levels of trust and a shared sense of corporate community (Boon and Den Hartog, 2011).

- *Job strain*: this refers to a psychological response to a demanding work context and can be a consequence of having the perception of having little control over one's work, while facing high job demands (House and Rizzo, 1972).

The data set that we use in this example is another that we have not used before: *Ch7_perf_2014_to_2015_sick_2014.xlsx*. The data looks like this:

1 ID (employee ID).

2 Gender (1 = female, 2 = male).

3 JobTenure2014 (years with the organization as at November 2014).

4 POS2014 (composite of perceived organizational support questions on a scale of 1 to 5 as at November 2014).

5 DistJust2014 (composite of distributive justice questions on a scale of 1 to 5 as at November 2014).

6 ProcJust2014 (composite of procedural justice questions on a scale of 1 to 5 as at November 2014).

7 JOBSAT2014 (composite of job satisfaction questions on a scale of 1 to 5 as at November 2014).

8 ValueFit2014 (composite of person organization fit questions on a scale of 1 to 5 as at November 2014).

9 JobStrain2014 (composite of job strain questions on a scale of 1 to 5 as at November 2014).

10 PerformanceRating2014 (performance rating given in January 2014 on a scale of 1 to 5, with 5 being the highest).

11 PerformanceRating2015 (performance rating given in January 2015 on a scale of 1 to 5, with 5 being the highest).

12 SickDays2014 (total number of sick days taken in 2014).

Predicting 2015 performance from survey measures and sickness absence

In selecting which model to test here, we can make many choices (a situation that the HR analyst will often find themselves in). The first choice to make is which measure of performance we should use. We have two measures – January 2014 and January 2015 (giving the ratings from the previous year's performance).

The temporal sequence of data included in the data set is of vital importance when considering which analytic model to run.

Our regression models make an implicit assumption that A causes B, or in this case that our independent variables may cause variation in performance. As such, if the independent variables available are collected in 2014, we probably want to make sure that the performance measure that we are to predict with these factors is the 2015 performance measure. If we try to predict the January 2014 performance measure with November 2014 staff attitudes then we are doing things backwards. So, we should choose the 2015 performance measure as a dependent variable here.

Let's first estimate a multiple regression model in R (as in the above examples), looking at the link between employee attitudes, sickness absence and performance. Hence we are testing the following model:

Performance Rating 2015 (January) =
$a + b_1$ (POS2014) + b_2 (DistJust2014) + b_3 (ProcJust2014) +
b_4 (JOBSAT2014) + b_5 (ValueFit2014) + b_6 (JobStrain2014) +
b_7 (sickdays2014)

Using exactly the same linear regression method we have used elsewhere and above, we can test this model. The code is in *Ch7_example_3_4_5.R*. We will load packages, set the working directory, and load the data with the following code.

```
if (!require("pacman")) install.packages("pacman")
pacman::p_load(readxl, dplyr, modelsummary, olsrr, this.path, huxtable)
setwd(this.path::here())
Ch7_ex3 <- read_excel("Ch7_perf_2014_to_2015_sick_2014.xlsx")
```

We can specify the following multiple regression model:

```
mod_perf <- lm(PerformanceRating2015 ~ POS2014 + DistJust2014 +
ProcJust2014 + JOBSAT2014 + ValueFit2014 + JobStrain2014 + SickDays2014,
data = Ch7_ex3)
```

We can see a summary of this model with the next line of code:

```
summary(mod_perf)
```

Which produces Figure 7.7:

7.7

```
> summary(mod_perf)

Call:
lm(formula = PerformanceRating2015 ~ POS2014 + DistJust2014 +
    ProcJust2014 + JOBSAT2014 + ValueFit2014 + JobStrain2014 +
    SickDays2014, data = Ch7_ex3)

Residuals:
      Min        1Q    Median        3Q       Max
 -3.00871  -0.67107  -0.01566   0.34531   2.50392

Coefficients:
                Estimate   Std. Error   t value   Pr(>|t|)
(Intercept)     0.958714     0.584229     1.641   0.102275
POS2014         0.195593     0.130405     1.500   0.135125
DistJust2014   -0.125878     0.101917    -1.235   0.218152
ProcJust2014    0.163098     0.140265     1.163   0.246219
JOBSAT2014      0.033225     0.100467     0.331   0.741189
ValueFit2014    0.062162     0.114183     0.544   0.586733
JobStrain2014   0.246692     0.072244     3.415   0.000764 ***
SickDays2014   -0.017989     0.008388    -2.145   0.033118 *
---
Signif. codes:  0 '***' 0.001 '**' 0.01 '*' 0.05 '.' 0.1 ' ' 1

Residual standard error: 0.8992 on 213 degrees of freedom
   (405 observations deleted due to missingness)
Multiple R-squared: 0.09726,  Adjusted R-squared: 0.06759
F-statistic: 3.278 on 7 and 213 DF, p-value: 0.002494
```

In the output above, we can see that the R-square = 0.097, or that 9.7 per cent (approximately one-tenth) of the variance in the performance rating given in January 2015 can be accounted for by the predictor variables used here.

Looking at the F-statistic, which tests the significance of how well the model predicts variation in the 2015 performance rating, we can see that the regression ANOVA F-value is 3.278, with an associated total degrees of freedom of 220 (7+213) and the significance level of 0.002 (p<0.01). So we could say it is less than 0.005, which means there is less than a 5 in 1,000 chance that we would randomly find this pattern of shared variance (between the 2015 performance ratings and the independent variables in the model). Hence the model is significant.

So, while the model only accounts for one-tenth of the output (2015 performance rating), it is significant. Hence we can be confident in recommendations that we make on the basis of the significant results produced with this model (in that we may have found factors that may impact the performance outcome). It is important to set the expectations in such a way that the impact will be conservative (and always caveat our claims on the basis that our regression findings do not definitively 'prove' causality).

This is a regression method where you put all factors in as predictors and see what come out as significant predictors. This helps control for multiple factors and takes into account noise and inter-correlations between the factors measured.

We can examine individual variables with *modelsummary* output:

```
mod1 <- modelsummary(mod_perf, output = "modelsummary_list")
mod2 <- modelsummary(mod_perf, output = "modelsummary_list", standardize
= "basic")
models <- list(
"Unstandardized" = mod1,
"Standardized" = mod2)
modelsummary(models, stars = TRUE, statistic = NULL, output =
"huxtable")
```

This produces Figure 7.8:

7.8

	Unstandardized	Standardized
(Intercept)	0.959	0.000
POS2014	0.196	0.168
DistJust2014	-0.126	-0.116
ProcJust2014	0.163	0.121
JOBSAT2014	0.033	0.037
ValueFit2014	0.062	0.041
JobStrain2014	0.247***	0.267***
SickDays2014	-0.018*	-0.144*
Num.Obs.	221	221
R2	0.097	0.097
R2 Adj.	0.068	0.068
AIC	590.0	590.0
BIC	620.6	620.6
Log.Lik.	-286.020	-286.020
RMSE	0.88	0.88

+ p < 0.1, * p < 0.05, ** p < 0.01, *** p < 0.001

By looking at the standardized coefficients (i.e. beta coefficients), you can see that the number of sick days taken in 2014 has a negative relationship with the 2015 performance rating, meaning more sick days taken in 2014 is associated with lower performance rating in 2015. Additionally, the amount of job strain has a significant and positive relationship with the 2015 performance rating, meaning greater job strain in 2014 is associated with higher performance rating in 2015 (we discuss this finding further in Chapter 11 where we present additional analytic strategies; this finding could be an example of where we might want to explore interactions between our predictors).

SNAPSHOT HIDDEN GEM

The perceived level of job strain and the number of sick days taken in 2014 are the key potential drivers of performance on ratings given in 2015. Interestingly, the more an individual feels they have job strain, the more likely they are to receive a higher performance rating.

You can, however, use a slightly different method called stepwise regression. This method, in effect, just selects the most important factors contributing to the prediction of your dependent variable. It looks at the independent variables, it finds the strongest relationship, and then it enters this as a regression model. Then it looks to see if the variable with the next strongest relationship adds to the regression model if it is included. This process continues until the prediction of the dependent variable is not improved any more. Thus you get your most efficient regression model. This process is called stepwise regression.

Example 4: using stepwise multiple linear regression to model performance

If we enter the above independent variables into a stepwise regression model predicting performance then we get a cleaner, simpler, more parsimonious model. The notion of parsimony here refers to not having unnecessary factors included in our model with the argument 'simple is better'. Bear in mind, however, that when we do this our model is not 'controlling' for the possible effect of other (excluded) variables, so the analyst needs to think carefully about what approach to take.

Here, we again use the data file: *Ch7_perf_2014_to_2015_sick_2014.xlsx*. To run stepwise regression with this example, we will look at code that continues in the file *Ch7_example_3_4_5.R*. This code follows from the example above, so you will need to run the code from the prior section to make the following work. First we will need to load a package that can perform backward stepwise regression, namely the *olsrr* package:

```
pacman::p_load(olsrr)
```

We then ask the program to conduct the backward stepwise regression. The *ols_step_backward_aic* program does this by starting the modelling process with all of the variables included in the model and gradually removes the variables with the largest (non-significant) p-value. This process is continued until all of the variables remaining in the model are significant. We will use the *mod_perf* regression result from the previous example – if you are starting with a clear workspace, you will need to estimate the model again for the remainder of the code in this example to work. Running the next line will conduct the stepwise regression. It runs the program and stores the results in the object *model_perf_back*:

```
model_perf_back <- ols_step_backward_aic(mod_perf)
```

The difference between the regression analyses we have been doing and stepwise regression is that we now are able to compare a few models with a view to finding the model that best fits in the most parsimonious way. It is important to consider that whilst stepwise regression has some advantages in that the models presented at the end *only* include significant predictors, therefore they are more simple and parsimonious models, there are some potential downsides to this approach. The main disadvantage is that you are not 'controlling' for the effects of other possible influencers of your dependent variable. It might actually be important to do this and demonstrate that you have control of the possible effects of other factors. If, for example, someone interrogating your findings felt that some other factors (that the stepwise regression analysis failed to include as a model) could be important, it may give you (and them) greater confidence if you actually include these other factors in your model, even though they do not come out as significant predictors.

We can look at the results of this analysis by calling the object:

```
model_perf_back
```

This produces the following output (Figure 7.9):

7.9   > model_perf_back

```
                              Stepwise Summary
------------------------------------------------------------------------
Step          Variable          AIC        SBC       SBIC     R2     Adj. R2
------------------------------------------------------------------------
0             Full Model      590.040    620.623   -36.533  0.09726  0.06759
1             JOBSAT2014      588.153    615.338   -38.562  0.09679  0.07147
2             ValueFit2014    586.452    610.239   -40.386  0.09557  0.07454
3             DistJust2014    586.167    606.556   -40.773  0.08852  0.07164
4             ProcJust2014    585.764    602.755   -41.260  0.08191  0.06922
------------------------------------------------------------------------


Final Model Output
------------------

                        Model Summary
-----------------------------------------------------------
R                  0.286      RMSE           0.890
R-Squared          0.082      MSE            0.807
Adj. R-Squared     0.069      Coef. Var     31.868
Pred R-Squared     0.038      AIC          585.764
MAE                0.666      SBC          602.755
-----------------------------------------------------------
RMSE: Root Mean Square Error
MSE: Mean Square Error
MAE: Mean Absolute Error
AIC: Akaike Information Criteria
SBC: Schwarz Bayesian Criteria

                           ANOVA
-----------------------------------------------------------
              Sum of
              Squares     DF     Mean Square  F      Sig.
-----------------------------------------------------------
Regression    15.626       3        5.209    6.454   3e-04
Residual     175.134     217        0.807
Total        190.760     220
-----------------------------------------------------------


                      Parameter Estimates
------------------------------------------------------------------------
model         Beta      Std. Error  Std. Beta    t       Sig    lower   upper
------------------------------------------------------------------------
(Intercept)    1.298      0.410                 3.162   0.002   0.489   2.107
POS2014        0.260      0.086       0.224      3.036   0.003   0.091   0.429
JobStrain2014  0.256      0.069       0.277      3.730   0.000   0.121   0.391
SickDays2014  -0.019      0.008      -0.151     -2.304   0.022  -0.035  -0.003
------------------------------------------------------------------------
```

You will see that the program has examined multiple models in the *Stepwise Summary* table. It first removed *JOBSAT2014* and then *ValueFit2014*, then *DistJust2014*, and finally removed *ProcJust2014*. It then settled on a final model which it could not improve, and shows us details about that model. Following the heading *Final Model Output*, we see details of this model.

The final model illustrates the predictors of the performance rating given in January 2015 as a combination of perceived organizational support (Beta = 0.224, $p < 0.05$) felt in November 2014, job strain (Beta = 0.277, $p < 0.05$) felt in November 2014 and the total number of days taken sick in 2014 (Beta = $- 0.151$, $p < 0.05$).

The raw regression model looks like this:

Performance Rating 2015 (January) =
1.298 + 0.260(POS2014) + 0.256(JobStrain2014) – 0.019(sickdays2014)

What does the data show us? Well, interestingly, it appears that the people who felt more under strain (who lost sleep worrying about work) in November 2014 seem to have higher performance appraisal ratings in January 2015. This is potentially problematic from a health and well-being perspective. More strain and worry tend to lead to higher performance? One would not want to consider trying to increase the strain and worry on individuals as an organizational performance improvement strategy. But it might be a reflection of the fact that people who work hard and are under pressure, and indeed who might lose sleep worrying about their work, are subsequently rewarded with a higher performance rating (regardless of whether they are actually performing at a higher level).

The story does not stop there, however. The second model indicates that the people who feel that their employer supports its staff also have higher performance ratings. Why might this be? Well, one could interpret this as the employees who feel their employer is not supportive may have lower levels of motivation or they may have a more disgruntled attitude than those who experience (or perceive) greater levels of support, thus this may play out in how their supervisor then rates them. It is worth considering for a moment how important it is to have the performance measure subsequent to the attitude survey rating in this model. If, for example, we inserted our 2014 performance measure here as a dependent variable instead of our 2015 performance measure, and we found a positive relationship between November 2014 perceived organizational support perceptions and January 2014 performance ratings, it might be that a lower performance rating produced negative perceptions of support, thus the causality would be reversed. Therefore it is essential that the performance rating that we use in our model (as a dependent variable) is given after the attitude/perceptual measure.

Strategically, how could we use this information to make recommendations? First, it is worth highlighting to senior leaders that the data suggests we may be rewarding people for being under strain. This could be damaging, because it is the high performers who are seen as role models in the organization – and if they are losing sleep and are under pressure, then it may be a signal to others that if they want to be rewarded also then they need to be putting more strain and pressure on themselves, which is not healthy for them or for the organization. A high level of job strain is likely to cause individuals to become ill, which would, in time, cause more days taken in sickness absence and eventually (according to this model) lead to a lower performance rating. So this approach would not lead to sustained, long-term, consistent high performance.

Let's look at the other key drivers: sickness absence and organizational support. First, sickness absence. Many organizations invest in employee well-being programmes to help employees remain mentally and physically healthy, and there are many specialists in the field who can advise on employee well-being programmes. Even small, simple, low-cost suggestions such as providing fresh fruit, encouraging exercise through lunchtime or after-work clubs, or obtaining discounted gym membership for staff can go a long way to help employees to stay healthy. Other suggestions include teaching healthy habits to employees through external speakers, employee assistance programmes to help employees who are experiencing stress, offering on-site flu vaccinations or even an on-site doctor's office.

Finally, perceived organizational support is important. The more employees perceive their employer to be supportive, the higher they are likely to perform. To improve this, it would almost certainly require further investigations into which HR policies are deemed supportive (and which are not) so that prescriptive action may be taken. This could be done through a review of processes combined with input from survey respondents.

SNAPSHOT HIDDEN GEM

The perceived level of job strain, the perceived level of organizational support felt and the number of sick days taken in 2014 are the key drivers of performance ratings given in 2015. Interestingly, the more an individual feels they have job strain, and the more they feel their employer supports employees, the more likely they are to receive a higher performance rating. The lower the number of sick days taken, the higher the performance rating that they tend to be given.

Example 5: using stepwise multiple linear regression to model change in performance over time

In this example, we are repeating the same model used in Example 4; however, here we are controlling for earlier levels of performance. In the example above we have predicted 2015 performance levels by exploring 2014 predictors. Our data set also has 2014 data that would be useful to use in our analysis. If we take earlier levels of performance into account we would, in effect, be able to filter out any role that earlier performance ratings may have in influencing our 2014 variables (which you would expect to be substantial as employees often get consistent performance ratings over the years). This is important because even though in our model above we are showing that 2015 performance may be influenced by 2014 experiences and perceptions, it is possible that these perceptions could have been influenced by 2014 performance ratings rather than the other way around. When we predict 2015 performance, if we have not controlled for earlier levels of performance we will not know for certain whether we are just showing relationships between 2014 performance and subsequent 2014 attitudes. If we include a 2014 performance measure in our regression model as an independent variable then we are in effect filtering out the impact that the January 2014 performance may have had on our November 2014 attitudes when accounting for variation in January 2015 performance. Importantly, when we include a 2014 performance measure as a control in our model, we are looking at the relationship between 2014 experiences (and sickness) on a *change* in performance rating between 2014 and 2015. This is actually a stronger predictive test and we are able to be more confident in any causal inferences that such analysis might identify. The R code for this example is in the file *Ch7_example_3_4_5.R*. The code follows from the previous examples in the file *Ch7_example_3_4_5.R*.

We define and estimate a new multiple regression model that includes the *PerformanceRating2014* variable:

```
mod_perf2 <- lm(PerformanceRating2015 ~ PerformanceRating2014 + POS2014 +
DistJust2014 + ProcJust2014 + JOBSAT2014 + ValueFit2014 +
JobStrain2014 + SickDays2014, data = Ch7_ex3)
```

And we use the same program to conduct the backwards stepwise regression on this new model, and display the results:

```
model_perf_back2 <- ols_step_backward_aic(mod_perf2)
model_perf_back2
```

This produces Figure 7.10:

7.10   `> model_perf_back2`

```
                              Stepwise Summary
-------------------------------------------------------------------------------
Step              Variable       AIC        SBC       SBIC       R2      Adj. R2
-------------------------------------------------------------------------------
0                 Full Model    539.966    573.811   -77.920   0.23207   0.20267
1                 ValueFit2014  538.003    568.463   -80.048   0.23193   0.20633
2                 JOBSAT2014    536.081    563.157   -82.114   0.23166   0.20981
3                 POS2014       534.792    558.483   -83.527   0.22915   0.21097
4                 DistJust2014  533.628    553.935   -84.795   0.22619   0.21165
-------------------------------------------------------------------------------
Final Model Output
------------------

                   Model Summary
-----------------------------------------------------------------
R                     0.476       RMSE          0.800
R-Squared             0.226       MSE           0.656
Adj. R-Squared        0.212       Coef. Var    28.894
Pred R-Squared        0.178       AIC         533.628
MAE                   0.646       SBC         553.935
-----------------------------------------------------------------
RMSE: Root Mean Square Error
MSE: Mean Square Error
MAE: Mean Absolute Error
AIC: Akaike Information Criteria
SBC: Schwarz Bayesian Criteria

                            ANOVA
-------------------------------------------------------------------------
              Sum of                Mean
              Squares     DF        Square     F        Sig.
-------------------------------------------------------------------------
Regression     40.831      4        10.208    15.565    0.0000
Residual      139.688    213         0.656
Total         180.518    217
-------------------------------------------------------------------------

                        Parameter Estimates
-----------------------------------------------------------------------------------
model                  Beta    Std. Error  Std. Beta  t        Sig    lower    upper
-----------------------------------------------------------------------------------
(Intercept)            0.467      0.400                1.166   0.245  -0.322    1.256
PerformanceRating2014  0.377      0.058     0.396      6.519   0.000   0.263    0.491
ProcJust2014           0.173      0.084     0.130      2.056   0.041   0.007    0.338
JobStrain2014          0.175      0.057     0.194      3.064   0.002   0.062    0.287
SickDays2014          -0.016      0.007    -0.127     -2.092   0.038  -0.030   -0.001
-----------------------------------------------------------------------------------
```

Looking at the *Model Summary* table, we can see that it has an adjusted R-square value of 0.226. This means that 22.6 per cent of the variance in the dependent variable (2015 performance ratings) is accounted for by the independent variables in the final model, i.e. 2014 performance ratings, job strain, sick days taken and procedural justice.

The ANOVA table tells us that, with total degrees of freedom of 217 and an F-value of 15.565, the final model is significant with p-value < 0.001. This means that there is less than 1 in 1,000 chance that we could come to this result through chance alone.

Looking at the coefficients for the model in the Parameter Estimates section, we can see that our raw regression model looks like this:

2015 performance ratings =
0.467 + 0.377 (2014 performance ratings) + 0.173 (procedural justice) + 0.175 (job strain) − 0.016 (sick days taken)

The above actually predicts an increase (or decrease) in performance between 2014 and 2015 and is thus much more interesting to us.

SNAPSHOT HIDDEN GEM

The biggest predictor of 2015 performance is 2014 performance; however, change in performance between 2014 and 2015 is largely driven by job strain, number of sick days taken and the employees' perceptions of procedural justice.

Interestingly, one of the things that often happens when one carries out some analysis is that some results often lead us to explore further. If it is the case that sickness absence predicts performance, what is it that predicts sickness absence?

Example 6: using multiple regression to predict sickness absence

Using the same data set, we can switch the dependent variable to the number of sick days taken, and include scores from the employee attitude survey as the independent variables. The R code for this example is in the file *Ch7_example_3_4_5_6.R*. The code continues from the previous example in that file. We first define the multiple regression model, which has the number of sick days in 2014 as the dependent variable (*SickDays2014*). The independent variables are taken directly from the employee opinion survey results: composite of job satisfaction (*JOBSAT2014*), composite of person organization fit (*ValueFit2014*), composite of job strain (*JobStrain2014*), composite of distributive justice (*DistJust2014*), composite of procedural justice (*ProcJust2014*) and composite of perceived organizational support (*POS2014*).

```
mod_sick <- lm(SickDays2014 ~ JOBSAT2014 + ValueFit2014 + JobStrain2014 +
DistJust2014 + ProcJust2014 + POS2014, data = Ch7_ex3)
```

We can then see the results of this model:

```
summary(mod_sick)
```

Which produces Figure 7.11:

7.11

```
> summary(mod_sick)

Call:
lm(formula = SickDays2014 ~ JOBSAT2014 + ValueFit2014 + JobStrain2014 +
    DistJust2014 + ProcJust2014 + POS2014, data = Ch7_ex3)

Residuals:
     Min      1Q  Median      3Q     Max
  -6.703  -2.684  -1.547  -0.121  55.510

Coefficients:
                Estimate    Std. Error    t value     Pr(>|t|)
(Intercept)      -0.8967       3.8632      -0.232       0.8166
JOBSAT2014       -1.1096       0.6728      -1.649       0.1003
ValueFit2014      1.0454       0.7595       1.376       0.1699
JobStrain2014     0.9282       0.4702       1.974       0.0494 *
DistJust2014      0.1503       0.6610       0.227       0.8203
ProcJust2014     -1.1795       0.9213      -1.280       0.2016
POS2014           1.8110       0.8596       2.107       0.0361 *
---
Signif. codes: 0 '***' 0.001 '**' 0.01 '*' 0.05 '.' 0.1 ' ' 1

Residual standard error: 6.713 on 265 degrees of freedom
  (354 observations deleted due to missingness)
Multiple R-squared: 0.04429,  Adjusted R-squared: 0.02265
F-statistic: 2.047 on 6 and 265 DF, p-value: 0.05987
```

Using the same analysis method as in the above example, we can see that in running a model that predicts number of days sick in 2014, the R-square = 0.044, or that 4.4 per cent of the variance in number of sick days taken is accounted for by the predictor variables used here.

Looking at the F-statistic, which tests the significance of how well the model predicts variation in number of sick days taken, there are some important indicators to pull out. First, the regression ANOVA F-value is 2.047, with associated total degrees of freedom of 271, giving the significance level of 0.060. So the model does not quite meet the $p<0.05$ threshold for significance. If we had more data perhaps this might become significant, but as it is we cannot confirm this. As it is so close to significance, let's take a look at what the results are hinting at. We can look at the coefficients more closely with tables generated using the *modelsummary* program:

```
mod3 <- modelsummary(mod_sick, output = "modelsummary_list")
mod4 <- modelsummary(mod_sick, output = "modelsummary_list", standardize
= "basic")
models <- list(
```

```
"Unstandardized" = mod3,
"Standardized" = mod4)
modelsummary(models, stars = TRUE, statistic = NULL, output =
'huxtable')
```

This produces Figure 7.12:

7.12

	Unstandardized	Standardized
(Intercept)	-0.897	0.000
JOBSAT2014	-1.110	-0.166
ValueFit2014	1.045	0.096
JobStrain2014	0.928*	0.140*
DistJust2014	0.150	0.019
ProcJust2014	-1.180	-0.120
POS2014	1.811*	0.215*
Num.Obs.	272	272
R2	0.044	0.044
R2 Adj.	0.023	0.023
AIC	1816.7	1816.7
BIC	1845.5	1845.5
Log.Lik.	-900.325	-900.325
F	2.047	2.047
RMSE	6.63	6.63

+ $p < 0.1$, * $p < 0.05$, ** $p < 0.01$, *** $p < 0.001$

The unstandardised regression model looks like this:

Number of days sickness absence =
−0.897 − 1.110 (job satisfaction) + 1.045 (person organization fit) + 0.928 (job strain) +
0.150 (distributive justice) − 1.180 (procedural justice) + 1.811 (perceived organizational
support)

Although we saw a positive relationship between job strain and performance in the
last example, we can see from this analysis that job strain also predicts sickness
absence. This suggests that people who feel under pressure may end up getting higher
ratings only if this does not make them sick. This is a well-known idea – that a bit of
pressure can increase performance but too much may have a negative effect (it can
make people sick). So our analysis here shows some evidence of this. Importantly,
however, we also see that the more employees experience support from their employer
then the more days off sick they tend to take. This can help us to understand some
of the processes involved in ensuring high sustainable performance: having demanding and challenging jobs, making sure procedures are in place at the organization

that are fair and just, and ensuring a supportive culture. From this set of analysis, we seem to have identified some conditions for a sustainable high-performance workplace. The research literature exploring possible stress reactions (see Cooper et al, 2001 for a review) identifies a number of factors that may intervene in experiences of workplace pressure – and 'support' is one of these possible 'buffers' that may mitigate the negative effects of workplace pressure. Such a process (i.e. a factor to potentially buffer a negative experience) is referred to as a moderating process (testing for moderation will be discussed in Chapter 11).

Growth trajectories and analytic demands

One of the things we may be interested in is identifying predictors of certain patterns of performance over time. For example, we might want to look at the changes in individual performance ratings or levels of engagement over three or four years of employment, and what factors may influence that over time; the more waves of data that we have, the more interesting and powerful our analysis can get. This type of analysis can be extremely useful in the long term, especially in terms of predictive utility, but it comes with its challenges and will be discussed further in Chapter 11.

Example 7: exploring patterns in performance linked to employee profile data

The data file we are using with this example is: *Ch7_MI_data_perf.xlsx*. The data here is from a large multinational manufacturing organization and contains details of 9,450 employees across four countries, looking at age, tenure, gender and benchmark position salary.

The data looks like this:

1 Perf (performance appraisal: 1 = low; 2 = medium; 3 = high).

2 Joiner (recent joiner: 1 = old timer, 2 = new hire).

3 SalaryBenchmark (benchmark salary: 1 = <80 per cent; 2 = 80–89.99 per cent; 3 = 90–109.99 per cent; 4 = 110–120 per cent; 5 = >120 per cent of benchmark).

4 CountryCode (country where employee is based: (1 = United States; 2 = UK; 3 = Netherlands; 4 = Russia).

5 Gender (1 = male; 2 = female).

6 AgeCat (age group: 1 = 20–29; 2 = 30–39; 3 = 40–49; 4 = 50–59; 5 = 60–64; 6 = 65+).

7 TenureCat (years with the organization: 1 = less than 1 year; 2 = 1–2 years; 3 = 3–5 years; 4 = 6–10 years; 5 = 11–15 years; 6 = more than 16 years).

8 Leaver (whether or not the employee left the organization: 1 = stayer; 2 = leaver).

Notice in the listed variables where there is more than one value such as *Perf* and *AgeCat* that the numbers assigned to the values have a numerical meaning, i.e. the higher the number in *Perf*, the higher the performance rating, so the number is meaningful numerically. In the *TenureCat* variable, although not interval-level data, the higher the number, the longer the person has been with the organization. This helps with our analysis in highlighting whether the dependent variable increases or decreases (and to what extent) with an increase or a decrease in the independent variable. In the *CountryCode* variable, however, the number assigned to the country has no numerical meaning, so a model like the one we have been using for the above examples does not work for a variable like country (i.e. an increment in the numeric value would *not* mean the employee moves closer to Russia – just as a mean value of 3.5 for a team would *not* suggest they are based somewhere between the Netherlands and Russia, say in Poland?); clearly in this variable, the numbers are just labels.

In this situation, in order to include these country categories in our analysis we need to set up new variables that we refer to as *dummy* variables.

We set up the new variables so that there are two choices in each, as follows:

9 USAdummy (shows if the employee is based in the United States or not: 1 = yes; 0 = no).

10 UKdummy (shows if the employee is based in the UK or not: 1 = yes; 0 = no).

11 Netherlandsdummy (shows if the employee is based in the Netherlands or not: 1 = yes; 0 = no).

12 Russiadummy (shows if the employee is based in Russia or not: 1 = yes; 0 = no).

After constructing dummy variables in this way, we now want to include them in the analysis; importantly, with dummy variables we choose one of them to act as a baseline or reference category (country in this case). To break down this idea further, say the United States is the head office of this particular organization. We might want to know whether performance ratings might be influenced by whether they work in a country *other* than the United States; does it make a difference if someone works in the UK, in the Netherlands or in Russia compared to the United States? So we would select United States as our reference. How do we reflect this in our analysis? As mentioned previously, we simply leave the reference category dummy variable out of the model but include all of the other country dummy variables. Although it is not intuitive to leave out the most strategically important country (or the country with the most employees), think of it as analysing the difference it makes if someone is not based in this country. This will become clearer as we discuss the results.

We will conduct a multiple regression in the same manner as the examples above. The R code for this example is in the file *Ch7_example_7.R*. We will load required packages, set the working directory, and load the data.

```
if (!require("pacman")) install.packages("pacman")
pacman::p_load(readxl, dplyr, modelsummary, olsrr, this.path, huxtable)
setwd(this.path::here())
Ch7_ex7 <- read_excel("Ch7_MI_data_perf.xlsx")
```

And, for convenience, we will recode the gender variable to be more interpretable, and convert it to a factor:

```
Ch7_ex7$Gender_text <- case_match(Ch7_ex7$Gender, 1 ~ "Male", 2 ~
"Female")
Ch7_ex7$Gender_text <- as.factor(Ch7_ex7$Gender_text)
```

We then define the multiple regression model, with performance appraisal as the dependent variable (*Perf*). The independent variables are salary benchmark (*SalaryBenchmark*), gender (*Gender_text*), age category (*AgeCat*), tenure category (*TenureCat*), and dummy variables for the UK (*UKdummy*) Netherlands (*Netherlandsdummy*), and Russia (*Russiadummy*).

```
mod_appraise <- lm(Perf ~ SalaryBenchmark + Gender_text + AgeCat +
TenureCat + UKdummy + Netherlandsdummy + Russiadummy,
data = Ch7_ex7)
```

We can see the summary of the model with the next line:

```
summary(mod_appraise)
```

Which produces Figure 7.13:

7.13

```
> summary(mod_appraise)

Call:
lm(formula = Perf ~ SalaryBenchmark + Gender_text + AgeCat +
    TenureCat + UKdummy + Netherlandsdummy + Russiadummy, data = Ch7_ex7)

Residuals:
     Min       1Q   Median       3Q      Max
 -1.5495  -0.2574  -0.1479   0.2306   1.7795

Coefficients:
                     Estimate   Std. Error    t value     Pr(>|t|)
(Intercept)          1.180937     0.037192     31.752     < 2e-16 ***
SalaryBenchmark      0.129841     0.007614      17.05     < 2e-16 ***
Gender_textMale      0.732047     0.021061     34.758     < 2e-16 ***
AgeCat              -0.071025     0.006369    -11.153     < 2e-16 ***
TenureCat            0.025867     0.004619      5.600    2.21e-08 ***
UKdummy              0.068118     0.013444      5.067    4.13e-07 ***
Netherlandsdummy     0.538236     0.030386     17.713     < 2e-16 ***
Russiadummy          0.661148     0.023224     28.469     < 2e-16 ***
---
Signif. codes: 0 '***' 0.001 '**' 0.01 '*' 0.05 '.' 0.1 ' ' 1

Residual standard error: 0.4872 on 8836 degrees of freedom
  (606 observations deleted due to missingness)
Multiple R-squared: 0.1399,      Adjusted R-squared: 0.1392
F-statistic: 205.3 on 7 and 8836 DF, p-value: < 2.2e-16
```

From the output, we can see from the R-square that 14 per cent of the variance in the dependent variable (performance appraisal rating) is accounted for by variance in the independent variables. The model is significant, with an F-statistic of 205.3, a regression degrees of freedom of 7, and a residual degree of freedom of 8,836.

We can now examine each independent variable by generating a table using the *modelsummary* program:

```
mod1 <- modelsummary(mod_appraise, output = "modelsummary_list")
mod2 <- modelsummary(mod_appraise, output = "modelsummary_list",
standardize = "basic")
models <- list(
"Unstandardized" = mod1,
"Standardized" = mod2)
modelsummary(models, stars = TRUE, statistic = NULL, output =
"huxtable")
```

Which produces this table (Figure 7.14):

7.14

	Unstandardized	Standardized
(Intercept)	1.181***	0.000***
SalaryBenchmark	0.130***	0.180***
Gender_textMale	0.732***	0.654***
AgeCat	-0.071***	-0.127***
TenureCat	0.026***	0.063***
UKdummy	0.068***	0.057***
Netherlandsdummy	0.538***	0.208***
Russiadummy	0.661***	0.563***
Num.Obs.	8844	8844
R2	0.140	0.140
R2 Adj.	0.139	0.139
AIC	12390.3	12390.3
BIC	12454.1	12454.1
Log.Lik.	-6186.137	-6186.137
F	205.281	205.281
RMSE	0.49	0.49

+ $p < 0.1$, * $p < 0.05$, ** $p < 0.01$, *** $p < 0.001$

The model predicting performance appraisal can be expressed in the following way using unstandardized coefficients:

Performance appraisal rating =
1.181 + 0.130 (benchmark salary) + 0.732 (gender) – 0.071 (age) + 0.026 (tenure) +
0.068 (UK) + 0.538 (Netherlands) + 0.661 (Russia)

With very large data sets, significance levels can often be rather unhelpful. This is one of the challenges with running inferential statistical models with 'big data'. The column of standardized coefficients, however, does give us some important information as to what are the most important factors that could be influencing performance across the organization and in what direction (and by how much). It is clear, for example, that gender seems to be very important in predicting performance rating. As males are coded as 1 and females as 2 in this data set, it seems that males get higher ratings, as this is a negative relationship (Beta = –0.654, $p < 0.001$).

The data also suggests that employees in the Netherlands (Beta = 0.208, $p <$ 0.001) and Russia (Beta = 0.563, $p < 0.001$) tend to receive higher performance ratings than their US counterparts. It would definitely be worth conducting further analysis to look at how the organization's performance appraisal ratings schemes are applied across different countries.

SNAPSHOT HIDDEN GEM

The biggest predictor of performance ratings in this organization is gender, showing that men receive significantly higher performance ratings than women. Employees from Russia and the Netherlands also receive significantly higher performance ratings.

The hidden gem above potentially points to procedural inconsistencies in the performance ratings process, so the recommendation on the back of this analysis would be to more strictly monitor the calibration process and the assessment process to ensure that line managers are not favouring male employees over female employees, and that employees in the Netherlands and Russia are being assessed against equivalent criteria (compared to the headquarters in the United States) to ensure a fair process.

Example 8a: exploring the use of supermarket checkout scan rates as a measure of employee performance

Many supermarkets in the UK impose a scan-rate target on their employees who work on the checkout. The *Daily Mail* newspaper reported on a leading supermarket imposing a target on staff whereby they must scan each item in three seconds or less, or face being moved to another department (2012).

The example given below explores patterns of checkout scan rates across various demographic employee characteristics of a 'fictitious' supermarket chain. The variables in the data sample are outlined below. The dependent variable measured in this example is the average number of items scanned per minute (per employee), and the target in this particular supermarket was 22 items per minute. Obviously, as we are exploring predictors of performance in this chapter, employee variation in this scan rate (ScanPminute) is the key performance indicator that we try to predict here (we use this data set again in Chapter 9). The data file we use here is *Ch7_supermarket_checkout.xlsx*:

1 id (unique ID for each employee).
2 educ (number of years of education of the employee).
3 jobtime (number of weeks working with the supermarket).
4 disability (whether or not the employee has stated they have a disability: 0 = no; 1 = yes).
5 Gender (1= male; 2 = female).
6 ScanPminute (average number of items scanned per minute this week).

7   Store (which store: 1 = Portsmouth North; 2 = Portsea Island).

8   weeksinjob (number of weeks working on the checkout).

9   AgeCAT (age category: 1 = 16–19; 2 = 20–24; 3 = 25–29; 4 = 30–34; 5 = 35–39; 6 = 40–44; 7 = 45–49; 8 = 50–54; 9 = 55–59; 10 = 60+).

10 Age 1 (16–19).

11 Age 2 (20–24).

12 Age 3 (25–29).

13 Age 4 (30–34).

14 Age 5 (35–39).

15 Age 6 (40–44).

16 Age 7 (45–49).

17 Age 8 (50–54).

18 Age 9 (55–59).

19 Age 10 (60+).

Let's look a bit more closely at the scan-rate data by age group. We will first load the data. The code is in the file *Ch7_example_8a_8b_9.R*. We will load required packages, set the working directory, and load the data.

```
if (!require("pacman")) install.packages("pacman")
pacman::p_load(readxl, dplyr, modelsummary, this.path, huxtable)
setwd(this.path::here())
Ch7_super <- read_excel("Ch7_supermarket_checkout.xlsx")
```

For readability, we will recode the AgeCAT variable and transform it to a factor:

```
Ch7_super$AgeCAT_text <- case_match(Ch7_super$AgeCAT, 1 ~ "16-19",
                    2 ~ "20-24",
                    3 ~ "25-29",
                    4 ~ "30-34",
                    5 ~ "35-39",
                    6 ~ "40-44",
                    7 ~ "45-49",
                    8 ~ "50-54",
                    9 ~ "55-59",
                    10 ~ "60+")
Ch7_super$AgeCAT_text <- as.factor(Ch7_super$AgeCAT_text)
```

We can now generate a table of scan-rate by age group:

```
datasummary((ScanPminute) * AgeCAT_text ~ N + Mean + SD + Min + Max,
    data = Ch7_super, output = "huxtable")
```

This produces Figure 7.15, which shows the number of employees in each age group, the average number of items scanned per minute, the standard deviation or spread of the values for each age group, as well as the minimum and maximum for that age category:

	AgeCAT_text	N	Mean	SD	Min	Max
ScanPminute	16-19	19	15.68	4.65	7.00	27.00
	20-24	111	20.13	3.26	5.00	27.00
	25-29	141	18.82	2.99	8.00	28.00
	30-34	36	20.46	3.98	14.00	28.00
	35-39	33	18.77	4.31	7.00	28.00
	40-44	35	22.17	4.90	6.00	32.00
	45-49	31	21.31	3.30	7.00	28.00
	50-54	29	20.99	2.26	16.00	27.00
	55-59	35	19.86	3.65	8.00	27.00
	60+	4	12.38	4.96	8.00	19.50

Some key things that Figure 7.15 tells us are that the supermarket employs almost three times the number of staff in the age categories 20–24 and 25–29 than in any other age category; that employees in the 40–44 age group are the only age group that meets the (22 items per minute) target on average, and that there is a lot of variation in the number of items scanned by those employees (this is also the case for age groups 16–19, 35–39 and 60+).

Example 8b: exploring patterns in supermarket checkout scan rates linked to employee demographic data

If we run a multiple regression analysis, we will be able to identify which of the demographic variables, if any, impact the number of items scanned per week. We will follow on from the code above. To make the gender variable more interpretable, we will recode it:

```
Ch7_super$Gender_text <- case_match(Ch7_super$Gender, 1 ~ "Male", 2 ~
"Female")
Ch7_super$Gender_text <- as.factor(Ch7_super$Gender_text)
```

We can define the multiple regression model as in the next lines of code. We will set the average number of items scanned per minute this week (*ScanPminute*) as the dependent variable, and set the independent variables to be gender (*Gender_text*), week in job (*Weeks*), stated disability (*disability*), educational level (*educ*), Portsmouth North versus Portsea Island (*Store*) and age category (*AgeCAT*).

```
mod_scans <- lm(ScanPminute ~ Gender_text + Weeks + disability +
educ + Store + AgeCAT, data = Ch7_super)
```

We can show the model summary:

```
summary(mod_scans)
```

Which produces Figure 7.16:

7.16

```
> summary(mod_scans)

Call:
lm(formula = ScanPminute ~ Gender_text + Weeks + disability +
    educ + Store + AgeCAT, data = Ch7_super)

Residuals:
      Min       1Q   Median       3Q      Max
  -13.8810  -1.3802   0.1576   1.7489  11.3988

Coefficients:
                   Estimate  Std. Error  t value  Pr(>|t|)
(Intercept)        21.197365    1.062151   19.957   < 2e-16 ***
Gender_textMale    -1.900011    0.349655   -5.434  8.89e-08 ***
Weeks               0.039248    0.005625    6.977  1.04e-11 ***
disability          0.235729    0.374747    0.629    0.5296
educ               -0.138297    0.059424   -2.327    0.0204 *
Store              -0.296129    0.305456   -0.969    0.3328
AgeCAT              0.079574    0.066990    1.188    0.2355
---
Signif. codes:  0 '***' 0.001 '**' 0.01 '*' 0.05 '.' 0.1 ' ' 1

Residual standard error: 3.293 on 467 degrees of freedom
Multiple R-squared: 0.2571, Adjusted R-squared: 0.2475
F-statistic: 26.94 on 6 and 467 DF, p-value: < 2.2e-16
```

We can see from the model summary in Figure 7.16 that the R-square is 0.257, which means that 25.7 per cent, or more than one-quarter, of the variation in the average number of items scanned per minute in this given week is shared with the independent variables in the model. The F-statistic is 26.94 with 473 degrees of freedom and the model has a significance level of $p < 0.001$ (our model is very significant). We can now examine each independent variable by examining a table of coefficients:

```
mod1 <- modelsummary(mod_scans, output = "modelsummary_list")
mod2 <- modelsummary(mod_scans, output = "modelsummary_list",
standardize = "basic")
models <- list(
  "Unstandardized" = mod1,
  "Standardized" = mod2)
modelsummary(models, stars = TRUE, statistic = NULL, output = "huxtable")
```

This produces Figure 7.17:

7.17

	Unstandardized	Standardized
(Intercept)	21.197***	0.000***
Gender_textMale	-1.900***	-0.250***
Weeks	0.039***	0.301***
disability	0.236	0.026
educ	-0.138*	-0.105*
Store	-0.296	-0.039
AgeCAT	0.080	0.050
Num.Obs.	474	474
R2	0.257	0.257
R2 Adj.	0.248	0.248
AIC	2484.0	2484.0
BIC	2517.3	2517.3
Log.Lik.	-1234.010	-1234.010
F	26.935	26.935
RMSE	3.27	3.27

+ p < 0.1, * p < 0.05, ** p < 0.01, *** p < 0.001

Looking at the standardized beta coefficients, we can see that gender (Beta = −0.250, p < 0.001) and weeks in job (Beta = 0.301, p < 0.001) are the most significant influencers with p-values less than 0.001 (p < 0.001). The gender value is negative, showing that women have a significantly faster scan rate than males. Education level is also significant (Beta = −0.105, p < 0.05), showing that more time in education does not seem to improve scan rates.

> SNAPSHOT HIDDEN GEM
>
> The biggest predictors of the average number of items scanned this week are gender and weeks in the job. Women have a significantly higher scan rate than men, and also the longer that employees are working on the checkout, the faster their scan rate. Interestingly, the educational level of employees had a negative impact (meaning the more time that employees spent in education, the lower their scan rate).

Example 9: determining the presence or otherwise of high-performing age groups

If we want to develop a profile of the employee who has the highest scan rate, we would need to break down key categories in our workforce data set, in particular the age category. At the moment when we just include this in the regression there is no evidence of a linear relationship between age category and scan rate (Beta = 0.050, p > 0.05). Given the variation in mean scan rates across the age groups (see Figure 7.15), however, we may obtain more diagnostic sensitivity by coding the age groups into separate dummy variables, in a similar way to what we did with the countries in Example 7 above. As there are 10 age categories to our *AgeCAT* variable, we create 10 new variables representing each of the age categories by themselves; we code the separate variables 1 and 0 depending on whether the employees' age falls into each of these categories. Let's conduct the multiple regression using the dummy age variables instead of the *AgeCAT* variable. Remember, with the country categories in Example 7 we selected the United States as the baseline. In this example, let's simply select the largest age group as the baseline/reference category. This is age 25–29, hence we leave this category out of the regression analysis and include all other age category dummies. Since we created a factor variable with 10 levels in Example 8a (*AgeCAT_text*), we can use this variable. We need to tell R what we would like the reference category to be and R will create dummy variables accordingly. The code for this example is in the file *Ch7_example_8a_8b_9.R*, and we follow from the previous example. To recode the variable, run the following line of code:

```
Ch7_super$AgeCAT_text <- relevel(Ch7_super$AgeCAT_text, ref = "25-29")
```

The line above uses the *rlevel* program to set the reference category to '25–29' for the variable *AgeCAT_text* in the dataframe Ch7_super. We can then define a new multiple regression model to include this variable in place of the *AgeCAT* variable:

```
mod_scans2 <- lm(ScanPminute ~ Gender_text + Weeks + disability +
educ + Store + AgeCAT_text, data = Ch7_super)
```

We can show the model summary:

```
summary(mod_scans2)
```

Which produces Figure 7.18:

7.18

```
> summary(mod_scans2)

Call:
lm(formula = ScanPminute ~ Gender_text + Weeks + disability +
    educ + Store + AgeCAT_text, data = Ch7_super)

Residuals:
      Min       1Q   Median       3Q      Max
  -13.1766  -1.4234  -0.0144   1.4947  10.8803

Coefficients:
                   Estimate   Std. Error   t value   Pr(>|t|)
(Intercept)        24.940589    1.051880    23.710   < 2e-16 ***
Gender_textMale    -2.734184    0.346196    -7.898   2.11e-14 ***
Weeks               0.027656    0.005319     5.200   3.01e-07 ***
disability         -0.298656    0.350958    -0.851   0.395228
educ               -0.287903    0.057903    -4.972   9.37e-07 ***
Store              -0.314438    0.277292    -1.134   0.257402
AgeCAT_text16-19   -6.033746    0.787036    -7.666   1.06e-13 ***
AgeCAT_text20-24   -0.692278    0.413170    -1.676   0.094511 .
AgeCAT_text30-34    2.011708    0.562317     3.578   0.000384 ***
AgeCAT_text35-39   -0.160372    0.585044    -0.274   0.784117
AgeCAT_text40-44    1.399338    0.591699     2.365   0.018448 *
AgeCAT_text45-49   -0.439121    0.633350    -0.693   0.488453
AgeCAT_text50-54   -0.213221    0.636572    -0.335   0.737814
AgeCAT_text55-59   -1.349806    0.621405    -2.172   0.030353 *
AgeCAT_text60+     -8.022047    1.544472    -5.194   3.10e-07 ***
---
Signif. codes:  0 '***' 0.001 '**' 0.01 '*' 0.05 '.' 0.1 ' ' 1

Residual standard error: 2.983 on 459 degrees of freedom
Multiple R-squared: 0.4011, Adjusted R-squared: 0.3829
F-statistic: 21.96 on 14 and 459 DF, p-value: < 2.2e-16
```

In Figure 7.18 we can immediately see that the R-square is now 0.401 rather than 0.257 as before, so we can be confident that 40 per cent of the variance in the 'average number of items scanned per minute this week' measure can be accounted for by this more elaborate model that divided the age category variable into separate dummy variables. The F-statistic is 21.96 with 473 degrees of freedom total and the model is significant with a p-value < 0.001. As you can see, by breaking the age category variable into separate age groups we have managed to account for 14.4 per cent more of the variation in our scan-rate performance measure. Clearly, the age category measure was not diagnostically sensitive enough as a basic ordinal variable (in linear relationship testing) and it needed to be broken up into smaller categories in order to be useful in our analysis. We can take a closer look at the independent variables by producing a table with the *modelsummary* program:

```
mod3 <- modelsummary(mod_scans2, output = "modelsummary_list")
mod4 <- modelsummary(mod_scans2, output = "modelsummary_list",
standardize = "basic")
models <- list(
  "Unstandardized" = mod3,
  "Standardized" = mod4)
modelsummary(models, stars = TRUE, statistic = NULL, output =
"huxtable")
```

This produces Figure 7.19:

7.19

	Unstandardized	Standardized
(Intercept)	24.941***	0.000***
Gender_textMale	-2.734***	-0.359***
Weeks	0.028***	0.212***
disability	-0.299	-0.033
educ	-0.288***	-0.219***
Store	-0.314	-0.041
AgeCAT_text16-19	-6.034***	-0.312***
AgeCAT_text20-24	-0.692+	-0.077+
AgeCAT_text30-34	2.012***	0.141***
AgeCAT_text35-39	-0.160	-0.011
AgeCAT_text40-44	1.399*	0.096*
AgeCAT_text45-49	-0.439	-0.029
AgeCAT_text50-54	-0.213	-0.013
AgeCAT_text55-59	-1.350*	-0.093*
AgeCAT_text60+	-8.022***	-0.193***
Num.Obs.	474	474
R2	0.401	0.401
R2 Adj.	0.383	0.383
AIC	2397.9	2397.9
BIC	2464.4	2464.4
Log.Lik.	-1182.928	-1182.928
F	21.961	21.961
RMSE	2.93	2.93

+ p < 0.1, * p < 0.05, ** p < 0.01, *** p < 0.001

The standardized coefficients table in Figure 7.19 tells us that the key predictors are gender (Beta = –0.359, p < 0.001), weeks in the job (Beta = 0.212, p < 0.001), education (Beta = –0.219, p < 0.001), age 16–19 (Beta = –0.312, p < 0.001), age 30–34 (Beta = 0.141, p < 0.001), age 40–44 (Beta = –0.096 p < 0.05), age 55–59 (Beta =

–0.093, p < 0.05) and age 60+ (Beta = –0.193, p < 0.001). Looking at the Beta values to get the direction, we can see that the criteria more likely to achieve a high number of scans per minute in this week are as follows:

SNAPSHOT HIDDEN GEM

The biggest predictors of higher average number of items scanned this week are gender, weeks in the job, education and age categories. Interestingly, those who have achieved the highest number of scans this week are women, those aged 30–34, those with a high number of weeks in the job and those who have spent less time in education.

Ethical considerations caveat in performance data analysis

But what do we recommend that the supermarket does with this information? Not hire employee school leavers or people over 60? This would be unfair and expose the organization to age discrimination claims. How about the financial services organization? Should we recommend that they only employ women in an effort to increase customer loyalty, because customers of female sales people have higher customer loyalty? This would obviously not be a fair, ethical or sensible recommendation. Indeed we also need to be careful with the sensitive nature of pulse survey data, just as we do with employee engagement data (as mentioned in Chapter 5). It is important here, as in all of our analysis, to review the results in context and consider the wider impact of what the results suggest. More information about the ethics of analysis and findings can be found in Chapter 12.

Considering the possible range of performance analytic models

You may have noticed that this case study chapter is the longest in the book; this reflects the emphasis that HR analytics as a discipline places on being able to predict performance and the need for us to present a number of different examples of models predicting performance. The types of analysis presented here only represent a small proportion of possible analytic models that can be run to predict performance. We touch on some other methods in Chapter 11 where we discuss more advanced analytic approaches, but ultimately there is no end to the forms of analysis that can be carried out.

The type of analysis carried out will always need to be carefully considered and, generally speaking, the analyst will choose a particular model set-up that has the potential to answer *specific business questions relevant to the context* of the organi-zation. As discussed above (and demonstrated in our examples) there are many types of metrics that can be considered to be an important performance measure (none are likely to be a perfect gauge of employee performance); the performance indices that the analyst chooses will always depend on the business question that they are trying to answer. However, it is important for the analyst to question and interrogate the legitimacy of any performance indicator that they explore (especially due to the danger that the reliance on one particular metric can end up institutionalizing metric-oriented behaviour, or IMOB for short; see Chapter 12). Where possible, the analyst should try to predict a *range* of performance measures so that when diagnosing factors that might predict performance they apply the principles of a 'balanced score-card' where possible.

Importantly, when analysts estimate specific models in predicting performance they will always need to ask themselves what the results actually mean in practice; they will need to question whether the results are producing findings that might lead to actionable interventions. They will also need to consider whether there are factors that might be influencing their results that have not been taken into account in their analytic models (this will be discussed further in Chapter 12). Having said this, when the analytic models produce some interesting significant results as predictors of performance, this information might be used to predict future performance (see Chapter 10); these factors can also (where appropriate) inform managerial practice and identify levers that can be focused on to help foster higher levels of organiza-tional performance.

References

Armstrong, M and Baron, A (2005) *Managing Performance: Performance management in action*, Chartered Institute of Personnel and Development, London

Bach, S (2012) Performance management, in *Managing Human Resources: HRM in transition*, 5th edn, ed S Bach and M R Edwards, John Wiley and Sons, New York

Bernstein, D A and Nash, P W (2008) *Essentials of Psychology*, 4th edn, Cengage Learning, Boston

Boon, C and Den Hartog, D N (2011) Human resource management, person–environment fit, and trust, *Trust and Human Resource Management*, pp 109–21

Brown, D and Hirsh, W (2011) Performance management: Fine intentions, *People Management*, September, pp 34–37

Colquitt, J A (2001) On the dimensionality of organizational justice: A construct validation of a measure, *Journal of Applied Psychology*, 86 (3), pp 386–400

Cooper, C L, Dewe, P J and O'Driscoll, M P (2001) *Organizational Stress: A review and critique of theory, research and applications*, Sage, California

Daily Mail (2012) One checkout item every three seconds, www.dailymail.co.uk/femail/article-2170377/Morrisons-imposes-new-second-targets-cut-till-queues.html (archived at https://perma.cc/R2XF-4RXJ)

Eisenberger, R, Huntington, R, Hutchison, S and Sowa, D (1986) Perceived organizational support, *Journal of Applied Psychology*, 71, pp 500–07

House, R J and Rizzo, J R (1972) Role conflict and ambiguity as critical variables in a model of organizational behavior, *Organizational Behavior and Human Performance*, 7, pp 467–505

Locke, E A (1976) The nature and causes of job satisfaction, in *Handbook of Industrial and Organizational Psychology*, pp 1297–349, ed M D Dunnette, Rand McNally, Chicago

08

Case study 5

Recruitment and selection analytics

In the process of recruiting and selecting new employees, organizations often collect and record a considerable amount of information that can be utilized in many ways by an HR analytics expert. Much of the recruitment- and selection-related analysis that an HR analytics team might wish to conduct could be considered a subset of other analysis forms that we present in other case study chapters. For example, an HR analyst may wish to explore factors and data collected in the recruitment and selection process in order to determine whether certain metrics, data or onboarding activities predict future performance. Thus, a case study of recruitment and selection analytics can include predictive models intended to account for employee performance after they join the firm (and the analyst should carefully study the predicting performance case study in Chapter 7). What makes such a model a recruitment and selection case study is the choice of independent variables, which will involve variables linked to data collected in the recruitment and selection phase.

Another type of predictive analysis that an HR analyst may wish to test is a model that explores recruitment- and selection-related predictors of employee turnover. As well as looking at predictors of new joiner performance, the analyst would want to predict factors related to the recruitment and selection process that help predict whether these joiners actually stay (or leave). Thus the analyst should read the predicting turnover case study in Chapter 6, in particular Example 3 (pages 203–12), where individual turnover is the phenomenon that we are trying to predict.

One of the key preoccupations that should be at the forefront of an HR analyst's priorities when conducting analysis in the recruitment and selection area is the degree to which recruitment and selection processes appear to be free from bias. Thus, diversity-related analysis of recruitment and selection activities (and data) should be a key subset of activities to focus on (and the analyst should carefully study the diversity case study in Chapter 4). For example, what are the gender male–female ratios of people who apply for jobs in the organization compared to the male–female ratios of people who are shortlisted, interviewed and ultimately offered a job? Also, the analyst may wish to conduct a similar analysis linked to ethnicity and other important demographic categorizations apart from gender. The fact that recruitment and selection analysis can be considered a subset of other predictive analysis questions, therefore, means that this chapter will only present a few examples of particular analyses that could be conducted with recruitment- and selection-related data.

Reliability and validity of selection methods

One of the key areas of debate within the area of recruitment and selection revolves around the issue of what selection method can be considered to be the 'best' way of selecting new candidates. What do we mean by 'best' here? Such a question is of key importance when we want to apply analytic techniques to the area of recruitment and selection. Both reliability and validity are important in this regard (see the discussion of reliability and validity in relation to engagement set out in Chapter 5); in the area of recruitment and selection analysis these relate specifically to the method or range of methods used to form a judgement on a candidate that will influence whether they are offered a job or not. Importantly, these judgements will lead to a metric (e.g. aptitude test score, competency rating, personality test score) and the metric will often be the determinant of a hiring decision. As these metrics will generally be driving hiring decisions, the reliability and validity of these metric creation methods are therefore of key concern.

What do we mean by reliability and validity of selection methods? By reliability of selection methods, we mean the degree to which a particular method will consistently lead to the same judgement about an individual on a particular feature or characteristic, often across different settings. Importantly, human beings are fallible, and judgements that we make about each other are fundamentally prone to bias; we are victims of the inevitability of human subjectivity. Thus, any selection method/ selection metric creation tool that increases the consistency and reliability in making judgements about potential recruits will be a 'better' selection method. Of course, it is well known (Schmidt and Hunter, 1998) that unstructured interviews (that amount to 'a bit of a chat' really) are one of the most unreliable methods of forming a judgement about potential recruits.

The validity of a selection method relates to the degree to which the particular method will accurately identify the people that the selectors intended to identify as being the right person for any particular job. In ensuring that the right person is identified, the methods will need to: 1) successfully discriminate between people who will perform well versus those who will struggle to perform well; and, 2) successfully discriminate between people who will want to stay versus people who will want to leave shortly after they join. Of course, 1) and 2) are inextricably linked, as someone who does not perform well is likely to not want to hang around for ever (though of course this statement makes certain assumptions about the nature of human motivation in the workplace...). Thus, we have two clear metrics that we can use to judge the validity of a metric: performance ratings and staff turnover data. From a predictive HR analytics point of view, given the considerable costs often incurred in the process of selecting the right candidate for a job (see Chapter 6 for a brief discussion of this), ensuring that the methods used are successfully predicting performance in the organization is an important analytic activity to carry out.

Human bias in recruitment selection

There is so much potential for human bias to come into play in the recruitment and selection process that an entire chapter could be devoted to discussing this (and how an analyst might try to expose its occurrence). Examples of such general everyday judgement biases include 'halo' effects (where one characteristic stands out and influences judgements of other characteristics), leniency tendencies and harshness tendencies, as well as first or last impression effects. However, one of the key biases that the predictive HR analytics expert will want to explore is that associated with stereotyping, prejudice and discrimination. Thus, one of the case study examples we present here revolves around an exploration into patterns of demographics that might be found associated with recruitment and selection stages; specifically, whether the patterns of gender or UG proportions in the applicant pool remain consistent through various stages of the recruitment and selection period. As with the other analyses that we are presenting for this chapter, analysis exploring bias and recruitment activities is in essence a subset of diversity analysis; thus the following example could equally be found within our diversity case study in Chapter 4.

Example 1: consistency of gender and UG proportions in the applicant pool

The following example involves a data set that has been compiled in order to specifically conduct inferential testing linked to gender and UG profiles of the pool of applications received, versus the applications shortlisted/interviewed and ultimately those who are offered a job. The following data set has information linked to 280 applications for graduate jobs in a large consultancy firm.

The data set that we use here is *Ch8_recruitment_applicants_2023.xlsx*. The applicant data set includes the following information within nine variables:

1 ApplicantCode (applicant code).

2 Gender (1 = male or 2 = female).

3 UGyn (underrepresented group: 1 = yes or 2 = no).

4 ShortlistedNY (0 = rejected or 1 = shortlisted).

5 Interviewed (0 = not interviewed or 1 = interviewed).

6 FemaleONpanel (1 = male only panel or 2 = female member on panel).

7 OfferNY (1= made an offer or 0 = not offered).

8 AcceptNY (1 = accepted or 0 = declined).

9 JoinYN (1 = joined or 0 = not joined).

As the variable and value labels indicate, the data set indicates the gender (*Gender* – variable 2) of each person that sent in an application for the graduate job as well as whether or not they were categorized as underrepresented group (*UGyn* – variable 3). Importantly, the *ShortlistedNY* variable indicates whether, after an initial review of their application, they were considered to be an appropriate candidate for interview (in other words, considered potentially employable). The *Interviewed* variable indicates whether they were interviewed or not, the *FemaleONPanel* variable indicates whether there was a female interviewer included on the interview panel. Then a key variable here is whether the applicant was offered a job or not (*OfferNY*) and the *AcceptNY* variable indicates whether they accepted the offer. Finally the *JoinYN* variable indicates whether the applicant joined the organization.

Patterns of gender and UG in the applicant pool

The first thing we will want to do is look at the patterns of gender and UG in the applicant pool in general. We will load the data and examine the frequencies of both variables. The code for this example is in the file *Ch8_examples_.R*. We first load packages, set the working directory, and load the data by running the code below. You can run each line of code by highlighting it and clicking the *Run* button, or through the keyboard shortcut *Control + Enter* (Windows and Linux) / *Command + Return* (MacOS). The first time you run this code, it may take a few minutes to download all of the required packages from the internet.

The first four lines load some required packages, set the working directory, and load the data:

```
if (!require("pacman")) install.packages("pacman")
pacman::p_load(readxl, dplyr, descr, modelsummary, this.path, huxtable)
setwd(this.path::here())
Ch8_ex1 <- read_excel("Ch8_recruitment_applicants_2023.xlsx")
```

For readability, we will transform numeric variables into factors. First, we transform the gender variable:

```
Ch8_ex1$Gender_text <- as.factor(case_match(Ch8_ex1$Gender, 1 ~ "Male",
2 ~ "Female"))
```

Where we used two lines of code to accomplish this in examples in a previous chapter, we will condense this into a single line, as you can see in the line of code above. We do this by nesting the *case_match* function within the *as.factor* function. What happens is that any time a *1* or a *2* is seen in the *Gender* variable in the *Ch8_ex1* dataframe, a value of *Male* or *Female* is generated accordingly, and this value is stored as a factor value (not as a character value) in the new variable *Gender_text*. Nesting functions within other functions can shorten code, but more than two levels of nested functions can get confusing. We recommend no more than two levels of nesting so that you maintain interpretable code. We will recode additional variables with the following lines:

```
Ch8_ex1$UGyn_text <- as.factor(case_match(Ch8_ex1$UGyn, 1 ~ "yes",
2 ~ "no"))
Ch8_ex1$ShortlistedNY_text <- as.factor(case_match(Ch8_ex1$ShortlistedNY,
0 ~ "rejected", 1 ~ "shortlisted"))
Ch8_ex1$Interviewed_text <- as.factor(case_match(Ch8_ex1$Interviewed,
0 ~ "not interviewed", 1 ~ "interviewed"))
Ch8_ex1$FemaleONpanel_text <- as.factor(case_match
(Ch8_ex1$FemaleONpanel, 1 ~ "male only panel", 2 ~ "female member on
panel"))
Ch8_ex1$OfferNY_text <- as.factor(case_match(Ch8_ex1$OfferNY,
1 ~ "made an offer", 0 ~ " not offered"))
Ch8_ex1$AcceptNY_text <- as.factor(case_match(Ch8_ex1$AcceptNY,
1 ~ "accepted", 0 ~ "declined"))
Ch8_ex1$JoinYN_text <- as.factor(case_match(Ch8_ex1$JoinYN,
1 ~ "joined", 0 ~ "not joined"))
```

We can then generate frequency tables for each variable of interest with the following lines of code.

```
datasummary((Gender_text + UGyn_text + ShortlistedNY_text + Interviewed_text +
    FemaleONpanel_text + OfferNY_text + AcceptNY_text + JoinYN_text) +
    1 ~ N + Percent(), data = Ch8_ex1, output = "huxtable")
```

Above, we use the *datasummary* program in the *modelsummary* package to generate
the frequency tables, which results in Figure 8.1.

8.1

		N	Percent
Gender_text	Female	202	72.14
	Male	78	27.86
UGyn_text	no	159	56.79
	yes	121	43.21
ShortlistedNY_text	rejected	192	68.57
	shortlisted	88	31.43
Interviewed_text	interviewed	55	19.64
	not interviewed	225	80.36
FemaleONpanel_text	female member on pan-el	22	7.86
	male only panel	33	11.79
OfferNY_text	not offered	27	9.64
	made an offer	28	10.00
AcceptNY_text	accepted	18	6.43
	declined	10	3.57
JoinYN_text	joined	18	6.43
	not joined	10	3.57
	All	280	100.00

When we look at the table generated in Figure 8.1, we can see that of the 280 applicants for these jobs, the majority are female (72.14 per cent) and just under half
(43.21 per cent) are categorized as underrepresented groups. Subsequently, 88 were
shortlisted and 55 were interviewed, leading to 28 offers and 18 joining.

Example 2: investigating the influence of gender and UG on shortlisting and offers made

A key question that we want to explore here is whether the proportion of those
shortlisted for interview who are female or UG are representative of these groups
from the applicant pool. If it is the case that the proportion of female applicants is
the same as the proportion of those shortlisted, then this immediately suggests that
there is no evidence of any particular gender bias. Just from looking at the gender
frequencies presented above, which indicate that 72 per cent of the applicant pool
are female, we should expect a similar proportion of females to be present in the
group of applicants that have been shortlisted, if the initial screening procedures
have no particular bias.

Importantly, as we discussed in the diversity case study in Chapter 4, the analysis required to test whether there is evidence for any meaningful bias would require a crosstabs analysis and, in particular, a chi-square test to check whether there is statistically significant evidence of any gender preferences in the process of shortlisting. Following on from the code above, we will first generate a cross-tabulation of *Gender_text* and *ShortlistedNY_text* variables. The following code follows from the example above, so you will need to run the code from the prior section to make the following work:

```
CrossTable(Ch8_ex1$Gender_text, Ch8_ex1$ShortlistedNY_text, prop.t =
FALSE, prop.chisq = FALSE, expected = TRUE)
```

This produces Figure 8.2:

8.2

```
> CrossTable(Ch8_ex1$Gender_text, Ch8_ex1$ShortlistedNY_text, prop.
t = FALSE, prop.chisq = FALSE, expected = TRUE)
   Cell Contents
|-------------------------|
|                       N |
|              Expected N |
|          N / Row Total |
|          N / Col Total |
|-------------------------|
```

	Ch8_ex1$ShortlistedNY_text		
Ch8_ex1$Gender_text	rejected	shortlisted	Total
Female	152	50	202
	138.5	63.5	
	0.752	0.248	0.721
	0.792	0.568	
Male	40	38	78
	53.5	24.5	
	0.513	0.487	0.279
	0.208	0.432	
Total	192	88	280
	0.686	0.314	

As we can see from the output, 38 out of the 78 males in the applicant pool were shortlisted and 50 from the 202 females were shortlisted. Also, although 72.1 per cent of the applicant pool are female, the proportion of those shortlisted who are female drops to 56.8 per cent. Thus the cross-tabulation provides some evidence that there may be a male-leaning preference in the shortlisting process (which could be due to the fact that the male candidates are stronger applicants; however, all things being equal we would not expect this pattern).

Although the frequency statistics above suggest that there may be some gender male preference in the shortlisting process, we do not at this stage know whether this could occur by chance alone. Therefore conducting chi-square analysis is required in order for us to understand how strong this tendency is and whether this is a statistically significant pattern. We conduct the analysis with the following code:

```
chisq.test(Ch8_ex1$Gender_text, Ch8_ex1$ShortlistedNY_text)
```

This produces Figure 8.3:

8.3
```
> chisq.test(Ch8_ex1$Gender_text, Ch8_ex1$ShortlistedNY_text)

    Pearson's Chi-squared test with Yates' continuity correction

data: Ch8_ex1$Gender_text and Ch8_ex1$ShortlistedNY_text
X-squared = 13.905, df = 1, p-value = 0.0001923
```

As Figure 8.3 shows, the Pearson's chi-square value of 13.905 is highly significant (with $p < 0.001$). Therefore we can be completely confident that there is definitely a pro-male preference in the shortlisting process somewhere (which would probably require further investigation); there is less than a 1 in 1,000 chance that we would find this pattern of gender proportions with the shortlisted versus not shortlisted populations by chance alone.

We would also need to carry out the same analysis on the shortlisted (versus non-shortlisted) applicant pool but this time comparing UG classification. We similarly generate a cross-tabulation:

```
CrossTable(Ch8_ex1$UGyn_text, Ch8_ex1$ShortlistedNY_text, prop.t =
FALSE, prop.chisq = FALSE, expected = TRUE)
```

Which produces Figure 8.4:

8.4
```
> CrossTable(Ch8_ex1$UGyn_text, Ch8_ex1$ShortlistedNY_text, prop.
t = FALSE, prop.chisq = FALSE, expected = TRUE)

   Cell Contents
|---------------------------|
|                       N |
|              Expected N |
|          N / Row Total |
|          N / Col Total |
|---------------------------|


===============================================================
                          Ch8_ex1$ShortlistedNY_text
Ch8_ex1$UGyn_text         rejected        shortlisted        Total
---------------------------------------------------------------
no                            90                69              159
                             109                50
                           0.566             0.434            0.568
                           0.469             0.784
---------------------------------------------------------------
yes                          102                19              121
                              83                38
                           0.843             0.157            0.432
                           0.531             0.216
---------------------------------------------------------------
Total                        192                88              280
                           0.686             0.314
===============================================================
```

As the cross-tabulation in Figure 8.4 shows, of the 280 applicants, 121 (43.2 per cent) are UG and of these only 19 were shortlisted. This amounts to 15 per cent of the UG part of the applicant pool. When you compare this to the fact that 43.4 per cent (69 applicants) of the non-UG applicant pool (159) were shortlisted, this seems to show a real preference for non-UG applicants in the shortlisting process. Importantly, as we did previously with gender, we need to test this pattern for significance using the chi-square test, which we conduct with the next line of code:

```
chisq.test(Ch8_ex1$UGyn_text, Ch8_ex1$ShortlistedNY_text)
```

Which produces the following output (Figure 8.5):

8.5
```
> chisq.test(Ch8_ex1$UGyn_text, Ch8_ex1$ShortlistedNY_text)

        Pearson's Chi-squared test with Yates' continuity correction

data: Ch8_ex1$UGyn_text and Ch8_ex1$ShortlistedNY_text
X-squared = 23.184, df = 1, p-value = 1.472e-06
```

Importantly, what we see here is that the likelihood of finding this pro-non-UG short-listing preference by chance alone (given the proportions of UG we find in our applicant pool) is less than a 1 in 1,000 chance (chi square = 23.184, p < 0.001). Thus, although lots of the applicant pool are UG, relatively few of them are shortlisted. Such a finding would need to be investigated further to make sure that these shortlisting preferences were not being driven by some systematic discrimination or prejudice.

Combining gender and UG in predicting shortlisting

In the above analysis we have explored the patterns of shortlisting across two varia-bles of gender and UG; however, our analysis explores the patterns of shortlisting across these two variables separately. Importantly, when we conduct analysis of factors that might predict shortlisting, we should ideally take these two demographic variables into account at the same time. One of the reasons to do this is that there may be a relationship between UG and gender in our applicant pool. If it were the case, for example, that most of the UG applicant group were female, the two different sets of findings above might actually be due to UG *or* gender preferences rather than both. Therefore it would be important to incorporate both into an analysis at the same time. One way of doing this is using logistic regression (as we did in the turnover case study in Chapter 6). We would use logistic rather than linear regression here because the outcome (shortlisted or not) is binary. We first load the *rcompanion* package to help with logistic regression, and *kableExtra* for positioning tables:

```
pacman::p_load(rcompanion, kableExtra)
```

To conduct the logistic regression, we can run the following line of code:

```
diversity_reg <- glm(ShortlistedNY ~ Gender_text + UGyn_text, data =
Ch8_ex1, family = "binomial")
```

And examine model fit with the next line of code:

```
nagelkerke(diversity_reg, restrictNobs = TRUE)
```

Which produces Figure 8.6:

8.6
```
> nagelkerke(diversity_reg, restrictNobs = TRUE)
$Models

Model: "glm, ShortlistedNY ~ Gender_text + UGyn_text, binomial, Ch8_ex1"
Null:  "glm, ShortlistedNY ~ 1, binomial, fit$model"

$Pseudo.R.squared.for.model.vs.null
                                 Pseudo.R.squared
McFadden                               0.120428
Cox and Snell (ML)                     0.139231
Nagelkerke (Cragg and Uhler)           0.195535

$Likelihood.ratio.test
 Df.diff LogLik.diff Chisq      p.value
     -2       -20.99 41.98    7.6581e-10

$Number.of.observations

Model: 280
Null:  280

$Messages
[1] "Note: For models fit with REML, these statistics are based on
refitting with ML"

$Warnings
[1] "None"
```

The statistics shown in Figure 8.6 tell us that gender and UG seem to account for just under 20 per cent of the variation in shortlisting (Nagelkerke pseudo R-square = 0.19355, thus 19.36 per cent) and this model (chi-square = 41.98) is highly significant (p<0.001). Importantly, we need to look at the model summary and coefficients in order to identify whether gender and UG *both* account for whether the applicants are shortlisted. First we examine the model:

```
summary(diversity_reg)
```

Which produces Figure 8.7:

8.7
```
> summary(diversity_reg)

Call:
glm(formula = ShortlistedNY ~ Gender_text + UGyn_text, family =
"binomial",
    data = Ch8_ex1)

Coefficients:
                  Estimate   Std. Error    z value    Pr(>|z|)
(Intercept)        -0.6032       0.1856     -3.250     0.00115 **
Gender_textMale     1.1957       0.3006      3.978    6.94e-05 ***
UGyn_textyes       -1.5157       0.3096     -4.895    9.83e-07 ***
---
Signif. codes:  0 '***' 0.001 '**' 0.01 '*' 0.05 '.' 0.1 ' ' 1


(Dispersion parameter for binomial family taken to be 1)

    Null deviance: 348.59  on 279   degrees of freedom
Residual deviance: 306.61  on 277   degrees of freedom
AIC: 312.61

Number of Fisher Scoring iterations: 4
```

We also generate a table with raw and exponentiated coefficients (i.e. odds ratios) with the next lines of code:

```
mod = list("Log Odds" = diversity_reg, "Odds ratio" = diversity_reg)
modelsummary(mod, exponentiate = c(FALSE, TRUE), statistic = NULL,
stars = TRUE, output = "huxtable")
```

Which produces Figure 8.8:

8.8

	Log Odds	Odds ratio
(Intercept)	-0.603**	0.547**
Gender_textMale	1.196***	3.306***
UGyn_textyes	-1.516***	0.220***
Num.Obs.	280	280
AIC	312.6	312.6
BIC	323.5	323.5
Log.Lik.	-153.306	-153.306
F	17.061	17.061
RMSE	0.43	0.43

+ p < 0.1, * p < 0.05, ** p < 0.01, *** p < 0.001

The set of results shown in Figure 8.8 tells us three very important bits of information. First, when modelled together in accounting for shortlisting likelihood, gender and UG demographic characteristics *both* independently (significantly) account for the likelihood of whether the applicant will be shortlisted. This information can be ascertained from the fact that the coefficients for both variables in Table 8.8 have three stars next to them. Second, the odds ratio column gives us information about the odds of males versus females and UG versus non-UG getting shortlisted. To understand these odds ratios we need to bear in mind how the data set is coded.

1 *Gender_text* ("Male" or "Female").

2 *UGyn_text* ("yes" or "no").

3 *ShortlistedNY* (0 = rejected or 1 = shortlisted).

The shortlisted dependent variable coding implies that as this variable increases to 1 from 0 then the applicant has been shortlisted. As the odds ratio for the *Gender_text* variable is 3.306 when it is equal to male (remember an odds ratio of 1 equates to 50:50 even odds), this tells us that males are 3.306 times more likely than females to be shortlisted. The odds ratio for *UGyn_text* variable of 0.220 tells us that UG applicants are less likely to be shortlisted than non-UG applicants. For every non-UG candidate chosen, only 0.220 UG candidates are chosen. Calculated another way, non-UG applicants are 4.545 times more likely to get shortlisted than UG applicants (1 / 0.220 = 4.545).

Comment and thoughts for additional analysis

The results here clearly suggest that there may be some bias in the shortlisting of the applicants in favour of male non-UG. It would be important to add additional data to the logistic regression that would help us to get a better picture of whether there is something about the female and UG applicants that might explain these preferences that is not linked to any kind of discrimination; for example it may be that the education or work experience patterns associated with these two groups could explain why they are not being shortlisted. Often, an interesting finding that an analysis uncovers will lead to the requirement of additional analysis to be conducted before the real picture of what is going on in the organization is obtained.

SNAPSHOT HIDDEN GEM

Male applicants are 3.3 times more likely to be shortlisted for jobs in our organization than women applicants; and non-UG applicants are 4.5 times more likely to be shortlisted than UG applicants. Analytics indicate that further investigation is required as to why this is the case.

Offers made – gender and UG

One final analysis before we go on to explore predictive models with our selection data is to see whether the non-UG and male preferences found in the shortlisting continues on into the selection phase after the interviews have been conducted. We can repeat the crosstabs and chi-square analysis that we conducted above, but look at who was made an offer after an interview compared to who was not made an offer. We run similar code to what we did previously, changing out the *ShortlistedNY* variable for *OfferNY* variable:

```
CrossTable(Ch8_ex1$Gender_text, Ch8_ex1$OfferNY, prop.t = FALSE, prop.
chisq = FALSE, expected = TRUE)
```

This produces Figure 8.9:

8.9

```
> CrossTable(Ch8_ex1$Gender_text, Ch8_ex1$OfferNY, prop.t =
FALSE, prop.chisq = FALSE, expected = TRUE)
     Cell Contents
|-------------------------|
|                       N |
|              Expected N |
|         N / Row Total |
|         N / Col Total |
|-------------------------|


===============================================================
                              Ch8_ex1$OfferNY
Ch8_ex1$Gender_text          0              1         Total
---------------------------------------------------------------
Female                      18             10            28
                          13.7           14.3
                         0.643          0.357         0.509
                         0.667          0.357
---------------------------------------------------------------
Male                         9             18            27
                          13.3           13.7
                         0.333          0.667         0.491
                         0.333          0.643
---------------------------------------------------------------
Total                       27             28            55
                         0.491          0.509
===============================================================
```

And we can conduct a chi-squared test with the following line:

```
chisq.test(Ch8_ex1$Gender_text, Ch8_ex1$OfferNY)
```

Which produces Figure 8.10:

8.10

```
> chisq.test(Ch8_ex1$Gender_text, Ch8_ex1$OfferNY)

        Pearson's Chi-squared test with Yates' continuity correction

data: Ch8_ex1$Gender_text and Ch8_ex1$OfferNY
X-squared = 4.1035, df = 1, p-value = 0.04279
```

With our first set of analysis output here (Figures 8.9), we can see that although approximately half of those interviewed are female (28 of 55), only about one-third (35.7 per cent) of the interviewees who are offered jobs are female. Importantly, this pro-male job-offer pattern is significant (continuity correction chi-square = 4.1035, p < 0.05; see Figure 8.10). Given that this finding is significant even with the relatively small sample size here (which is not huge), this indicates that our pro-male bias is rather severe.

We now conduct similar analysis with the *UGyn* variable:

```
CrossTable(Ch8_ex1$UGyn_text, Ch8_ex1$OfferNY, prop.t = FALSE, prop.
chisq = FALSE, expected = TRUE)
```

This produces Figure 8.11:

8.11

```
> CrossTable(Ch8_ex1$UGyn_text, Ch8_ex1$OfferNY,
  prop.t = FALSE, prop.chisq = FALSE, expected = TRUE)
     Cell Contents
  |-------------------------|
  |                       N |
  |              Expected N |
  |           N / Row Total |
  |           N / Col Total |
  |-------------------------|


  ===============================================================
                          Ch8_ex1$OfferNY
  Ch8_ex1$UGyn_text           0               1             Total
  ---------------------------------------------------------------
  no                         22              20                42
                           20.6            21.4
                          0.524           0.476             0.764
                          0.815           0.714
  ---------------------------------------------------------------
  yes                         5               8                13
                            6.4             6.6
                          0.385           0.615             0.236
                          0.185           0.286
  ---------------------------------------------------------------
  Total                      27              28                55
                          0.491           0.509
  ===============================================================
```

And we can conduct a chi-square test with the following line:

```
chisq.test(Ch8_ex1$Gender_text, Ch8_ex1$OfferNY)
```

Which produces Figure 8.12:

8.12

```
> chisq.test(Ch8_ex1$UGyn_text, Ch8_ex1$OfferNY)

        Pearson's Chi-squared test with Yates' continuity correction

data: Ch8_ex1$UGyn_text and Ch8_ex1$OfferNY
X-squared = 0.31342, df = 1, p-value = 0.5756
```

When we look at the UG analysis with the interview offer, we see that UG applicants who get to interview (8 from 13) are as likely to get a job offer as the non-UG who get to interview (20 from 42) (see Figure 8.11). This is supported by the non-significant chi-square result (chi-square = 0.313. p > 0.05) (see Figure 8.12).

SNAPSHOT HIDDEN GEM

The bias in the recruitment within our organization that favours male applicants at the early stages of the process (shortlisting) continues into the selection phase of hiring, as males are more likely to be offered a job after an interview than women. Although UG applicants are less likely to be shortlisted and asked along for an interview (compared to non-UG applicants), if they get to interview, they do not tend to experience the same level of bias at this stage (they are as likely to get a job offer as non-UG).

Obviously, further analysis can be carried out that explores various combinations of other decisions made in the recruitment and selection process (e.g. such as whether a female member on the panel might be linked to offer/acceptance frequencies, etc). By now the analyst should be able to apply the above analytic techniques to explore these questions.

Validating selection techniques as predictors of performance

As discussed above, a key activity that an HR analytics expert would wish to conduct is explore what selection factors (from data collected or associated with the selection process) predict post-hire employee performance. One reason to do this is to test how valid the selection processes are; a second reason is to identify selection factors that will predict who is likely to turn out to be a high performer. In the next example we have compiled a data set that merges HR information collected at the selection stage, specifically scores and ratings taken at graduate assessment centres; this particular organization is a large financial consultancy firm and hires a large cohort of graduates each year. The data file used for this analysis is called 'Ch8_selection. xlsx' and contains data linked to 360 graduates within 30 different variables.

The variables are:

1	GradID	Employee Identifier
2	Gender	Male (1) or Female (2)
3	EducationHighest	Education Category: BSc (1) MSc (2) PhD (3)
4	UGYN Underrepresented group: Yes (1) or No (2)	
5	WorkExperience	Worked Before: Yes (1) No (2)
6	GradJOBfunction	Function Joined:

(1) HR
(2) Finance
(3) Marketing
(4) Sales
(5) Risk
(6) Legal
(7) Operations

7	ACPersonalityO	Assessment C Personality Openness (percentage)
8	ACPersonalityC	Assessment C Personality Conscientious (percentage)
9	ACPersonalityE	Assessment C Personality Extraversion (percentage)
10	ACPersonalityA	Assessment C Personality Agreeable (percentage)
11	ACPersonalityN	Assessment C Personality Neuroticism (percentage)
12	ACRatingINTCOMPA	Assessment C Competency Technical (1–5)
13	ACRatingINTCOMPB	Assessment C Competency Team Player
14	ACRatingINTCOMPC	Assessment C Competency Critical Thought
15	ACRatingINTCOMPD	Assessment C Competency Business Aware
16	ACRatingINTCOMPE	Assessment C Competency Drive Innovation
17	ACRatingAPTnumerical	Numerical Aptitude Test Score
18	ACRatingAPTverbal	Verbal Reasoning Aptitude Test Score
19	InductionDay	Attend Induction Day: No (0) Yes (1)
20	InductionWeek	Attend Induction Week: No (0) Yes (1)
21	OnBoardingBuddy	Given Joining Buddy: No (0) Yes (1)

22 Year1performanceRating   Year 1 Performance Rating:

    (1) Fails to Meet Expectations
    (2) Just Meets Expectations
    (3) Meets Expectations Comfortably
    (4) Exceeds Expectations
    (5) A Star Performer

23	LeaverYr2	Leaver in First 24 Months (0) No (1) Leaver
24	HRDummyV	HR Dummy Variable
25	FinanceDummyV	Finance Dummy Variable
26	MarketingDummyV	Marketing Dummy Variable
27	SalesDummyV	Sales Dummy Variable
28	RiskDummyV	Risk Management Dummy Variable
29	LegalDummyV	Legal Dummy Variable
30	OperationsDummyV	Operations Dummy Variable

The 30 variables in this data set contain some demographic and CV-related information associated with the graduates (*Gender, EducationHighest, UG, Work Experience*) and indicate which function the graduate joined (*GradJOBfunction*) and a set of variables that represent dummy variables for each function (see Chapter 7 for a discussion of dummy variables); these are the last seven variables in the data set (24–30 above). Variables 7–11 above indicate the score that each applicant was given with a personality assessment; these represent scores on personality dimensions of openness, conscientiousness, extraversion, agreeableness and neuroticism. Each graduate gets a percentage score for each of these personality dimensions.

The next five variables (12–16 above) represent a competency rating score given (agreed by an interview panel) on the organization's core competencies: A = technical capabilities, B = team player, C = critical thinking, D = business awareness and E = drive and innovation. Note that the competency rating scales range from 1 to 5, but we only have scores of 4 and 5 here because the applicants were not hired unless they were given 4 or 5 on all ratings. Then variables 17 and 18 are aptitude test scores conducted at the assessment centre: *ACRatingAPTnumerical*, which rates the graduate on numerical reasoning; and *ACRatingAPTverbal*, which rates them on verbal reasoning. Then there are three variables (19–21) that indicate whether the graduate attended the induction day (variable 19 above), an induction week (variable 20) and whether the graduate was assigned an 'onboarding buddy' (variable 21) after they joined. All of these 21 variables represent data that was collected at the selection stage/joining stage.

The next two variables include data drawn from the HR information system some time after the graduate joined; this includes the graduate performance appraisal rating at the end of year 1 (Year1performanceRating rated on a scale of 1 = fails to meet expectations to 5 = star performer) and whether they left the company in the first two years of their job

(LeaverYr2). Importantly, some of the graduates left in the first year and as such will not have any performance rating on the Year1performanceRating variable.

Note here that although 106 of the graduates left before the two-year anniversary, the fact that 42 graduates did not get a performance rating may well indicate that these 42 had left before their year-one performance rating was given, thus they left in the first 12 months of their tenure (this needs further investigation).

We will first load the data:

```
Ch8_sel <- read_excel("Ch8_selection.xlsx")
```

And recode some categorical variables so that they are more interpretable:

```
Ch8_sel$Gender_text <- as.factor(case_match(Ch8_sel$Gender,
1 ~ "Male", 2 ~ "Female"))
Ch8_sel$EducationHighest_text <- as.factor(case_match
(Ch8_sel$EducationHighest, 1 ~ "BSc", 2 ~ "MSc", 3 ~ "PhD"))
Ch8_sel$UGYN_text <- as.factor(case_match(Ch8_sel$UGYN, 1 ~ "Yes",
2 ~ "No"))
Ch8_sel$WorkExperience_text
<- as.factor(case_match
(Ch8_sel$WorkExperience, 1 ~ "Yes", 2 ~ "No"))
Ch8_sel$GradJOBfunction_text
<- as.factor(case_match
(Ch8_sel$GradJOBfunction,
                          1 ~ "HR",
                          2 ~ "Finance",
                          3 ~ "Marketing",
                          4 ~ "Sales",
                          5 ~ "Risk",
                          6 ~ "Legal",
                          7 ~ "Operations"))
Ch8_sel$InductionDay_text <- as.factor(case_match(Ch8_sel$InductionDay,
0 ~ "No", 1 ~ "Yes"))
Ch8_sel$InductionWeek_text <- as.factor(case_match (Ch8_sel$InductionWeek,
0 ~ "No", 1 ~ "Yes"))
Ch8_sel$OnBoardingBuddy_text <-
as.factor(case_match
(Ch8_sel$OnBoardingBuddy, 0 ~ "No", 1 ~ "Yes"))
Ch8_sel$Year1performanceRating_text
<- as.factor(case_match
(Ch8_sel$Year1performanceRating,
                          1 ~ "Fails to Meet Expectations",
                          2 ~ "Just Meets Expectations",
                          3 ~ "Meets Expectations Comfortably",
                          4 ~ "Exceeds Expectations",
                          5 ~ "A Star Performer"))
Ch8_sel$LeaverYr2_text <- as.factor(case_match(Ch8_sel$LeaverYr2,
0 ~ "No", 1 ~ "Yes"))
```

We can generate a compact summary of all of the numeric variables with the *data-summary_skim* program in the *modelsummary* package:

```
datasummary_skim(Ch8_sel, type = "numeric", output = "huxtable")
```

This produces Figure 8.13:

8.13

	Unique	Missing Pct.	Mean	SD	Min	Median	Max
GradID	360	0	180.5	104.1	1.0	180.5	360.0
Gender	2	0	1.4	0.5	1.0	1.0	2.0
EducationHighest	3	0	1.6	0.5	1.0	2.0	3.0
UGYN	2	0	1.8	0.4	1.0	2.0	2.0
WorkExperience	2	0	1.7	0.5	1.0	2.0	2.0
GradJOBfunction	7	0	3.7	2.1	1.0	3.0	7.0
ACPersonalityO	10	0	49.3	15.1	26.0	46.0	97.0
ACPersonalityC	20	0	62.4	21.1	23.0	57.0	98.0
ACPersonalityE	19	0	57.3	21.1	26.0	57.0	98.0
ACPersonalityA	14	0	56.9	21.9	26.0	57.0	98.0
ACPersonalityN	31	0	59.0	22.1	12.0	57.0	98.0
ACRatingINTCOMPA	2	0	4.4	0.5	4.0	4.0	5.0
ACRatingINTCOMPB	2	0	4.8	0.4	4.0	5.0	5.0
ACRatingINTCOMPC	2	0	4.2	0.4	4.0	4.0	5.0
ACRatingINTCOMPD	2	0	4.6	0.5	4.0	5.0	5.0
ACRatingINTCOMPE	2	0	4.2	0.4	4.0	4.0	5.0
ACRatingAPTnumerical	15	0	84.2	8.0	56.0	83.0	98.0
ACRatingAPTverbal	14	0	83.3	6.1	67.0	83.0	97.0
InductionDay	2	0	0.9	0.3	0.0	1.0	1.0
InductionWeek	2	0	0.8	0.4	0.0	1.0	1.0
OnBoardingBuddy	2	0	0.9	0.3	0.0	1.0	1.0
Year1performanceRating	6	12	3.4	1.2	1.0	3.0	5.0
LeaverYr2	2	0	0.3	0.5	0.0	0.0	1.0
HRDummyV	2	0	0.2	0.4	0.0	0.0	1.0
FinanceDummyV	2	0	0.2	0.4	0.0	0.0	1.0
MarketingDummyV	2	0	0.2	0.4	0.0	0.0	1.0
SalesDummyV	2	0	0.1	0.3	0.0	0.0	1.0
RiskDummyV	2	0	0.1	0.3	0.0	0.0	1.0
LegalDummyV	2	0	0.2	0.4	0.0	0.0	1.0
OperationsDummyV	2	0	0.1	0.3	0.0	0.0	1.0

We can also get a summary of the factor variables we just recoded with the following code:

```
datasummary_skim(Ch8_sel, type = "categorical", output = "huxtable")
```

This produces Figure 8.14:

8.14

		N	%
Gender_text	Female	150	41.7
	Male	210	58.3
EducationHighest_text	BSc	144	40.0
	MSc	206	57.2
	PhD	10	2.8
UGYN_text	No	280	77.8
	Yes	80	22.2
WorkExperience_text	No	240	66.7
	Yes	120	33.3
GradJOBfunction_text	Finance	66	18.3
	HR	62	17.2
	Legal	60	16.7
	Marketing	70	19.4
	Operations	44	12.2
	Risk	30	8.3
	Sales	28	7.8
InductionDay_text	No	46	12.8
	Yes	314	87.2
InductionWeek_text	No	81	22.5
	Yes	279	77.5
OnBoardingBuddy_text	No	32	8.9
	Yes	328	91.1
Year1performanceRating_text	A Star Performer	64	17.8
	Exceeds Expectations	84	23.3
	Fails to Meet Expectations	27	7.5
	Just Meets Expectations	29	8.1
	Meets Expectations Comfortably	114	31.7
LeaverYr2_text	No	254	70.6
	Yes	106	29.4

Example 3: predicting performance from selection data using multiple linear regression

The first analysis that we present here involves predicting year-one performance appraisal ratings from demographic and CV information, assessment centre ratings (that include personality, competency and aptitude scores), attendance at induction days and weeks, whether they were given an onboarding buddy as well as the 'function joined' information. Thus, as our dependent variable is a 1-to-5 scale variable we will conduct a multiple linear regression analysis. Our dependent variable is *Year1performanceRating*, while our independent variables are most of the other variables (excluding *GradID, GradJOBfunction, LeaverYr2* and *HRDummyV* variables). This code follows from the example above, so you will need to run the code from the prior examples to make the following work.

We can estimate the model with this code:

```
perf_reg <- lm(Year1performanceRating ~ Gender_text + EducationHighest +
        UGYN_text + WorkExperience_text + ACPersonalityO +
        ACPersonalityC + ACPersonalityE + ACPersonalityA +
        ACPersonalityN + ACRatingINTCOMPA + ACRatingINTCOMPB +
        ACRatingINTCOMPC + ACRatingINTCOMPD + ACRatingINTCOMPE +
        ACRatingAPTnumerical + ACRatingAPTverbal + InductionDay_text +
        InductionWeek_text + OnBoardingBuddy_text +
        GradJOBfunction_text, data = Ch8_sel)
```

We can see the model summary with this code:

```
summary(perf_reg)
```

Which produces Figure 8.15:

8.15

```
> summary(perf_reg)

Call:
lm(formula = Year1performanceRating ~ Gender_text + EducationHighest +
    UGYN_text + WorkExperience_text + ACPersonalityO + ACPersonalityC +
    ACPersonalityE + ACPersonalityA + ACPersonalityN + ACRatingINTCOMPA +
    ACRatingINTCOMPB + ACRatingINTCOMPC + ACRatingINTCOMPD +
    ACRatingINTCOMPE + ACRatingAPTnumerical + ACRatingAPTverbal +
    InductionDay_text + InductionWeek_text + OnBoardingBuddy_text +
    GradJOBfunction_text, data = Ch8_sel)

Residuals:
     Min          1Q      Median          3Q         Max
-2.05797    -0.30754     0.00088     0.41912     1.62688

Coefficients:
                        Estimate    Std. Error    t value    Pr(>|t|)
(Intercept)           -6.3016453     1.2266092     -5.137    5.10e-07 ***
Gender_textMale        0.8578881     0.1306267      6.567    2.34e-10 ***
EducationHighest       0.1384466     0.0825704      1.677    0.09467  .
UGYN_textYes           0.0193234     0.1039189      0.186    0.85262
WorkExperience_textYes -0.0606132    0.0892045     -0.679    0.49737
ACPersonalityO        -0.0034899     0.0037530     -0.930    0.35319
ACPersonalityC         0.0079011     0.0026536      2.978    0.00315 **
ACPersonalityE         0.0097542     0.0035029      2.785    0.00571 **
ACPersonalityA         0.0009825     0.0030945      0.317    0.75110
ACPersonalityN        -0.0009245     0.0022080     -0.419    0.67574
ACRatingINTCOMPA       0.3638584     0.1381901      2.633    0.00891 **
ACRatingINTCOMPB       0.1306136     0.1197009      1.091    0.27610
ACRatingINTCOMPC       0.0903146     0.1402235      0.644    0.52003
ACRatingINTCOMPD       0.3592834     0.1125143      3.193    0.00156 **
```

```
ACRatingINTCOMPE              0.3456275    0.1654996    2.088     0.03763 *
ACRatingAPTnumerical          0.0099152    0.0070480    1.407     0.16055
ACRatingAPTverbal             0.0077312    0.0100409    0.770     0.44194
InductionDay_textYes          0.3567033    0.1412323    2.526     0.01208  *
InductionWeek_textYes         0.0234061    0.1286484    0.182     0.85576
OnBoardingBuddy_              0.2318439    0.2521455    0.919     0.35860
textYes
GradJOBfunction_textHR       -0.1540589    0.2537409   -0.607     0.54422
GradJOBfunction_              0.9969515    0.2196078    4.540     8.25e-06 ***
textLegal
GradJOBfunction_              0.4696088    0.2082127    2.255     0.02485  *
textMarketing
GradJOBfunction_              0.2478106    0.1950781    1.270     0.20498
textOperations
GradJOBfunction_              0.7688165    0.1879488    4.091     5.57e-05 ***
textRisk
GradJOBfunction_             -0.2177445    0.2401891   -0.907     0.36539
textSales
---
Signif. codes:  0 '***' 0.001 '**' 0.01 '*' 0.05 '.' 0.1 ' ' 1

Residual standard error: 0.6991 on 292 degrees of freedom
  (42 observations deleted due to missingness)
Multiple R-squared: 0.6639, Adjusted R-squared: 0.6352
F-statistic: 23.08 on 25 and 292 DF, p-value: < 2.2e-16
```

We can also put the coefficients in a table:

```
mod1 <- modelsummary(perf_reg, output = "modelsummary_list")
mod2 <- modelsummary(perf_reg, output = "modelsummary_list", standardize
= "basic")
# Create a list of models
models <- list(
  "Unstandardized" = mod1,
  "Standardized" = mod2)
# Show models
modelsummary(models, stars = TRUE, statistic = NULL, output =
"huxtable")
```

This produces Figure 8.16:

8.16

	Unstandardized	Standardized
(Intercept)	-6.302***	0.000***
Gender_textMale	0.858***	0.362***
EducationHighest	0.138+	0.064+
UGYN_textYes	0.019	0.007
WorkExperience_textYes	-0.061	-0.024
ACPersonalityO	-0.003	-0.045
ACPersonalityC	0.008**	0.144**
ACPersonalityE	0.010**	0.179**
ACPersonalityA	0.001	0.018
ACPersonalityN	-0.001	-0.016
ACRatingINTCOMPA	0.364**	0.155**
ACRatingINTCOMPB	0.131	0.046
ACRatingINTCOMPC	0.090	0.032
ACRatingINTCOMPD	0.359**	0.150**
ACRatingINTCOMPE	0.346*	0.123*
ACRatingAPTnumerical	0.010	0.070
ACRatingAPTverbal	0.008	0.039
InductionDay_textYes	0.357*	0.102*
InductionWeek_textYes	0.023	0.007
OnBoardingBuddy_textYes	0.232	0.035
GradJOBfunction_textHR	-0.154	-0.049
GradJOBfunction_textLegal	0.997***	0.309***
GradJOBfunction_textMarketing	0.470*	0.168*
GradJOBfunction_textOperations	0.248	0.071
GradJOBfunction_textRisk	0.769***	0.182***
GradJOBfunction_textSales	-0.218	-0.053
Num.Obs.	318	318
R2	0.664	0.664
R2 Adj.	0.635	0.635
AIC	701.7	701.7
BIC	803.2	803.2
Log.Lik.	-323.832	-323.832
F	23.075	23.075
RMSE	0.67	0.67

+ $p < 0.1$, * $p < 0.05$, ** $p < 0.01$, *** $p < 0.001$

Note that we are including the *GradJOBfunction_text* despite the fact that it is a categorical variable with multiple levels. Usually, a change in a level of a categorical variable is not a change of numeric quantities (i.e. a change in going from HR to the marketing department is not the same as a change from 2 to 3 years of work experience). However, we can include factor variables because R recognizes these automatically and generates dummy variables for us (see Chapter 7, pages 261–66, for a discussion of dummy variables).

The regression model shown in Figure 8.15 tells us a number of interesting things. First, our demographic, assessment centre, function and induction data accounts for a good deal of the variation (R-square = 0.664) in performance ratings (some 66.4 per cent of this variation) and this model is significant (F-statistic = 23.075, 317 degrees of freedom total, $p < 0.001$). If one looks at the individual standardized coefficients in Figure 8.16 and their corresponding significance levels, we see that there are 10 key variables that can be identified as significant 'drivers' of subsequent performance ratings.

Three of the functional dummies are shown to be significant and all Betas are positive. As our 'finance' category is not visible and was thus the reference category, these indicate that graduates from marketing (Beta = 0.470, $p < 0.05$), risk (Beta = 0.769, $p < 0.001$) and legal (Beta = 0.997, $p < 0.001$) all tend to get more positive performance ratings than those in finance. It seems that those who did attend the induction day are slightly more likely to get a better performance rating (Beta = 0.102, $p < 0.05$). As for the assessment-centre competency ratings, graduates tended to perform better who were rated as more positive on the three competencies: technical capabilities (*ACRatingINTCOMPA*; Beta = 0.155, $p < 0.01$), business awareness (*ACRatingINTCOMPD*; Beta = 0.150, $p < 0.01$), drive and innovation (*ACRatingINTCOMPE*; Beta = 0.123, $p < 0.05$).

The results also indicate that graduates scoring more highly on conscientiousness and extraversion personality characteristics tended subsequently to get higher performance ratings (Beta = 0.144, $p < 0.01$ and Beta = 0.179, $p < 0.01$ respectively). Finally, the coefficient for the gender variable indicates that male employees are more likely to get a positive performance rating compared to female employees as we have a positive coefficient for gender (Beta= 0.362, $p < 0.001$).

SNAPSHOT HIDDEN GEM

Key aspects of assessment-centre activities are found to predict post-joining performance and this provides validating evidence for a range of selection practices used.

The fact that personality factors predict performance provides evidence that the use of personality tests in the assessment centre is a valid selection technique. The same can be argued for the use of competency-based interviews, the ratings from which are significant predictors of performance. The results also indicate that investing in an induction day has benefit too (as attendance on this predicts performance, we discuss this further in Chapter 10).

Before we move on to using this selection data to predict subsequent graduate turnover, we would want to reflect on some of the findings above. We can see that the function that the graduate is in tends to account for a fair bit of the variance in the performance appraisal ratings. This would probably need some investigating in order to understand whether there are some systematic differences in the performance scores given in different departments; such a difference may or may not be a problem, depending upon company policy regarding performance appraisal-rating calibration. Also, we can see that the aptitude test scores do not predict performance. If we assume that aptitude tests should predict performance in jobs, it may be the case that the verbal and numerical reasoning might have an influence on jobs in a varied fashion across different functions (e.g. numerical reasoning may be an important predictor of performance only in certain jobs, such as highly technical roles within the finance or risk division). The analysis here has not tested this and it might be something that the analytics expert should explore further (by looking at the correlations between these scores and performance with the separate functional groups).

Also, in reflecting on the results of the above analysis, it seems to show that female graduates do not perform as well as male graduates. Before drawing any conclusions from this, the analyst would need to consider (and explore analytically) whether there are functional variations in how performance appraisal ratings are applied in practice (managers across functions may vary in their generosity when giving ratings). Related to this, the analyst would need to consider whether the functions vary in male and female ratios. This apparent gender effect could also be demonstrating a gender bias in performance appraisal practices and the finding definitely needs to be investigated further. We will return to this analysis in Chapter 10 where we use the results of these regression models to predict expected levels of performance of candidates in an assessment centre (to potentially aid selection decisions).

Example 4: predicting turnover from selection data – validating selection techniques by predicting turnover

For our last recruitment and selection example we continue to use the same graduate selection data set that we introduced in the previous example (in predicting performance): *Ch8_selection.xlsx*. Although this is the same data set, we set out details of the variables and coding again for ease of reference:

1 GradID   Employee Identifier

2 Gender   Male (1) or Female (2)

3 EducationHighest   Education Category: BSc (1) MSc (2) PhD (3)

4 UGYNUnderrepresented group: Yes (1) or No (2)

5 WorkExperience   Worked Before: Yes (1) No (2)

6 GradJOBfunction   Function Joined:

   (1) HR
   (2) Finance

    (3) Marketing
    (4) Sales
    (5) Risk
    (6) Legal
    (7) Operations

7	ACPersonalityO	Assessment C Personality Openness (percentage)
8	ACPersonalityC	Assessment C Personality Conscientious (percentage)
9	ACPersonalityE	Assessment C Personality Extraversion (percentage)
10	1ACPersonalityA	Assessment C Personality Agreeable (percentage)
11	1ACPersonalityN	Assessment C Personality Neuroticism (percentage)
12	1ACRatingINTCOMPA	Assessment C Competency Technical (1–5)
13	ACRatingINTCOMPB	Assessment C Competency Team Player
14	ACRatingINTCOMPC	Assessment C Competency Critical Thought
15	ACRatingINTCOMPD	Assessment C Competency Business Aware
16	ACRatingINTCOMPE	Assessment C Competency Drive Innovation
17	ACRatingAPTnumerical	Numerical Aptitude Test Score
18	ACRatingAPTverbal	Verbal Reasoning Aptitude Test Score
19	InductionDay	Attend Induction Day: No (0) Yes (1)
20	InductionWeek	Attend Induction Week: No (0) Yes (1)
21	OnBoardingBuddy	Given Joining Buddy: No (0) Yes (1)
22	Year1performanceRating	Year 1 Performance Rating:

    (1) Fails to Meet Expectations
    (2) Just Meets Expectations
    (3) Meets Expectations Comfortably
    (4) Exceeds Expectations
    (5) A Star Performer

23	LeaverYr2	Leaver in First 24 Months (0) No (1) Leaver
24	HRDummyV	HR Dummy Variable
25	FinanceDummyV	Finance Dummy Variable
26	MarketingDummyV	Marketing Dummy Variable
27	SalesDummyV	Sales Dummy Variable
28	RiskDummyV	Risk Management Dummy Variable
29	LegalDummyV	Legal Dummy Variable
30	OperationsDummyV	Operations Dummy Variable

Here, we are going to predict whether our demographic or our selection-centre data predicts graduate turnover. Thus, as our dependent variable here is the *LeaverYr2* binary variable (variable 23 set out in our list), we can set up a logistic regression to investigate. We will use most of the variables excluding the *GradID* as independent variables. This code follows from the example above, so you will need to run the code from the prior section to make the following work. We can set up the estimation with the following code:

```
leaver_reg <- glm(LeaverYr2 ~ Gender_text + EducationHighest +
            UGYN_text + WorkExperience_text + ACPersonalityO +
            ACPersonalityC + ACPersonalityE + ACPersonalityA +
            ACPersonalityN + ACRatingINTCOMPA + ACRatingINTCOMPB +
            ACRatingINTCOMPC + ACRatingINTCOMPD + ACRatingINTCOMPE +
            ACRatingAPTnumerical + ACRatingAPTverbal +
            InductionDay_text + InductionWeek_text +
            OnBoardingBuddy_text + GradJOBfunction_text +
            Year1performanceRating, data = Ch8_sel, family = "binomial")
```

We can check overall model fit with this code:

```
nagelkerke(leaver_reg, restrictNobs = TRUE)
```

Which produces Figure 8.17:

8.17

```
> nagelkerke(leaver_reg, restrictNobs = TRUE)
$Models

Model: "glm, LeaverYr2 ~ Gender_text + EducationHighest + UGYN_text +
WorkExperience_text + ACPersonalityO + ACPersonalityC + ACPersonalityE +
ACPersonalityA + ACPersonalityN + ACRatingINTCOMPA + ACRatingINTCOMPB +
ACRatingINTCOMPC + ACRatingINTCOMPD + ACRatingINTCOMPE +
ACRatingAPTnumerical + ACRatingAPTverbal + InductionDay_text +
InductionWeek_text + OnBoardingBuddy_text + GradJOBfunction_text +
Year1performanceRating, binomial, Ch8_sel"
Null: "glm, LeaverYr2 ~ 1, binomial, fit$model"

$Pseudo.R.squared.for.model.vs.null
                                         Pseudo.R.squared
McFadden                                        0.307662
Cox and Snell (ML)                              0.308147
Nagelkerke (Cragg and Uhler)                    0.441465

$Likelihood.ratio.test
 Df.diff  LogLik.diff   Chisq      p.value
    -26      -58.573   117.15    1.5541e-13

$Number.of.observations

Model:318
Null: 318

$Messages
[1] "Note: For models fit with REML, these statistics are based on
refitting with ML"

$Warnings
[1] "None"
```

The likelihood ratio test in Figure 8.17 is significant (chi-square = 117.15, p < 0.001) and the Nagelkerke pseudo R-square is .441, thus the model accounts for a good amount of the turnover (approximately 44.1 per cent) that we have in our model. We can examine each of the independent variables after we examine the model summary and put the results in a table:

```
summary(leaver_reg)
```

This produces Figure 8.18:

8.18
```
> summary(leaver_reg)

Call:
glm(formula = LeaverYr2 ~ Gender_text + EducationHighest + UGYN_text +
    WorkExperience_text + ACPersonalityO + ACPersonalityC + ACPersonalityE +
    ACPersonalityA + ACPersonalityN + ACRatingINTCOMPA + ACRatingINTCOMPB +
    ACRatingINTCOMPC + ACRatingINTCOMPD + ACRatingINTCOMPE +
    ACRatingAPTnumerical + ACRatingAPTverbal + InductionDay_text +
    InductionWeek_text + OnBoardingBuddy_text + GradJOBfunction_text +
    Year1performanceRating, family = "binomial", data = Ch8_sel)

Coefficients:
                             Estimate  Std. Error  z value  Pr(>|z|)
(Intercept)                  7.254072    5.636040    1.287  0.198064
Gender_textMale             -1.475599    0.591895   -2.493  0.012667 *
EducationHighest            -0.061308    0.356463   -0.172  0.863446
UGYN_textYes                -0.117642    0.436138   -0.270  0.787363
WorkExperience_textYes       0.076379    0.357292    0.214  0.830725
ACPersonalityO              -0.022576    0.016252   -1.389  0.164796
ACPersonalityC              -0.008892    0.011291   -0.788  0.430971
ACPersonalityE               0.017251    0.014956    1.153  0.248744
ACPersonalityA               0.001325    0.013808    0.096  0.923532
ACPersonalityN               0.020552    0.009650    2.130  0.033196 *
ACRatingINTCOMPA            -0.500084    0.563797   -0.887  0.375083
ACRatingINTCOMPB             0.129340    0.480134    0.269  0.787634
ACRatingINTCOMPC            -0.325908    0.558909   -0.583  0.559816
ACRatingINTCOMPD            -0.496656    0.457434   -1.086  0.277593
ACRatingINTCOMPE             0.437630    0.692689    0.632  0.527528
ACRatingAPTnumerical        -0.060629    0.036303   -1.670  0.094906 .
ACRatingAPTverbal            0.039984    0.043247    0.925  0.355199
InductionDay_textYes        -1.969398    0.568591   -3.464  0.000533 ***
InductionWeek_textYes        0.053869    0.510772    0.105  0.916006
OnBoardingBuddy_textYes     -0.531975    1.086876   -0.489  0.624521
GradJOBfunction_textHR      -3.269841    1.249043   -2.618  0.008848 **
GradJOBfunction_textLegal   -1.574230    1.058902   -1.487  0.137104
GradJOBfunction_           -0.374598    0.879887   -0.426  0.670302
textMarketing
GradJOBfunction_           -0.503548    0.849578   -0.593  0.553380
textOperations
GradJOBfunction_textRisk    -0.407120    0.865539   -0.470  0.638094
GradJOBfunction_textSales   -0.635664    1.011591   -0.628  0.529755
Year1performanceRating       0.086310    0.241503    0.357  0.720802
---
Signif. codes:  0 '***' 0.001 '**' 0.01 '*' 0.05 '.' 0.1 ' ' 1

(Dispersion parameter for binomial family taken to be 1)

    Null deviance:  380.76  on 317  degrees of freedom
Residual deviance:  263.62  on 291  degrees of freedom
  (42 observations deleted due to missingness)
AIC: 317.62

Number of Fisher Scoring iterations: 5
```

We can put the coefficients in a table with the following lines of code:

```
mod = list("Log Odds" = leaver_reg, "Odds ratio" = leaver_reg)
modelsummary(mod, exponentiate = c(FALSE, TRUE), statistic = NULL, stars
= TRUE, output = "huxtable")
```

Which produces Figure 8.19:

8.19

	Log Odds	Odds ratio
(Intercept)	7.254	1413.851
Gender_textMale	-1.476*	0.229*
EducationHighest	-0.061	0.941
UGYN_textYes	-0.118	0.889
WorkExperience_textYes	0.076	1.079
ACPersonalityO	-0.023	0.978
ACPersonalityC	-0.009	0.991
ACPersonalityE	0.017	1.017
ACPersonalityA	0.001	1.001
ACPersonalityN	0.021*	1.021*
ACRatingINTCOMPA	-0.500	0.606
ACRatingINTCOMPB	0.129	1.138
ACRatingINTCOMPC	-0.326	0.722
ACRatingINTCOMPD	-0.497	0.609
ACRatingINTCOMPE	0.438	1.549
ACRatingAPTnumerical	-0.061+	0.941+
ACRatingAPTverbal	0.040	1.041
InductionDay_textYes	-1.969***	0.140***
InductionWeek_textYes	0.054	1.055
OnBoardingBuddy_textYes	-0.532	0.587
GradJOBfunction_textHR	-3.270**	0.038**
GradJOBfunction_textLegal	-1.574	0.207
GradJOBfunction_textMarketing	-0.375	0.688
GradJOBfunction_textOperations	-0.504	0.604
GradJOBfunction_textRisk	-0.407	0.666
GradJOBfunction_textSales	-0.636	0.530
Year1performanceRating	0.086	1.090
Num.Obs.	318	318
AIC	317.6	317.6
BIC	419.2	419.2
Log.Lik.	-131.808	-131.808
F	2.639	2.639
RMSE	0.35	0.35

$+ \ p < 0.1, \ * \ p < 0.05, \ ** \ p < 0.01, \ *** \ p < 0.001$

The output table in Figure 8.19 gives us information about how important each of the variables is in predicting graduate turnover, and indeed the odds of the graduate being a leaver linked to what value they may have in each of the variables. We can see that there are four significant predictors of graduate turnover. The first is gender, which has log odds of 1.476 (p < 0.05) and an odds ratio of 0.229. This tells us that female graduates are 4.367 times more likely to leave than males in the first two years (1 / 0.229 = 4.367).

One of the function dummy variables is also significant, with those in HR less likely to leave than those in finance, the reference group. In fact, those in finance are 26.3 times more likely to leave than HR graduates (1 / .038 = 26.3).

Those graduates who show higher levels of neuroticism are more likely to leave within the first two years (odds ratio = 1.021, log odds = 0.021, p < 0.05). Finally, if the graduate went on the induction day they are less likely to leave (odds ratio = 0.14, log odds = −1.969, p < 0.001) in the first two years. Again, it is not straightforward to conceptualize as we have an odds ratio lower than 1 (0.14); therefore it is often easier to transform the odds ratio to represent the odds of being the lower coded category of the predictor (in this case induction-day absentee). When we do this, we see that absent graduates are 7.14 times more likely to be a leaver within two years than those who attended (1 / 0.14 = 7.14).

SNAPSHOT HIDDEN GEM

Key aspects of assessment-centre activities are found to predict graduate turnover. It is clear that the HR function has higher retention than the finance, marketing, risk and operations functions. Female graduates are much more likely to leave than male graduates; this needs further investigation. Also, non-attendance of induction day should be a key warning flag for possible future turnover (as attendance is significant it does, however, validate induction days as a useful onboarding activity).

Further considerations

As mentioned elsewhere, it is often the case that when one begins to analyse and diagnose predictors of various important outcomes (such as turnover or low performance), the analysis uncovers diagnostic clues pointing towards what is going on within the organization and further analysis is often required. The fact that turnover varies considerably across the functions, and women are more likely to leave, means that it might be worth exploring whether the gender ratio of leavers varies considerably over the different functions. It might be the case that female turnover is extremely high in some of the functions with high turnover; this would be worth exploring. This is in effect an interaction analysis (we explain this in Chapter 11). Ultimately, as the HR analytics expert becomes more experienced, they will begin to see clues in the data that help them to really understand (and predict) what is going on in their organization.

Other considerations for analytic applications

Here, as with all the chapters, we have only presented some examples of the kind of models that an analytics team could begin to explore with each topic or area. There are obviously many different types of analysis that focus on the area of recruitment and selection analytics that we do not cover here. One thing that analysts linked to recruitment and selection teams may want to consider is the cost of recruitment and selection activities (and the cost per successful hire). This kind of information would be useful to feed into analysis where the HR analytics team want to validate particular selection techniques/activities. Cost information can be linked to analysis that we have carried out above.

Once the HR analytics team increase in their level of experience, the potential and opportunities for integrating different data (e.g. cost information) into models, interpretations and recommendations linked to analysis examples we present here will begin to expand.

Reference

Schmidt, F and Hunter, J (1998) The validity and utility of selection methods in personnel psychology: Practical and theoretical implications of 85 years of research findings, *Psychological Bulletin*, 124 (2), pp 262–74

Case study 6

Monitoring the impact of interventions

Tracking the impact of interventions

One of the key tasks that an HR analytics practitioner will be involved in is helping to evaluate the impact of an HR intervention. Often these interventions can involve a considerable financial investment and there may be an expectation that the intervention will have an impact. The obvious example is something like the introduction of a training programme; training programmes cost money and the evaluation of the effectiveness of training can be considered to be an activity that any good HR function should do automatically (there are literally hundreds of books out there explaining how to do this). The cost of any HR intervention, and its potential return, is something that HR practitioners have to consider in the planning and inception stage. It is often the case that before the intervention gets a sign-off HR will have to explicitly anticipate and present expected outcomes as part of a business case to justify the investment. Thus, having expertise in helping to track and monitor the potential impact of HR interventions is an essential capability that an HR analytic expert would be required to have.

Ultimately, to properly assess the impact or efficacy of any intervention programme, some assessment of *change* will be required. This may be, for example, a change in employee attitudes, perceptions or behaviour. For an intervention to have had an impact, some change must occur following its introduction. In the majority of cases, the only reason to introduce an HR intervention is to create change of some sort. Having said this, there may of course be a situation where the HR function wants to introduce an intervention to stop change (e.g. to make sure that positive attitudes or behaviours do not decline). In general the HR function wants to impact something, and something is expected to change after the intervention. Importantly, the HR analytics expert will be completely aware of this fact, as often the only way to track the impact of an intervention is to demonstrate and interrogate change in one or more appropriate metrics.

What intervention; what measure?

When contemplating how to track the impact of an intervention, the HR analytics expert will need to carefully consider what metric should be used. It is possible that some simple metrics may exist already that can be monitored over time and can give information that indicates impact. For example, if you were to implement an HR initiative (such as training) to improve performance, there may be performance indicators that are regularly collected (such as customer feedback results) that you could just track and watch for any change subsequent to implementation. Another example where a relevant direct metric may already exist (that can just be monitored) is where an HR intervention has been introduced to have a positive impact on well-being; sickness absence rates (assuming that these are recorded) and changes in these could simply be tracked. Thus some metrics will exist that can be accessed to track the impact of an intervention.

Importantly, great care must be taken to ensure that the metric used to track the impact is actually a valid indicator of something that the HR function hopes to influence with the intervention. The metric must fit the intended impact of an intervention in order to track the impact properly. As mentioned, in some cases this is simple and a metric exists; however, in other cases this is not possible. Although in Chapter 7 we gave an example of sickness absence rates as a possible measure of well-being, and this may be a reasonable indicator of well-being, it may not be the only or best measure. There may be a case for identifying other indicators as well: for example, employee levels of engagement, job satisfaction and/or levels of stress or psychological strain.

So the HR analytics expert needs to address each intervention and ask three key questions:

1 What exactly would we expect this intervention to impact/what do we expect/ hope to see a change in if it is successful?

2 What possible measures or metrics exist at the moment that might help test for this change?

3 Do we need to create a measure/index/metric that we can track to assess the impact of the intervention?

It may be that the analytics expert recommends that the organization create new methods to measure and track particular perceptions, attitudes, behaviours or performance indicators in order to monitor the effectiveness of an HR intervention. Importantly (ideally) this needs to be done before the intervention is implemented; a key way to be able to identify the impact of an intervention is to track the impact from before, after and beyond. Ultimately, from an analytics point of view, this requires a solid understanding of the analysis of 'change'.

A simple example might be if we are trying to improve the mathematics skills of cashier staff. We might give them a simple test at time zero, then another test just after some basic mathematics training and then another test six months later to track progress and see if the knowledge has been retained. The test is a measure that we have had to introduce in order to track the impact of the intervention.

Simple change testing

Importantly, when we introduce an intervention, what sort of change are we looking for? Depending on the metric and what we are hoping to affect, we would generally want an improvement of some sort. If, for example, we were trying to improve well-being, then we might want to track sickness absence rates and the change we would be looking for following an intervention would be a reduction in sickness absence rates. So the change would be downward change in sickness absence. An improvement in performance would imply a change in performance; depending upon the performance metric being considered this could involve an increase (e.g. increase in scan rate of checkout staff) or decrease (e.g. average length of calls in a call-centre environment). Regardless of the nature of the required change for an intervention to be considered, an ideal platform to assess change is where a *before-and-after* metric can be monitored; before-and-after monitoring of key metrics is often the only way to obtain a clear picture of the efficacy of any intervention. Aside from tracking established metrics or newly introduced metrics, conducting surveys to provide rich information before and after an intervention might often be the most sensible option. In this situation, the HR function may need to consider introducing either a panel or a pulse survey.

Panels and pulses

The word 'panel' in research and analytics is a term that is used a lot. It is important to understand what it means and why it is a useful research tool that opens up analytic and diagnostic options. A panel is where a collection or sample of people is tracked over time, often multiple times.

In market research, panels are regularly used to monitor and understand consumer behaviour. Often, a sample of shoppers are paid to monitor and keep track of where they shop or what they buy over a period of time; market research companies are able to judge trends and patterns of change in purchasing behaviour. These panels can be monitored and employee purchasing behaviour, and change in this (e.g. following an advertising campaign on certain products), can be monitored and tracked. In addition to this, these people can also be interviewed and surveyed at various points to ask them about their reasons for buying certain products and reactions to certain products. Such a panel of consumers can provide invaluable information that would otherwise not be obtainable. Ultimately, though, from an HR point of view, an ideal 'panel' would be a sample of employees whose perceptions, attitudes and behaviour are tracked over multiple time points.

Due to the inevitable power dynamic between employees and the employer, there will be confidentiality issues and sensitivities in asking employees their attitudes and perceptions about their employment experiences. In the very nature of a panel, employees are identified in some way so that their perceptions, behaviour and attitudes can be tracked over time (thus enabling change to be observed). Therefore an organization has to be very careful as to how these confidentiality issues are handled if part of the data (metric) collection exercise includes surveys. However, with regard to monitoring the impact of intervention, tracking employees over time and monitoring change in a particular metric allows considerable opportunities to evaluate the impact of an intervention.

Distinct from a 'panel', a 'pulse' survey is something that HR functions often carry out; this often involves a short survey sent to a sample of staff carried out over regular intervals; thus multiple waves of data are often collected. Pulse surveys are used to provide a regular picture of staff perceptions and attitudes that can also potentially provide a picture of change occurring within the organization. The difference between a pulse and a panel is that a pulse does not necessitate the same people being monitored over time to observe their change; the ideal pulse does, however, need to involve the collection of a random sample from the organization in each wave of data collection to help ensure that the sample observed on each occasion is representative of the organization's population. In some ways, when tracking change, both the panel and the pulse as methods should theoretically provide information about change over time. For example, if we surveyed a random selection of 850 employees (from an organization that employed 10,000 people) a month before the introduction of an HR intervention (e.g. a work–life balance programme) and then another random selection of 850 employees again six months afterwards, we could potentially obtain a picture of how 'the organization' may have changed over time because each pulse should theoretically represent the organization (assuming the employee samples were a random sample). We could also survey a random selection of 100 employees one month before the HR intervention, track their responses and survey them again six months afterwards; with this panel we should be able to see whether this sample has changed over the time period. Importantly, with panels, our sample size does not need to be as big as with a pulse as we do not have to make absolutely sure that the two data collection samples 'represent' the organization.

Sampling issues and representativeness

One of the reasons we have to use random samples in our analysis is that we want our data set to reflect characteristics of our organization, but we might not want to have to collect metrics or measures for an entire organization. Although we might want to understand the impact of an intervention on an entire organization and were considering setting up a survey to assess its impact (involving either a pulse or a panel), due to our understanding of sampling theory and something called the 'central limit theorem' we do not actually need to survey our entire organization.

The central limit theorem tells us that assuming we carefully sample from our organizational population, only a relatively small sample of employees need to be surveyed if we wish to begin to understand general characteristics of the organization (this is discussed again in Chapter 12). Therefore, even if we are conducting analysis with an extremely large organization with many thousands of employees globally, and we need to conduct surveys to track employee responses to enable an understanding of the possible impact of the intervention, only a sub-sample is required. As statisticians like to say: 'You don't need to eat the whole bowl of soup to get an idea of what the soup tastes like' (as long as you are careful how you select your spoonful). Thus, conducting a mini research project to track employee responses to an intervention may not be prohibitively expensive or as time-consuming as one might assume.

The use of control conditions

In scientific research, experiments are considered to be the only sufficient way of testing for some kind of causal impact. Even with sophisticated modelling of change and variance patterns using regression models, the problem of isolating causality in data will always still be present. As such, if one needs to try to assess the impact of interventions, it is always worth considering whether there may be a possible group of employees who could be compared to our target group as some kind of control condition. For example, if an organization wanted to introduce a new training initiative to increase staff performance, the analyst tracking the impact might want to compare a group of workers who have received the training with a group who have not. Even if training is provided for most of the organization, this is often staggered; thus conditions may be set up to enable the existence of a quasi control group.

Testing for embedded and sustainable impact of initiatives

A famous finding from a ground-breaking series of workplace performance studies carried out in the early 1900s is that change can occur in employees purely when they are being observed. Elton Mayo and colleagues entered the Hawthorne plant of an electric component manufacturing company and carried out numerous experiments on workers to try to understand what factors helped lead to high performance and worker productivity. The so-called 'Hawthorne effect' refers to the situation where employees' performance and productivity seemed to change (and improve) in the workplace studies regardless of the actual experimental conditions that were introduced. Thus, the so-called 'Hawthorne effect' describes the phenomenon whereby, in the act of trying to assess the impact of an intervention, purely by paying attention to employees, a short-term boost in performance and productivity is often witnessed. A key implication that this has for the HR analytics expert who needs to track the impact of an intervention is that any observations of a change that follows the intervention need to be repeated over the long term. This has implications for the time period that is required to assess any sustainable impact of an intervention. Ideally, any analysis of change should incorporate an assessment of change before the intervention and immediately after, as well as at a reasonable period after this.

Time versus intervention effects: isolating the effects of an intervention

Temporal causes of change will often naturally occur in the workplace and, when testing for the possible causal effects of the introduction of an HR initiative or programme, the HR analyst needs to be able to isolate and separate natural temporal effects from the possible 'causal' effects of a new initiative. For example, if a doctor prescribes an intervention of antibiotics for tonsillitis, and then the patient gets better after one month, how do we know that the patient might not have got better after one month due to the passing of time (and the workings of the body's immune system) rather than due to the antibiotics? To assess the effectiveness of an intervention, we need to create comparison groups: a group that experiences the intervention and a control group that does not. This allows us to isolate the intervention effect. At the same time, we must account for natural variations to distinguish between changes caused by the intervention and others that occur due to the passage of time. In the analysis we carry out, every effort should be made to identify and measure both causes of change in the dependent variable. This usually requires the use of temporal analysis that incorporates the assessment of change across groups who may have different experiences throughout the intervention period.

Thus rigorous statistical analysis will need to be conducted that tests change in different groups who may have been exposed to different experiences at the same time, as well as testing for general change in employees over time. One of the best ways to understand the impact of an event is to see change over time before and after an intervention. However, if a 'before' scenario has not been enabled then the analyst needs to do their utmost to be able to isolate groups of employees who have experienced different conditions, so as to strengthen the 'post-intervention' impact conclusions that they can draw. As you will see in one of the examples we give in this chapter, we introduce a training programme to try to improve (increase) checkout scan rate. One way to assess the impact of this is to compare the scan rate of employees who have been on a training course with a group of employees who have not been on a training course. This would, of course, only be possible if not all staff received training. However, an assessment of the true impact of the training intervention would not really be possible if some 'before' data was not obtained; because as the analysis shows here, the before-and-after change in scan rate varies considerably across the group who received training versus the group who did not. Thus, at the very least, an analyst should always try to get two simple measures of a before-and-after metric from a group of employees who have had direct experience of the intervention at hand. Below we go through various examples of different analytic techniques to apply to different types of change-related data; we start with the simplest.

Using a related/repeated/paired sample t-test

If you are interested in exploring change over time linked to the same object or entity (e.g. team) or the same group of individual employees then the simplest form of statistical analysis that you can conduct is the paired sample t-test, also known as the repeated sample t-test or the related sample t-test. With this test, you obtain two sets of data from the same individual or object (e.g. team) and conduct a simple analysis to find out whether there are any statistical differences between each individual's scores over the two occasions; thus whether there has been a significant change in the metrics or measurements over time.

Example 1: stress before and after intervention

In this example, a market research firm has identified a problem with stress in the workplace; an engagement survey identified work pressure and work hours as being positively associated with well-being indices of anxiety, depression and reported sleeping problems. Following a series of focus groups the HR function has identified that a work–life balance intervention is needed to alleviate the problem. Data that the analyst explored can be found in the data set *Ch9_intervention_WLB.xlsx*. This file is a relatively simple data set with four variables:

1 EmployeeID.
2 Gender (1 = male; 2 = female).
3 stressT1 (1–5 where 1 = very low stress; 5 = very high stress).
4 stressT2 (1–5 where 1 = very low stress; 5 = very high stress).

The organization introduced a work–life balance (WLB) programme that included working from home and flexible hours. The survey measured stress levels as part of a simple survey before the change (*stressT1*); it introduced the new programme and then three months later distributed questionnaires again to measure the same stress measure (*stressT2*) a second time. Importantly, there is an employee ID column that the analyst used to match the two waves of data.

As the analyst needs to track employee stress levels over time, some way of linking findings from the two questionnaires was required. To do this the employees were asked to enter their email address on the questionnaires; when circulating the questionnaire the analyst made a commitment that identifying information would never be stored in the same data set as the responses to the other attitude questions. The analyst allocated separate employee identification codes to email addresses in a separate Excel spreadsheet and linked the two sets of email addresses and ID codes separately in order to link the data for analysis. Importantly, this data set remains anonymous even though the stress measures have been linked to individuals across time.

The Excel file here includes basic data collected from 534 employees; the stress measure used is a very basic single item: 'In the past week, what levels of stress would you say you have experienced?' with a scale of 1 = 'very low stress' to 5 = 'very high stress'. The R code for this chapter is in the file *Ch9_examples.R*.

Before we conduct a paired samples t-test the analyst should check the mean stress levels at Time 1 compared to Time 2. The first set of lines load needed packages, set the working directory, and load the data. The first time you run this code, it may take a few minutes to download all of the required packages from the internet.

```
if (!require("pacman")) install.packages("pacman")
pacman::p_load(readxl, modelsummary, broom, rempsyc, modelsummary,
this.path, huxtable, modelbased)
setwd(this.path::here())
Ch9_ex1 <- read_excel("Ch9_intervention_WLB.xlsx")
```

We can then generate descriptive statistics using the *datasummmary_skim* program in the *modelsummary* package.

```
datasummary(stressT1 + stressT2 ~ N + Mean + SD + Min + Max, data = Ch9_
ex1, output = "huxtable")
```

Note the code above asks R to generate descriptive statistics for just the two variables of interest, namely *stressT1* and *stressT2*. This results in Figure 9.1:

9.1

	N	Mean	SD	Min	Max
stressT1	525	3.17	1.03	1.00	5.00
stressT2	300	2.90	1.08	1.00	5.00

The output from this analysis (Figure 9.1) shows the descriptive information about the two stress level variables in the data set. The average of stress at Time 1 is 3.17 (on the 1-to-5 scale) and this is higher than at Time 2 where the average stress level is 2.90. Other information is presented, for example the N associated with the Stress 1 measure is 525. This means that of the 534 respondents in the data set, there were nine cases of missing data for this measure. At Time 2, however, the N was 300 employees, which means that a considerable number of employees who filled out the first questionnaire did not do so the second time.

Because of the uneven Ns across the two waves of stress data, we would have to be very careful drawing any conclusions about change in stress between Time 1 and Time 2 as these are in effect two very different groups of employees. One is made up of over 500 employees, whereas the sample of the latter time period has more than 200 fewer employees. Therefore, if we just looked at the stress level mean of the full Time 1 data and compared this to the lower stress mean at Time 2, we could not be sure as to whether the difference in the average stress levels indicates a reduction in stress or whether it indicates that the people who did not respond across both times had higher stress than those who did respond (which might actually make a lot of sense). Because of this we should really compare the two stress levels when there are 'pairs' of data at Time 1 and Time 2; when we do this we can check for the significance of the paired differences/changes that may have occurred. Simply checking for changes on one particular metric for a group of individuals over time requires a particular statistical test – here you would use a repeated/paired samples t-test. To conduct this test run the code below:

```
t.test(Ch9_ex1$stressT1, Ch9_ex1$stressT2, paired = T)
```

This produces Figure 9.2:

9.2

```
> t.test(Ch9_ex1$stressT1, Ch9_ex1$stressT2, paired = T)

      Paired t-test

data: Ch9_ex1$stressT1 and Ch9_ex1$stressT2
t = 3.9233, df = 293, p-value = 0.0001089
alternative hypothesis: true mean difference is not equal to 0
95 percent confidence interval:
 0.1525583 0.4596866
sample estimates:
mean difference
       0.3061224
```

The results in Figure 9.2 provide us with some key information. The 'mean difference' of stress at Time 1 and Time 2 is 0.306. Interestingly, we can see that the degrees of freedom is 293 (indicated by *df*). In a paired t-test, the total number of people is one greater than the number of degrees of freedom (i.e. df = N -1). This means we only managed to collect stress data at both time points from 294 employees out of 534. In other words, 240 employees that responded to the survey did not complete the survey at Time 1 *and* Time 2. This is very important information that the analyst needs to bear in mind when analysing the responses; who are these 240 employees? Why did they not complete the surveys at both time points? We then might ask whether there are characteristics that we could identify with this group that could have a bearing on the results. Putting these questions aside, we will want to find out the mean and standard deviation of stress at Time 1 and 2 for those who completed the survey at both times. The means and standard deviations shown in Figure 9.1 are based on any response at Time 1 or Time 2. To look at the mean stress for only those who completed surveys at both time points, run the following line of code:

```
stress_df <- na.omit(Ch9_ex1)
datasummary(stressT1 + stressT2 ~ N + Mean + SD + Min + Max, data =
stress_df, output = "huxtable")
```

The first line of code creates a new data set. We use the *na.omit* program to say that we want a version of the *Ch9_ex1* dataframe where we exclude any rows with missing data. This new dataframe is stored as *stress_df* and we use near-identical code as previously to find out the mean and standard deviation of the stress variables for this new dataframe. Running the code above produces Figure 9.3:

9.3

	N	Mean	SD	Min	Max
stressT1	294	3.20	1.04	1.00	5.00
stressT2	294	2.90	1.09	1.00	5.00

From Figure 9.3, it looks like the Time 2 mean stress level (mean = 2.90) is lower than it was at Time 1 (mean = 3.20). As these are matched pairs of stress variables, these employees seem to have shown a reduction in stress levels after the WLB programme was introduced.

Importantly, however, we need to check whether these changes are significant or not. To check for significance, we go back to Figure 9.2 and look at the key statistic, which is the t-value of 3.923. The test is significant at the $p < 0.001$ level. Thus, in summary, stress levels are lower at Time 2 than Time 1, the mean stress levels reduced from 3.2 to 2.9 and this change is significant, $t(293) = 3.923$, $p < 0.001$. Thus, there is evidence here to suggest that the WLB intervention has had a positive impact on stress levels across the market research firm.

Example 2: stress before and after intervention by gender

In the above analysis we conduct a straightforward t-test comparing the entire data set across the two time points. If, however, we want to check whether these differences occur with two different groups (e.g. males versus females) then we will need to use a more complicated analysis. The statistical test we will be using here consists of a particular subset of an analysis referred to as general linear model (GLM).

GLM: within and between repeated measures

Here we are using the same data set again: *Ch9_intervention_WLB.xlsx*.

You will recall that this simple data set has four variables:

1 EmployeeID.

2 Gender (1 = male; 2 = female).

3 stressT1 (1–5, where 1 = very low stress; 5 = very high stress).

4 stressT2 (1–5, where 1 = very low stress; 5 = very high stress).

Here we are going to ask R to test for: a) the significance of a general change in stress levels across Time 1 and Time 2; b) any general gender differences in stress levels; and c) differences in the change in stress when comparing men with women. Thus this analysis performs a number of different statistical checks. This code follows from the example above, so you will need to run the code from the prior section to make the following work. First we load some required packages:

```
pacman::p_load(tidyr, dplyr, ggplot2, rstatix)
```

To do this kind of repeated measures analysis, we need the data to be in a long format. By 'long format' we mean that each row of the dataframe shows a single level of a factor along with the dependent variable. To more concretely explain what we mean, we will examine the current structure of the data, which is in wide format, with this code:

```
head(stress_df)
```

This code produces Figure 9.4:

9.4

```
> head(stress_df)
# A tibble: 6 × 4
      EmployeeID      gender      stressT1      stressT2
         <dbl>        <dbl>         <dbl>         <dbl>
1         1003           1             3             4
2         1004           1             3             3
3         1005           1             3             2
4         1006           1             1             2
5         1007           1             2             3
6         1009           1             4             4
```

The *head* program shows us the first six rows of the dataframe. This data set is in a 'wide' format, because each row captures all of the data for a particular employee. So the first row in the wide format of the data (i.e. first row of *stress_df*) represents employee ID number 1003 who is male and responded to both the Time 1 and Time 2 survey. It's a compact way of recording the data, so this format is very popular. But some programs require the data to be in 'long' format. In 'long' format, we will want one row for their response in Time 1 and another row for their response in Time 2. To keep track of when they answered with which value, it would be preferable to have an additional variable to keep track of Time 1 vs Time 2 responses. There are numerous advantages to storing data in long format, but they are beyond the scope of this chapter. For now, we will focus on transforming from wide to long format, with the following code:

```
stress_df_long <- gather(data = stress_df, key = time, value = stress_lev,
stressT1, stressT2)
```

Here we use the *gather* program in the *tidyr* package. We specify our data set *stress_df*, and tell it that our key variable, or the variable we use to keep track of Time 1 vs Time 2 records, should be called *time*. We then say that the value variable, or the actual stress levels reported, should be called *stress_lev*. We then list the variables to be gathered into long format, namely *stressT1* and *stressT2*. We store this result in a new dataframe called *stress_df_long*. We can then examine the first few rows of this data set with the following code:

```
head(stress_df_long)
```

Which produces Figure 9.5:

9.5

```
> head(stress_df_long)
# A tibble: 6 × 4
        EmployeeID        gender            time        stress_lev
            <dbl>         <dbl>           <chr>             <dbl>
1            1003             1         stressT1                 3
2            1004             1         stressT1                 3
3            1005             1         stressT1                 3
4            1006             1         stressT1                 1
5            1007             1         stressT1                 2
6            1009             1         stressT1                 4
```

We now see four variables, some of them familiar. *EmployeeID* and *gender* are the same, but a new variable *time* records when a response was given and *stress_lev* shows the response at that time. Further down the dataframe will be records for stress levels at Time 2 for the same group of employees.

As in previous examples, we will transform the gender variable to be more interpretable:

```
stress_df_long$gender_text <- as.factor(case_match(stress_df_
long$gender, 1 ~ "Male", 2 ~ "Female"))
```

To get a better idea of the stress levels at each time, within genders and by a combination of both times by gender we will need to generate estimated marginal means – simply generating means might be misleading if there are unequal numbers of genders completing measures at different time points or if factors affect groups differently. Generating estimated marginal means adjusts for unequal numbers and influence of factors; for example, one group may be more affected by stress at T2 than the other. This is an issue when we examine more than one factor at a time. We can generate estimated marginal means by gender, time and a combination of gender and time, and standard deviations using the *estimate_means* program:

```
model <- lm(stress_lev ~ time * gender_text, data = stress_df_long)
estimate_means(model, at = "time")
estimate_means(model, at = "gender_text")
estimate_means(model, at = c("time", "gender_text"))
```

These produce Figures 9.6, 9.7 and 9.8:

9.6

```
> estimate_means(model, at = "time")
NOTE: Results may be misleading due to involvement in interactions
Estimated Marginal Means
```

time	Mean	SE	95% CI
stressT1	3.17	0.06	[3.05, 3.29]
stressT2	2.89	0.06	[2.77, 3.01]

```
Marginal means estimated at time
```

9.7

```
> estimate_means(model, at = "gender_text")
NOTE: Results may be misleading due to involvement in interactions
Estimated Marginal Means
```

gender_text	Mean	SE	95% CI
Female	3.16	0.06	[3.05, 3.27]
Male	2.90	0.07	[2.77, 3.03]

```
Marginal means estimated at gender_text
```

9.8

```
> estimate_means(model, at = c("time", "gender_text"))
Estimated Marginal Means
```

time	gender_text	Mean	SE	95% CI
stressT1	Female	3.39	0.08	[3.23, 3.54]
stressT2	Female	2.93	0.08	[2.77, 3.09]
stressT1	Male	2.95	0.10	[2.76, 3.14]
stressT2	Male	2.85	0.10	[2.67, 3.04]

```
Marginal means estimated at time
```

The means in Figure 9.6, 9.7 and 9.8 tell you a number of important things. First, in Figure 9.6, we see the mean stress levels at Time 1 and Time 2, which shows the mean stress levels in general have gone down between the timepoints. Second, in Figure 9.7, the average stress levels are 2.90 for males and 3.16 for females when you combine the two sets of temporal stress data together. This is called a main effect of gender and the means indicate that females in general seem to express higher stress levels than males. Third, in Figure 9.8, we see males and females separately at the two timepoints. As you can see, the average stress levels of males go down slightly from 2.95 at Time 1 to 2.85 at Time 2, and for females the stress levels go down from 3.39 at Time 1 to 2.93 at Time 2. We can see this graphically if we plot these means with the next lines of code:

```
ggplot(stress_df_long, aes(x = time, y = stress_lev, group = gender_text,
color = gender_text)) +
geom_line(stat = "summary", fun = "mean")
```

This generates Figure 9.9:

9.9

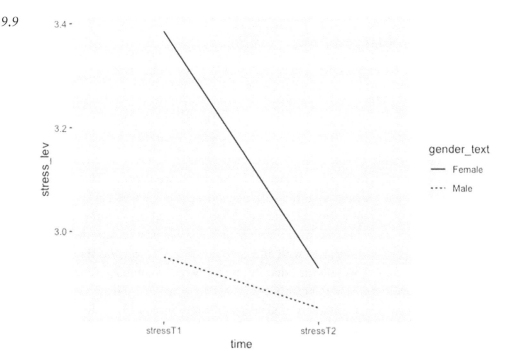

The plot visually represents what has happened with stress in our organization across time and between genders. Importantly we need to check various aspects of these findings (gender differences in stress in general, temporal changes in stress in general across time and temporal changes in stress across time when comparing men with women). To assess this we need to conduct the within and between repeated measures analysis, which is shown in the next lines of code:

```
stress_mod <- anova_test(data = stress_df_long, dv = stress_lev, wid =
EmployeeID, within = time, between = gender_text)
```

We use the *anova_test* program to specify the data set *stress_df_long*, the dependent variable *stress_lev*, the identifier for individuals *EmployeeID*, the within-subjects factor *time*, and the between-subjects factor *gender_text*. We store the results in the *stress_mod* object. We can show the results with the next line of code:

```
stress_mod
```

Which produces Figure 9.10:

9.10
```
> stress_mod
ANOVA Table (type III tests)

              Effect   DFn   DFd       F         p    p<.05      ges
1        gender_text     1   292   6.971   0.00900      *      0.014
2               time     1   292  12.430   0.00049      *      0.017
3   gender_text:time     1   292   5.213   0.02300      *      0.007
```

To interpret these results let us first look at the time result in Figure 9.10. Remember we defined this as the within-subjects factor, or the difference between Time 1 and Time 2. The F-statistic for *time* is 12.430 with a significance of p < 0.001. This is very similar to the paired samples t-test conducted above and it tells us that the general change (drop in this case) in stress over time is significant. We next look at the result for *gender_text*, which is associated with an F-statistic of 6.971, which is significant to the level of p < 0.01. This indicates that in general (when combining Time 1 and Time 2 results), men report significantly less stress than women. Finally, *gender_ text:time* represents the combination of gender and time, specifically if the change between Time 1 and Time 2 are different for women and men. This is associated with an F-statistic of 5.213 and this is significant at the p < 0.05 level. This information is key here, as combined with the plot presented in Figure 9.9 it tells us that females show a significant reduction in stress between Time 1 and Time 2 at a significantly greater level of change than the reduction that men seemed to show between Time 1 and Time 2; this suggests that there is a significant 'interaction' between gender and change in stress across Time 1 and Time 2.

Example 3: value-change initiative

The following example takes us through a scenario where a financial advisory company wants to introduce a new set of socially responsible corporate values and is investing in a 'Values Festival' event, which involves a full day of activities (that all employees participate in) where the new values, and how they translate into every-day behaviour, are introduced:

> *'Our Values'*
> RESPECT *for Key Stakeholders:*
> *Communities, Customers, Shareholders and Employees*

Because the organization is investing a considerable sum of money into this activity, the management want to make sure that the values take hold. Therefore they ask their engagement survey (six-monthly panel) provider to include some questions that can give an indication of the level of employee commitment to these new values. Just before the values event, the managers (who wanted to check for the impact of the values festival) were able to include a set of questions in this externally organized survey sent to a random sample of the organization (800 employees from four key strategically important functions within the organization). The employees were sent the online questionnaires six months later and then another six months after this. The following items were included (note that the name of the organization has been replaced with 'ORG'):

1   In my actions I am always respectful of the local communities associated with ORG.

2   In my actions I am always respectful of ORG's customers.

3   In my actions I am always respectful of ORG's shareholders.

4   In my actions I am always respectful of ORG's employees.

An anonymized data set has been provided to the HR analytics team. This data includes three waves of data collection with 438 employees from the panel; the data can be found in the following Excel data file: *Ch9_value_change.xlsx*.

Here there are 16 variables, the first of which (*FUNCTION*) outlines which of four functions the employee works for (HQ admin, sales, HR, marketing). Twelve of the variables include employee responses to the four individual value questions for each of the three waves. The final three variables are average composite measures of the four items for each of the waves:

1   FUNCTION (department the employee works in 1: HQ Admin; 2: Sales; 3: HR; 4: Marketing).

2   Vals1t1 (value commitment community Time 1).

3   Vals2t1 (value commitment customers Time 1).

4   Vals3t1 (value commitment shareholders Time 1).

5   Vals4t1 (value commitment employees Time 1).

6   Vals1t2 (value commitment community Time 2).

7   Vals2t2 (value commitment customers Time 2).

8   Vals3t2 (value commitment shareholders Time 2).

9   Vals4t2 (value commitment employees Time 2).

10   Vals1t3 (value commitment community Time 3).

11   Vals2t3 (value commitment customers Time 3).

12   Vals3t3 (value commitment shareholders Time 3).

13   Vals4t3 (value commitment employees Time 3).

14 ValsCompositeT1 (composite of the four value commitment items at Time 1).

15 ValsCompositeT2 (composite of the four value commitment items at Time 2).

16 ValsCompositeT3 (composite of the four value commitment items at Time 3).

GLM: repeated measures

The first analysis that we do here is to see whether the staff commitment to the values changes over time; if the value-change programme is to have an impact on staff then we would hope to see an increase in the commitment over the three waves of data collection. Here, we need to test for a significant change over time in the three sets of values, and we use the three composite measures of value commitment six months apart. The statistical analysis that we use for this is GLM repeated measures. This code follows from the example above, so you will need to run the code from the prior section to make the following work.

```
Ch9_ex3 <- read_excel("Ch9_value_change.xlsx")
```

Since the data is in wide format, we will need to transform it into long format. First, we will need to create an ID variable so we can keep track of how each employee responded over time. An easy way to do this is to treat each row number as a separate ID (i.e. the first row is assigned the ID number 1, the second number is assigned ID number 2, etc.), which we can do with the following code:

```
Ch9_ex3$id <- rownames(Ch9_ex3)
```

We can then select just the variables we need to conduct the analysis, namely the three composite variables and the ID variable.

```
values <- Ch9_ex3[, c("id", "ValsCompositeT1", "ValsCompositeT2",
"ValsCompositeT3")]
```

We now transform the dataframe from wide format to long format with the following code:

```
values_long <- gather(data = values, key = time, value = value_level,
ValsCompositeT1, ValsCompositeT2, ValsCompositeT3)
```

We can take a look at the resulting dataframe to see if it is in the intended format. We should have: 1) a variable to indicate each employee *id*, 2) a variable called *time* that records when the variable was measured and 3) a numeric variable that indicates the level of values at a particular time *value_level*. We can check this with the following code:

```
head(values_long)
```

This produces Figure 9.11:

9.11
```
> head(values_long)
# A tibble: 6 × 3
                  id                time            value_level
                  <chr>             <chr>               <dbl>
       1          1                 ValsCompositeT1       4.25
       2          2                 ValsCompositeT1       3.5
       3          3                 ValsCompositeT1       4
       4          4                 ValsCompositeT1       3.5
       5          5                 ValsCompositeT1       3.25
       6          6                 ValsCompositeT1       3.25
```

This data structure is what we expected and what we need for further analysis. As in the previous example, we can now generate some means to gauge change over time. Since we are only looking at one factor we do not need to generate estimated marginal means (and if we did using the code example used previously, we would get the same result). We can generate means with the following code:

```
datasummary(value_level * time ~ N + Mean + SD + Min + Max, data =
values_long, output = "huxtable")
```

Which results in Figure 9.12:

9.12

	time	N	Mean	SD	Min	Max
value_level	ValsCompositeT1	434	4.11	0.45	3.00	5.00
	ValsCompositeT2	438	4.12	0.49	2.00	5.00
	ValsCompositeT3	438	4.19	0.45	2.75	5.00

First let's look at the average level of value commitment over the three time points. The mean level of value commitment (see Figure 9.12) increases from 4.11 at Time 1, to 4.12 at Time 2 and finally 4.19 at Time 3. These averages are linked to a scale of 1 = strongly disagree to 5 = strongly agree; so, in general, people are fairly committed to each of the values; neutral levels of commitment would have a mean of 3. These increases do not seem too large in themselves, though there is an increase (that we will need to test for significance). We can visually examine the pattern through a plot, generated by the following lines of code:

```
ggplot(values_long, aes(x = time, y = value_level, group = 1)) +
   geom_line(stat = "summary", fun = "mean")
```

This produces Figure 9.13, where we can see the increase visually; there seems to be a steeper increase in commitment in the later six-month period compared to the slight increase in the first six-month period.

9.13

We next conduct the analysis with the following code (you may see a warning message about dropping rows that contain missing data):

```
value_mod <- anova_test(data = values_long, dv = value_level, wid = id,
within = time)
```

As we have done with t-tests, we should check assumptions important to the integrity of the test. The repeated measures ANOVA test makes the assumption of something called sphericity. Sphericity is the assumption that the variance of the differences between each pair of scores is equal. So in our example, the test of sphericity is testing for whether the variance of the difference between scores at Time 1 and at Time 2 is the same as the variance of the difference between scores at Time 1 and at Time 3, and the same as the variance of the difference between scores at Time 2 and Time 3. This test applies when there are more than two points of data from the same participant (just as we have here with data from the same people at more than two time points). The Mauchly test, then, explores whether the variance patterns of the differences between the sets of time-point data look different (when looking at particular combinations of time-point data). If the test is violated, the *anova_test* program will run similar (robust) statistical tests alongside the within-subjects ANOVA part of the test, namely the Greenhouse-Geisser tests, which should be used (if the Mauchly test for sphericity is significant, which ideally we do not want it to be).

So, once again, the test for sphericity examines whether the pattern of differences across the different sets of repeated measures violates the assumption of sphericity. Ideally we do not want this test to be significant, as it would be saying that the variance of differences in our data looks unusual when you compare across the particular time phases. The *anova_test* program conducts the test automatically, and we can see the result if we look for it. It is one part of the *value_mod* object and we can see it when we ask for the model results:

    value_mod

Which produces Figure 9.14:

9.14

```
> value_mod
ANOVA Table (type III tests)

$ANOVA
      Effect        DFn    DFd     F       p       p<.05    ges
1     time          2      866   6.159   0.002      *      0.005

$'Mauchly's Test for Sphericity'
      Effect      W       p     p<.05
1     time     0.979    0.01      *

$'Sphericity Corrections'
      Effect       GGe    DF[GG]   p[GG]   p[GG]<.05       HFe    DF[HF]   p[HF]   p[HF]<.05
1     time     0.979 1.96,  847.92   0.002       *      0.984 1.97,  851.73  0.002       *
```

In our case, Mauchly's test is significant (Figure 9.14, p<0.05). Because of this, when considering whether the repeated measures of value commitment change significantly over time we need to consider adjustments to standard test. Fortunately, the *anova_test* program automatically shows the appropriate results in the '$ANOVA' section depending on the significance of Mauchly's test. If the test is not significant, it shows the unadjusted test results. If the test is significant, it shows the figures with the appropriate corrections in the 'Sphericity Corrections' section.

We can now check the result of the repeated measures ANOVA in the section labelled '$ANOVA' in Figure 9.14. We can see that the F-statistic associated with time is significant, indicating that there is significant chance in value commitment across the 12-month period.

The finding here is that, across the three waves of data collection, commitment to the company's new values appears to increase steadily. This provides evidence that the values are potentially being embedded within the workforce.

Something that is important to check for, however, is whether this value 'embedding' is found across all parts of the workforce (such as the different functions).

Example 4: value-change initiative by department

In Example 2, we tested for a change in stress across different groups (male/female) within our workforce. Here, we can conduct an analysis that examines whether the value commitment change we witness over time occurs within different groups of workers. For this we use a GLM repeated measures within and between test (where the value commitment measures are the repeated 'within' element, and the functions are the 'between' group comparison element).

GLM: within and between repeated measures

The statistical analysis that we use for this is similar to the example above, but we will specify a between-subjects factor. Because we are using the same data as in example 3 above, we will be using the same dataframe. So this code follows from the example above, and you will need to run the code from the prior section to make the following work. First, we will recode the *FUNCTION* variable to be more interpretable:

```
Ch9_ex3$function_text <- as.factor(case_match(Ch9_ex3$FUNCTION,
1 ~ "HQ Admin",
                          2 ~ "Sales",
                          3 ~ "HR",
                          4 ~ "Marketing"))
```

Next, we will create a dataframe of just the variables we will need. We follow on in the same example file as above.

```
values_function <- Ch9_ex3[, c("id", "function_text", "ValsCompositeT1",
"ValsCompositeT2", "ValsCompositeT3")]
```

We then transform the data from wide to long format:

```
values_function_long <- gather(data = values_function, key = time,
value = value_level, ValsCompositeT1, ValsCompositeT2, ValsCompositeT3)
```

We then inspect the data to see if the transformation took place as expected:

```
head(values_function_long)
```

Which produces Figure 9.15:

9.15
```
> head(values_function_long)
# A tibble: 6 × 4
         id          function_text      time                value_level
         <chr>       <fct>              <chr>                      <dbl>
  1      1           HQ Admin           ValsCompositeT1             4.25
  2      2           HQ Admin           ValsCompositeT1             3.5
  3      3           HQ Admin           ValsCompositeT1             4
  4      4           HQ Admin           ValsCompositeT1             3.5
  5      5           HQ Admin           ValsCompositeT1             3.25
  6      6           HQ Admin           ValsCompositeT1             3.25
```

The data is in the long format we need, with each row having an ID variable, indicates the function that person is in, has a separate row for each time period, and the level of value commitment recorded within each time. We will remove any rows without reported value commitment with the following command:

```
values_function_long <- na.omit(values_function_long)
```

We can now generate estimated marginal mean levels of value commitment for each time:

```
model <- lm(value_level ~ time * function_text, data =
values_function_long)
estimate_means(model, at = "time")
```

Which produces Figure 9.16:

9.16
```
> estimate_means(model, at = "time")
NOTE: Results may be misleading due to involvement in interactions
Estimated Marginal Means

time              |    Mean   |     SE     |            95% CI
----------------------------------------------------------------------
ValsCompositeT1   |    4.08   |    0.03    |        [4.02, 4.14]
ValsCompositeT2   |    4.09   |    0.03    |        [4.03, 4.15]
ValsCompositeT3   |    4.21   |    0.03    |        [4.15, 4.27]

Marginal means estimated at time
```

And for each function:

```
estimate_means(model, at = "function_text")
```

Which produces Figure 9.17:

9.17

```
> estimate_means(model, at = "function_text")
NOTE: Results may be misleading due to involvement in interactions
Estimated Marginal Means
```

function_text		Mean		SE		95% CI
HQ Admin		4.07		0.02		[4.04, 4.11]
HR		4.23		0.02		[4.19, 4.27]
Marketing		4.05		0.05		[3.94, 4.15]
Sales		4.16		0.04		[4.08, 4.23]

```
Marginal means estimated at function_text
```

We can also generate means by time and function:

```
estimate_means(model, at = c("time", "function_text"))
```

This produces Figure 9.18:

9.18

```
> estimate_means(model, at = c("time", "function_text"))
Estimated Marginal Means
```

time		function_text	Mean		SE		95% CI
ValsCompositeT1		HQ Admin	4.05		0.03		[3.99, 4.11]
ValsCompositeT2		HQ Admin	4.04		0.03		[3.97, 4.10]
ValsCompositeT3		HQ Admin	4.13		0.03		[4.07, 4.20]
ValsCompositeT1		HR	4.22		0.04		[4.15, 4.29]
ValsCompositeT2		HR	4.26		0.04		[4.19, 4.33]
ValsCompositeT3		HR	4.22		0.04		[4.15, 4.29]
ValsCompositeT1		Marketing	4.00		0.09		[3.82, 4.18]
ValsCompositeT2		Marketing	3.98		0.09		[3.80, 4.16]
ValsCompositeT3		Marketing	4.17		0.09		[3.98, 4.35]
ValsCompositeT1		Sales	4.05		0.07		[3.92, 4.19]
ValsCompositeT2		Sales	4.10		0.07		[3.97, 4.23]
ValsCompositeT3		Sales	4.32		0.07		[4.18, 4.45]

```
Marginal means estimated at time
```

And we can visualize these trends over time through a plot:

```
ggplot(values_function_long, aes(x = time, y = value_level, group =
function_text)) +
geom_line(stat = "summary", fun = "mean", aes(linetype = function_text))
```

Which produces Figure 9.19:

9.19

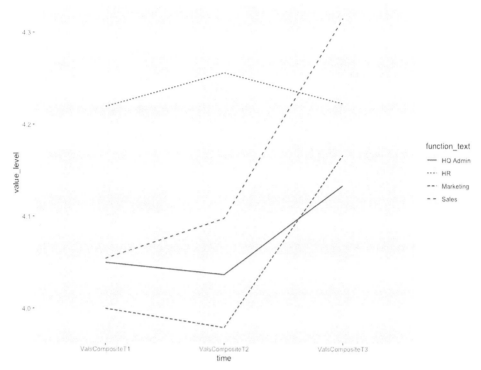

The first set of information that we would probably want to look at here (Figure 9.16) is the means for the three sets of value commitment measures across the three occasions and the value commitment means associated with the four functions. As before, there is some increase between Time 1 and Time 2 but a greater increase occurs between the second and third phases of data collection. Whenever variables are combined with another variable in GLM analysis there is always the possibility that statistics from the samples might vary, as missing data alters the actual sample being used each time. It is important that you are sensitive to these issues. The second set of results in Figure 9.17 shows that there are some differences in the means across the functions (in general; disregarding the temporal differences) with the mean level of value commitment being highest in the HR function and lowest in the marketing function. However, when we look at the third set of results in Figure 9.18 we see that the means of the value commitment differ quite a bit across the three waves, depending upon what function we are considering. For example, the HQ row shows a very slight dip between waves 1 and 2 and an increase between waves 2 and 3; the sales function shows a general increase across all three waves. To further understand the apparent patterns of change we can look at the plot (Figure 9.19).

From the looks of this graph the four functions have slightly different trajectories of change across the three time periods, which may hold some important information if we want to understand the impact of the value-change event (which occurred between waves 1 and 2). However, we need to test for significant differences across the waves, taking into account the differences across the functions. We can do this with the following lines of code:

```
value_function_mod <- anova_test(data = values_long, dv = value_level,
  wid = id, within = time, between = function_text)
```

We can examine the sphericity assumption by examining a specific part of the model output:

```
value_function_mod
```

Which produces Figure 9.20:

9.20

```
> value_function_mod
ANOVA Table (type III tests)

$ANOVA
              Effect    DFn    DFd      F        p      p<.05      ges
1      function_text      3    430   6.404   0.000298      *      0.027
2               time      2    860   9.176   0.000114      *      0.008
3 function_text:time      6    860   2.912   0.008000      *      0.008

$'Mauchly's Test for Sphericity'
              Effect      W      p      p<.05
1               time  0.981  0.017       *
2 function_text:time  0.981  0.017       *

$'Sphericity Corrections'
              Effect    GGe        DF[GG]      p[GG]  p[GG]<.05    HFe        DF[HF]      p[HF]  p[HF]<.05
1               time  0.981 1.96,  844.03  0.000128      *      0.986 1.97,  847.86  0.000124        *
2 function_text:time  0.981 5.89,  844.03  0.009000      *      0.986 5.92,  847.86  0.008000        *
```

We can see Mauchly's test is significant ($p < 0.05$), so we know that the anova_test program will report adjusted results when we look at the summary of the model in the '$ANOVA' section.

When we considering whether the repeated measures of value commitment change significantly over time, the *time* variable is associated with an F-statistic of 9.176, which is significant at $p < 0.001$. Thus we can say that our results change over the three time points. So we see a significant increase in value commitment across the 12-month period here (we would expect this from the previous example).

Before we move on to see whether there are differences in changes across time in value commitment when comparing our functions, we should look at whether there are significant differences between the value commitment of the four functions in general. For this, we look at the between-subjects set of results. The *function_text* variable is associated with an F-statistic of 6.404, which is significant at $p < 0.001$; this part of the test is similar to a one-way ANOVA result that we looked at in Chapter 6 (page 194).

The next thing we need to consider is how our patterns of change over time vary across the different functions. The *function_text:time* result shows a significant interaction between function and value change ($F = 2.912$, $p < 0.01$). This indicates that we can confidently say that there are significant differences in the changes in value commitment when we compare our four functions; our plot graph above (Figure 9.19) helps explain the pattern that we find. There is clearly less of an increase in the value commitment with the HR function (that does not really increase much over the three periods) compared to say the sales function (that shows a greater increase).

Looking at the pattern of results, the HR function might be a little disappointed that there was not an immediate increase in value commitment between the first and the second wave of data collection. But some context is required to fully understand the results. A new performance appraisal system was introduced between the second and third waves that included judging employees on whether they showed commitment to the values of the organization. Thus it makes sense that the value commitment was found in the long term once this performance-appraisal value benchmark was introduced. When examining changes over time it is always important to consider what events were going on during the time of data collection; contextual information is often important to consider when interpreting change over time.

Before we move on from this example, one thing we need to consider is the nature of the sample that we are effectively analysing. In the frequency output in Figure 9.17, it is clear that the sample sizes in our four functions vary considerably. The marketing group has only 24 employees, the financial sales group has only 46 employees, the HR function has 164 and HQ has 200. Whilst we can be confident that the panel results do show significant changes over time, an analyst will need to consider the degree to which there may be something meaningful in the pattern of responses that have been provided for analysis. The analyst will need to check a number of things. The first thing to check is the relative size of the four functions in the organization itself; second, the degree to which these differences in employee numbers across the functions in the data set represent the variation in relative size of the functions in both the organization itself and target population that the survey company sampled from. If these proportions are not in line with what is expected then further investigation needs to be carried out to understand why these samples vary as they do.

Example 5: supermarket checkout training intervention

In Chapter 7 we presented supermarket checkout performance data with the explanation that many supermarkets have a scan-rate target with their employees who work on the checkout. The management of this supermarket introduced a special training programme (for staff who wanted to attend; participation was voluntary) to share good scan-rate techniques. One of the features of the course included training on how to manage overly talkative customers who interfere with the scan rate, without coming across as rude. Given that such a training programme is quite specific and it has a clear aim of improving scan rates of checkout staff, deciding on a metric to track its efficacy is fairly straightforward (and we do not have to collect any more data than the HR systems routinely collect in this organization). We simply identify who went on the (voluntary) training course and track their scan rate in the week following the training course. We have inserted data on this into the previous data set that we used in Chapter 7. The new data set is called *Ch9_supermarket_checkout_training.xlsx* and it has the following variables:

1 id (unique ID for each employee).

2 educ (number of years of education of the employee).

3 disability (whether or not the employee has stated they have a disability: 0 = no; 1 = yes).

4 Gender (1 = male; 2 = female).

5 Scanspminute (average number of items scanned per minute this week).

6 Store (which store: 1 = Portsmouth North; 2 = Portsea Island).

7 weeks (number of weeks working on the checkout).

8 AgeCat (age category: 1 = 16–19; 2 = 20–24; 3 = 25–29; 4 = 30–34; 5 = 35–39; 6 = 40–44; 7 = 45–49; 8 = 50–54; 9 = 55–59; 10 = 60+).

9 Age 1 (16–19).

10 Age 2 (20–24).

11 Age 3 (25–29).

12 Age 4 (30–34).

13 Age 5 (35–39).

14 Age 6 (40–44).

15 Age 7 (45–49).

16 Age 8 (50–54).

17 Age 9 (55–59).

18 Age 10 (60+).

19 Training (whether or not the employee participated in the training course: 0 = no; 1 = yes).

20 ScanPminuteTime2 (average number of items scanned per minute in the week after training).

You will see that two variables have been added to the data set, which represent a new variable that indicates whether the checkout operator went on the training course and the new average scan rate in the week after the training course was delivered.

Here we initially analyse this data using the same GLM analysis utilized with the values change example (as it takes into account change over time and compares between groups at the same time). Here, we have two groups now, those who participated in the training and those who did not. We also have two waves of scan-rate data for all (regardless of whether the checkout operator attended the training course). This code follows from the example above, so you will need to run the code from the prior section to make the following work.

As with the analysis examples presented above, we will load the data.

```
Ch9_ex5 <- read_excel("Ch9_supermarket_checkout_training.xlsx")
```

And we will recode the *Training* variable to make it more interpretable:

```
Ch9_ex5$training_text <- as.factor(case_match(Ch9_ex5$Training, 0 ~
"no", 1 ~ "yes"))
```

Next we select just the variables we need, and then transform it from wide to long format:

```
scan_df <- Ch9_ex5[, c("id", "training_text", "ScanPminute",
"ScanPminuteTime2")]
scan_df_long <- gather(data = scan_df, key = time, value = scans,
ScanPminute, ScanPminuteTime2)
```

We can examine the resulting dataframe:

```
head(scan_df_long)
```

This produces Figure 9.21:

9.21

```
> head(scan_df_long)
# A tibble: 6 × 4
            id      training_text    time               scans
         <dbl>      <fct>            <chr>               <dbl>
1           1      no               ScanPminute            18
2           2      no               ScanPminute          19.5
3           3      no               ScanPminute          19.5
4           4      no               ScanPminute            22
5           5      no               ScanPminute            22
6           6      no               ScanPminute            17
```

This is the format we need. We can remove rows with missing data with the follow-ing code:

```
scan_df_long <- na.omit(scan_df_long)
```

As in previous examples, we will generate estimated marginal means, as we are look-ing at more than one factor. We can then generate some means, first by time:

```
model <- lm(scans ~ time * training_text, data = scan_df_long)
estimate_means(model, at = "time")
```

This produces Figure 9.22:

9.22

```
> estimate_means(model, at = "time")
NOTE: Results may be misleading due to involvement in interactions
Estimated Marginal Means

time                 |         Mean  |             SE  |          95% CI
-------------------------------------------------------------------------
ScanPminute        |       |19.00  |          0.18  |  [18.65, 19.35]
ScanPminuteTime2  |       |20.70  |          0.18  |  [20.34, 21.06]

Marginal means estimated at time
```

And then marginal means by training status:

```
estimate_means(model, at = "training_text")
```

This produces Figure 9.23:

9.23

```
> estimate_means(model, at = "training_text")
NOTE: Results may be misleading due to involvement in interactions
Estimated Marginal Means
```

training_text		Mean	SE	95% CI
no		20.11	0.15	[19.82, 20.40]
yes		19.59	0.21	[19.17, 20.00]

```
Marginal means estimated at training_text
```

And marginal means by time and training status:

```
estimate_means(model, at = c("time", "training_text"))
```

This produces Figure 9.24:

9.24

```
> estimate_means(model, at = c("time", "training_text"))
Estimated Marginal Means
```

time		training_text		Mean	SE	95% CI
ScanPminute		no		19.80	0.21	[19.40, 20.20]
ScanPminuteTime2		no		20.42	0.21	[20.01, 20.83]
ScanPminute		yes		18.20	0.30	[17.62, 18.78]
ScanPminuteTime2		yes		20.98	0.30	[20.38, 21.57]

```
Marginal means estimated at time
```

And we can examine a plot with the following code:

```
ggplot(scan_df_long, aes(x = time, y = scans, group = training_text)) +
geom_line(stat = "summary", fun = "mean", aes(linetype = training_text))
```

This produces Figure 9.25:

9.25

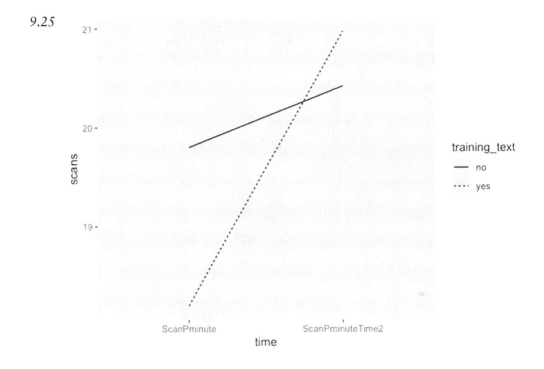

We can now conduct the analysis with the next lines of code:

```
scan_mod <- anova_test(data = scan_df_long, dv = scans, wid = id,
         within = time, between = training_text)
```

We can see the results of the analysis with the next line:

```
scan_mod
```

This produces Figure 9.26:

9.26
```
> scan_mod
ANOVA Table (type III tests)

            Effect   DFn   DFd        F          p    p<.05      ges
1    training_text     1   450    2.439   1.19e-01             0.005
2             time     1   450  151.284   3.56e-30      *      0.045
3  training_text:time   1   450   62.205   2.37e-14      *      0.019
```

Because we are only using two waves of data the sphericity assumptions are not important and Mauchly's test is not reported by the *anova_test* program. Here the main result of the time variable (i.e. the within-subjects factor) is significant (F = 151.284, p < 0.001). The *time* by *training_text* interaction is also significant F = 62.205, p < 0.001. This suggests that there is a change over time in the scan-rate performance data, and that there is an interaction between scan-rate change and whether people have been on a training course or not. The above results also show the effect of *training_text* on its own as it shows that the general effect of training is not significant (when disregarding change over time). This is an interesting null finding; however, the significant interaction between *time* by *training_text* suggests that the story is going to be more complicated. To interpret what is going on we need to look at the marginal means (Figures 9.22, 9.23 and 9.24) and the mean plot (Figure 9.25), which we selected in our analysis set-up.

We first examine the descriptive statistics for the different 'marginal means'. The mean scan rate in general (Figure 9.23, combining Time 1 and Time 2 data) for the people who did not participate (mean = 20.11) is higher than for those who did participate in training (mean = 19.59). Our analysis above suggests that these between-subjects differences are not significant, however. Our *time* marginal means (Figure 9.22) show that, regardless of training, participation the overall scan-rate mean has increased from 19.00 before the training to 20.70 after the training. As mentioned above, this is a significant temporal effect.

The key set of statistics, however, is the scan-rate means at Time 1 versus Time 2 for employees who participate in training versus those who did not (Figure 9.24); especially as the analysis results indicate that there is a significant *training_text* by *time* interaction (indicated by *training_text:time* in the output). Clearly, those who chose to go on the training course tended to have a lower scan-rate mean before the training course (mean = 18.20) compared to those who did not participate (mean = 19.80). This may be explained by the fact that those with lower scan rates are under pressure from management to increase this and they are probably more likely to volunteer for the training course than those with higher scan rates. The results also show that whilst there seems to be some increase in scan rate for the training non-participators from Time 1 to Time 2 (mean = 20.42) this rate of increase was not as much as for those who did participate (Time 2 mean = 20.98) and this interaction was significant (p < 0.001). The mean plot figure clearly demonstrates that the training course seems to have had an effect on scan rate. One of the strengths of this particular analysis compared to the change analysis conducted previously is that we actually include a 'treatment' versus 'control' condition in our analysis. By treatment, we mean that we have a subset of our organization that has been 'treated' differently to a 'control' group; in this case the treatment is attendance on a training course. In effect we are setting up a quasi-experiment, and when we show that change occurs with those receiving the treatment, but others who have not received this treatment do not show as much of a change, then this gives us strong confidence that the training course has had an impact (we need to consider whether we have a Hawthorne effect, of course… yet regardless of this possibility the training course seems to have had an impact).

Example 6: supermarket checkout training course – Redux

Conditional panel regression models assessing change in metrics whilst controlling for other factors

So far, the change analysis that we have carried out above tends to involve fairly straightforward mean testing and the data sets have also tended to be fairly straightforward; we have not tended to try to test for change effects whilst controlling for other factors that could be influencing change in the possible dependent variable. When we have two groups in the organization where one has experienced an intervention and another has not, a powerful way of testing for the impact of such an intervention whilst controlling for other factors is an analytic approach called conditional panel regression (Finkel, 1995). Here, we use multiple regression analysis to predict our Time 2 scan rate whilst controlling for our baseline Time 1 scan rate (as we did in Chapter 7 when modelling performance ratings whilst controlling for the previous year's ratings); in doing this we are in effect predicting 'change' in scan rate.

The logic of this analysis might not immediately seem obvious, so we will discuss this a little more here. When you conduct a regression analysis you are in effect trying to predict variation in a particular dependent variable. In Chapter 7 we predicted checkout scan rate as a dependent variable; in doing this we were trying to see whether variation in certain independent variables predicts the variation in checkout scan rate. Importantly, when you have two phases, or waves, of scan-rate data per individual taken at different time points (Time 1 scan rate versus Time 2 scan rate) you can set the latter scan-rate data as a dependent variable and insert the earlier scan rate as an independent variable.

Assuming that individual differences are an important factor accounting for scan rate (if someone is fast at Time 1 then they are likely to be fast at Time 2), operators' Time 1 scan rate is likely to predict the Time 2 scan rate; thus accounting for variation in the Time 2 scan rate to a considerable degree. It is *very* unlikely that the Time 2 scan rate will be exactly the same as the Time 1 scan rate for each checkout operator; as such there will be some error in prediction of Time 2 scan rate when using Time 1 scan rate as an independent variable. The more there is a difference in employee scan rates when comparing Time 1 with Time 2 then the greater the 'error' in prediction; where Time 1 scan rate differs from Time 2 scan rate then the predicted value that we would get for Time 2 scan rate if we just used Time 1 scan rate as a guide would not always be correct – it would have some error (in prediction of Time 2 scan rate). Importantly, if we set up a model where scan rate at Time 2 is regressed onto a number of independent variables and we tried to account for variation in this scan rate but we included Time 1 scan rate as a control, the relationship that Time 1 scan rate shares with these independent variables and Time 2 scan rate is filtered out of the regression model. In effect we are no longer predicting variation in Time 2 scan rate; we are predicting the difference in scan rate between Time 1 and Time 2 (Time 2 scan rate – Time 1 scan rate). Thus, we are predicting a change in scan rate between Time 1 and Time 2.

Using a multiple regression analysis as a change model enables us to include an independent variable that signifies whether someone has been on a training course; thus we can test whether training-course attendance seems to have an impact on change in scan rate. In addition to this, we can also control for a whole range of other factors that we know might be important in accounting for individual scan rate (see Chapter 7, pages 266–68) at the same time. Hopefully this will become clearer when we look at the conditional change panel regression analysis output. We are using the same supermarket data set as above: *Ch9_supermarket_checkout_training.xlsx*. Example code is in the same file as used in the previous examples *Ch9_examples.R*. This code follows from the example above, so you will need to run the code from the prior section to make the following work.

Since we are conducting multiple regression without any within subjects component, we can use the dataframe loaded in the previous example, namely *Ch9_ex5*. For convenience, we can recode some categorical variables to be more interpretable:

```
Ch9_ex5$disability_text <- as.factor(case_match(Ch9_ex5$disability,
0 ~ "no", 1 ~ "yes"))
Ch9_ex5$gender_text <- as.factor(case_match(Ch9_ex5$Gender, 1 ~ "male",
2 ~ "female"))
Ch9_ex5$store_text <- as.factor(case_match(Ch9_ex5$Store, 1 ~
"portsmouth", 2 ~ "portsea"))
```

In the previous example, we already coded the *Training* variable to *training_text*, which we will use in this analysis also.

We then specify a multiple regression model using the *lm* program. The dependent variable should be *ScanPminuteTime2*. We then need to specify the following 16 variables as independent variables. Note that the 'Age 3 (25–29)' category is excluded from the analysis as we want this to be our reference age category (see Example 9 in Chapter 7, page 271):

1 educ (number of years of education of the employee).

2 disability (whether or not the employee has stated they have a disability: 0 = no; 1 = yes).

3 Gender (1 = male; 2 = female).

4 Store (which Store: 1 = Portsmouth North; 2 = Portsea Island).

5 Weeks (number of weeks working on the checkout).

6 Age 1 (16–19).

7 Age 2 (20–24).

8 Age 4 (30–34).

9 Age 5 (35–39).

10 Age 6 (40–44).

11 Age 7 (45–49).

12 Age 8 (50–54).

13 Age 9 (55–59).

14 Age 10 (60+).

15 Training (whether or not the employee participated in the training course: 0 = no; 1 = yes).

16 ScanPminute (average number of items scanned per minute this week, our Time 1 scan-rate measure).

Translating the above requirements into R code:

```
scan_change <- lm(ScanPminuteTime2 ~ educ + disability_text +
        gender_text + store_text + Weeks + age1 + age2 + age4 +
        age5 + age6 + age7 + age8 + age9 + age10 + training_text +
        ScanPminute, data = Ch9_ex5)
```

Notice that in the code above, the *ScanPminute* variable inserted as an independent variable is in effect a control variable that means we are actually predicting change in scan rate; also note that the training variable included as an independent variable is the key intervention variable, as it will tell us whether going on a training course accounts for Time 1 to Time 2 change in scan rate.

We can see the results of this model with the next line of code:

```
summary(scan_change)
```

This produces Figure 9.27:

9.27

```
> summary(scan_change)

Call:
lm(formula = ScanPminuteTime2 ~ educ + disability_text + gender_text +
    store_text + Weeks + age1 + age2 + age4 + age5 + age6 + age7 +
    age8 + age9 + age10 + training_text + ScanPminute, data = Ch9_ex5)

Residuals:
    Min      1Q  Median      3Q     Max
-5.3632 -1.3270 -0.2482  0.5133 14.7039

Coefficients:
                       Estimate   Std. Error   t value   Pr(>|t|)
(Intercept)            9.634524     1.187572     8.113   5.1e-15 ***
educ                  -0.076569     0.049291    -1.553    0.1211
disability_textyes    -0.161796     0.299946    -0.539    0.5899
gender_textmale       -0.991085     0.312102    -3.176    0.0016 **
store_textportsmouth  -0.033067     0.236569    -0.140    0.8889
Weeks                  0.006808     0.004629     1.471    0.1420
age1                  -1.579620     0.719322    -2.196    0.0286 *
age2                  -0.109422     0.354331    -0.309    0.7576
age4                   0.434264     0.481295     0.902    0.3674
age5                   0.786402     0.494642     1.590    0.1126
age6                   1.010018     0.501923     2.012    0.0448 *
age7                   0.123312     0.561286     0.220    0.8262
age8                  -0.116486     0.547664    -0.213    0.8317
age9                  -0.353469     0.520244    -0.679    0.4972
age10                  0.675008     1.314692     0.513    0.6079
training_textyes       1.599696     0.260295     6.146   1.8e-09 ***
ScanPminute            0.609897     0.038280    15.932   < 2e-16 ***
---
Signif. codes:  0 '***' 0.001 '**' 0.01 '*' 0.05 '.' 0.1 ' ' 1

Residual standard error: 2.476 on 435 degrees of freedom
  (22 observations deleted due to missingness)
Multiple R-squared: 0.5535,        Adjusted R-squared: 0.537

F-statistic: 33.7 on 16 and 435 DF, p-value: < 2.2e-16
```

The first thing to notice here is that the regression model accounts for 55.4 per cent of variance in our dependent variable and our model is highly significant ($F(16, 435) =$ 33.7, $p < 0.001$). Thus we can account for 55.4 per cent of variation on our Time 2 scan rate with this model (which, as models go, is quite good).

As in prior examples, we can put the coefficients in a table that makes it easier to interpret, with the following code:

```
mod1 <- modelsummary(scan_change, output = "modelsummary_list")
mod2 <- modelsummary(scan_change, output = "modelsummary_list",
standardize = "basic")
```

```
# Create a list of models
models <- list(
  "Unstandardized" = mod1,
  "Standardized" = mod2)
# Show models
modelsummary(models, stars = TRUE, statistic = NULL, output = "huxtable")
```

This produces Figure 9.28:

9.28

	Unstandardized	Standardized
(Intercept)	9.635***	0.000***
educ	-0.077	-0.061
disability_textyes	-0.162	-0.018
gender_textmale	-0.991**	-0.136**
store_textportsmouth	-0.033	-0.005
Weeks	0.007	0.054
age1	-1.580*	-0.083*
age2	-0.109	-0.013
age4	0.434	0.032
age5	0.786	0.055
age6	1.010*	0.073*
age7	0.123	0.008
age8	-0.116	-0.008
age9	-0.353	-0.026
age10	0.675	0.017
training_textyes	1.600***	0.206***
ScanPminute	0.610***	0.630***
Num.Obs.	452	452
R2	0.553	0.553
R2 Adj.	0.537	0.537
AIC	2120.8	2120.8
BIC	2194.9	2194.9
Log.Lik.	-1042.423	-1042.423
F	33.696	33.696
RMSE	2.43	2.43

+ p < 0.1, * p < 0.05, ** p < 0.01, *** p < 0.001

Out of all 16 independent variables in the model, five are significant. As we would expect with a panel model like this, the Time 1 scan rate is the biggest predictor of Time 2 scan rate with a Beta of 0.630 ($p < 0.001$); the more the checkout person scans at Time 1 then the more they tend to scan at Time 2 – this is a fairly strong positive coefficient. Of vital importance, however, is that the training course variable is also significant (Beta = 0.206, $p < 0.001$), providing strong evidence that the training programme has a significantly positive impact on change (an increase) in scan rates of checkout operatives; thus training potentially increases scan rates. In addition, gender is a significant predictor of change, with a Beta of -0.136, $p < 0.01$, suggesting that women tended to show an increase over time; 40- to 44-year-olds (*age6* variable; Beta = 0.073, $p < 0.05$) seemed to show more of an increase in scan rates across time than our reference age category of 25- to 29-year-olds; and 16- to 19-year-olds (*age1* variable) showed a greater decrease over time compared to the same reference category (Beta = −0.083). Obviously, of these results, the key finding is that attendance at the scan-rate training leads to a greater increase in scan rate than you see with people who did not attend.

Evidence-based practice and responsible investment

The above are generally examples of where either organizations have deliberately set up conditions where important predicted outcomes of an intervention are created, or metrics are made available to monitor whether an intervention has the desired impact. This is obviously very sensible management practice and indeed something that an effective HR function will want to do; both to help set up conditions where the expected returns from an investment can be identified and also to be able to ensure that the intervention has positive returns. It is as important to identify when an intervention has a negative outcome as it is to identify when it has a positive outcome; something can be done about an intervention that is not working when the impact of the intervention is monitored. Without tracking the impact of an intervention, it may be the case that management will never know whether the investment has paid off or whether it is having negative consequences.

See no evil, hear no evil, speak no evil

Whilst many organizations make investment decisions based on what management think is the best thing to do, it might often be the case that a decision has been made by management to introduce a change or HR intervention on grounds that do not necessarily make rational sense. Sometimes management can make decisions to implement a change on ideological grounds, on grounds that competitors are doing it or for irrational reasons, even; these decisions can sometimes be made even when the case for interventions might not be very strong. Indeed, often, investments into a new intervention can be so huge or so difficult to undo that the last thing management would want is a set of metrics that could risk the exposure of this. Ultimately, in the spirit of accountable and sustainable treatment of employees, the HR analytics expert should always try to present a case for tracking the impact of an intervention wherever possible; the HR analytics function should always be on the lookout for situations where the impact of any management change can be monitored and tracked on its workforce.

Reference

Finkel, S E (1995) *Causal Analysis With Panel Data: Quantitative applications in the social sciences*, Sage, California

10

Business applications

Scenario modelling and business cases

So far in this book we have set out and discussed a variety of different analytic techniques and walked through the analysis of various models. Whilst we have in general used predictive analytic techniques, these have tended to be used to diagnose key drivers of important HR outcomes (such as employee turnover and performance) or to help us evaluate the effectiveness of an initiative or intervention. Once a budding HR analytics expert has gone through the case study chapters and run various analyses for themselves with his or her organization's own HR data, perhaps the following might happen.

The analyst goes into the boardroom/executive committee/senior management group/HR director's office and she/he presents the sophisticated predictive analysis and the models, pointing out the significant findings that include drivers of HR outcomes and a proposed course of action. Four of the five people in the room nod in affable agreement, impressed at the analyst's skills and clearly enlightened by what the analysis shows. Then the analyst looks at David in the corner. David is not smiling; instead he is frowning. He looks up and the long pause causes others to look at David also. There is an air of anticipation in the room. He takes one last observable glance at the meeting papers outlining the analysis before raising his head, taking off his reading glasses and uttering the words 'So what?'

It feels like a slap in the face and a bit rude actually. Where are his manners? Maybe he didn't understand? But then the words that follow suggest he understood completely.

'Should I now go and change my departmental plan, my day-to-day tasks, the management of my team leaders?' he asks. 'What is to stop us from all agreeing that this "statistically significant" model,' he says (doing finger quotation marks around the words 'statistically significant'), 'is great to have, but then leaving this meeting, going back to our jobs, and never giving it another thought?'

The others in the room start to look uncomfortable and a little embarrassed. At this point the analyst realizes that David is actually on his/her side. Despite his spikey exterior, David is impressed with the model and actually wants to use it. So do the others; the problem is, they just don't know how. In other words, nice model, but 'So what?'

The important question now is how you can translate these analyses and results into tangible predictive business applications. Aside from the obvious business implications of being able to diagnose drivers of HR outcomes, we might now want to ask the 'So what?' question. From the types of analyses that we have carried out so far, there are a number of things that the HR analytics expert can do with the knowledge gained that can help us to answer this 'So what?' question.

Here lies the real value in statistical models. The models have been created and analyses run. In this chapter we can present a few examples of how the statistical models that we outline can be applied further; some of these examples demonstrate how the analyst can make real and tangible predictions from the analysis conducted. In this chapter we discuss the following:

Predictive modelling scenarios

Using the regression models we built in the 'turnover and performance' case studies (Chapters 6 and 7) to model future scenarios, we will work out who is more likely to leave and how their performance might be impacted when environmental factors change. We will also use financial models to build a business case for particular HR initiatives.

Evidence-based decision making

We will use the models that we built in the recruitment and selection case studies (Chapter 8) as a basis for making important people-related decisions, thus helping to reduce the likelihood for bias by adding additional evidence-based information to our decision-making process.

Predictive modelling scenarios

Here we use an example model that we ran in Chapter 7 to explore predictors of customer satisfaction with financial sales representatives. We will briefly revise the analysis and show how you can take the findings in order to model the potential impact of focusing on particular drivers with a view to understanding how this could lead to an increase in our factor of interest; with the modelling we can potentially draw some conclusions about how our particular HR outcome (in this case customer reinvestment intentions) could be influenced.

Example 1: customer reinvestment

In Chapter 7 we explored predictors of customer reinvestment intentions in a financial sales environment. This was example 1b in Chapter 7 (performance case study, see pages 239–41) (using the data file: *Ch7_customer_satisfaction.xlsx*).

You may recall that we looked at the results of a customer satisfaction survey in a financial services organization in order to determine the drivers of customer reinvestment intentions (expressed in a customer satisfaction survey). To recap, the survey asked investing customers to grade their sales person on a scale of 1 to 5, where 1 was 'dissatisfied' and 5 was 'extremely satisfied' on the following measures:

1 Sales person understanding your needs (*Sat1*).

2 Sales person seems confident (*Sat2*).

3 Sales person has a recommendation (*Sat3*).

4 Sales person is knowledgeable (*Sat4*).

Then the survey asked customers to rate themselves on two measures that indicate a degree of customer loyalty (a 1-to-5 scale was used in each case). The first loyalty measure related to intentions to reinvest and the second measure indicated how much they intended to reinvest. The response items for these two measures used the following 1-to-5 response scales:

5 Likelihood of reinvesting (*CustLoyalty*):
   - 1 = Definitely going to go elsewhere with my investments.
   - 2 = Thinking about going elsewhere with my money.
   - 3 = Not sure about where I will place my future investments.
   - 4 = Thinking about investing here again.
   - 5 = Definitely will invest here again.

6 How much they may or may not reinvest (*INvestMore*):
   - 1 = Definitely will not invest more than now here.
   - 2 = Unlikely to invest more than now here.
   - 3 = Planning to invest 0–50 per cent more than now in this organization.
   - 4 = Planning to invest 50–100 per cent more in this organization.
   - 5 = Going to double my investment or more in this organization.

The final question was about the gender of the sales person:

7 Sex of sales person: 1 = female; 2 = male (*SexOfSalesperson*).

If we present the predictive model that we analysed in Chapter 7 (see Figure 7.3, page 240) as a diagram, when we run the multiple regression equation, the model would look like Figure 10.1:

10.1 Diagram of the regression model predicting customer reinvestment intentions from customer satisfaction data (analysis presented in Figure 7.5 of Chapter 7)

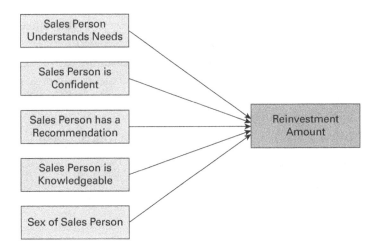

And the resulting output from the analysis can be found in Figure 10.2:

10.2

	Unstandardized	Standardized
(Intercept)	1.740***	0.000***
Sat1	0.176***	0.219***
Sat2	0.030	0.034
Sat3	0.140***	0.186***
Sat4	0.012	0.014
SexOfSalesperson	-0.020	-0.010
Num.Obs.	1772	1772
R2	0.170	0.170
R2 Adj.	0.168	0.168
AIC	3998.1	3998.1
BIC	4036.4	4036.4
Log.Lik.	-1992.030	-1992.030
RMSE	0.74	0.74

$+ \ p < 0.1, \ * \ p < 0.05, \ ** \ p < 0.01, \ *** \ p < 0.001$

When we translate the model results to a raw regression equation we have the following:

Customer reinvestment =

1.740 + 0.176 (understanding customer needs) + 0.030 (sales confidence) +

0.140 (giving a recommendation) + 0.012 (product knowledge) – 0.020 (gender)

And the significant drivers (independent variables) came out to be:

understanding customer needs (p<0.001); and

giving a recommendation (p<0.001).

With this information, we realized the Snapshot hidden gem:

Understanding customer needs and having a recommendation are the two key drivers of customer reinvestment indices.

In considering what we can do with this information, we can now take this further and look at the potential impact that bespoke changes would have on customer reinvestment.

The independent variables are on a scale of 1 to 5 that looks like this:

1 Very dissatisfied.

2 Somewhat dissatisfied.

3 Neither satisfied nor dissatisfied.

4 Somewhat satisfied.

5 Extremely satisfied.

Currently, the average scores for the independent variables on these scales (in our data set) are:

- Understanding customer needs is 3.47.
- Sales confidence is 3.79.
- Giving a recommendation is 3.43.
- Product knowledge is 3.59.

And knowing that we have set the value of 1 as female and 2 as male for the gender variable, then the average gender score is 1.78.

If we plug those average values into the model equation, we should get a value for the dependent reinvestment variable that is close to the average figure for this variable (*INvestMore*) in our data set, which is 2.92:

Customer reinvestment

= 1.740 + 0.176 (3.47) + 0.030 (3.79) + 0.140 (3.43) + 0.012 (3.59) − 0.020 (1.78)

= 2.95

The value of 2.95 is the predicted/expected level of customer reinvestment based on our model when inputting average values for each independent variable. In conducting some modelling with our equation, we can translate this predicted value to be the average of the customer reinvestment scores with the sales people that our model included (not all people were included as there was some missing data with particular individuals on certain variables). We established in our case study that the model was significant with a p-value of 0.001, so there is less than a 1 in 1,000 chance that we would find this pattern of shared variance (between the customer reinvestment scores and the other survey questions) by chance alone. Hence the model is significant. Note that while we performed this calculation by hand here to demonstrate the logic of this approach, an example of how to do this R using code is shown in the file *Ch10_example.R*. Code for other examples in this chapter are also available in that file.

So, back to David's big 'So what?' question. Knowing from the R-square value of 0.170 and the p-value of less than 0.001 in the case study, we can be 99.9 per cent confident that the model 'accounts for' almost 20 per cent, or approximately one-fifth of the variance in the dependent variable. Let's try a couple of scenarios.

Something we can do with these results is model the impact of a hypothetical increase with particular drivers of probable reinvestment amounts; we can see how our predicted level of reinvestment changes when we adjust significant drivers of dependent variable. We could, for example, ask: 'What if we managed to increase our level of understanding customer needs to a point where the average customer rating was 4.00 (somewhat satisfied) rather than the current average of 3.47 (somewhere between neither satisfied nor dissatisfied and somewhat satisfied)?'

To recap, the survey response values for our outcome customer reinvestment variable are:

How much they may or may not reinvest:

  1 = Definitely will not invest more than now here.

  2 = Unlikely to invest more than now here.

  3 = Planning to invest 0–50 per cent more than now in this organization.

  4 = Planning to invest 50–100 per cent more in this organization.

  5 = Going to double my investment or more in this organization.

And we are working with an average value for this in our data set of 2.95.

We then plug our new value for understanding customer needs into the model regression equation (in much the same way as we did in the previous calculation) and we can work out the expected level of customer reinvestment; all other things remaining the same, we get the following result:

= 1.740 + 0.176 (**4.00**) + 0.030 (3.79) + 0.140 (3.43) + 0.012 (3.59) – 0.020 (1.78)

= 3.04

We can see that changing our understanding customer needs value from 3.47 (some-where between neither satisfied nor dissatisfied and somewhat satisfied) to 4.00 (somewhat satisfied) increases the average expected level of customer reinvestment and pushes the average further into level 3 (planning to invest 0–50 per cent more than now). This is a substantial move in the right direction for organizational revenue.

But what if we also trained our sales people so that they had an increased under-standing of customer needs, and were 'always' able to give a recommendation that met each customer's needs? What if the average score was 4.5 for both of the two key drivers of our customer reinvestment outcome?

Plugging those two new values into the model:

$$= 1.740 + 0.176\ (\mathbf{4.5}) + 0.030\ (3.79) + 0.140\ (\mathbf{4.5}) + 0.012\ (3.59) - 0.020\ (1.78)$$
$$= 3.28$$

This is a much higher value and shows how much a change in the two variables we know to have the most impact ('understanding customer needs' and 'giving a recom-mendation') will impact the outcome we are interested in, i.e. the amount of customer reinvestment. This is very powerful modelling.

Moving the average from 2.95 to 3.24 in monetary terms means there are more customers who plan to invest 0–50 per cent more than they do now, and for the aver-age now to be quite a bit over 3, it also means we have a much greater prevalence of customers who would indicate a '4' value on the survey, which means they intend to invest 50–100 per cent more than they do now. So, let's extrapolate and say that an increase of .29 on a scale of 1 to 5 is an average increase in likelihood to reinvest of .29/5 = 0.058, or let's round it to 6 per cent.

We could use this information to build an estimate of the possible increase in reinvestment to enable a business case for investing in training. If you were writing a business case for a new training programme to increase the ability of sales people to understand customer needs and make a recommendation, you might show a potential business case for investing in training on the basis that this training will help increase customers' satisfaction. You could suggest that the return on that investment might be a 6 per cent increase in the amount your customers invest if you were able to increase average customer satisfaction ratings on these two driver variables by 0.5 (on the 1-to-5 scales). Whilst we recognize here that we are work-ing with a 1-to-5 scale that is not exactly discrete in terms of the amount of customer reinvestment that a customer is saying that they may invest, it would be reasonable to translate an increase in the scale to a rough estimate of the potential increase in investment potential (our analyst would have to explain this assump-tion and caveat that this is a rough estimate; but an estimate based in rigorous modelling nonetheless).

SNAPSHOT HIDDEN GEM

If the annual customer investment figures totalled US $1.2 billion last year, and our model suggests that an increase in understanding customer needs and giving a recommendation should influence an increase in customer investment by 6 per cent, then we predict a possible increase of approximately $72 million of additional customer investment by getting more customer satisfaction in those two factors.

Obviously this would be a very big and specific claim to make and there is no guarantee that your training will definitely lead to a 0.5 increase in satisfaction on the two driver dimensions. It would be sensible for the analyst to model a range of possible increases and translate these to some kind of discrete sensitivity analysis of potential financial returns that various scenarios of different increases in the two satisfaction drivers could lead to. Importantly when we are talking about such large sums of money, even a relatively small increase in customer satisfaction could lead to a decent return, thus covering the costs of new training initiatives.

Remembering that this is a linear regression model, it is important to keep in mind that it does not prove causality, and our results give us information about relationships between variables and the probabilities that these relationships are not products of random factors. So while the levels of significance that our results presented above are considerable, and we can be 99.9 per cent confident that the independent variables in our model 'account for' or 'share' variation in our customers' reports of intended investment increases, the results do not offer 'proof' for causality. We should be careful to caveat our claims on the basis that our regression findings show statistical relationships between variables but do not prove that one thing causes another; i.e. while increasing an understanding of customer needs and the ability to make a recommendation will result in an increase in customer reinvestment, we cannot be sure that this is the direct *cause* – there may be other factors at play.

It would also be sensible to caveat our business-case predictions with the reminder that these are customers' self-report predictions of their reinvestment intentions and that self-report intentions do not always lead to action (their intentions might not lead to actual investments – for many reasons). The analyst needs to be aware that there are a number of different ways of modelling the possible impact of increases in predictors and this is just one possible way.

However, despite these caveats, the analytical evidence-based rigour used in the modelling here can be presented and defended, and assumptions can be set out. Here, the analyst will have:

1 conducted rigorous statistical analysis exploring the drivers of customer reinvestment intentions;

2 identified how much the key drivers predict variations in reinvestment intentions;

3 demonstrated how focusing on the key drivers could influence customer reinvestment;

4 developed a model that can help get a sense of potential financial return that might be possible with a training initiative that could increase the drivers by a range of possible values.

At this point, it would be worth pointing out an additional analysis linked to the above that the analytics team could undertake to follow this up. Given that the analysts must know who the sales representatives are and who the customers are in this scenario (otherwise they would not have been able to link the customer surveys with the analysts), the analyst could also track how much the customers did invest the following year and conduct this analysis with actual increases (or decreases) in investment rather than self-report customer intentions. With actual monetary figures to play with as a dependent outcome variable, the power of this kind of analysis (and the accuracy of the claims made) increases considerably; the analyst could actually model the monetary value of potential increases in our drivers rather than an estimate based on a less accurate 1-to-5 Likert scale (that requires assumptions to be made).

Example 2: modelling the potential impact of a training programme

In scenario one we explored and modelled the drivers of potential customer reinvestment on the basis of sales representative-linked customer satisfaction survey data. Here we turn to an example predictive modelling scenario where we model the potential tangible impact (on individual employee performance) of a training programme; we conduct some scenario modelling using an example used in both Chapter 7 and Chapter 9, where we explored factors predicting supermarket scan rate with checkout operators.

As a recap, in Chapter 7 we presented supermarket checkout performance data with the explanation that many supermarkets have a scan-rate target with their employees who work on the checkout. The management of this supermarket introduced a special training programme (for staff who wanted to attend; i.e. participation was voluntary) to share good scan-rate techniques. We then introduced a new data set in Chapter 9 where we included additional data in the data set that showed who participated in the training course, and new scan-rate (post-training period) data.

The new data set was called *Ch9_supermarket_checkout_training.xlsx* and it has the following variables:

1 id (unique ID for each employee).

2 Educ (number of years of education of the employee).

3 Disability (whether or not the employee has stated they have a disability: 0 = no; 1 = yes).

4 Gender (1 = male; 2 = female).

5 Scanspminute (average number of items scanned per minute this week).

6 Store (which store: 1 = Portsmouth North; 2 = Portsea Island).

7 Weeks (number of weeks working on the checkout).

8 AgeCat (age category: 1 = 16–19; 2 = 2–24; 3 = 25–29; 4 = 30–34; 5 = 35–39; 6 = 40–44; 7 = 45–49; 8 = 50–54; 9 = 55–59; 10 = 60+).

9 Age 1 (16–19).

10 Age 2 (20–24).

11 Age 3 (25–29).

12 Age 4 (30–34).

13 Age 5 (35–39).

14 Age 6 (40–44).

15 Age 7 (45–49).

16 Age 8 (50–54).

17 Age 9 (55–59).

18 Age 10 (60+).

19 Training (whether or not the employee participated in the training course: 0 = no; 1 = yes).

20 ScanPminuteTime2 (average number of items scanned per minute in the week after training).

For convenience, we recoded the categorical variables that were encoded with numbers to make them more interpretable in the output. The variable *disability_text* had the values 'no' or a 'yes' to indicate disability status, *gender_text* had the values 'male' and 'female' to indicate gender, *store_text* had the values 'portsmouth' or 'portsea' to indicate store location, and training_text had the values 'no' or 'yes' to indicate training status. We used these variables in the regression model in place of the variables encoded with numbers.

With the 'Redux' model (example 6) that we estimated in Chapter 9 (pages 343–48) we predicted Time 2 (post-training) scan rate with demographic factors, pre-training scan rate and whether the operator participated in a training session.

This model therefore predicted 'change' in scan rate (see Figure 10.3 for a visual presentation of the model tested).

The code to conduct the analysis can be found in the file *Ch10_examples.R*.

Notice here that the *Scanspminute* (average number of items scanned per minute this week) variable was as an independent variable (this means we are actually predicting change in scan rate – see discussion on this in Chapter 9). Also note that the 'Training' variable included as an independent variable is the key intervention variable as it will tell us whether attending a training course accounts for Time 1 to Time 2 change in scan rate. The output for this model can be found in Figures 10.4 and 10.5.

10.3   Diagram of the regression model predicting post-training scan rate when controlling for pre-training scan rate and training participation (example 6 in Chapter 9)

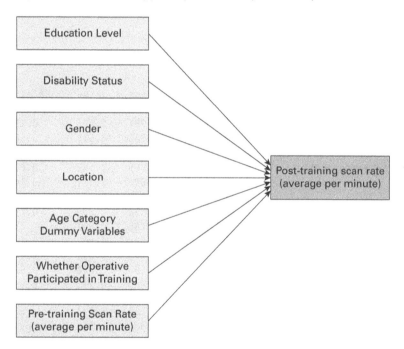

To conduct the analysis, we first load packages, set the working directory and load the data:

```
if (!require("pacman")) install.packages("pacman")
pacman::p_load(readxl, dplyr, modelsummary, this.path, huxtable)
setwd(this.path::here())
Ch9_ct <- read_excel("Ch9_supermarket_checkout_training.xlsx")
```

We then specify the model:

```
scan_change <- lm(ScanPminuteTime2 ~ educ + disability_text + gender_text +
        store_text + Weeks + age1 + age2 + age4 + age5 + age6 + age7 +
        age8 + age9 + age10 + training_text + ScanPminute,
        data = Ch9_ex5)
```

We can see the results of the model with this next line of code:

```
summary(scan_change)
```

10.4

```
> summary(scan_change)

Call:
lm(formula = ScanPminuteTime2 ~ educ + disability_text + gender_text +
    store_text + Weeks + age1 + age2 + age4 + age5 + age6 + age7 +
    age8 + age9 + age10 + training_text + ScanPminute, data = Ch9_ex5)

Residuals:
      Min        1Q    Median        3Q       Max
   -5.3632   -1.3270   -0.2482    0.5133   14.7039

Coefficients:
                        Estimate   Std. Error  t value   Pr(>|t|)
(Intercept)             9.634524     1.187572    8.113   5.1e-15 ***
educ                   -0.076569     0.049291   -1.553    0.1211
disability_textyes     -0.161796     0.299946   -0.539    0.5899
gender_textmale        -0.991085     0.312102   -3.176    0.0016  **
store_textportsmouth   -0.033067     0.236569   -0.140    0.8889
Weeks                   0.006808     0.004629    1.471    0.1420
age1                   -1.579620     0.719322   -2.196    0.0286  *
age2                   -0.109422     0.354331   -0.309    0.7576
age4                    0.434264     0.481295    0.902    0.3674
age5                    0.786402     0.494642    1.590    0.1126
age6                    1.010018     0.501923    2.012    0.0448  *
age7                    0.123312     0.561286    0.220    0.8262
age8                   -0.116486     0.547664   -0.213    0.8317
age9                   -0.353469     0.520244   -0.679    0.4972
age10                   0.675008     1.314692    0.513    0.6079
training_textyes        1.599696     0.260295    6.146   1.8e-09 ***
ScanPminute             0.609897     0.038280   15.932   < 2e-16 ***
---
Signif. codes:  0 '***' 0.001 '**' 0.01 '*' 0.05 '.' 0.1 ' ' 1

Residual standard error: 2.476 on 435 degrees of freedom
  (22 observations deleted due to missingness)
Multiple R-squared: 0.5535,        Adjusted R-squared: 0.537
F-statistic: 33.7 on 16 and 435 DF, p-value: < 2.2e-16
```

We can get a table of the unstandardized and standardized betas in a table with this code:

```
mod1 <- modelsummary(scan_change, output = "modelsummary_list")
mod2 <- modelsummary(scan_change, output = "modelsummary_list",
standardize = "basic")
models <- list(
  "Unstandardized" = mod1,
  "Standardized" = mod2)
modelsummary(models, stars = TRUE, statistic = NULL, output =
"huxtable")
```

10.5

	Unstandardized	Standardized
(Intercept)	9.635***	0.000***
educ	-0.077	-0.061
disability_textyes	-0.162	-0.018
gender_textmale	-0.991**	-0.136**
store_textportsmouth	-0.033	-0.005
Weeks	0.007	0.054
age1	-1.580*	-0.083*
age2	-0.109	-0.013
age4	0.434	0.032
age5	0.786	0.055
age6	1.010*	0.073*
age7	0.123	0.008
age8	-0.116	-0.008
age9	-0.353	-0.026
age10	0.675	0.017
training_textyes	1.600***	0.206***
ScanPminute	0.610***	0.630***
Num.Obs.	452	452
R2	0.553	0.553
R2 Adj.	0.537	0.537
AIC	2120.8	2120.8
BIC	2194.9	2194.9
Log.Lik.	-1042.423	-1042.423
F	33.696	33.696
RMSE	2.43	2.43

+ p < 0.1, * p < 0.05, ** p < 0.01, *** p < 0.001

We can see that the regression model accounted for 55.3 per cent of variance in our dependent variable and our model is highly significant ($F(16, 435) = 33.7, p < 0.001$). See Figure 10.4 for the statistics relating to each of our independent (driver) variables.

From these model results, if we insert our coefficients into an unstandardized raw regression equation, we get the following:

Average (post-training) scan rate =

9.635

– 0.077 Education Level

– 0.162 stated disability

– 0.991 Male gender

– 0.033 Portsmouth Location

+ 0.007 Week in job

– 1.580 Age 16–19

– 0.109 Age 20–24

+ 0.434 Age 30–34

+ 0.786 Age 35–39

+ 1.010 Age 40–44

+ 0.123 Age 45–49

– 0.116 Age 50–54

– 0.353 Age 55–59

+ 0.675 Age 60+

+ 1.600 Participated in training

+ 0.610 Pre-training scan rate

We can see that out of all 16 independent variables in the model, five are significant (these are highlighted in bold). What we are most interested in here is the impact of participation in the checkout training. We can see that the unstandardized coefficient for the variable that indicates participation in this training course is B=1.600 and this is highly significant ($p < 0.001$). Before we move on to model the impact of participation in training on scan rate we need to consider some descriptive information. See the code below to obtain descriptive statistics once the file and packages outlined in the example are loaded:

```
datasummary_skim(Ch9_ct, fmt = 2, type = "numeric", output = 'huxtable')
```

The code above uses the *datasummary_skim* program, and asks it to generate a summary of the numeric variables dataframe *Ch9_ct*. The extra piece of code *fmt = 2* asks it to generate descriptive statistics to two decimal places. We can also ask for a summary of categorical variables:

```
datasummary_skim(Ch9_ct, fmt = 2, type = "categorical", output =
'huxtable')
```

The descriptive information for the variables in our dataframe is presented in Figures 10.6a and 10.6b.

10.6a

	Unique	Missing	Pct.	Mean	SD	Min	Median	Max
id	474	0		237.50	136.98	1.00	237.50	474.00
educ	10	0		13.49	2.88	8.00	12.00	21.00
disability	2	0		0.22	0.41	0.00	0.00	1.00
AgeVariable	45	0		32.75	11.87	17.00	28.00	61.00
Gender	2	0		1.46	0.50	1.00	1.00	2.00
ScanPminute	28	0		19.28	3.78	5.00	19.50	32.00
Store	2	0		1.47	0.50	1.00	1.00	2.00
Weeks	29	0		36.66	29.14	1.00	27.00	103.00
AgeCAT	10	0		4.19	2.38	1.00	3.00	10.00
age1	2	0		0.04	0.20	0.00	0.00	1.00
age2	2	0		0.23	0.42	0.00	0.00	1.00
age3	2	0		0.30	0.46	0.00	0.00	1.00
age4	2	0		0.08	0.27	0.00	0.00	1.00
age5	2	0		0.07	0.25	0.00	0.00	1.00
age6	2	0		0.07	0.26	0.00	0.00	1.00
age7	2	0		0.07	0.25	0.00	0.00	1.00
age8	2	0		0.06	0.24	0.00	0.00	1.00
age9	2	0		0.07	0.26	0.00	0.00	1.00
age10	2	0		0.01	0.09	0.00	0.00	1.00
Training	2	0		0.32	0.47	0.00	0.00	1.00
ScanPminuteTime2	38	5		20.60	3.64	5.50	21.50	32.50

10.6b

		N	%
disability_text	no	370	78.06
	yes	104	21.94
gender_text	female	216	45.57
	male	258	54.43
store_text	portsea	221	46.62
	portsmouth	253	53.38
training_text	no	320	67.51
	yes	154	32.49

There are two key values in Figure 10.6 that we could use to (very quickly) begin to model the impact on scan rates of the training programme. First, the mean value for participation in training = 0.32. This variable is coded 0 = not participated and 1 = participated. Therefore a mean of 0.32 indicates that just under one-third of the organization participated in the training programme. The second useful value is average number of items scanned per minute after the training programme, which comes to 20.60. We can immediately see that there is a difference in scan rate at the pre-training versus the post-training levels (pre-training average scan rate per minute = 19.28). For a number of reasons, we cannot just take the difference in these two scan rates as the impact of the training. First, this increase happened across the board regardless of who went on the training; second, just looking at the increases overall does not tell us anything about what factors are linked to this increase. Thus to model the impact of our training course we need to look at the regression model output in Figure 10.6, which tells us the potential contribution that participation in the training course had, taking into account all other factors in the model. The unstandardized beta coefficient for the training participation was B = 1.600. This suggests that all other things being equal, participation in training in our organization can have 1.6 item-per-minute scan-rate improvement. We can check this using the following set of calculations:

Average post-training scan rate = (all other things being equal) + 1.6(average value for participation in the training course)

This is a variation on our raw regression equation without including all other factors in our model (we do not need to include each of these because we can calculate an estimate of their contribution to the equation, as follows) and inputting the average participation value as our actual variable data.

As we know the average value for our training participation variable, we can set out the following:

Post-training scan rate = (all other things being equal) + 1.6(participated in training)

As we know the average post-training scan rate (20.60) and the training participation rate (0.32) we can also set out the following:

20.60 = (all other things being equal) + 1.6(0.32)

Because we know the mean post-training scan rate (20.60) and we know the coefficient contribution to training course (1.6) and the mean of the training participation variable (0.32), we can transpose the equation to calculate what we need to insert into our (all things being equal) part of the equation:

All other things being equal = 20.60 – 1.6(0.32)
Thus we can calculate:
20.088 = 20.60–1.6(0.32)

And if we retransform this back to our regression equation predicting post-training scan rate we get the following:

$20.60 = (20.088) + 1.6(0.32)$

With this we can conduct some modelling of what the impact would be on our scan rate with various levels of participation on the training course. If we assume that all of our staff participated in the training course then our mean level for our participation variable would be 1 rather than 0.32 (which indicates that about one-third of the organization participated). Thus our equation would read the following with 100 per cent participation:

$21.688 = (20.088) + 1.6(\mathbf{1})$

Furthermore, if no one participated our equation would read the following (our mean level for our participation variable would be 0 rather than 0.32):

$20.088 = (20.088) + 1.6(\mathbf{0})$

We could run variations of this with different levels of participation in training and see what the potential impact on scan rate would be. However, clearly, with all other things being equal, full versus no participation in the training course changes the scan rate by an average of 1.6 items per minute in our entire organization. This is extremely powerful information that we can then use to help evaluate and justify the impact of our training course in our organization – especially when we start to consider what impact this would have across all our employees.

If we assume that each of our 452 checkout operators works 35 hours per week on the checkouts and that these operators are working at full productivity, each employee works for 2,100 minutes scanning items per week (35×60). Working on the average scan-rate per minute of 20.6, at the moment if all employees participated in the training course this should lead to 43,260 items scanned per week ($2,100 \times 20.6$) per employee.

Without the training programme, the average scan-rate per minute would be 20.088; this amounts to a total of 42,184.8 items scanned in an average week per employee ($2,100 \times 20.088$).

Compared to not running the training course, if full participation in the new training programme occurred, this should increase the average scan rate to 21.688 from 20.088, which amounts to an additional average scan potential of 3,360 scans per employee (($2,100 \times 21.688$) – ($2,100 \times 20.088$)). Thus with 452 employees this increases the potential number of items scanned in a week by 1,518,720 items. As with the previous example, you will be able to see how this can be done in R in the file *Ch10_example.R*.

SNAPSHOT HIDDEN GEM

Using our model, we can say that if all employees went on the customer service training programme, we predict the potential number of items scanned in a week could increase by over 1.5 million items.

This is just one example of the kind of predictive modelling that we can do with the results of our scan-rate regression modelling. Obviously here we are making a number of assumptions that would need consideration if we were to try to present the implications of our analysis to a board of directors (to justify the investment in our training programme). These assumptions would need nuanced modelling themselves (e.g. assumptions such as all operators work 35 hours a week at full scan-rate productivity). However, hopefully the reader can begin to see some of the potential of applying our analytic results to actual business scenarios.

Obtaining individual values for the outcomes of our predictive models

In considering how else we might be able to use our regression models in an applied way to answer the 'So what?' question, there is a particularly useful feature of R that we can use to help apply our regression results to create predictive models. R has a very practical tool (that most statistical programs should also have) that can be used to review predicted model values for all individuals in our data set and to help translate your model findings into a truly predictive tool.

You can get R to estimate your regression model and save the values of our outcome variable that our model predicts on the basis of: 1) our regression equation results; and 2) the actual values of each individual independent variable for each employee that we have in our data set (and that helped to produce 1) in the first place). The benefit of this tool is that (after you have saved the data file as a different name so that you don't mess with the original data) you can add new employees where you have data values for the predictor (independent) variables and run the analysis again, saving predicted values in our predicted dependent variable for the new cases. This is particularly useful when we want to use existing patterns with our organization to make predictions about new cases. This also allows you to enter as many 'what if' scenarios as you like (by adjusting various values of your independent variables with a particular individual) to get a (new) predicted value of our particular outcome. The opportunities to use this predictive modelling tool are considerable (we go on to show other examples of using this tool below).

The process for getting R to apply a regression model and save a predicted value of our outcome variable is quite simple. We demonstrate this below in an application where we make predictions about future behaviour of graduate candidates on the basis of behaviour (performance and leaving behaviour) exhibited by previously hired graduates.

Example 3: predicting the likelihood of leaving

For our next model we intend to apply our predictive models that we ran with employees in Chapter 6 (prediction of turnover case study) to obtain data that tells us the likelihood of leaving for each employee within our organization. In the employee turnover case study, Chapter 6 (see pages 203–12), we used binary logistic regression to predict individual turnover using gender of the employee and of the immediate manager, age, length-of-service, performance appraisal rating, country and leaver status. The model we tested is presented diagrammatically in Figure 10.7 and our data set used was *Ch6_Individual_Turnover.xlsx*.

10.7

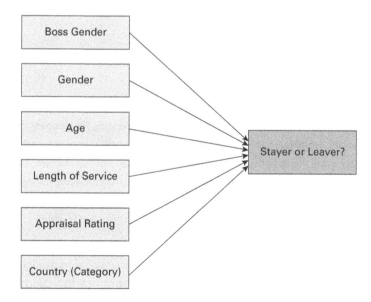

The output that this model produced can be found in Figure 10.8. The code to conduct this analysis is also in the file *Ch10_examples.R*.

10.8

	Log Odds	Odds Ratio
(Intercept)	0.168	1.183
BossGender	-0.184	0.832
Gender	-0.608***	0.544***
Age	-0.001	0.999
LengthOfService	-0.017	0.983
AppraisalRating	-0.248*	0.780*
Country_textBelgium	-0.249	0.779
Country_textFrance	-0.455	0.634
Country_textItaly	-0.059	0.943
Country_textMexico	-0.415	0.660
Country_textPoland	-0.734	0.480
Country_textSpain	-0.572	0.565
Country_textSweden	0.002	1.002
Country_textUK	-0.506	0.603
Country_textUnited States	-0.698	0.497
Num.Obs.	1650	1650
AIC	1234.2	1234.2
BIC	1315.3	1315.3
Log.Lik.	-602.101	-602.101
F	3.498	3.498
RMSE	0.33	0.33

+ p < 0.1, * p < 0.05, ** p < 0.01, *** p < 0.001

From Chapter 6 (pages 223–27) we can tell the following:

> Country differences do not come out as significant in accounting for turnover in our model; however, women are more than twice as likely to leave as men are, and a higher appraisal rating will increase the chances of employees staying (thus women and employees who get low performance ratings are a 'higher risk of leaving' category than other employees).

Recall from Chapter 3 that the structure of the logistic regression model (those who find equations intimidating can read on without worrying too much about the mechanics of what is going on here; our application will begin to make sense) looks like this:

LOGISTIC REGRESSION MODEL

$$Ln(p/(1-p)) = b_0 + b_1x_{1i} + b_2x_{2i} + b_nx_{ni}$$

where p is the probability that Y=1, or, put another way:

$$P(Y) = 1/(1+e^{-(b_0 + b_1x_{1i} + b_2x_{2i} + \ldots + b_nx_{ni})})$$

where 'e' is the base of natural logarithms, i is the instance of the variable, Y is the dependent variable, x(1 to n) are the n independent variables and b is the degree to which that independent variable impacts the dependent variable in the equation.

So, in other words, the regression model can calculate the probability that $Y = 1$ (whether someone is likely to be a leaver) and in a retention risk analysis project this is exactly what we want to know. In this example, $Y =$ turnover, so the probability that $Y = 1$ is the probability that someone in our organization will leave. With R, we can use our regression model (above) to determine the probability that any given individual will leave. This is particularly useful because we have no idea what the likelihood is of anyone leaving until we have run our turnover regression model. All we really knew about turnover before we created the model was whether employees have already left or whether they are still there.

By estimating our regression models, identifying drivers of turnover, we can then apply our regression equation to everyone's data values linked to these 'drivers' and we can get R to make predictions as to the probability of each person leaving. We could, for example, determine that the likelihood of someone leaving was 20 per cent, or 40 per cent, or 60 per cent, or 80 per cent, etc. This would have extremely useful applications in talent management and succession planning.

Having a good idea of the risk of an individual resigning when having career discussions, reviewing top talent and planning succession for senior roles in the organization is critical. It may indeed flag when to take action that may turn things around for an individual to prevent them from resigning and, particularly for senior roles, save the organization a considerable amount of money.

With this example, we can estimate the logistic regression model and save the regression model equation's predicted output for each individual in our organization; R applies the regression equation to the data in the predictor variable columns in the data set and saves the solution of the regression equation (the probability that someone is going to be a leaver) in a new column.

To do this we estimate our binary logistic regression model with the code below, which can be found in the file *Ch10_example.R*. We first load the required packages, and load the data file (the working directory was set in the prior example, and we follow on from that example).

```
pacman::p_load(readxl, modelsummary, dplyr, rcompanion, kableExtra)
Ch6_it <- read_excel("Ch6_Individual_Turnover.xlsx")
```

We then recode some variables for readability:

```
Ch6_it$Country_text <- case_match(Ch6_it$Country, 1 ~ "Belgium",
                2 ~ "Sweden",
                3 ~ "Italy",
                4 ~ "France",
                5 ~ "Poland",
                6 ~ "Mexico",
                7 ~ "Spain",
                8 ~ "UK",
                9 ~ "United States",
                10 ~ "Australia")
Ch6_it$Country_text <- as.factor(Ch6_it$Country_text)
```

We can then estimate the model:

```
logit_reg <- glm(LeaverStatus ~ BossGender + Gender + Age + LengthOfService +
            AppraisalRating + Country_text, data = Ch6_it, family =
            "binomial")
```

We then use this model to predict the probability of each person leaving, and label the classification with 'leaver' or 'stayer'. If their probability of leaving is 50 per cent or greater, we will classify them as a 'leaver', and if it is less than 50 per cent, we will classify them as a 'stayer'. We can do this with the following lines of code:

```
Ch6_it$probabilities <- logit_reg %>% predict(Ch6_it, type = "response")
Ch6_it$predicted.group <- ifelse(Ch6_it$probabilities > 0.5, "leaver",
"stayer")
```

We can look at the created probability variable with the following code:

```
summary(Ch6_it$probabilities)
```

Which produces Figure 10.9:

10.9

```
> summary(Ch6_it$probabilities)
   Min.   1st Qu.   Median     Mean   3rd Qu.      Max.  NA's
0.03786   0.08189  0.11515  0.12663   0.15239   0.45640     2
```

In Figure 10.9 we see the minimum, 1st quartile, median, mean (i.e. average), 3rd quartile, maximum and number of missing values for the newly created probability variable. You can see that the highest probability of leaving in our particular screen-shot (Figure 10.9) is 0.4564. Although this is closer to 0 than 1, many would agree that 45.64 per cent chance of leaving the organization is substantial. You can also see that the lowest figure goes down to 0.03786, or about 3.8 per cent.

Clearly, the difference between someone having a risk of leaving of nearly 46 per cent and a risk of leaving of 3.8 per cent is quite high. Indeed, it may be that all that needs to happen with someone who is at 46 per cent before they resign is a small nudge from a competitor (or an unfair decision from their line manager or co-worker). If this individual is on the succession plan for the future leadership of the organization it is useful to have this information, which may help to prevent a resignation before it happens. The reader will see that in some cases the leaver status with each employee in our data set is .00 and in some cases 1. The employees who have a 1 in this column have already left. It is the people who are still in the organization (with .00 in the leaver column) that have a higher *probabilities* value who may need special attention to make sure that they don't leave.

Another really useful way of using this method to predict individual turnover is with new recruitment and selection contexts. Many organizations run very expensive and detailed assessment centres to assist in decisions when selecting new joiners into the organization. The application of our regression models that we use in the previous example can be applied to help selectors make some 'evidence-based' decisions on who to hire. For example, models could be developed to predict expected post-hire performance levels with new assessment-centre candidates as well as the likelihood that they will not leave within a short period after coming on board. These models could be run using assessment-centre data input as the independent variables. The information that these models produce could provide critical input into selection decisions (and associated courses of action required for hiring using the model to predict likely outcomes).

Making graduate selection decisions with evidence obtained from previous performance data

As discussed in previous sections of this book, decisions made about people are often subjective, relying on gut instinct and involving bias (that may or may not be unconscious). While gut instinct can be valuable in technical and procedural contexts, it's less reliable when making decisions about people. Leaders do, however, often rely on instinct rather than evidence when making decisions about people (Ulrich, in Fitzenz, 2010). Ulrich suggests that 'most leaders would not make product decisions based on feelings alone; rather they use data based on how different product features meet or do not meet customer expectations. We should expect no less from people analytics.'

Recruitment and selection is one of the key areas of the employee process where the decisions we make have an enormous impact on the organization for years to come. In the recruitment and selection case study (Chapter 8), we discovered that key aspects of assessment-centre activities are found to predict post-joining performance. In this model, we also found that the onboarding activity of induction had a positive impact on first-year performance.

Specifically, we developed a complex model to predict performance after one year with newly recruited graduates. We constructed a model based on data available from a range of sources; our predictor variables (independent variables) included assessment-centre scores, gender, highest level of education reached, whether they had previous work experience and which department of the organization they had joined. We also included onboarding factors such as whether graduates attended an induction day or induction week, and whether they had an onboarding buddy.

The reader may recall that we used the data file *Ch8_selection.xlsx*: this file had a number of variables containing data linked to 360 graduates. The file contained the following variables:

1 GradID — Employee Identifier

2 Gender — Male (1) or Female (2)

3 EducationHighest — Education Category: BSc (1) MSc (2) Ph.D. (3)

4 UGYN — Underrepresented group: Yes (1) or No (2)

5 WorkExperience — Worked Before: Yes (1) No (2)

6 GradJOBfunction — Function Joined:

(1) HR
(2) Finance
(3) Marketing
(4) Sales
(5) Risk
(6) Legal
(7) Operations

7 ACPersonalityO — Assessment C Personality Openness (percentage)

8 ACPersonalityC — Assessment C Personality Conscientious (percentage)

9 ACPersonalityE — Assessment C Personality Extraversion (percentage)

10 ACPersonalityA — Assessment C Personality Agreeable (percentage)

11 ACPersonalityN — Assessment C Personality Neuroticism (percentage)

12	ACRatingINTCOMPA	Assessment C Competency Technical (1-5)
13	ACRatingINTCOMPB	Assessment C Competency Team Player
14	ACRatingINTCOMPC	Assessment C Competency Critical Thought
15	ACRatingINTCOMPD	Assessment C Competency Business Aware
16	ACRatingINTCOMPE	Assessment C Competency Drive Innovation
17	ACRatingAPTnumerical	Numerical Aptitude Test Score
18	ACRatingAPT	verbal Verbal Reasoning Aptitude Test Score
19	InductionDay	Attend Induction Day: No (0) Yes (1)
20	InductionWeek	Attend Induction Week: No (0) Yes (1)
21	OnBoardingBuddy	Given Joining Buddy: No (0) Yes (1)
22	Year1performanceRating	Year 1 Performance Rating:

(1) Fails to Meet Expectations
(2) Just Meets Expectations
(3) Meets Expectations Comfortably
(4) Exceeds Expectations
(5) A Star Performer

23	LeaverYr2	Leaver in first 24 Months (0) No (1) Leaver
24	HRDummyV	HR Dummy Variable
25	FinanceDummyV	Finance Dummy Variable
26	MarketingDummyV	Marketing Dummy Variable
27	SalesDummyV	Sales Dummy Variable
28	RiskDummyV	Risk Management Dummy Variable
29	LegalDummyV	Legal Dummy Variable
30	OperationsDummyV	Operations Dummy Variable

The complex model that we ran (see Chapter 8, Figure 8.16, page 300) was significant and confirmed that it is possible to predict graduates' 12-month performance ratings from the information held and collected during recruitment, selection and onboarding.

In Figure 10.10, we can recall the results of our model. The code to estimate the model is also in the file *Ch10_examples.R*.

10.10

	Unstandardized	Standardized
(Intercept)	-6.302***	0.000***
Gender_textMale	0.858***	0.362***
EducationHighest	0.138+	0.064+
UGYN_textYes	0.019	0.007
WorkExperience_textYes	-0.061	-0.024
ACPersonalityO	-0.003	-0.045
ACPersonalityC	0.008**	0.144**
ACPersonalityE	0.010**	0.179**
ACPersonalityA	0.001	0.018
ACPersonalityN	-0.001	-0.016
ACRatingINTCOMPA	0.364**	0.155**
ACRatingINTCOMPB	0.131	0.046
ACRatingINTCOMPC	0.090	0.032
ACRatingINTCOMPD	0.359**	0.150**
ACRatingINTCOMPE	0.346*	0.123*
ACRatingAPTnumerical	0.010	0.070
ACRatingAPTverbal	0.008	0.039
InductionDay_textYes	0.357*	0.102*
InductionWeek_textYes	0.023	0.007
OnBoardingBuddy_textYes	0.232	0.035
GradJOBfunction_textHR	-0.154	-0.049
GradJOBfunction_textLegal	0.997***	0.309***
GradJOBfunction_textMarketing	0.470*	0.168*
GradJOBfunction_textOperations	0.248	0.071
GradJOBfunction_textRisk	0.769***	0.182***
GradJOBfunction_textSales	-0.218	-0.053
Num.Obs.	318	318
R2	0.664	0.664
R2 Adj.	0.635	0.635
AIC	701.7	701.7
BIC	803.2	803.2
Log.Lik.	-323.832	-323.832
F	23.075	23.075
RMSE	0.67	0.67

+ p < 0.1, * p < 0.05, ** p < 0.01, *** p < 0.001

In terms of using the model to answer the 'So what?' question, two particular uses come to mind. One application is that this analysis may help us try to quantify the value of continuing with expensive onboarding activities whilst controlling for assessment-centre scores. The model could help to determine whether the return on the investment put into onboarding activity is worthwhile. The second is to assist with selection decisions. If we removed the onboarding piece from the model and looked at the pre-hiring information only, along with its impact on first-year performance, we could indeed use the model to help select new employees based on expected first-year performance (we outline this in examples 5 and 6 below). Before we do this, however, let's explore what impact the induction day might have on graduate performance and consider a model where we might be able to ascertain how important such an investment might be.

Example 4: constructing the business case for investment in an induction day

Here we explore the above model to help us build a business case for continuing to invest in the organization's induction day. We follow a similar approach to evaluating the impact of the checkout scan-rate training, as above. When we set out the raw regression equation based on the results of the regression model output presented in Figure 10.10, it looks like this (the significant drivers are highlighted in bold):

Performance rating year =

− 6.302

+ 0.858 Male Gender

+ 0.138 Education category

+ 0.019 UG

− 0.061 Worked before

− 0.003 Openness percentile score

+ 0.008 Conscientiousness percentile score

+ 0.010 Extraversion percentile score

+ 0.001 Agreeableness percentile score

− 0.001 Neuroticism percentile score

+ 0.364 Technical capabilities rating

+ 0.131 Team player rating

+ 0.090 Critical thinking rating

+ 0.359 Business awareness rating

+ 0.346 Drive and innovation rating

+ 0.010 Numeric reasoning test score

+ 0.008 Verbal reasoning test score

+ 0.357 Induction day attendance Yes

+ 0.023 Induction week attendance Yes

+ 0.232 Onboarding buddy Yes

– 0.154 HR dept

+ 0.997 Legal dept

+ 0.470 Marketing dept

+ 0.248 Operations

+ 0.769 Risk dept

– 0.218 Sales dept

So how will we use this model to determine the return on investment in onboarding? We can do this simply by using 'what if' statements and asking questions. For example: If no one went on the induction day, what would be the impact on average year-one performance of the new graduates? What if everyone went on the induction day? The answer to this question is quite simple to estimate, because we are just looking at the difference in performance in scenarios where no one versus everyone went on the induction day. This means we just need to look at the unstandardized coefficient. So, according to the model, individuals who attend the induction day are awarded, on average, a performance rating 0.357 points higher on the 1-to-5 scale than those who do not. This may be for a number of reasons that we might want to explore in another analytic research activity (we can only work with the data that we have here for now). Possible reasons for why induction-day presence could be important in predicting performance include: the induction helps ensure a quicker time to productivity due to 'knowing where everything is' or that it ensures a faster building of informal networks due to people met on the induction day, or many other things. According to Taylor (2010), benefits of an induction day include person–job fit, reducing intentions to leave and absenteeism, increasing employee commitment and job satisfaction.

Again here, it might be important to look at some descriptive statistics with our data set context for our scenario. Let's take a look at the descriptive statistics again. We can generate means, standard deviations, minimums and maximums with the following code, and we will start by loading packages, setting the working directory and loading the data (code available in the file *Ch10_examples.R*):

```
if (!require("pacman")) install.packages("pacman")
pacman::p_load(readxl, dplyr, modelsummary, rcompanion, this.path,
huxtable)
setwd(this.path::here())
Ch8_sel <- read_excel("Ch8_selection.xlsx")
```

We can then generate some descriptive statistics:

```
datasummary(Year1performanceRating + InductionDay + InductionWeek +
OnBoardingBuddy ~ N + Mean + SD + Min + Max, data = Ch8_sel,
output = "huxtable")
```

This produces Figure 10.11:

10.11

	N	Mean	SD	Min	Max
Year1performanceRating	318	3.41	1.16	1.00	5.00
InductionDay	360	0.87	0.33	0.00	1.00
InductionWeek	360	0.77	0.42	0.00	1.00
OnBoardingBuddy	360	0.91	0.28	0.00	1.00

From this output we know the current mean of graduates' first-year performance rating is 3.41 with 87 per cent of new graduates attending induction day. If we were to increase this to 100 per cent, then we can model the resultant increase on the first-year performance rating.

The regression coefficient that our model produces in predicting performance for our graduates associated with induction day is unstandardized coefficient = 0.357 ($p < 0.05$). We could use this to develop a model to assess the importance of the induction day.

All other things being equal, the first-year average performance rating = all other values (being equal) + 0.357 (average induction day attendance).

Currently, we have:

3.41 = all other values (being equal) + 0.357 (0.87)

We can transpose the equation to calculate what we need to insert into our (all other values being equal) part of the equation:

All things being equal = 3.41 – 0.357 (0.87)

Thus:

3.099 = 3.41 – 0.357 (0.87)

Now if we were able to update the attendance to 100 per cent, the predicted average performance would be:

3.099 + 0.357 (1) = 3.456

Or if we had no induction day, hence reducing the attendance to zero, the associated first-year performance would be:

3.099 + 0.357 (0) = 3.099

We have coded the variable such that the first-year performance variable is:

1 = Fails to Meet Expectations by Some Margin.

2 = Just Meets Expectations.

3 = Meets Expectations Comfortably.

4 = Exceeds Expectations.

5 = A Star Performer.

So we can say that the presence of an induction day improves the overall average performance from 3.099 to 3.456, significantly lifting performance towards the high-performer end. So a key part of evaluating a business case for investment into the induction day is that it can help improve employee performance. You can see how this can be done using R code in the file *Ch10_example.R*.

SNAPSHOT HIDDEN GEM

Using our model, we can predict that attendance at induction day for new joiners improves their performance rating by more than one-third of a rating point.

Example 5: using predictive models to help make a selection decision in graduate recruitment

The modelling scenario where we can use analytics to provide predictive information at selection stage involves the use of evidence from our regression model to help supply additional information that can help make a decision on who we should hire.

The above model included information on what features known at selection stage predicted future performance. This is very useful information that can be used by selectors. Of course, when making the selection decision, we have yet to carry out onboarding (as we have not yet hired any candidates), so let's look at our graduate performance regression model again without the induction variables included. We run the above model again (see Figure 8.19, page 307, for how we previously set this up, also in the file *Ch10_examples.R*); importantly this time we run it without the three onboarding variables and the following output is produced (Figure 10.12):

10.12

	Unstandardized	Standardized
(Intercept)	-5.359***	0.000***
Gender_textMale	0.910***	0.384***
EducationHighest	0.150+	0.069+
UGYN_textYes	0.017	0.006
WorkExperience_textYes	-0.058	-0.023
ACPersonalityO	-0.003	-0.040
ACPersonalityC	0.008**	0.146**
ACPersonalityE	0.010**	0.190**
ACPersonalityA	0.000	-0.007
ACPersonalityN	-0.002	-0.028
ACRatingINTCOMPA	0.387**	0.165**
ACRatingINTCOMPB	0.133	0.047
ACRatingINTCOMPC	0.084	0.030
ACRatingINTCOMPD	0.380***	0.158***
ACRatingINTCOMPE	0.327+	0.116+
ACRatingAPTnumerical	0.007	0.046
ACRatingAPTverbal	0.006	0.029
GradJOBfunction_textHR	-0.145	-0.046
GradJOBfunction_textLegal	0.994***	0.308***
GradJOBfunction_textMarketing	0.364+	0.130+
GradJOBfunction_textOperations	0.243	0.070
GradJOBfunction_textRisk	0.740***	0.175***
GradJOBfunction_textSales	-0.249	-0.061
Num.Obs.	318	318
R2	0.654	0.654
R2 Adj.	0.628	0.628
AIC	704.8	704.8
BIC	795.1	795.1
Log.Lik.	-328.422	-328.422
F	25.356	25.356
RMSE	0.68	0.68

+ p < 0.1, * p < 0.05, ** p < 0.01, *** p < 0.001

The model was significant with an R-square of 0.654. The new model results enable us to produce a regression equation predicting graduate performance with information known before onboarding. The raw regression model (with unstandardized coefficients) is outlined below (note, bold variables are the significant contributors):

Performance rating year =

− 5.359

+ 0.910 Male Gender

+ 0.150 Education category

− 0.017 UG

+ 0.058 Worked before

− 0.003 Openness percentile score

+ 0.008 Conscientiousness percentile score

+ 0.010 Extraversion percentile score

+ 0.000 Agreeableness percentile score

− 0.002 Neuroticism percentile score

+ 0.387 Technical capabilities rating

+ 0.133 Team player rating

+ 0.084 Critical-thinking rating

+ 0.380 Business awareness rating

+ 0.327 Drive and innovation rating

+ 0.007 Numeric reasoning test score

+ 0.006 Verbal reasoning test score

− 0.145 HR dept

+ 0.994 Legal dept

+ 0.364 Marketing dept

+ 0.243 Operations

+ 0.740 Risk dept

− 0.249 Sales dept

We can now use this model for subsequent recruitment exercises. So, say for the following year's graduate recruitment, we run the same assessment centre and gather the same information about candidates. This time, we can predict the first-year performance based on this information collected at the selection stage. For the purpose of this example, let's look at the candidates for the first assessment centre in the following year's graduate recruitment exercise, which took 10 candidates through the process to hire marketing graduates.

We can open the file containing the additional candidates with this code (working directory and required packages already loaded from previous examples):

```
Ch10_new <- read_excel("Ch10_new_candidates.xlsx")
```

The data for these recruits are in the last 10 rows of the data (rows 361–70). So we can examine their data with the following code:

```
datasummary_skim(Ch10_new[361:370,], output = 'huxtable')
```

This produces Figure 10.13:

10.13

	Unique	Missing Pct.	Mean	SD	Min	Median	Max
GradID	10	0	365.5	3.0	361.0	365.5	370.0
Gender	2	0	1.7	0.5	1.0	2.0	2.0
EducationHighest	3	0	1.4	0.7	1.0	1.0	3.0
UGYN	2	0	1.7	0.5	1.0	2.0	2.0
WorkExperience	2	0	1.8	0.4	1.0	2.0	2.0
GradJOBfunction	1	0	3.0	0.0	3.0	3.0	3.0
ACPersonalityO	4	0	38.2	6.5	26.0	35.5	45.0
ACPersonalityC	4	0	38.2	6.5	26.0	35.5	45.0
ACPersonalityE	6	0	88.5	6.4	78.0	89.0	98.0
ACPersonalityA	4	0	38.2	6.5	26.0	35.5	45.0
ACPersonalityN	8	0	73.3	19.5	45.0	77.5	97.0
ACRatingINTCOMPA	2	0	4.3	0.5	4.0	4.0	5.0
ACRatingINTCOMPB	2	0	4.7	0.5	4.0	5.0	5.0
ACRatingINTCOMPC	2	0	4.1	0.3	4.0	4.0	5.0
ACRatingINTCOMPD	2	0	4.4	0.5	4.0	4.0	5.0
ACRatingINTCOMPE	1	0	4.0	0.0	4.0	4.0	4.0
ACRatingAPTnumerical	4	0	81.6	2.6	78.0	82.5	84.0
ACRatingAPTverbal	4	0	81.6	2.6	78.0	82.5	84.0
HRDummyV	1	0	0.0	0.0	0.0	0.0	0.0
FinanceDummyV	1	0	0.0	0.0	0.0	0.0	0.0
MarketingDummyV	1	0	1.0	0.0	1.0	1.0	1.0
SalesDummyV	1	0	0.0	0.0	0.0	0.0	0.0
RiskDummyV	1	0	0.0	0.0	0.0	0.0	0.0
LegalDummyV	1	0	0.0	0.0	0.0	0.0	0.0
OperationsDummyV	1	0	0.0	0.0	0.0	0.0	0.0

You will see from Figure 10.13 data for the latest set of 10 graduates; these graduates are all going into the marketing function (see the 1.00 entries in the *MarketingDummyV* section of Figure 10.13) and as yet we do not have onboarding information; there is also no *Year1performanceRating* data in the data file associated with these potential employees (because we have not yet hired them).

Now, to get information on which of these 10 candidates is most likely to perform best as an employee we rerun the linear regression model. Because this dataframe does not have the numeric variables coded into factor variables, we will need to transform those variables with the code below.

```
Ch10_new$Gender_text <- as.factor(case_match(Ch10_new$Gender,
1 ~ "Male", 2 ~ "Female"))
Ch10_new$EducationHighest_text <- as.factor(case_match
(Ch10_new$EducationHighest, 1 ~ "BSc", 2 ~ "MSc", 3 ~ "PhD"))
Ch10_new$UGYN_text <- as.factor(case_match(Ch10_new$UGYN,
1 ~ "Yes", 2 ~ "No"))
Ch10_new$WorkExperience_text <- as.factor(case_match
(Ch10_new$WorkExperience, 1 ~ "Yes", 2 ~ "No"))
Ch10_new$GradJOBfunction_text <- as.factor(case_match
(Ch10_new$GradJOBfunction,
                         1 ~ "HR",
                         2 ~ "Finance",
                         3 ~ "Marketing",
                         4 ~ "Sales",
                         5 ~ "Risk",
                         6 ~ "Legal",
                         7 ~ "Operations"))
Ch10_new$InductionDay_text <- as.factor(case_match(Ch10_new$InductionDay,
0 ~ "No", 1 ~ "Yes"))
Ch10_new$InductionWeek_text <- as.factor(case_match(Ch10_new$InductionWeek,
0 ~ "No", 1 ~ "Yes"))
Ch10_new$OnBoardingBuddy_text <- as.factor(case_match
(Ch10_new$OnBoardingBuddy, 0 ~ "No", 1 ~ "Yes"))
Ch10_new$Year1performanceRating_text <-
as.factor(case_match(Ch10_new$Year1performanceRating,
                         1 ~ "Fails to Meet Expectations",
                         2 ~ "Just Meets Expectations",
                         3 ~ "Meets Expectations Comfortably",
                         4 ~ "Exceeds Expectations",
                         5 ~ "A Star Performer"))
Ch10_new$LeaverYr2_text <- as.factor(case_match(Ch10_new$LeaverYr2,
0 ~ "No", 1 ~ "Yes"))
```

We can now conduct the regression with the following code as we did in Chapter 8, excluding the onboard variables:

```
perf_reg_new <- lm(Year1performanceRating ~ Gender_text + EducationHighest +
UGYN_text + WorkExperience_text + ACPersonalityO + ACPersonalityC +
ACPersonalityE + ACPersonalityA + ACPersonalityN + ACRatingINTCOMPA +
ACRatingINTCOMPB + ACRatingINTCOMPC + ACRatingINTCOMPD + ACRatingINTCOMPE +
ACRatingAPTnumerical + ACRatingAPTverbal + GradJOBfunction_text,
data = Ch10_new)
```

We can now generate predictions for all individuals in the dataframe using the following code:

```
Ch10_new$pred_perf <- perf_reg_new %>% predict(Ch10_new, type =
"response")
```

This will give the estimated first-year performance for all cases.

We can look at the predicted performance for the candidates using the following code:

```
Ch10_new$pred_perf[361:370]
```

This produces Figure 10.14:

10.14

```
> Ch10_new$pred_perf[361:370]
      361        362        363        364        365        366        367        368        369        370
3.743976   2.741671   3.801049   2.195371   2.773115   2.337597   2.889746   3.075819   3.884443   3.144249
```

You can see, then, that many of the candidates are predicted to be low performers. There are three of the 10 candidates who are predicted to be high performers, gaining a score near 4, candidates 361, 363 and 369. We have two additional candidates who are expected to be average performers with a score very close to 3, candidates 368 and 370, with the rest of the candidates coming in with low expectations of performance. The recommendation, then, based on this model, would be to put forward candidates 361, 363 and 369 for interview. Depending on the resources available, the organization may also carry out further assessment on candidates 368 and 370 before recommending them for interview.

Careful consideration with the use of predicted performance values

Obviously this information should not be used solely as the decision-making tool for selection of our graduates, as our regression models only ever work on probabilities (and significance of our predictors is determined on the basis of the probabilities) of patterns emerging from our historical data (which does not always translate to what happens today or in the future). If you peruse down the predicted values *pred_perf* column for existing graduates in our data set and compare these values with the actual performance data for the existing graduates, you will see that the predictions are not always accurate. Although our model is significant in predicting performance, it does not predict 100 per cent of the variation in performance – it is not perfect. Thus, even if our model predicts that a candidate's performance will not be high, if hired they may well end up being a star performer (our model will never take into account all factors that account for performance). We should, of course, never assume that our model predictions would always come true... However, the analysis produces very useful evidence-based predictions that should help our selectors come to a decision (especially if they are vacillating over who to hire).

Example 6: which candidate might be a 'flight risk'?

As discussed in Chapter 8, this same data set is also used to predict whether our existing graduates have chosen to leave the organization before completing two years of service. The same method can be used to determine which of our new marketing candidates are more likely to leave, although whether this should be used as a selection technique is a question of ethics. The model may, however, be better used to flag up any potential high performers we wish to hire but who are more at risk of leaving early – so that they may be managed accordingly.

Because leaving the organization or not leaving the organization is a binary decision, or a binary/categorical variable, we would use a binary logistic regression with 'left by year two' as the dependent variable, as we did in Chapter 8 (rather than a linear regression). So again we are using the new graduate selection data set (Ch10_new_candidates.xlsx) in which we have entered data for our 10 new marketing graduate candidates.

These predicted probabilities will then be saved in an additional column in exactly the same way as the predicted performance in example 5.

We can set up the logistic regression model predicting early leavers (notice again that we do not include onboarding/induction information or Year 1 performance rating as predictors because we have not yet hired these candidates) by using the following code. We follow on from the previous example, and we assume the working directory, data and required packages are already loaded:

```
leaver_reg <- glm(LeaverYr2 ~ Gender_text + EducationHighest_text +
UGYN_text + WorkExperience_text + ACPersonalityO + ACPersonalityC +
ACPersonalityE + ACPersonalityA + ACPersonalityN + ACRatingINTCOMPA +
ACRatingINTCOMPB + ACRatingINTCOMPC + ACRatingINTCOMPD + ACRatingINTCOMPE +
ACRatingAPTnumerical + ACRatingAPTverbal + GradJOBfunction_text,
data = Ch10_new, family = "binomial")
```

And as with previous examples, we can generate probabilities and predicted group using this code:

```
Ch10_new$probabilities <- leaver_reg %>% predict(Ch10_new, type =
"response")
Ch10_new$pred_group <- ifelse(Ch10_new$probabilities > 0.5, "leaver",
"stayer")
```

We can examine the predicted performance and probabilities of leaving generated for the 10 candidates with this code:

```
Ch10_new$pred_perf[361:370]
Ch10_new$probabilities[361:370]
```

This produces Figure 10.15:

10.15

```
> Ch10_new$pred_perf[361:370]
      361       362       363       364       365       366       367       368       369       370
 3.743976  2.741671  3.801049  2.195371  2.773115  2.337597  2.889746  3.075819  3.884443  3.144249
> Ch10_new$probabilities[361:370]
      361       362       363       364       365       366       367       368       369       370
0.6475131 0.9464330 0.3807404 0.9228281 0.9429330 0.9474130 0.8584299 0.8928189 0.3353703 0.7534021
```

You will see (from Figure 10.15) that candidate 361 is predicted to have a fairly high performance rating (3.74) but there is a 65 per cent chance that this individual would be an early leaver. If a decision is made to hire this individual then their line manager should pay particular attention to making sure their needs are met in the early phase of employment.

In Chapter 6, the turnover case study, we discussed the costs involved in employee turnover. These included separation costs, replacement costs and training costs, which were estimated to cost the organization between 93 per cent and 200 per cent of each single leaver's salary, depending on certain job factors. A poor hiring decision may not only include the cost of turnover as discussed, but may also include the costs involved due to the operational 'damage' caused by having a person in position who is not suited to the role. According to Kiazim (2015), the types of problems could include: attrition and wasted hiring budgets; theft; embezzlement; damaged morale; endangerment of clients, business associates and other employees; loss of productivity; litigation; or even public scandal and negative publicity. It is, hence, recommended to try to avoid these types of problems by taking an analytic decision-making approach to hiring.

Further consideration on the use of evidence-based recommendations in selection

In Chapter 12, we discuss ethical issues that should be considered in making decisions based on data and HR analysis; selection decisions are a particularly relevant area in this regard. So, although gender, ethnicity and even the highest level of education are part of the model created (indeed gender being a significant 'driver' of performance ratings), it does not mean that significant results with these should be used as a means for selecting the predicted highest performers. It is important to realize that there are always other factors at play that our models do not take into account; thus although demographic factors may show significance in some model it is almost never the demographic features themselves that directly cause variation in our dependent variables. Such a belief would be totally deterministic and would not show any consideration for the likely complex nature of behaviour. There could be so many reasons that we need to consider, for example, as to why females seem to show lower levels of performance in our models here. For example a high prevalence of male senior managers may be part of the reason why male graduates are more likely to receive higher performance ratings – due to possible biases at play. This does not mean that we shouldn't hire women, but that we should do something about our managers demonstrating discrimination in their performance appraisal judgements! The same is true for ethnicity and even higher levels of education, which are often linked to socio-economic background and not necessarily capability or aptitude/competencies – for which one may argue that the assessment-centre results are a better measure. So, when using a model for specific decision making and recommendations for action, it is worth considering what should and should not be included in our interpretations of what is going on in our organization.

References

Fitz-enz, J (2010) *The New HR Analytics: Predicting the economic value of your company's human capital investment*, AMACOM, New York

Kiazim, O (2015) The real cost of a bad hiring decision, HR Zone, www.hrzone.com/talent/acquisition/the-real-cost-of-a-bad-hiring-decision (archived at https://perma.cc/S7GP-LZ72)

Taylor, T S (2010) *Resourcing and Talent Management*, 5th edn, Chartered Institute of Personnel and Development, London

11

More advanced HR analytic techniques

This book is designed to be an introduction for an HR professional who wants to add statistical competencies to their analytic capabilities. If this is indeed your first introduction to statistics, we would recommend putting this chapter to one side until you are confident with the techniques discussed in the rest of the book. Once you have had the opportunity to run the analyses yourselves again and again on your own data, the day-to-day basic techniques will become second nature and you may well want to understand more complex analyses procedures that have the power to do even more.

Up until this point, we have restricted the statistical modelling in this book to a range of statistical analyses that an HR analyst is most likely to conduct on a day-to-day basis. There is, however, a whole range of much more sophisticated statistical procedures that can be used to help answer a range of different and more complex HR analytic research questions. As you become more advanced, you will start to look beyond the basic techniques and realize that the possible analytic questions that could be explored go on and on.

The aim of this chapter is to provide an introduction to some of the more widely used advanced analytic techniques, so that you are aware of them, and to provide you with some recommendations for further reading. We will cover:

- Mediation processes: when the independent (predictor) variable has an indirect relationship with the dependent variable rather than a direct one. In other words, a serial (sequential) 'causal' process is occurring. We describe the analytic process to explore such a pattern of relationships.

- Moderation and interaction analysis: when two independent predictor variables combine or interact to account for variation in the dependent variable. In other words, the effect of a predictor variable on our dependent variable is contingent on another contextual factor.

- Multi-level linear modelling: when the data you are looking at is in a hierarchical structure of levels, for example individual → team → department.

- Curvilinear relationships: when a relationship exists between two variables that is not linear. For example, when a relationship between two variables drawn on a graph shows a curve rather than a straight line. The increase in an independent variable may initially be associated with an increase in a dependent variable, but as the independent variable continues to increase, we begin to see a decrease in the dependent variable (or vice versa).

- Structural equation models: a form of analysis that tests data against some form of theoretical predicted model generally involving a number of variables usually arranged in a predicted causal sequence; this analysis tends to involve the exploration of a number of regression equations simultaneously. These models can be made up of either observed variables or latent variables (or concepts) measured by multiple items (see Chapter 5 for a discussion of latent variables).

- Growth models: when analysis is conducted that predicts growth or change over time in the dependent variable by collecting data over a number of time points.

- Latent class analysis: a subset of structural equation modelling, its main purpose is to conduct analysis with a number of metrics in order to identify particular groups within a sample or population (on the basis of each individual's profile of scores across the range of metrics).

- Response surface methodology and polynomial regression analysis: polynomial regression explores the relationship between one or more independent variables and a dependent variable, taking into account the potential for curvilinear relationships between the independent variable(s) and the dependent variable. Polynomial analyses can be extended to explore curvilinear relationships and interactions between two independent variables and a dependent variable, taking into account the apparent level of the dependent variable expected at any particular level of one or more independent variables. Response surface methodology plots these relationships and interactions on 3D graphs.

- Machine learning: machine learning (ML) and automated machine learning (AML) refer to the process by which machines learn from data, much in the same way that humans learn every day from all the information that comes our way. We learn what is right and what is wrong. We grow to understand what causes an 'error' and we learn from this, correct our behaviour accordingly and improve with experience. Of course, this may not be true for every human! In predictive HR analytics, this translates to systematically building a model based on the entire data set (after first using a smaller training sample) considering all the variables available, regardless of their meaning, to form an optimal model with the aim of reducing the error.

Some of these statistical procedures could be very useful to HR analysts as they become more capable; for example, the moderation and interaction testing and the curvilinear relationship analysis. Most if not all of these tests can be carried out with R, although they will require learning about additional packages not covered in this book. However, we explain these conceptually and point you to packages that can be used to conduct some of these more sophisticated modelling techniques.

Mediation processes

In many of the predictive analyses models presented in this book, it may appear that we often seem to look for evidence of a fairly straightforward cause-and-effect process where X is assumed to influence Y. However, in many cases a possible causal flow may involve a more complex serial process where one factor influences another only if it has an effect on a third factor, referred to as a mediator. With mediation, the effects of X on Y are expected to occur through an intervening causal process or a serial chain of causal reactions.

A simple example might be whether a challenging experience at work leads to someone leaving his or her job. Let's say, for example, that employees experience an increase in their workload. An increase in workload may only cause someone to look for work elsewhere when it has led to some dissatisfaction with their job. An employee may not start looking for work at another organization if the increase in workload did not lead to dissatisfaction; importantly, it is dissatisfaction that has a direct impact on people leaving, not the increased workload. The impact of an increase in workload (X) on people leaving (Y) is indirect through dissatisfaction (M) rather than direct. We could represent this possible causal flow in a diagram (see Figure 11.1).

11.1   Mediation process

Recent decades have witnessed a shift in how mediation processes are tested analytically. For more than two decades, the Baron and Kenny (1986) method of mediation testing was the approach taken to examine the existence of mediation in the social science and management field. This involved conducting a series of three separate regression analyses. With the Baron and Kenny approach, to test for the above mediation model you needed to follow three steps:

- **Step one**
  We conduct a regression that predicts job dissatisfaction with increases in workloads. Thus the regression equation for this step looks like: job dissatisfaction = a + b_1 (*increase in workload*); and the standardized regression equation for this step looks like: job dissatisfaction = Beta$_1$ (*increase in workload*).

  If mediation exists as per Figure 11.1, increases in workload must be a significant predictor of job dissatisfaction.

- **Step two**
  We conduct a regression that predicts intention to leave with increases in workloads. Thus the regression equation for this step looks like: intention to leave = a + b_1

(*increase in workload*); and the standardized regression equation for this step looks like: intention to leave = Beta$_1$ (*increase in workload*).

If mediation exists as per Figure 11.1, increase in workload must be a significant predictor of intention to leave.

- **Step three**

  We conduct a regression that predicts intention to leave with increases in workloads as well as job dissatisfaction as independent variables. Thus the regression equation for this step looks like: intention to leave = a + b$_1$ (*increase in workload*) + b$_2$ (*job dissatisfaction*); and the standardized regression equation for this step looks like: intention to leave = Beta$_1$ (*increase in workload*) + Beta$_2$ (*job dissatisfaction*).

  If mediation exists as per Figure 11.1, then:

  - Our mediator *job dissatisfaction* must be a significant predictor of Y *intention to leave* in step 3.

  - The increase in workload (X) Beta$_1$ in step 3 must be less than Beta$_1$ in step 1, so the *increase in workload* has less of an impact on *intention to leave* when we account for *job dissatisfaction*.

  - If *increase in workload* is no longer significant in step 3, then we would say there is full mediation.

  - If there is no reduction in Beta$_1$ from step 1 to step 3 and the impact that an *increase in workload* has on *intention to leave* does not change across these two steps when we account for *job dissatisfaction*, then we would say there is no mediation.

  - If *increase in workload* still has a significant impact on *intention to leave* but Beta$_1$ in step 3 is smaller than Beta$_1$ in step 1, we would say there is partial mediation.

The good thing about these steps is that they can be followed very easily and carried out with R by running a few regressions.

There are, however, some challenges with this approach, some of which have been discussed in depth by Andrew Hayes (2009) in his paper 'Beyond Baron and Kenny: Statistical mediation analysis in the new millennium'. One of the problems with the Baron and Kenny approach is that it requires a series of separate regression analysis to be conducted, which never actually give a robust statistic that can be used as an indicator of the extent of mediation. This has led to a new statistical approach often referred to as the Preacher and Hayes approach.

The Preacher and Hayes approach to analysing mediation involves creating a measure or coefficient of the degree of mediation (or indirect effects) to be produced and the significance of this coefficient to be tested using 'bootstrapped' confidence intervals. Hayes has authored an R program for this new approach, and a link to it, as well as additional information, is available on the following website: www.afhayes.com/introduction-to-mediation-moderation-and-conditional-process-analysis.html.

It is relatively easy to estimate mediation models with the Preacher and Hayes approach using Hayes' R program. For example, you can specify the dependent variable, the mediator variable, and the independent variable in a single line of code. To illustrate, let's imagine a hypothetical data set called *org_data*. It contains the variables in Figure 11.1, namely *increase_workload*, a numeric variable to measure perceived increase in workload, *job_dissatisfaction*, a numeric variable to measure level of job dissatisfaction and *intent_leave*, a numeric variable to indicate how seriously people are considering leaving. All of the variables are measured on a 1–7 scale with higher ratings indicating a greater level of perceived workload, dissatisfaction, and intent to leave, respectively. Conducting this analysis would involve running the following line of code:

```
process(data = "org_data", y = "intent_leave",
x = "increase_workload", m = " job_dissatisfaction", model = 4)
```

Of course, you will have to load the Hayes' program and load the data set before attempting this. But you will see that the code itself is straightforward. However, it takes some time to familiarize yourself with the different types of models that 'Process' can run in order to make sure that you have the correct set-up. The output is not always straightforward and takes a bit of getting used to; however, further discussion on this should be left for a more advanced HR analytics text. We provide an alternative way to conduct mediation analysis in the file *Ch11_examples.R*. It involves job strain predicting lower job satisfaction, which in turn predicts job performance. We leave it to the reader to examine this relationship.

Before finishing up on the discussion of mediation analysis, there is some debate within the organizational sciences about how the temporal element of mediation processes should be set up. As mediation models involve serial causal processes (i.e. X leads to M, which then leads to Y), there is an explicit assumption of causality implied with such models. One of the key challenges with such models is that often they are tested using correlation analysis or regression analyses, and, whilst these approaches can identify the existence of the necessary relationships that should exist if the causal model were 'true', the existence of relationships between variables does not imply causality. As we know from our discussion on regression and correlation in Chapter 3, whilst regression and correlation do indicate a relationship, relationships do not necessarily imply causality (just as, as pointed out in Chapter 3, a high correlation between ice cream consumption and skin cancer does not mean that ice cream gives you skin cancer – there may be other factors involved, such as time spent in the sun, for example). It is often the case that an analyst conducting mediation testing is inferring causality from the pattern of data even despite this issue. The HR analyst should always bear this in mind.

Moderation and interaction analysis

Most of the predictive models that we have explored in this book include examples where the analyst makes some kind of assumption that one or more factors may be influencing or driving a particular metric (such as performance or engagement, etc) in a linear or direct way (whilst taking into account how our collection of potential 'drivers' are related to each other). With the multiple regression and the binary logistic regression examples in this book, we are exploring the degree to which we can *directly* account for variance in our dependent variables by looking at our collection of potential 'drivers'. It is, however, sometimes the case that we can uncover really important patterns in our data by exploring how two potential drivers combine or interact to account for variation in our predicted metric. Thus, we might want to explore *interaction effects* in our predictive models.

A very straightforward example of an interaction effect that we do explore in the book (though with an ANOVA rather than a 'predictive regression model') is the differential impact that the introduction of a work–life balance (WLB) programme has on stress levels (across time) when males and females are compared. Whilst, from our example, there was evidence of a direct effect on stress levels from the WLB programme introduction (in that our organization showed a reduction in stress levels after the introduction of the WLB programme) and gender (in that women in our organization tended to report higher stress levels), the really important finding in accounting for stress levels was the interaction between gender and the WLB programme introduction. We found that the stress levels reduced to a greater extent for women compared to men, following the WLB programme introduction. Thus, gender and WLB programme introduction interact as possible 'drivers' of stress levels.

A classic example of an interaction effect from the organizational psychology literature would be the demands-control 'stress' model presented by Karasek (1979). Karasek presented a model that aims to account for variation in occupational stress levels. The model tries to account for variation in employees' 'stress' levels (or psychological strain); so psychological strain can be considered to be our dependent variable. Karasek presented two main potential predictors of employee psychological strain: 1) the level of job demand (or pressure) that an employee experiences; and 2) the level of control (or autonomy) that an employee has over how they do their job. Both of these factors may indeed have *direct* effects on employees' psychological strain: the higher the job demands experienced then the more strain an employee feels; and the greater the level of job control a person has then the less psychological strain they will experience. However, Karasek argues that these two factors should interact in explaining possible positive or negative employee reactions. The negative impact of job demands may actually be dependent upon (or influenced by) how much job control they have.

One can infer from Karasek's model that if someone has a high level of job control, then they may generally be less stressed at work than if they have low control; one could also infer that people with high demands may generally be more stressed than people with low demands. Importantly, the model implies an interaction between these two factors, in that someone who experiences high job demands may not experience psychological strain if they have the decision latitude/ability to control how they respond to the high job demands. Thus job control interacts with job demands in accounting for employees' level of psychological strain. An indicative graphical representation of this interaction effect is presented in Figure 11.2.

Importantly, the interaction here indicates that the impact that job demands have on employees' levels of psychological strain is contingent on how much decision latitude or autonomy they have in their jobs. Thus, autonomy moderates the impact that job demands have on strain.

11.2   Example impact of an interaction between job demands and job control on employees' level of psychological strain

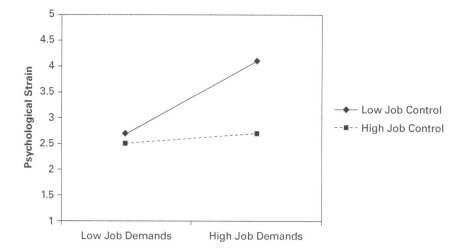

Calculating interaction effects with an ANOVA example has been discussed in Chapters 7 and 9. However, we have not outlined how to calculate interactions between independent variables in a multiple regression model. When two independent variables are continuous, where we believe that these factors may influence a particular dependent variable and furthermore we believe that the influence may involve an interaction effect, we can include such an analysis in our multiple regression predictive model.

An additional example of a possible interactional analysis, linking to a case study that we have presented, is our prediction of increases in performance ratings between

2014 and 2015. We presented this analysis in Chapter 7. In this example we were predicting increases in performance ratings that were given between 2014 and 2015; we included a measure of the degree to which individuals express that they experience work-related pressure and strain (to the point that they sometimes worry about work and lose sleep). We also included a measure of sickness absence in the model. Individual sickness absence and expressed levels of strain were both shown to be related to increases in performance rating; absence rates with a negative relationship and psychological strain with a positive relationship. We could easily conceive that there may be an interplay between pressure/strain and sickness absence and whether or not someone gets a higher performance rating than the previous year. Maybe people who are under strain but do not take time off sick are the ones who get the performance rating increase rather than those who are not under strain but take time off sick. This is easy to test with our regression. First, in accordance with the recommended approach to testing for moderation set out by Cohen and Cohen (1983), you need to standardize your two variables of strain and sickness absence. We recommend the approach of converting the data within the two metrics into z-scores, which equalizes the scale for both measures. To convert the variables *JobStrain2014* and *SickDays2014* to z-scores, you can run the following code, which is available in the file *Ch11_examples.R*. We first set the working directory, load required packages, and the data:

```
if (!require("pacman")) install.packages("pacman")
pacman::p_load(readxl, dplyr, modelsummary, this.path, huxtable,
interactions, ggplot2)
setwd(this.path::here())
Ch7_ex3 <- read_excel("Ch7_perf_2014_to_2015_sick_2014.xlsx")
```

We can then convert the *JobStrain2014* and *SickDays2014* to z-scores:

```
Ch7_ex3$JobStrain2014_z <- scale(Ch7_ex3$JobStrain2014)
Ch7_ex3$SickDays2014_z <- scale(Ch7_ex3$SickDays2014)
```

The code above assumes the variables are in a dataframe named *Ch7_ex3*, as in the instructions for example 3 in Chapter 7. The code defines new variables in that dataframe (*JobStrain2014_z*; *SickDays2014_z*) that are z-scored versions of the *JobStrain2014* and *SickDays2014* variables, as computed by the *scale* program.

Then once you have these two new variables, you include them as independent variables in a regression that predicts 2015 performance (whilst controlling for 2014 performance, which enables a prediction of change in performance – see discussion on this in Chapter 7, page 255). Example code for this regression is below:

```
perf_sick_mod <- lm(PerformanceRating2015 ~ PerformanceRating2014 +
JobStrain2014_z * SickDays2014_z, data = Ch7_ex3)
```

The asterisk in between the *JobStrain2014_z* and *SickDays2014_z* variables tells R to create an interaction term in the model, which represents the multiplication of those two variables. If that interaction term is significant ($p < 0.05$) then we know that the two variables interact in their relationship with change in performance. After estimating this model, we can create a table of results using the code below, with the result shown in Figure 11.3:

```
mod1 <- modelsummary(perf_sick_mod, output = "modelsummary_list")
mod2 <- modelsummary(perf_sick_mod, output = "modelsummary_list",
standardize = "basic")
models <- list(
"Unstandardized" = mod1,
"Standardized" = mod2)
modelsummary(models, stars = TRUE, statistic = NULL, output =
"huxtable")
```

11.3

	Unstandardized	Standardized
(Intercept)	1.399***	0.000***
PerformanceRating2014	0.399***	0.419***
JobStrain2014_z	0.156**	0.172**
SickDays2014_z	-0.274**	-0.186**
JobStrain2014_z × SickDays2014_z	0.262*	0.148*
Num.Obs.	218	218
R2	0.230	0.230
R2 Adj.	0.215	0.215
AIC	532.6	532.6
BIC	552.9	552.9
Log.Lik.	-260.304	-260.304
RMSE	0.80	0.80

+ $p < 0.1$, * $p < 0.05$, ** $p < 0.01$, *** $p < 0.001$

To further understand the interaction, the easiest thing to do is to plot the results on an interaction graph (such as that presented in Figure 11.2). You can do this in R with the *interact_plot* program in the *interactions* package. For the model above, we can use the following code:

```
interact_plot(perf_sick_mod, pred = SickDays2014_z,
modx = JobStrain2014_z)
```

We specify the model, the predictor variable and the moderating variable. This produces Figure 11.4:

11.4

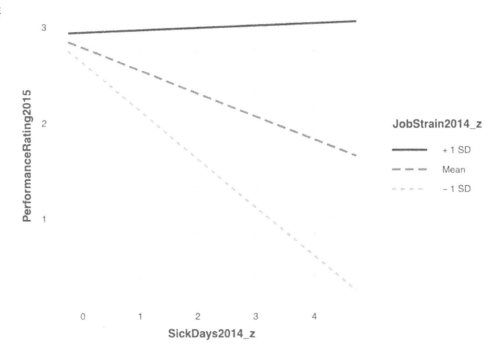

For a thorough discussion of interaction and moderation effects, a comprehensive paper written by Dawson (2014) would be a good reference to follow up.

The previous explanation outlines how to set up interaction analysis with a multiple regression that has a continuous dependent variable and two continuous independent variables. If the predictive model involves a binary variable such as that used with individual turnover analysis, and we are interested in whether two categorical variables might interact, we can very simply use a similar approach conduct such an analysis. In Chapter 6 we have a predictive model that tries to account for individual leavers. So our dependent variable is a binary variable. Two of the predictor variables included are categorical (gender of employee and gender of boss). If we think that the genders of the employee and their boss may be important in predicting turnover patterns, the interaction between these two gender variables may be worth exploring. To check for this in a predictive model we can ask R to check for the interaction between gender of individual by gender of boss. To do this, you would again put an asterisk (*) between the two variables of interest when setting up the regression. Again, if this interaction term is significant in the model output then we can assume that the two variables interact.

Multi-level linear modelling

The very nature of HR data means that HR analysts will intuitively be aware of the fact that data can be presented at different levels. For example, data can be at the individual employee level, the team level, the department level, the function level, the country level and the organization level. Often with HR data, analysis at one level (e.g. the individual employee) has been or needs to be manipulated so that it can be analysed at another level (e.g. team). Employee engagement scores are a classic example of this – often when a survey company conducts an employee attitude/engagement survey where each employee is given a questionnaire to fill out and given an 'engagement' score (as well as scores on measures for other constructs). However, due to issues of confidentiality, the data that they then provide to the organization is usually a computed average (engagement) or percentage (engaged) scores aggregated to a higher level such as team, department or organization (which might be benchmarked against other organizations within the industry). This is why in the engagement case study in Chapter 5 we conduct analysis at the aggregate team level; often this is the lowest level of engagement data that is available to an HR analyst. In the engagement modelling and in various other analyses these team-level engagement scores are then used to predict other metrics (such as team turnover statistics and team diversity data). Below we make this level data structure a little clearer in a simplistic scenario of five levels:

- Level 1: individual data relating to a particular employee. This could be data held or recorded in an HR database.

- Level 2: team-level data where the individual employees are nested into teams as groups – some data might only be available at a team level (e.g. team sales figures).

- Level 3: departmental-level data where the individual employees are nested into teams as groups and these teams are further nested into departments as groups.

- Level 4: country-level data where the countries include individual employees nested into teams as groups and further nested into departments as groups.

- Level 5: organizational-level data that characterizes something at the organization level.

It is important to understand that using different levels of data in some statistical procedures (without considering this) can potentially create problems for the analyst for a number of reasons. One of these reasons might be that when a statistic is aggregated or created at a particular group level, and included in an analysis that includes individual-level data, the sensitivity of the analysis may be reduced. To make this point clearer we will use a hypothetical situation where we have 5,000 employees in an organization organized into 300 teams (of on average 16–17 team members) in 10 departments across 10 countries. If we had team-level statistics (e.g. percentage of engaged team members in each team) linked to each individual and we used this team engagement score as a possible factor to try to predict what made individual employees leave in the last 12 months, each team member would be given the same team engagement score when we try to predict why and whether they left. Probably, the analysis would be more sensitive if we had individual engagement scores, as it would take into account individual variation in engagement rather than use a blunt aggregated team figure for each individual. Playing this out, we might be trying to predict whether an individual will leave, but with a measure that has something to do with the team rather than the individual. It might be the case that the reason an individual left was because they were disengaged, even though their team was highly engaged; thus team-level engagement might not be likely to predict whether this individual was going to be a leaver.

A second reason why it might not always be sensible to use group-level statistics that have been aggregated or created at a particular group level, and include them in analysis that has involved working with individual-level data, is that many statistical procedures such as multiple linear regression may include some assumptions that the individual employees or objects of study (e.g. teams) are 'independent'. By this it means that the individual elements are free to vary at the individual level that is not explained as a function of some grouping. If people are actually organized into a group and this grouping could well explain the particular phenomenon that we are trying to predict, it would be quite important to take this grouping (or lack of independence) into account in the analysis.

In this book we do not discuss or present multi-level linear modelling, which is a form of predictive modelling that can take into account some of the complications associated with multi-level nested data. In short, multi-level analysis enables a researcher to predict particular outcomes at one level whilst taking into account the nesting within the data. For example, with multi-level analysis you could model individual turnover or engagement data by incorporating both the individual and the nested (e.g. team) nature of the data structure. The results would be able to identify the importance of individual versus group-level predictors of individual turnover or engagement data. As explained, however, we do not set out this type of analysis in this book. The main reason for this is that multi-level analysis is considered an advanced analytic method that is beyond the scope of this text. Once you open up a multi-level box with HR data, the statistical and mathematical foundations become really quite complex. The second reason for this is that there are so many possible multi-level nested data structures with HR-related data that this would take up too much of this introductory text. For a further discussion on multi-level modelling please refer to Tabachnick and Fidell (2013) and Field (2013) on multi-level linear modelling. Note that there are a number of ways to do this kind of analysis in R, using packages such as *lme4* and *nlme*.

Curvilinear relationships

Sometimes, we may test our data for relationships but not find any evidence of a significant statistical linear relationship. Testing for correlations and running regression analysis will, as a default, test for linear relationships between variables. Even if there is no evidence that there might be linear relationships in our HR data, it may be the case that a curvilinear relationship exists. With linear relationships, as one variable increases then the values of a second variable will either increase (with a positive linear relationship) or decrease (negative linear relationship). The following situation may, however, exist: as we witness cases increase with one variable (A) we see a corresponding increase on a second variable (B) but after we find that our first variable (A) increases beyond a certain point we then see a decrease in our second variable (B). Or, alternatively, we witness an initial decrease in our variable (B) followed by an increase in (B) as (A) increases from the lowest point to the highest point. Either of these would be a curvilinear rather than a linear relationship.

A good HR-related example of a possible curvilinear relationship would be job pressure and performance: as pressure goes up people may begin to rise to the occasion and perform better, but their performance may well start to go down once the job pressure gets too high.

One of the challenges with curvilinear relationships is that with most predictive models, unless you specifically look for a curvilinear relationship, analysis output may suggest that either: 1) no relationship exists between two variables; or 2) the relationship that exists is linear in nature. As an example of 2), we can consider our team-level case study presented in Chapter 5. In this example we were predicting team-level engagement and one of the factors that seemed to predict team engagement was the percentage of the team who were male; the analysis indicated that the higher the percentage of males in the teams, then the lower the team engagement scores were found to be (Beta = –0.303, p < 0.001). This clearly indicates that as the teams become more male dominated, team engagement seems to go down. However, if the analyst interrogated the relationship between the percentage of the teams that were made up of males and team engagement, he or she would have found that the relationship in this organization is curvilinear. Of the 928 teams in the data set, the lowest proportion of males is 1 per cent and the highest is 100 per cent. The Beta of –0.303 would suggest that the teams with the highest level of engagement would be with the almost all female teams, and engagement gradually goes down to its likely lowest level when we have all male teams. However, this is not the case with our data. As teams go from 1 per cent male to 40 per cent male there tends to be an increase in engagement, and as the percentage tips over towards 100 per cent the engagement levels tend to go down. How do we know this?

We can ask R to check for quadratic curve estimation in the relationship between male team percentage and team engagement.

To do this you would conduct a regression with a special kind of interaction variable, namely a variable multiplied by itself (i.e. variable squared). To do this in R, we first create a z-scored variable. In this case, we compute a z-score of the percentage of male employees in a team. The following code can be found in the file *Ch11_examples.R*:

We first load required packages, set the working directory, and the data file:

```
if (!require("pacman")) install.packages("pacman")
pacman::p_load(readxl, dplyr, modelsummary, this.path, huxtable,
ggplot2)
setwd(this.path::here())
Ch5_eng <- read_excel("Ch5_Engagement_CASE_Group_level_data_2023.xlsx")
```

Then we z-score the *PercentMale* variable:

```
Ch5_eng$PercentMale_z <- scale(Ch5_eng$PercentMale)
```

We then create a squared version of that z-scored variable:

```
Ch5_eng$PercentMale_z2 <- Ch5_eng$PercentMale_z * Ch5_eng$PercentMale_z
```

Now we can estimate two regression models, one using the z-scored variable, and another using a square of the z-scored variable:

```
linear_mod <- lm(EMPsurvEngagement ~ PercentMale_z, data = Ch5_eng)
curv_mod <- lm(EMPsurvEngagement ~ PercentMale_z2, data = Ch5_eng)
```

We can create a table of the unstandardized and standardized coefficients for these models with the code below:

```
linear_mod <- lm(EMPsurvEngagement ~ PercentMale_z, data = Ch5_eng)
curv_mod <- lm(EMPsurvEngagement ~ PercentMale_z + PercentMale_z2,
data = Ch5_eng)
linear_mod1 <- modelsummary(linear_mod, output = "modelsummary_list")
linear_mod2 <- modelsummary(linear_mod, output = "modelsummary_list",
standardize = "basic")
curv_mod1 <- modelsummary(curv_mod, output = "modelsummary_list")
curv_mod2 <- modelsummary(curv_mod, output = "modelsummary_list",
standardize = "basic")
models <- list(
"Unstand., linear" = linear_mod1,
"Stand., linear" = linear_mod2,
"Unstand., curvilinear" = curv_mod1,
"Stand., curvilinear" = curv_mod2)
modelsummary(models, stars = TRUE, statistic = NULL, output = "huxtable")
```

This generates Figure 11.5:

11.5

	Unstand., linear	Stand., linear	Unstand., curvilinear	Stand., curvilinear
(Intercept)	81.176***	0.000***	82.781***	0.000***
PercentMale_z	-3.757***	-0.375***	-4.368***	-0.436***
PercentMale_z2			-1.607***	-0.228***
Num.Obs.	927	927	927	927
R2	0.141	0.141	0.189	0.189
R2 Adj.	0.140	0.140	0.187	0.187
AIC	6767.1	6767.1	6715.3	6715.3
BIC	6781.6	6781.6	6734.6	6734.6
Log.Lik.	-3380.573	-3380.573	-3353.652	-3353.652
F	151.472	151.472	107.807	107.807
RMSE	9.28	9.28	9.01	9.01

+ p < 0.1, * p < 0.05, ** p < 0.01, *** p < 0.001

As you will see from the output (Figure 11.5) the linear regression term is significant (standardized Beta = –0.375, p < 0.001) with an R-square of 0.141, but a quadratic regression term is also significant (standardized Beta = –0.228, p < 0.001, when controlling for the negative linear relationship) with an R-square of 0.189. We can visualize the relationship with this code:

```
ggplot(Ch5_eng, aes(x = PercentMale_z, y = EMPsurvEngagement)) +
geom_point() +
stat_smooth(method = "lm", formula = y ~ x, linetype = "solid") +
stat_smooth(method = "lm", formula = y ~ poly(x, 2), linetype =
"dashed")
```

Which produces Figure 11.6:

11.6

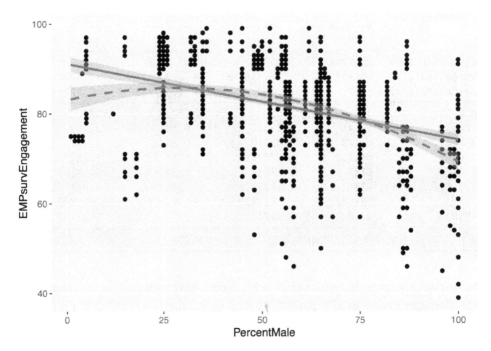

As the scatter graph shows (which includes a dashed curvilinear line of best fit through the plots), engagement initially increases as the proportion of males in each team goes up from 1 per cent; then team engagement starts to go down after the percentage of males starts to go above 30 per cent or 40 per cent.

Structural equation models

Structural equation modelling (SEM) is a form of analysis that tests data against some form of theoretical predicted model that generally involves a number of variables usually arranged in a predicted causal sequence. In its simplest form it involves a number of sequential regression analyses with multiple observed dependent variables, where the researcher indicates the expectation that particular predictive relationships should exist. The HR analyst also can conduct analysis that, in effect, takes into account the complexities and imperfections ('error' in measurement) of multi-item measurement metrics and model expected predictive relationships (referred to as 'structural' relationships) at the same time. Often with SEM the researcher is interested in testing a particular process of causality between a range of different variables. Imagine extending the simple mediated model presented in Figure 11.1 to include multiple independent variables, multiple mediators and multiple dependent variables. These models can incorporate interactions, mediation and multi-level structural relationships; the possible complexities of models that can be tested with SEM are considerable. Importantly, the researcher may have a number of different possible theoretical models that they may want to test for in order to identify which one 'fits the data' the best.

In order to carry out structural equation modelling, you can use the *lavaan* or *OpenMx* packages in R. The potential for variations and complications in the types of models that you can run with SEM programs is endless; discussing these is far beyond the remit of this book. Whilst it is useful for the analyst to be aware of SEM, it is quite unlikely that an HR analytics team would have much need to conduct this form of complex 'theory testing' analysis. For further reading, a good introductory book on SEM with Mplus is Geiser (2013); and Kelloway (2014) is also recommended.

Growth models

Growth models are specifically designed to predict growth or change over time in particular variables and therefore require data to be collected over a number of time points with each individual or object (such as a team). In essence, growth models involve a sophisticated form of modelling change. In Chapter 9 (on monitoring the impact of interventions) we do look at some forms of change, indeed we see whether checkout scan rates change over two time points, whether employee commitment to the organization's values changes over three time points, and we also predict performance whilst controlling for an earlier performance rating (that in effect predicts change in performance). Some of these forms of analyses are really looking at average change linked to a particular sample. However, with growth models we specifically identify growth patterns with individual cases (e.g. with employees) and try to predict and account for these growth patterns. From an HR analytics point of view, some examples of how these types of models might be useful in analysis could include the prediction of individuals who show a constant growth or increase in a particular performance dimension (e.g. sales or general increase in performance appraisal ratings). Such a model could be very useful, for example, to identify factors in a recruitment and selection process that predict high achievers and people who show continual growth in their development (rather than trying to predict performance taken just at one time point). There is more than one method of exploring and analysing growth models. In general, they involve more complex methods than we have presented in this book; however, two methods of growth analysis utilizing different analysis techniques are outlined below: multi-level modelling: individual growth models; and latent growth modelling.

Multi-level modelling: individual growth models

One of the approaches that can be used for growth modelling is referred to as multi-level modelling: individual growth models. In effect, this utilizes multi-level linear modelling techniques mentioned above. This approach treats multiple waves of data collection linked to each individual (or entity such as a team) modelled as nested or grouped data in a multi-level model. If you think about it, if you have five or so data points collected for each employee, in a data set of a whole workforce that has these multiple waves of data collection the multiple waves will be linked across the individual employees. Thus, the analysis treats the five (or more) data points per employee as being 'nested' with that individual. The growth model then explores the degree to which the data set as a whole seems to find particular individual growth patterns (e.g. a linear increase or decrease) over the five waves, but it allows for (and models) the existence of variation in the growth patterns for each individual. Using this technique, the researcher can incorporate and identify various predictors of particular growth patterns (e.g. linear increases, linear decreases, curvilinear increases or decreases).

Translating this into an HR analytics example, to explain this further we could use an example of a workforce of financial sales staff who sell insurance products for a bank. With such a workforce we could monitor their quarterly sales in dollars ($), and let's say we have two years of quarterly sales figures amounting to eight data points per sales staff. If we had 200 sales staff where we tracked their sales figures from the day they started, we could have a data set of sales staff in their first two years. We could then model certain sales trajectories, e.g. they start high and show no increase over time, they show a linear increase over time, they show a linear decrease or they show a curvilinear growth in sales, where the sales person either starts off selling well but this flattens out or they take a while to get going but then they increase later on in the period (see the examples in Figure 11.7).

11.7   Example sales trajectory profiles

Once the researcher identifies these possible growth trajectories they could then look for possible predictors of the different profiles of performance. These predictors could be something like scores given on an assessment centre in recruitment (which could evaluate assessment centre efficacy), education level, previous experience and induction training provision, amongst other possible factors. This kind of analysis is quite complicated to get to grips with; however, it can be conducted with R. A good reference for this is by Singer and Willett (2003). An additional reference for this form of analysis is Hoffman (2015).

Latent growth modelling

A second form of growth modelling involves the use of structural equation modelling and is referred to as latent growth modelling (LGM). Because this involves structural equation modelling analytics this requires an SEM package such as *lavaan*. It is also only really feasible to use this with more than three waves of data. It can be done with three but the set-up becomes much more complicated and there will be limits to what type of trajectories can be examined (e.g. curvilinear/quadratic trajectories cannot be examined with three waves). However, assuming that the analyst has a good understanding of the *lavaan* package and more than four waves of data, the opportunities that this analysis approach enables are considerable. It is similar to the above-mentioned multi-level modelling: individual growth model approach in that it enables the researcher to predict particular patterns of growth over time; however, the diagnostic sophistication of LGM is much greater. It can pretty much do all of the analysis that we set out with the multi-level modelling: individual growth modelling, but it can easily incorporate additional types of analysis that the previous type struggles with. For example, it can have multiple slopes with multiple growth trajectories. If we use our sales example again, you could model a scenario where commission payments were also modelled over time for each sales person. So you could have eight waves of data associated with sales and eight waves of data associated with commission paid each quarter. You could then explore the degree to which certain types or patterns of commission payments were associated with certain types of sales growth pattern. For example, you could test whether paying certain types of remuneration deal and growth trajectories of bonus payments were linked to certain trajectories of sales growth. For example, if you do not increase bonus payments over time does this tend to be followed by a flattening out of sales performance; or is the provision of a base salary (with no commission) linked to a high immediate sales performance and a flatter increase over time (assuming that the organization had such variation in their remuneration practices, of course)? Although the learning investment required to be able to understand and carry out LGM is quite considerable, the potential for the advanced analyst to identify really important patterns of behaviour is considerable.

Latent class analysis

Latent class analysis is a powerful analytic tool that could potentially play a role in helping answer certain types of HR analytic questions. In essence, it helps an analyst to create employee profiles within a particular data set from a range of different metrics or indices. This analytic tool could be used with HR analytic activities that involve the imperative to identify particular groups of employees that behave in a particular way. Classic examples might be identifying talent pools using a range of different metrics. The HR analyst might be tasked to identify 'key talent' using a range of indices (e.g. performance ratings, ratings of potential, position in competency band, etc).

Latent class analysis enables the analyst to explore and produce a range of different classes within the organization based on how employees 'score' on a range of indices;

for example, the analyst could produce and explore three or four different profiles within the organization to classify them (e.g. as 'key talent', 'potential key talent', etc).

Another example could be with appraisals where a range of different performance material is collected across a number of dimensions; how the organization deals with multiple and varying appraisal information for each individual could be more complicated than one might think. If there were six different appraisal dimensions representing different competencies, the organization might want to have a particular matrix where people who get certain scores on different dimensions will be given particular performance ratings. Of course, the more dimensions that are involved, the more complicated this gets. For example, if someone gets an above-average score on four of the six but below average on the remaining two, should they get a different rating than someone who got four average and two above-average ratings? The possible combinations represent a real complication to determining performance-rating classes with multiple indices. If, in the end, the organization wanted to create, say, four different classes of performance rating, it would be perfectly sensible to see if various performance clusters naturally occurred in the data across the six dimensions. Latent class analysis could well become a very useful tool in such situations. We will not, however, go into any more depth on this topic given the fact that it is beyond the scope of this book. This kind of analysis can be conducted in R with the *poLCA* package.

Response surface methodology and polynomial regression analysis

Response surface methodology is an analysis tool that is specifically designed to explore the implications (in an outcome variable) of two particular independent variable measures matching at different levels on their dimensions; the analysis utilizes polynomial regression analysis. On the flip side of this, the analysis specifically enables the exploration of the implications if there are mismatches or gaps at different levels of two dimensions. In some ways, this form of analysis is an extension to moderation or interaction testing mentioned earlier in this chapter, as the analysis explores what level employees (or teams) tend to have on a given dependent variable, given the levels that they have on two separate independent variables. Response surface analysis is, however, a much more sophisticated version of interaction testing as not only does it take into account the linear impact on a particular dependent variable that the interaction between two independent variables has, but it also takes into account curvilinear relationships and interactions (hence the polynomial regression element) and the implications of a mismatch/gap or congruence between the two independent variables. If we use our earlier 'stress' and 'job demands' as an example, the suggestion by the Karasek model is that the interplay between job demands and decision latitude may be key in determining employees' psychological well-being.

11.8   RSM surface plot of a hypothetical relationship between job demands and decision latitude that has psychological well-being as the dependent variable

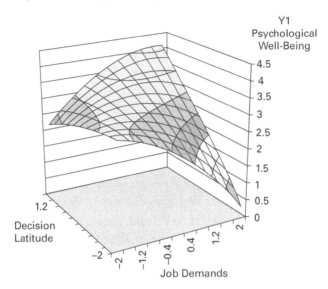

NOTE The different shades in the 3D shape assist in determining the incremental position along the well-being scale.

Figure 11.8 shows an RSM surface plot of a hypothetical relationship between job demands and decision latitude (autonomy) at various levels in our organization. The two X axis scales are z-scores, hence we have a negative and positive, and the Y axis is psychological well-being. From this graph we can see that the optimal scenario of well-being is a scenario where employees have high demands but they also have higher-than-average levels of decision latitude; when the incongruence of demands and latitude levels is on the high demands and low latitude levels, we see lower levels of well-being.

With this particular example (Figure 11.8), the main interesting feature of the analysis is not necessarily the gap or mismatch between the two independent variables, but what happens to the well-being at different levels of the two independent variables. Because this example does not necessitate a 'match' between the two variables, the power of this analysis is not fulfilled; it is not much more than a sophisticated interaction analysis that incorporates curvilinear relationships (that polynomial regression analysis enables). Where RSM really comes into its own is when the idea of congruence or incongruence becomes more important for our dependent variable.

To demonstrate our point further here we can present another hypothetical example where a match of some sort could be important. Organizations that place great emphasis on customer focus often have this as a key competency in performance appraisal ratings, where all employees are rated on the degree to which they demonstrate 'customer focus' when going about their everyday job. When it comes to performance appraisal time, employees' supervisors will rate their subordinates on customer focus and supervisors will also be rated themselves. Here we hypothesize that the degree to which the supervisor has a customer focus may have important consequences for employees in that this will determine the implications of the employee themselves getting rated as high or low customer focus. Figure 11.9 shows an RSM graph of the supervisor versus employee customer focus ratings being plotted together, along with the employees' performance ratings. As we can see, the consequences of incongruence between the employee and customer ratings seem quite important. If the employee is rated highly on customer focus but the supervisor is not so customer focused then the employee is not rewarded (with a high-performance appraisal) for their customer focus; the rewards for high levels of employee customer focus seem greater, however, when the supervisor is highly customer focused (the high point of the surface).

11.9   Hypothetical RSM graph showing the importance of congruence/incongruence in employee versus supervisor customer focus (on employee performance ratings)

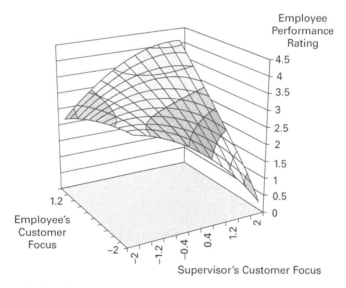

NOTE The different shades in the 3D shape assist in determining the incremental position along the well-being scale.

Interestingly, as shown in Figure 11.9, employees with a low level of customer focus seem to be punished to a much greater degree when the supervisor cares a lot about customer focus, especially when compared to employees who have supervisors who are not rated highly on customer focus. This pattern of results actually indicates a curvilinear pattern of incongruence effects on performance ratings. Interestingly, we do not witness any curvilinear effects where there tends to be congruence between the employee and the supervisor ratings of customer focus. Where employees and super-visors have low customer focus the employee does not get a particularly low rating.

The polynomial regression analysis and RSM graphs give us a range of statistical tests for congruence and incongruence effects; they tell us whether any congruence and incongruence effects are linear/curvilinear. The analysis gives us significance levels for these effects and a range of Excel tools exist that plot various effects. Probably one of the main experts in polynomial analytic and RSM techniques is Professor Jeffrey Edwards (no relation to either author) who is currently based at the University of North Carolina at Chapel Hill. Resources he has created for SPSS and Stata are available on his website: tarheels.live/jeffreyedwardswebsite/home/resources. An additional collection of resources on response surface analysis is available on the Open Science Foundation website, including workshop slides and research papers: osf.io/9vk3h/wiki/home.

In R, response surface analysis can be conducted using the *RSA* package. Using this approach, it is possible to plot a incongruence graph (Y = –X) as shown in Figure 11.10 for the hypothetical model shown in Figure 11.9.

11.10   Incongruence graph

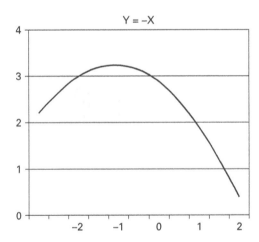

This graph demonstrates a curvilinear incongruence effect of employee versus super-visor customer focus on the employees' performance ratings. The plots also show that this is not the case where there is congruence between employee versus supervi-sor customer focus; though there is a slight positive relationship (linear increase) along the congruence line (Y = X) (see Figure 11.11).

The potential for exposing some really interesting HR analytic insights with RSM is, we hope, quite obvious. Where congruence or incongruence of any particular two factors is expected to have an important impact on a particular metric, it is undoubt-edly the ideal advanced form of analysis that can expose what is really going on in the organization.

11.11 Congruence graph

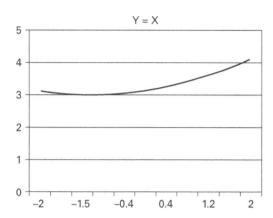

Machine learning

This section will give you a high level understanding of what machine learning is, some of its benefits and limitations, and how it might be applied to HR analytics.

What it is and how it works

Most of us will have come across machine learning already, perhaps without being aware. For example, when a spam filter decides that an email you receive is different from what you usually get and decides to put it in a spam folder instead of your inbox; when Netflix suggests programmes you may like to watch; when Facebook directs you towards products that you may want to buy; or when the fraud prevention team at your bank calls you to say your credit card has just been used for some designer clothes in Milan and it doesn't seem like normal behaviour for you, these are all examples of machine learning at work. The machine devours all the data coming its way and uses it to model behaviours and make predictions about your next move. Importantly, machines do this using particular algorithms.

The term 'algorithm' has been used in places throughout this book, often with an assumption that the reader knows what an algorithm is. In many statistical procedures set out in the book, algorithms are being applied without us making this explicit. In the field of machine learning, the term algorithm is used extensively so it is worth defining this here before going on to discuss the topic.

What is an algorithm? According to Corman et al (2009), an algorithm is 'any well-defined computational procedure that takes some value, or set of values, as input and produces some value or set or values as output: an algorithm is thus a sequence of computational steps that transform the input into the output' (p 5). In some ways this definition seems quite broad, as it could encompass almost all activities that we have conducted in this book; where we get R to look at the data (input) and apply various computational formulae to produce some statistical output. Thus the definition may not help us to understand what people mean by algorithm in machine learning.

However, if we consider our linear regression model, this can help us to understand the meaning of an algorithm with machine learning. With regression, we try to account for variance in a particular dependent variable. We do this by looking at the degree to which variation in a particular independent variable (e.g. motivation) 'accounts for' (or shares) variation in a dependent variable (e.g. performance rating). With linear regression, we get a data set and try to identify particular patterns of linearity in shared variance between motivation and performance; if such a linear relationship exists we can then apply a set of rules that can help us predict performance from motivation levels. With linear regression we do this with a linear regression equation (e.g. performance=constant + beta × motivation level). The application of this equation to data is an application of a linear regression algorithm. Here it is as a set of rules: that if you multiply a given level of motivation (say 3) by a beta weight (e.g. 0.5) and add this to a constant value (mean levels of performance in your data, e.g. 3), you can 'predict' performance. Importantly, the value of the beta/slope is identified from a pattern of linear association between motivation and performance in our observed data set. If our linear regression algorithm is good at successfully/accurately predicting performance in our data set then we have a good algorithm that, when applied, helps us account for (or predict) variation in performance ratings. We can test how good our algorithm is by applying the equation to all of our values of motivation in our data set (along with the mean levels of performance in our data set) and examine the degree to which the equation produces accurate predictions of performance (to what degree does the application of the linear regression algorithm lead to accurate/inaccurate predictions of performance?).

If we have a good predictive algorithm (in this case linear regression), we might want to test this (by applying the equation) on new data (say 100 new recruits) that includes values of motivation (taken or measured at the point of induction) and make predictions as to their expected levels of performance. We have followed some of these procedures in the book using R. If we are manually learning from our data, we might see if the addition of a new variable (e.g. how many months/years someone has been in their job) improves the prediction of performance when applied to the data that we have; we can add job tenure to the regression model and see whether this improves the R square of the regression. We might also find that if we include a slightly different function to our regression equation (e.g. we add a curvilinear as well as a linear function to the equation model) this improves our ability to predict performance. If our model is improved, we will be able to make increasingly certain predictions (in terms of probability of getting a particular level of performance) given certain values of motivation and job tenure.

Importantly, what we have described here is a manual process of learning. With machine learning, we effectively get a computer program to follow such steps. As long as everything is set up correctly, the machine is likely to do this a lot quicker than a person.

As many aspects of machine learning rest on pre-existing statistical models (or algorithms), the fundamentals of machine learning are not new. For example, as early as the late 1700s and early 1800s Bayes' theorem and the least squares method were recorded and published. Bayes' theorem, a conditional probability theory, is the probability of an event occurring, given certain known conditions. Put simply, it is the probability of A, given B. For example, any person sitting happily working at their desk may estimate their probability of being made redundant as relatively low, say 20 per cent. This would be the probability of A. If, however, during the course of the day they learn that the company they work for has just gone into liquidation, that knowledge will impact their calculation of the probability they will be made redundant, which they will now estimate to be much higher, say 80 per cent. Thus gaining more knowledge, or more data (and new variables), will help to make the probability estimate more accurate.

With linear regression, we rely on the least squares method to get a sense of how good our equation/applied algorithm is at successfully making predictions with our dependent variable – this method is widely used for data fitting. When we develop a model, as we would in linear regression, we are finding a line of best fit. This line of best fit is where we draw a line that most closely fits the data points. If we measure the distance between the line and each data point, we get the error measure. In the least squares method, we square this (i.e. multiply it by itself) for each data point, thus ending up with only positive values. We then add these all up and the line of best fit minimizes the sum of squared errors (thus the 'least squares'). The more data we have, the more accurate the line of best fit will be.

As far back as 250 years ago people were already thinking about, talking about, writing about algorithms to better predict the future based on what is known and reducing the error in doing so.

Defining machine learning

There are many definitions available for machine learning, from one of the very first recorded definitions:

> [Machine learning is the] field of study that enables computers to learn without being explicitly programmed.

SOURCE Arthur Samuel, 1959

to this more recent definition:

> Machine learning is the science of getting computers to learn and act like humans do
> and improve their learning over time in autonomous fashion, by feeding them data and
> information in the form of observations and real-world interactions.

SOURCE Daniel Faggella, 2018

All machine learning programs must consist of the three component parts: representation, evaluation and optimization:

1 *Representation*: consisting of a group of classifiers or a basic language the computer can understand.

2 *Evaluation*: taking data and scoring it based on the program's objective.

3 *Optimization*: the strategy that gets you from the input data to the expected output.

The computer should generalize and process data so it can interpret new data that it hasn't worked on before.

Machine learning systems tend to be grouped, as they are by Sullivan (2018), Smith (2018) and Faggella (2018), according to the level of human interaction they need to operate. At the simplest level, this is supervised learning and unsupervised learning. Let's take a look at each in turn.

Supervised learning

Supervised learning refers to when a human has trained the machine. It has been provided with some training data and the answer is given in some cases so the machine knows what it is looking for. The machine learns the algorithm by trying to guess the answer from the data. If the expected answer is very different from the result, the machine will recalculate the algorithm using the data to get closer the next time. The algorithm corrects and improves based on the data. Supervised learning can fall into two categories – classification and regression:

- Classification: this involves predicting which category the output value will belong to, given particular input values. For example, given the input gender, department and performance rating (or specifically the values: female, finance, below expectation), the classification process will predict whether the risk of leaving will be high, medium or low.

- Regression: in machine learning, the regression process predicts a continuous value given particular input values. For example, given the input: average team age, average team tenure and team leader leadership index score, the regression process will predict average team performance, which will be a number on a continuous scale between 0 and 5.

Algorithms commonly used in supervised learning include:

- K-nearest neighbours
- linear regression
- neural networks
- support vector machines
- logistic regression
- decision trees
- random forests.

RANDOM FOREST EXAMPLE

To illustrate an instance of machine learning in R, we will explore a case of classifying employees using the random forest algorithm. One reason for classifying employees for an HR analytic purpose might be: 'Can we distinguish employees according to their respective job functions (e.g. HR, finance, etc.) based on their skills and personality?' This question has strategic HR value as it can reveal whether people in the organization are sufficiently differentiated in terms of abilities. For instance, individuals with high numeric ability are best suited to roles such as finance, while those with a strong aptitude for language might be ideal for legal functions, where many tasks involve working with documents. For this purpose, we use the random forest algorithm, which constructs multiple decision trees to effectively distinguish between categories. For example, the algorithm might identify in the data that individuals with a numeric ability score over 80 typically belong to the finance function. A decision tree might then categorize anyone with a numeric ability score over 80 as belonging to the finance function. You might wonder how the algorithm develops such a decision rule. The 'random' part of the algorithm's name clues us into the process of selecting a random subset of the attributes at each split in the construction of the trees. The algorithm constructs many such trees – hence the 'forest' in its name – helping to build a diverse set that is relatively free of bias. Another way randomness is used involves the data itself through a process called resampling. In this process, we construct a data set with the same number of rows and columns, but rows are randomly selected with replacement. This creates diversity in the training data and ensures that no decision tree is overly specific to the training data set, aiding in the development of a model that generalizes well to new data.

We will use the selection data from Chapter 8, namely *Ch8_selection.xlsx*. R code for this example is in the file *Ch11_examples.R*. We will attempt to use the personality characteristics (openness, conscientiousness, agreeableness, neuroticism), assessment centre competencies (technical, team player, critical thought, business aware and drive innovation), as well as general abilities (numerical and verbal aptitude) scores to predict job function.

We first load required packages, set the working directory and load the data. The first time you run this code, it may take a few minutes to download all of the packages from the internet.

```
if (!require("pacman")) install.packages("pacman")
pacman::p_load(readxl, dplyr, caret, randomForest, this.path)
setwd(this.path::here())
Ch8_mi <- read_excel("Ch8_selection.xlsx")
```

We then explicitly define *Ch8_mi* as a dataframe, to avoid compatibility issues later on with the *caret* package.

```
Ch8_mi <- as.data.frame(Ch8_mi)
```

Recall that in the data set, job functions are coded with numbers, so we will convert them to a factor variable for ease of interpretation.

```
Ch8_mi$Function <- ifelse(Ch8_mi$GradJOBfunction == 1, "HR",
        ifelse(Ch8_mi$GradJOBfunction == 2, "Finance",
        ifelse(Ch8_mi$GradJOBfunction == 3, "Marketing",
        ifelse(Ch8_mi$GradJOBfunction == 4, "Sales",
        ifelse(Ch8_mi$GradJOBfunction == 5, "Risk",
        ifelse(Ch8_mi$GradJOBfunction == 6, "Legal",
        ifelse(Ch8_mi$GradJOBfunction == 7, "Operations",
        "Unknown")))))))
Ch8_mi$Function <- as.factor(Ch8_mi$Function)
```

The steps that follow involve random selection. To ensure we obtain the same results across multiple runs of this code, we can set a 'seed' for the randomization process. This seed ensures that we get the same set of pseudo-random selections every time.

```
set.seed(123)
Ch8_mi <- Ch8_mi[sample(nrow(Ch8_mi)), ]
```

With the code above, we randomly ordered the rows of the *Ch8_mi* dataframe, since the data was somewhat grouped in terms of job functions.

```
training_rows <- sample(Ch8_mi$GradID, .7 * length(Ch8_mi$GradID))
```

The code above randomly selects 70 per cent of the employee identifiers, and puts them in the object *training_rows*.

```
select_train <- subset(Ch8_mi, GradID %in% training_rows)
select_test <- subset(Ch8_mi, !(GradID %in% training_rows))
```

The code above splits the data into two separate dataframes, a training set and a test set. This is determined by employee identifiers being in *training_rows* or not. Now we are ready for the random forest algorithm.

```
select_model <- train(select_train[, 7:18], select_train$Function,
method ='rf', importance = TRUE)
```

The code above uses the train program in the caret package to use the random forest algorithm. We first specify a set of predictors with the code *select_train[, 7:18]*, which tells the program to look at columns 7 to 18 of the training data set. Because we did not modify the order of the columns, they are in the same order as the *Ch8_mi* dataframe and include the variables from *ACPersonalityO* (openness personality factor) to *ACRatingAPTverbal* (verbal reasoning aptitude test score). Then we specify the classifications to predict (*select_train$Function*), the machine learning algorithm ('rf' for random forest), and ask the program to save the importance of each predictor. This code may take some time to run. Once complete, we can examine the output with the following line:

```
print(select_model)
```

This produces Figure 11.12:

11.12
```
> print(select_model)
Random Forest

251 samples
 12 predictor
    7 classes: 'Finance', 'HR', 'Legal', 'Marketing', 'Operations', 'Risk',
    'sales'

No pre-processing
Resampling: Bootstrapped (25 reps)
Summary of sample sizes: 251, 251, 251, 251, 251, 251, ...
Resampling results across tuning parameters:

  mtry  Accuracy   Kappa
   2    0.8511779  0.8200179
   7    0.8520113  0.8218511
  12    0.8310173  0.7968958

Accuracy was used to select the optimal model using the largest value.
The final value used for the model was mtry = 7.
```

The output above summarizes what was done. We gave the model a training data set with 251 rows (called *samples* in the output), gave the number of predictors considered (12), and listed the classification categories (finance, HR, etc.). It reports resampling the data set 25 times and lists how large each resampled data set was (251, 251, 251, etc.). It also shows something we haven't discussed before, which is the number of predictors the algorithm considers when making a classification choice (*mtry*). In this case, the highest accuracy was achieved by considering 7 predictors at each decision point. This model will be retained. We can now look at the importance of each variable for the various categories:

```
        varImp(select_model, scale = TRUE)
```

This produces Figure 11.13:

11.13
```
> varImp(select_model, scale = TRUE)
rf variable importance

   variables are sorted by maximum importance across the classes
                      Finance    HR   Legal  Marketing Operations  Risk   Sales
ACPersonalityE         41.931  58.21  45.711    100.00    51.342   25.49  39.379
ACRatingAPTnumerical   95.586  52.23  44.533     56.87    58.156   51.75  24.305
ACRatingAPTverbal      59.313  36.52  95.290     53.55    54.886   32.09  18.516
ACPersonalityA         61.525  91.86  45.570     36.83    42.856   33.21  24.171
ACPersonalityC         43.056  43.27  62.467     63.12    48.507   40.81  32.734
ACPersonalityN         35.728  21.65  25.187     44.16    40.956   33.67  13.158
ACRatingINTCOMPE       26.037  33.23  20.017     39.21    37.641   14.93   5.602
ACRatingINTCOMPA       24.789  27.90  32.902     35.84    39.207   19.70  20.293
ACRatingINTCOMPD       22.605  24.37  30.932     38.51    35.552   17.91   0.000
ACPersonalityO         26.728  31.17  20.403     31.67    31.808   27.59  20.628
ACRatingINTCOMPB        6.212  25.30  27.035     11.80    28.182   15.83   4.696
ACRatingINTCOMPC       17.007  16.90   8.411     16.08     9.921   16.07   4.358
```

We can see that importance of predictors varies considerably across functions. The numbers in each column indicate the importance of the variable that ranges from 0 to 100. Numeric ability is very important for classifying those in finance, and verbal ability is important for those in the legal function. Interestingly, agreeableness scores are important for those in HR and extraversion is important for marketing. There are no such important variables for those in operations, risk, and sales, presumably because we have much fewer people in those functions to provide data. There are more than 60 people each in the finance, HR, legal and marketing functions, and an average of 34 people in operations, risk and sales – about half. An alternative explanation is that the people in those functions have varied characteristics, making them more difficult to classify with the variables we have. We can now apply the model to our test data to see how well it predicts the 30 per cent of the sample we set aside earlier, and we can compare the predicted function to their actual function:

```
funct_predictions <- predict(select_model, select_test)
confusionMatrix <- table(Predicted = funct_predictions, Actual = select_
test$Function)
print(confusionMatrix)
```

This produces Figure 11.14:

11.14

```
> print(confusionMatrix)
                Actual
Predicted       Finance    HR   Legal  Marketing  Operations   Risk   Sales
   Finance         15       0      0        0          0         5       0
   HR               0      20      0        3          0         4       0
   Legal            0       2     22        0          0         0       0
   Marketing        0       1      0       13          0         0       2
   Operations       0       0      0        0         10         0       0
   Risk             0       0      0        0          0         4       0
   Sales            0       0      0        2          0         0       6
```

We can see the predictions and the actual functions in this figure. If the predictions are perfect, all of the numbers in the diagonals should correspond to the actual numbers of people in that function. We can see that the model did a reasonable job with the finance, HR, legal, marketing, operational, and sales functions, correctly classifying the vast majority. We can calculate the accuracy of the model with the following lines of code:

```
accuracy <- sum(diag(confusionMatrix)) / sum(confusionMatrix)
print(paste("Accuracy:", round(accuracy, 3)))
```

This produces Figure 11.15:

11.15

```
> print(paste("Accuracy:", round(accuracy, 3)))
[1] "Accuracy: 0.826"
```

An accuracy of 82.6 per cent is quite respectable and suggests that assessment-centre assessed personality and abilities are useful in predicting who ends up in what function.

In this example, we described an example involving classifying individuals to discrete categories, but there are many different kinds of machine learning algorithms and applications. For example, the logic of the random forest algorithm can be used for a continuous variable, such as performance evaluations. Other types of machine learning algorithms exist that use an entirely different logic and approach compared to this one – at time of writing, the *caret* package could handle working with 238 different machine learning algorithms. Awareness of the major types and their utility will allow the HR analyst to broaden the range of tools they can work with to bring about useful insights.

Unsupervised learning

Unsupervised learning is less common than supervised learning, but it is where we really start to understand the power of 'artificial intelligence' because in unsupervised learning the machine teaches itself without any help from a human. It is let loose on the data and allowed to analyse it freely. It looks at all the data and tries to make sense of it – just as we do as humans with all the information that comes our way. We look for trends and patterns, group like things together and in that way we learn about the world. We then use that information to help us determine what to expect in the future. As with humans, the value comes when we are able to recognize we have made a mistake, then make the necessary adjustments to reduce the chance of making the same mistake again.

Examples of unsupervised learning are:

- Clustering: when the program finds inherent groupings in the data. An example would be grouping employees together who share similar characteristics across a number of dimensions. For example, we might want our employees clustered together into five groups when we provide the machine with age and performance rating (there are similarities to clustering and latent class analyses mentioned above).

- Association rules: when the program finds a rule that describes a large proportion of the data. Essentially it uncovers a relationship that we may not have realized existed before. This has been used extensively in analytics linked to retail with a classic example like 'People who buy cornflakes are also likely to buy milk.' When thinking about employees, an example might be 'People who apply for a flexible working arrangement are also more likely to value healthcare benefits.'

Algorithms commonly used in unsupervised learning are:

- clustering: K-means, hierarchical cluster analysis
- association rule learning: eclat, priori
- visualization and dimensionality reduction.

Semi-supervised and reinforcement learning

There are also various degrees of learning in between these two, so you may also hear the phrases 'semi-supervised' and 'semi-unsupervised' in this context, which refer to a solution that is a hybrid between the two. The other important term to be aware of is 'reinforcement learning'. In reinforcement learning there is a 'reward' function that helps the machine to identify when it is on the right track.

The data

Because the algorithms in machine learning are entirely based on the data, the quality of the data is absolutely critical. An analyst involved in a machine learning undertaking will spend a lot of time making sure the data is in good shape. If there are errors and inaccuracies, this will make it very difficult for the machine to learn. Machines are a little like babies at the beginning of the learning process in that they don't have common sense or any frame of reference to even tell simple things apart, like a shoe from an umbrella. They learn from scratch, and so if there are errors in the data the machine will learn assuming that the error is supposed to be there.

The data on which machine learning is based may be structured or unstructured.

STRUCTURED DATA

For structured data, think of a spreadsheet or table. All of the case studies throughout this book are based on structured data, for example performance data, HR bio data, L&D history, promotions data, talent management data, recruitment data tables, etc. The data is organized in some sort of database and the variables are labelled.

UNSTRUCTURED DATA

Unstructured data, however, is not generally organized and labelled. It typically has a mix of text, dates and numbers all in together. In HR we often have very important information tucked away in unstructured data. Consider the following:

- the contents of a CV
- text in tweets or other social media posts by employees
- unstructured text summaries in performance reviews.

Machine learning can be used to analyse unstructured data and pull out important insights using the following methods:

- text mining
- social network analysis
- rare event detection
- sentiment analysis
- trending topics.

But it is far from perfect

Interestingly, the ability of machine learning to process data and make accurate predictions quickly is a big plus compared to human learning. However, sometimes the machine learning algorithm will make a mistake that a human would almost never make; it would also not have the context to be aware of how big the mistake is. For example, if your email system/spam algorithm puts an email from your spouse straight into the spam email folder it will not be aware of how wrong it has been (and how much trouble this could cause).

We discuss problems and bias with algorithms in the next chapter. The application of algorithms used in machine learning can unfortunately lead to deeply problematic predictions/recommendations in the output. Sometimes, of course, this requires humans to understand the context of these biases and may indeed lead to these algorithmic applications being scrapped (such as the time Amazon ditched their machine learning based recruiting tool that favoured men for technical jobs because it was being driven by historical data, which had an overrepresentation of males in these roles) (*Guardian*, 2018).

Tom Mitchell and colleagues at the School of Computer Science at Carnegie Mellon University (2018) discuss the important difference between the way that humans learn and the way that machines learn, and why results such as this are likely to keep occurring using current methods of machine learning. Looking at people first, we gain our knowledge over many years through diverse and varied experiences. We learn from others as well as from our own experiences, and as time goes on we become better learners, taking in many different types of knowledge.

How does a machine learn? It starts with a single data set, carries out statistical analysis on this data set and then learns from the data model that has been created. By comparison, it is very narrow. How can it compare with the diverse experiences of a human? The simple answer is that it can't. Whilst it may not be surprising to learn that machine learning research is constantly improving and looking for ways to close this gap, it is not there yet. At best, machine learning is a fantastic analytics tool to process data much more quickly than we can and inform the decisions that people make.

References

Baron, R M and Kenny, D A (1986) The moderator–mediator variable distinction in social psychological research: Conceptual, strategic and statistical considerations, *Journal of Personality and Social Psychology*, 51, pp 1173–82

Cohen, J and Cohen, P (1983) *Applied Multiple Regression/Correlation Analysis for the Behavioral Sciences*, 2nd edn, Erlbaum, New Jersey

Corman, T H, Leiserson, C E, Rivest, R L and Stein, C (2009) *Introduction to Algorithms*, 3rd edn, MIT press, Cambridge, MA

Dawson, J F (2014) Moderation in management research: What, why, when, and how, *Journal of Business Psychology*, 29, pp 1–19

Faggella, D (2018) What is machine learning? Techemergence, web.archive.org/web/20170128121606/https://www.techemergence.com/what-is-machine-learning/ (archived at https://perma.cc/E8Z2-DZ75)

Field, A (2013) *Discovering Statistics Using IBM SPSS Statistics*, 4th edn, Sage, London

Geiser, C (2013) *Data Analysis with Mplus*, Guilford, New York

Guardian (2018) Amazon ditched AI recruiting tool that favoured men for technical jobs, www.theguardian.com/technology/2018/oct/10/amazon-hiring-ai-gender-bias-recruiting-engine (archived at https://perma.cc/HXT9-6L25)

Hayes, A F (2009) Beyond Baron and Kenny: Statistical mediation analysis in the new millennium, *Communication Monographs*, 76, pp 408–20

Hoffman, L (2015) *Longitudinal Analysis: Modelling within-person fluctuation and change*, Routledge, New York

Huebner, R (2018) kMeans clustering with HR-related data, rpubs.com/rhuebner/kmeans_hr (archived at https://perma.cc/B55U-SKNX)

Karasek, R A (1979) Job demands, job decision latitude, and mental strain: Implications for job redesign, *Administrative Science Quarterly*, 24, pp 285–308

Kelloway, K E (2014) *Using Mplus for Structural Equation Modeling: A researcher's guide*, 2nd edn, Sage, California

Mitchell, T, Cohen, W, Hruschka, E, Talukdr, P, Yang, B, Betteridge, J, Carlson, A, Balvi, B, Gardner, M, Kisiel, B, Krishnamurthy, J, Lao, N, Maziatis, K, Mohamed, T, Nakashole, N, Platanios, A, Ritter, A, Samadi, M, Settles, R, Rang, D, Wijaya, D, Gupta, A, Chen, X, Saparov, A, Greaves, M and Welling, J (2018) Never-ending learning, *Communications of the ACM*, 61 (5), pp 103–15

Samuel, A L (1959) Some studies in machine learning using the game of checkers, *IBM Journal of Research and Development*, 3 (3), pp 210–29

Singer, J D and Willett, J B (2003) *Applied Longitudinal Data Analysis: Modelling change and event occurrence*, Oxford University Press, New York

Smith, H (2018) *Machine Learning: The absolute beginner's guide to learn and understand machine learning effectively*, CreateSpace Independent Publishing Platform, Scotts Valley, CA

Sullivan, W (2018) *Python Programming and Machine Learning With Python: Best starter pack illustrated guide for beginners and intermediates: The future is here!*, CreateSpace Independent Publishing Platform, Scotts Valley, CA

Tabachnick, B G and Fidell, L S (2013) *Using Multivariate Statistics*, 6th edn, Pearson, Boston

12

Reflection on HR analytics

Usage, ethics and limitations

This chapter is intended to serve as a reflective seminar where key issues and challenges with the activity of predictive HR analytics are explored. Often, with texts, blogs and discussions on the subject of HR analytics, authors only focus on the promise and potential of the discipline. The HR analytics expert, however, needs to be as aware of the challenges that the activity might lead to as well as the potential for considerable business benefits. Some of these challenges are linked to practical difficulties that arise when attempting to conduct sophisticated HR analytics; some are important challenges linked to debates in research science; some involve management challenges and behavioural issues; and some involve important ethical challenges.

HR analytics as a scientific discipline

Carrying out HR analytics is a scientific activity and the HR analyst is in effect acting as a research scientist. They are exploring aspects of the empirical world, attempting to answer research questions and using statistical techniques to interrogate data, test or check for patterns or causal factors that are apparent in the organizational world, with the intention of drawing conclusions from the analysis. A capability and area of expertise that a scientist will need to develop as they become more of an expert is the ability to understand what constitutes a good research design and what the limitations of particular types of research methods may be. In this regard the master HR analyst needs to be aware of the potential problems and methodological limitations inherent in the field of HR analytics. Some of the challenges in this regard include the following:

- Constraints on objectivity: as a representative of the organization, and ultimately representing the leadership within the organization, the analyst's 'objectivity' may not be guaranteed.

- Constraints on the analyst's ability to 'experiment' in order to discover possible and causal features of the environment.

- Constraints on data availability and quality to discover possible and causal features of the environment.

Constraints on objectivity

Ultimately, the HR analyst will often be operating within certain constraints. They will be working in a context where they are expected to carry out analysis that will identify factors that could potentially improve the bottom line of the organization. Also, as we discussed in Chapter 9 in our case studies exploring the impact of interventions, sometimes management decisions have been made and the investment might be so considerable that the organization's leaders may not want to hear that it has not led to the outcomes that were intended. This could put the analyst in a difficult position if they explore and find evidence that a decision made has cost the organization. A scientific approach to investigating workplace scenarios would actively involve looking for things that do not work – looking for evidence that decisions have produced negative results. Also the analyst may be assigned to a particular research question that could necessitate (politically) a particular finding.

It may be the case that an analyst discovers, through exploratory analysis, that there is a problem with something fundamental that the organization has done or is doing. Hopefully, this will lead the analyst to action change within the organization, in order to improve the situation or resolve the problem. However, they may operate within a context that may restrict their ability to try to uncover certain insights. For example, the organization may hold individual achievement as a central value, which leads to a focus on personal characteristics (e.g. incentive schemes or educational achievement) rather than properties of groups (e.g. team design or diversity metrics). Such focus can shape the kinds of questions asked and problems tackled.

Constraints on the ability to experiment

As an HR analytics professional, you may find yourself wanting to test a hypothesis – such as the hypothesis that excessive levels of stress will increase employee turnover, or that a higher bonus payment will translate into higher employee performance. It is important in these circumstances to accept that you can only analyse the data you have in the organization. Indeed, due to the power imbalance between employers and employees, it is not ethical (even if it were possible) to experiment on employees, at least without their willing participation. For example, you cannot give a bonus to some staff, and not others, in order to conduct an experiment on the impact of a bonus scheme. While this creates a treatment and control group from which to compare differences in performance, it will create a sense of inequity among staff. We talk later in the chapter about the data always being linked to human beings, so even if you did have a budget or leadership support to conduct experiments to test hypotheses, it is not ethical to do so. As we discussed in Chapter 9, however, there may be conditions that occur in the organization that enable a natural control group to exist, which can fundamentally strengthen the analyst's ability to infer causality from the analysis undertaken.

Constraints on data availability and data quality

Often there will be problems with the availability of data, either that it has not been collected, or that there are missing groups or missing data, which we talk about later in this chapter. The management information (MI) function has a responsibility to ensure the integrity and completeness of the data, and indeed many MI functions will conduct regular data audits and 'amnesty' exercises to encourage completion of the data. Nevertheless, it is rare for the data to be 100 per cent complete and you can only conduct analysis on those people for whom you have complete information (on whatever it is that you are testing). A separate question from availability concerns data quality. As the field of HR analytics has developed over recent years, the challenge of ensuring that the HR related data on which an HR analytic project is built on is reliable and of good quality is a major undertaking for the HR analytic team. Before an HR analytic project can start, many hours will need to be spent obtaining data, checking its quality and engineering it to ensure that it has solid foundations. The challenges of ensuring data quality cannot be underestimated and the analyst needs to recognize that their ability to uncover true insights may be limited by both the availability and quality of HR related data.

The metric becomes the behaviour driver: institutionalized metric-oriented behaviour

Chasing and monitoring certain numbers and performance metrics can become an automatic activity that the HR analyst will become engaged in. As discussed in Chapters 1 and 3, much current practice is oriented around producing descriptive reports and monitoring particular metrics (such as turnover or particular performance metrics across different parts of the organization). Once a particular metric has been identified as being an important one to focus on, then managers and the HR analyst may well treat such a metric as an indicator of a key performance measure. However, when investigating a particular aspect of employee behaviour in the workplace, rather than the metric representing a factor of interest (e.g. performance) the metric sometimes *becomes* the performance measure that all involved focus on. There is a danger, however, that once a particular performance metric becomes institutionalized, the metric starts to drive a particular type of performance. Behaviour and management focus within the organization starts to become oriented towards the achievement of a particular metric. Thus the phenomenon of institutionalized metric-oriented behaviour (IMOB) occurs. The problem with such activities is that an inordinate amount of attention and people effort becomes oriented around such metrics. This has a number of implications:

1 Line managers have a tendency to manage and monitor the metrics rather than carry out proper people-management activities.

2 Employees become overly focused on ensuring that they perform well on this particular metric.

3 Behaviours important to overall broad good performance either tend to be ignored by employees and managers or, in the worst case scenario, are actively discouraged in favour of behaviours that will reflect well in the metrics.

4 Certain staff members may be more or less disadvantaged by their inability to reach full potential on achievement of particular metrics.

As a hypothetical example of how IMOB can lead to points 1, 2 and 3 above, we can consider the supermarket performance metric case study example discussed in Chapter 7. Many supermarkets monitor and manage scan rates of checkout operatives. Common sense might suggest that a key performance metric that can be applied to a checkout operator would be how fast they process products. The slower the scan rate, the longer the queues of shoppers and the slower the rate of income generation in a particular period. There is evidence that shoppers will be put off going to a shop if queues get too long (Briggs, 2015).

It makes sense, therefore, that some supermarkets might focus on this particular metric. Certain supermarkets we have spoken to actively communicate weekly averages of scan rate per minute to staff as a performance management indicator. Presumably those who have low scan rates may be under pressure to speed up. When such a metric becomes the focus of IMOB, the line managers will place too much emphasis on each of their employees' scan rates and employees will become overly focused on increasing it, potentially at the expense of other behaviours. Obviously in a context such as a supermarket that has an IMOB of scan rate, the HR analyst may well spend some time predicting scan rates. As the HR analyst explores some predictive models and finds key trends and patterns, this reinforces the IMOB. The danger in such a situation is that one piece of knowledge (that customers do not like queues) leads to the monitoring of one particular metric at the expense of another piece of knowledge (for example, that customers might like a pleasant interaction at the checkout). Thinking through the possible implications of the IMOB of scan rate in supermarkets, the checkout operatives might be discouraged from engaging in a meaningful conversation with customers as this may inhibit fast scan rate. Thus the metric could actually be discouraging quality customer-oriented behaviour and be all about the quantity metric. It is also possible that some members of staff may be disadvantaged with this particular metric. It may be that some staff with disabilities, for example, may struggle to reach the full potential of extremely fast scan rate; it might also be the case that staff on certain shifts at certain times of day/certain times of the week (where there may be less customer flow-through) might also be disadvantaged. Some of these issues were mentioned as being instrumental in one particular supermarket that decided to remove the practice of monitoring checkout scan rate (*Yorkshire Post*, 2015).

Checkout scan rates at supermarkets are just one example where a performance measure can become an example of IMOB; many different examples could be presented. In academia, for example, some teaching quality metrics can become institutionalized (e.g. student evaluation scores). In environments where engagement surveys are conducted, the team engagement scores can become institutionalized. In call centres, incoming call rates, call lengths and percentage of time on the phone can become institutionalized. In consultancy or law firms, time reporting metrics and 'billable hours' are another example. Most readers may well be able to reflect on how their organization operates and whether there are examples of IMOB within their own work environment.

Because of the dangers of unintended consequences that can occur with IMOB, as an HR analyst you must always ask yourself: 'Are there any unintended consequences that might occur with a particular focus on any one metric?' You also need to be highly sensitive to the potential for a particular focus on any metric to foster and indeed help create instances of IMOB.

Balanced scorecard of metrics

One of the main reasons practitioners and theorists recommend a 'balanced scorecard' in performance management and performance metrics is to avoid problems associated with a mono-metric focus and target or metric-oriented behaviour. The problems associated with IMOB mentioned in the previous section will be inherent wherever performance is judged against one metric. Thus, it is recommended that any attempt to predict or model any metric or aspect of organizational performance should include a number of different indices or metrics in order to judge the full range of the particular performance, success of a function or employee behaviour.

Whenever the HR analytic expert is tasked with investigating a particular issue or factor, they should generally be on the lookout for more than one form of metric. As mentioned in the performance case study (Chapter 7), there are many ways to measure and monitor different types of performance. The HR analyst should always be thinking about different possibilities of data indicators that might provide information about different types of or aspects of performance. Similarly, if the phenomenon under investigation is diversity, then a range of different diversity indicators will need to be considered. For example, the analyst could consider the percentage of women in each team, the proportion of underrepresented groups in teams, the proportion of team leaders who are female *and* from underrepresented groups, the proportion of team leaders who are female *or* from underrepresented groups, the proportion of people promoted within teams over a recent period who are female or from underrepresented groups, the engagement scores of females versus males and from underrepresented groups within a team, etc. Ultimately the analyst should be on the lookout for as wide a range of different metrics on a particular measure as possible. Aside from the importance of avoiding the likelihood of institutionalizing metric-oriented behaviour, the sophistication of possible diagnostic and predictive modelling becomes much greater with an awareness of the potential differential meaning and implications of a range of different indicators and metrics of a phenomenon (e.g. diversity in this case).

What is the analytic sample?

In many analytic models that the HR analyst might want to explore, the sample to be utilized may be the entire organization. If this were the case, one would assume that the data sets to be used for the analysis will represent the entire organization. Importantly, this may not always be the case either, because the analyst is only interested in a particular subsection of the organization or because the data available (or indeed unavailable) might end up meaning that the sample at hand is not the entire organization. An example of the former might be some analysis that has a specific focus on part of the organization: for example, predicting customer satisfaction of financial advisers within a bank (Chapter 7), in which only the financial advisers are considered. Another example might be checkout operators within one supermarket who were employed within a given period.

As employees are always joining and leaving organizations, even if we decided to try to utilize the whole organization we may need to restrict the sample to cover those employed within a certain time period; this decision may of course end up restricting the sample that the analyst uses, and indeed the nature of the interpretations that can be drawn from analysis conducted with the HR data. Often, in designing models and analytic strategies, the HR analyst will have to make explicit choices around who to include in the analysis and who not to; however, deciding who is to be included in the analysis may not always be as simple as one might expect.

Ultimately the sample used in the analysis may end up being restricted by the fact that there may not always be a full set of data across all chosen measures for each employee. If we consider a potential model where we try to predict an increase in individual financial sales figures over a one-year period, the factors that we consider to predict these figures could include performance appraisal ratings of particular competencies as well as customer satisfaction ratings linked to each employee. The potential for some of the data required to not be available with some employees is quite high. To run these models, we would need two years of sales figures. So we can only analyse the data with employees who have been in the organization for two years or more; thus anyone who has not been employed in the organization for at least two years will not be included. Similarly, it may be the case that some information has not been collected for every employee (e.g. customer satisfaction surveys may not have been responded to by all customers; thus immediately these employees will not be included in the analysis). So this model will exclude employees who have been employed for less than two years and people who have not had customer satisfaction ratings taken. Immediately, therefore, if the analyst wanted to make assumptions about the workforce they would have to recognize that the modelling is based on a particular sample in its foundation. When there has been a restriction of the sample, not only does this mean that there may be restrictions on whether the analyst can comfortably generalize the findings to the rest of the organization but this may also imply that there is some bias to the analysis. The analyst must always consider who has been excluded from the sample.

Whilst the analytic example mentioned here would exclude any employee who has been employed within the last 24 months, even if the analyst wanted to explore a cross-sectional (single time point of data collection) model with current data, some information may be missing depending on when each aspect of data is collected and whether an employee was employed at the time of data collection (e.g. if a performance appraisal is conducted annually, the timing of the analysis will be important – some people may not have had an appraisal yet if they had joined within the last 12 months).

Another example where an analyst needs to carefully consider the potential sample is when we explore some model that included team employee engagement. As most engagement surveys are voluntary and the employee does not have to complete the questionnaire, it is possible for a team engagement score to represent a portion of the team rather than the whole team. The team engagement scores, therefore, may have an inherent bias in that they only represent the people who wanted to complete the survey; this may well have been people who had higher levels of engagement. Importantly, this issue needs to be considered when the analyst tries to link team engagement scores with some other team figures (e.g. team sales that are compiled from all team members' sales figures); it may be the case that the two sets of data actually represent different groups or samples. The analyst needs to carefully consider these issues; such problems may well mean that the relationships between two sets of measures might not be found because the two sets of data are associated with fundamentally different groups.

To make this more complicated, there could be country-specific differences in the data stored for each employee. This could be due to differences in legislation regarding data that can be collected and stored on employees; it can also be due to differences in meaning and interpretation of a particular metric. As an example, the meaning and country norms of who might be considered an employee can have a profound impact on what any analysis of employees might mean. As a specific example, the governments of some countries have employment policies linked to immigration and dictate that all organizations above a certain size must employ a certain proportion of local nationals (rather than expats). This can have profound implications on who is considered an employee because many organizations employ local workers on a zero-hours contract so that they can comply with these legislative requirements. The implication might be that the organization appears to have many more employees than actually do work within the organization. Thus the analyst needs to be aware that what might be in the database – and the meaning of particular data – is likely to vary across countries.

The missing group

Linked to the issue above about cross-country differences in data retention is systematic missingness of some groups. Some groups may not be represented and thus not be included in some analyses. This could be problematic in terms of the legitimacy or the representativeness of the data. Thus the analyst always needs to look at what the final number (N) is that R uses in a particular analysis. If it is lower than it should be then it might be the case that some groups have missing data on one of the metrics included in the analysis; an investigation may need to be carried out to explore who has the missing data and why.

An example might be in a multinational organization where the employee engagement survey asks a number of diversity-related questions, including sexual orientation. Whilst this is common practice in many countries in the West, in other countries, for example, homosexuality is considered a crime – hence it would not be appropriate to ask people to confirm their sexual orientation on an employee attitude survey. This has repercussions on how you might choose to analyse the diversity data across countries in a multinational organization.

The missing factor

Any research endeavour designed to determine the cause of events or the impact of a potential intervention will only be a worthwhile project if the measures and indices included in the project are valid, appropriate and (more importantly) comprehensive enough to sufficiently provide answers to the analytic research question. Something to watch out for when conducting statistical analysis utilizing predictive models with

HR-related data is that some key factors could be missing in the analysis and this factor may actually explain some of the results that the analyst relies on. The analyst will need to be particularly sensitive to possible factors that are not included in the analysis, which could actually play a key role in influencing the results. In research methodology terminology, such a factor is referred to as an 'extraneous variable'. A straightforward example of such a factor could be analysis that looks at job satisfaction, pay levels or employee engagement across particular teams, without taking into account some fundamental differences (e.g. gender or occupational job role) that could be associated with or explain variation across the teams. To some extent, the issue of the missing factor is partially addressed when we include control variables in the analysis (see examples in Chapter 5); for example, when we try to predict team engagement we can include as many control variables that are available and that we think are appropriate (e.g. gender percentage in the team, average team age, average job tenure, etc). However, sometimes the missing factor may be the fact that two or more of our possible variables may interact or there are contingencies to the effect that any one factor may have on another. Thus the interaction may be the missing factor. Ultimately, any modelling will involve judgement on the part of the analyst, and as the person driving and testing the models becomes more experienced they may intuitively get a sense of what possible extraneous variables might be influencing the results. Importantly, to get the most out of predictive modelling, an analyst will want to spend a good deal of time thinking about how to set up a data set. The early data manipulation/variable construction stage (which might involve creating different forms of dummy variables to be able to explore different features of how predictors may combine) is a very important stage of the analytics project. The more effort that is put into making sure the data used is set up to be able to able to uncover unique aspects/possible predictors, the more likely the model will produce some insightful output.

Carving time and space to be rigorous and thorough

Almost without fail, when providing HR analytics training to HR metrics/HR information teams, there is often the response that the potential opportunities for enabling considerable insights are recognized but there is a concern or expectation that the analytics team will not be given the required amount of time and space to be able to conduct the analysis. Whilst it is very quick to actually conduct analyses with R if you know what you are doing, the analyst will have to be given enough time and space to be able to thoughtfully set up data sets and explore and experiment with the various analytic models in order to get the most out of the data. Often when one estimates some sophisticated models, in interrogating the data and results an analyst discovers that they should go back and test the data for problems (e.g. a lack of reliability, missing data, etc). Carrying out analysis and perfecting predictive models are not linear processes. It is very important that before any results are pulled together and presented, the predictive analyst is given space and time to:

1 explore and understand the data available

2 consider the most appropriate research questions

3 test and explore particular models

4 conduct the analysis

5 interrogate the analysis

6 rerun the analysis

7 subject the analysis and results to further interrogation.

As it stands at the moment, in most large organizations, MI teams have to be constantly producing descriptive report after descriptive report to support IMOB behaviour and often have very little time available to go offline and start exploring and conducting HR analytic models. Thus, in the management and culture of any developed HR analytics team, there must be an acceptance that in carrying out and conducting predictive HR analytics time needs to be given to the analyst to go through the steps outlined above. In essence, creative space also needs to be provided for the analyst to be able to draw on their analytic imagination. Indeed, there will be little likelihood of determining the correct prescriptive action to address the reports if the analysis is not conducted properly and the bulk of the time is spent producing more and more descriptive reports. As an aside, advanced users of R will be able to automate aspects of report generation and free up time for predictive analyses. Such abilities are possible if the analytics team understands programming aspects of R.

Be sceptical and interrogate the results

If one believes some of the highly optimistic claims made by proponents of HR analytics (about how predictive analytics can transform your organization) then there will be an expectation that the predictive models and analytic insights will produce ground-breaking information that can change how they do business and thus lead to enormous business benefits.

Whilst it is possible that highly experienced HR analytics experts could identify some important insights that could save the organization vast sums of money – or identify factors that, if the organization focused on them, would lead to higher performance – it is important that the analytics expert always looks at the results with a slightly sceptical eye. Before reporting on/acting on any insights gained, the analyst needs to be extremely comfortable that the recommendations made have been carefully interrogated and that any assumptions made with the data (e.g. who is and is not represented by the numbers) are made very clear; transparency in the analysis approach is important in order to ensure that the audience of any recommendations is aware of any assumption made.

Importantly, whilst it will be imperative for the HR analytics expert to be an advocate of the benefits of careful statistical analysis, conducting predictive analytics is not an exact science and the insights that can be gained will often be limited by the quality of the data, and how rigorous the analyst has been undertaken. The expert HR analyst will be just as aware of the limitations with predictive analytics as they are of the benefits. An example of particular limitations that the analyst should always be aware of includes the key adage that 'correlations do not imply causality'. Even when the models include the tracking of changes over time, it is often the case that the analysis used with the predictive models relies on the observation of correlations/relationships between data in the data set.

The importance of quality data and measures

As any HR or MI analyst will understand, records within HR information databases are often incomplete and there are often gaps in information collected or stored in different regions and functions. One of the key things that the HR analytic team would need to do is to undertake an audit of the quality of information that is collected in different parts of the organization and identify any areas where there may be gaps or problems with the quality of data that is collected and stored. As discussed above, it may be the case that if particular data is missing in particular parts of the organization, this could end up excluding these groups from the analysis. Also, if the analyst is to rely on certain measures when designing and conducting particular predictive models, the measures need to be accurate measures of the concept at hand. With analytic techniques such as regression analysis, where we try to account for variation in a particular factor, some part of the variance in our dependent variable will be due to error in measurement. This issue was discussed in Chapter 5 in our discussion of measures of engagement. Aside from ensuring that the appropriate measures are used in the analysis conducted, which is an essential requirement of any good analytics model, the measures themselves need to be reliable and valid. As the maxim of 'garbage in, garbage out' implies, if the quality of the data being entered into the analysis is not at a required level, then what comes out of the analysis is likely to be of questionable quality.

The area of data governance is outside the scope of this book and indeed deserves its own book. But it is a critical piece of the HR analytics ecosystem. It refers to the practices such as ensuring data is easy to find, is of high quality, and that sufficient security is enabled by job role to allow people to use it. Good data governance will keep organizations within the parameters of data privacy law and mitigate organizational risk associated with data breaches. It includes practices such as regular data audits, clear data ownership by subject matter and a well-maintained business glossary of key metrics such as the definition of headcount or turnover. The guardrails put in place by good data governance policy and practice should provide freedom and the ability to innovate through employee trust, seamless access to data and faster turnaround times on analytics.

The evolution of AI in HR

Artificial intelligence (AI) can perform some of the tasks typically performed by people. It has some ability to learn and make decisions, mimicking cognitive functions. Its performance in serving as an accurate, reliable tool fit for the organization's purpose depends on how well it is designed and trained (McKinsey & Company, 2024). Some terms you may have heard of that are fast growing applications of AI in organizations are machine learning, deep learning and generative AI.

Machine learning gets computers to make predictions and decisions based on data – often observations captured in text (e.g. emails, message board comments, survey responses) and photos set in the real world. Machine learning algorithms can improve over time without human intervention. One example of machine learning is the recommendation systems in Netflix or Spotify, which learn what we like and get better over time at making recommendations for users. We covered some of the different types of machine learning in Chapter 11 and applications in HR may be to make predictions about who is more likely to resign or make a recommendation about the next career move for an employee.

Deep learning is a subset of machine learning that uses neural networks to process data. Neural networks process data through multiple layers and decision nodes, ultimately generating an outcome such as a classification or a prediction. They can process complex features in pictures, text, sounds, videos and other data to generate insights and predictions (IBM, 2023). A more recent development is generative AI, which extends the capabilities of these systems from merely classifying or predicting to generating novel outputs such as chat messages or pictures. One particular generative AI model, DALL-E 3, can take a text prompt and generate pictures based on the prompt. Similarly, ChatGPT can respond to instructions in text format and generate responses in kind.

Like a person, AI can learn, but it is not perfect. For instance, it can be trained with a specific purpose in mind but produce unexpected results. As mentioned earlier, Amazon scrapped an AI tool that was designed to help with recruitment because it recommended biased decisions that disadvantaged women (BBC, 2018). The data used to train the machine learning model was taken from 10 years of recruitment and selection decisions. In this data, most of the applicants had been men and the decisions tended to treat men more favourably. This meant that the machine learning tool mimicked this pattern and also favoured men, and tended not to shortlist CVs that indicated women applicants. While this may seem like a failure, there are multiple lessons to be learned. This tool could have been very helpful for HR professionals to automate repetitive tasks caused by the high volume of applicants. But any system used to make decisions about people should incorporate the attention of people who act with values in mind. We think the team at Amazon should be applauded for their willingness to be open about issues they faced so that others can learn from their experience.

People are inherenly biased, and so too are AI tools based on sampling people's decisions. Many readers of this book will have a background in psychology and will be aware of the first part of the prior statement. We can be biased towards thinking we are better than we are at making good hiring decisions; biased towards preferring candidates who are more similar to ourselves when it comes to background, gender, age, schooling or other characteristics; or biased towards the first impression, to name just a few ways in which bias comes into hiring decisions. So training AI tools based purely on human decisions is likely to result in a biased tool.

AI provides an opportunity to train a tool based on our best version of ourselves. To teach the tool based on examples of the decisions that we would want to replicate, i.e. good decisions such as those based on critical role criteria or required technical certifications.

Regardless of how good the tool is, and despite what we have said above about bias, there will always be a need for a human who is a domain expert to review and test the predictions or decisions made by AI. As this is a rapidly developing field, experimentation and continued learning will improve our understanding about the strengths and limitations of this tool. We are in a unique position in the Human Resources domain because decisions made by AI tools can have a significant impact on the lives of people. We need to be aware of and strive to remove bias in our data and ensure that AI does not unfairly evaluate a person or some groups disadvantageously. AI could increase diversity in recruitment if developed thoughtfully and deployed carefully.

Some other examples of using AI in the field of HR (Eubanks, 2022) include workforce planning, learning and development, talent management and reward.

Like people, AI needs guidance. Furthermore, we need to ensure AI tools incorporate transparency, explainability and fairness. It is also important in this domain that AI tools are explainable. Tools built on explainable AI have the benefit of transparency in decision-making, showing the reasons why the tool made the prediction it did and retaining human oversight of the model.

A note of caution when selecting an AI partner or consultancy if you don't have the in-house capability. Many consultancies do not offer explainable AI in their tools, meaning they cannot fully explain some components, including training data, method of training and the intent underlying the design of the tool. Instead, they offer an unexplainable but quicker to deploy 'black box' systems – pre-trained models of unknown, or partially unknown, quantity that may not include HR specific information. Their promise of speed to insights can seduce executives. But an approach that involves putting HR data into a pre-trained tool and obtaining predictions and/or prescriptive insights can be damaging. It may lead to decisions made without any consideration for bias, ethics or privacy that can be damaging for the organization and lose the trust of its people. In a recent example, a consultancy shared an automated recommendation phone app designed for executives. The app recommended hiring people in a specific age category. This would be discriminatory in many countries. But also by bypassing HR professionals, this recommendation might have been actioned without adequate consideration of its impact on the organization. Because the tool was a 'black box', the intended audience for the app were not provided with the rationale underlying such recommendations. Decisions made with such systems could challenge unfavourable hiring decisions with unknown consequences. Useful implementation of AI systems requires transparency, explainability, fairness and ensuring HR domain knowledge is a key part of the process.

Taking ethical considerations seriously

Over the past decade, as the field of HR analytics has developed, the challenges of ethics in have become more apparent, with commentators noting their concerns. In both academia and the professional realm, much is now written and spoken about linked to the ethical challenges faced by HR analytic teams (see Edwards et al., 2022). The concerns raised have become magnified as the sophistication of HR analytic technology has increased, in particular with the increasing use of systems that automate analytic activities and potentially apply AI to people data.

Employee confidentiality and willing participation

HR functions, as a norm, store and are privy to a huge amount of sensitive information on each employee. Some of this is personal information that employees voluntarily provide. Other data, created by the organization itself, such as bonus payments or performance ratings, is still personal in nature. Although organizations typically claim ownership of most of this information, employees often agree contractually that the organization can use this data for business purposes.

Big Brother concerns

The available technology in the current workplace means that data associated with employees may well be collected and stored without their knowledge or awareness. If HR Analytics teams try to use this data for analysis it will raise ethical concerns.

One example of an analytic project that employees may not have been aware of (and therefore they may not have been comfortable with) is modelling conducted at a global financial institution that linked food bought in the staff canteen and gym equipment used in the staff gym. This story was passed to one of the authors by the HR analytics director who helped to conduct the analysis. This particular organization used employee identity cards to enable employees to access various non-work-related facilities such as catering facilities and gym facilities. The information stored by this organization on each employee was so fine-grained that an HR analyst had access to what employees ate at the staff dining room during the day and what gym equipment they used (and for how long) when they went to the staff gym during the day.

The HR analytics team at this organization linked this data to the individual employee performance data within a call-centre function at the financial institution. They were able to model the ideal profile of meals, exercise period, workout pattern and ideal gym equipment that was associated with high performance at the call centre in the afternoon. Whilst there may be some potential for this information to be quite useful in terms of helping to identify the best profile of high performers, the Big Brother or surveillance implications of this kind of analysis are really quite profound. The implications of having bad health and dietary habits identified and used in a performance management discussion when someone is not performing in the call centre raises serious ethical concerns. One needs to question where the boundaries may lie as to what is information of a personal nature that the employer should not really be using for the purposes of HR analytics. It is quite normal for gym companies, canteens and shops to track and profile consumer behaviour, however. So some of this analysis is not particularly different from the activities that marketing analysts may conduct in terms of consumer behaviour; the difference is of course that there is a distinct power relationship present between the employer and employee that may not exist between service providers and customers.

As the HR analytic field matures, the potential for different analytic projects to be crossing ethical lines and straying into areas that can be considered either an invasion of employees' rights to privacy or an overstep of what can reasonably considered legitimate within reasonable bounds of managerial control increases. An example of analytic activities that can stray into a grey ethical area is the trawling, processing and analysis of employee electronic activities, including (for example) email correspondence. Although we do not cover this in the current book, organizational network analyses techniques enable organizations to model employee networks of communication. Such analyses can be carried out actively (where employees may be surveyed to find out who their networks are) or passively (where the organization tracks electronic activity that is already collected or stored by IT systems). Most analytic experts who undertake this kind of analyses will be aware of the privacy challenges; however, the potential for such analyses to easily stray into an invasion of employee privacy exists.

Ultimately, the analyst should always ask this question: 'If this analysis was being conducted on me or a member of my family without my or their knowledge would there be a level of discomfort?' Ultimately, if there are potential questions around a particular type of analysis then the right thing to do is to communicate with the employee group and probably give them the opportunity to opt out of the analysis.

Who owns the data?

In many cases, when an analyst is about to embark on an analytics activity, the legitimacy of the analysis in terms of invading employees' privacy is likely to be clear cut and well within managerial prerogative to carry out. However, where there is a possible challenge to this managerial prerogative, a source of this problem may be that the data might not really be owned by the organization.

Often, when an employee starts work, the contract can state that any HR information that the organization collects and stores is 'owned' by the organization. Whilst the data governance framework should clearly outline ownership for domains such as talent or compensation, in some situations, data ownership and use may fall outside formal agreements. These cases should be discussed with organisational data privacy experts.

HR data security issues

Even without considering HR information from an HR analytics perspective, the HR function will be highly aware of the importance of data security. As HR information systems become more sophisticated, the sheer amount of possible private information (e.g. salaries, bank account details, date-of-birth information, eating habits from the staff canteen) that can be stored becomes massive. Most organizations large enough to have an HR analytics team will also have a dedicated cyber security function who will work with analytics teams and provide support and guidance on managing the risk associated with data security. Indeed, it is commonplace for the cyber security function to have a well-developed process to undertake a security risk assessment before any material analytics project. This team is your friend and trusted ally. The responsibility that the HR analyst needs to take on board to ensure data security is of paramount importance – especially as one of the key things they will be doing is gathering considerable amounts of information from a variety of sources. The analyst may indeed be linking this information to an individual employee in order to draw conclusions about some aspect of their psychological state, behaviour or expected behaviour. We will not go into detail here about the importance of data security; many geographical regions have different legislative guidelines around the globe (e.g. the EU has quite strict data security guidelines) and it is the HR analytic expert's job to be aware of these regulatory frameworks and accord with them in conducting their HR analytic activity. Ultimately, taking data security seriously can be considered to be a key ethical standard that an HR analytics expert should abide by (see below).

Problems with using targeted demographic profiles – stereotyping, prejudice and discrimination

In the performance case study (Chapter 7) we presented an analytic scenario where age categories were interrogated in order to explore the possible profiles of top performers with average checkout scan rates. It was found that women of a particular age and education profile were the fastest checkout scanners. If the organization conducted this analysis and identified a particular profile such as this, a big question that the analyst (and the managers) will face is what should be done with this information. One response would be to introduce a policy of only hiring women between the ages of 30 and 35 to work on the checkouts. Such an approach, whilst rational to some degree, may have a number of implications. It would, of course, end up exposing the organization to potential gender and age discrimination challenges.

Everybody is different and the basis of predictive analysis revolves around patterns in the data rather than definitive certainties. In a sense, predictive analysis risks creating a stereotyped picture of the workforce based on profiles and categories identified in the analysis. A grave danger that could occur with a reliance on stereotypes is the tendency of people to be lazy thinkers (or so-called 'cognitive misers': see Fiske and Taylor, 1984) and not try to challenge stereotypes. This stereotyping can often lead to outright prejudice and discrimination (Brown, 2010). As with any stereotype, the differences within a social category will almost always be as big as the differences between categories. As such, where a recognizable demographic pattern is exposed in predicting any particular type of behaviour such as performance, the analyst should, ethically, go out of their way to demonstrate that although certain profiles may be associated with the highest level of performance, there will always be cases within the 'ideal' profile that do not accord with the expectations that the modelling has produced. Similarly, there will always be cases where employees in a non-ideal profile perform particularly well. One of the challenges that an expert predictive HR analyst might be faced with is how to identify patterns within the workforce without actively stereotyping the organization; without creating evidence that might support a simplified view of the world that may lead to the creation of prejudicial perceptions and discriminatory mindsets. One possible way around such a dilemma is for the analyst to try always to explore the data to identify complexity in the data and to accept that there will always be exceptions to scenarios identified in any predictive model. The analyst should always try to identify contingencies, contextual moderators or boundary conditions (see the discussion on interactions and curvilinear relationships in Chapter 11) that challenge a simple view; in doing so, the analyst will identify a more sophisticated model and will reduce the likelihood that any overly simplistic profiling ends up stereotyping the workplace.

Problems of biased algorithms

Over recent years, some of the challenges faced by analysts when trying to use analytic models to make decisions have begun to surface as a legitimate critique of the practice of applying automated algorithms (e.g. O'Neil, 2016 and Canhoto, 2017) to help speed up decision process, for example the use of automated selection processes (such as automated online video interview scoring) to make initial filtering decisions in the selection process. Some of this critique will be very important for an analytic team to ensure that their activities are not reinforcing or propagating biased decision making. Predictive models are necessarily based on the identification of patterns and trends from historical data.

If, however, the data analysed is linked to historically rated behaviour, such as performance ratings, and these historical ratings are problematic or built on biased, prejudicial or discriminatory decisions (made by certain individuals within the organization), the application of analytics could cause big problems for the organization. For example, if the organization historically employed sexist and biased managers who rated females as worse performers than men, then the application of an algorithm (modelled to identify high performers) to make selection decisions (using this historical data) will only serve to propagate the historical biases. So, if women managers or team leaders are discriminated against in an organization (and disadvantaged) and an analytic model identified gender as a predictor of performance, the application of this algorithm to make predictions about future expected performance would be propagating the previous historical bias. In this scenario, the results of the application of the algorithm (automated or otherwise) would point toward a recommended decision that a male employee would be a better hire (or have higher potential) than a female employee purely because males had an advantage in the organization in the past (and thus they would be expected to get higher performance ratings in the future).

Therefore, the potential for algorithms to reinforce and foster historical biases in their application is something an analyst must reflect upon, as we discussed in the Amazon example.

Algorithmic transparency and accountability

A related point here is the issue that organizations (and analytic teams) could potentially be using algorithms to make decisions without fully understanding how these algorithms work (or how they were derived). Such issues are a particularly important consideration if the HR function uses off-the-shelf predictive modelling products from existing providers without having knowledge of the algorithms themselves or how they work when they are being used to make predictions. For example, analytic products do exist that, when applied to HR data, can give an indication of 'likelihood of leaving' or 'expected performance level' based on an applied predictive model that has been developed in other organizations. This raises further areas of possible critique or challenges to the field with the application of predictive HR analytics; thus a field of debate is growing within the analytics community discussing the importance of 'algorithmic transparency' and 'algorithmic accountability'. The more that predictive analytics is applied to HR and used to make decisions, the more important these issues will become in the future.

Ethical standards for the HR analytics team

Given that predictive HR analytics is an emerging but growing field, it will be important that some kind of ethical principles can be identified to potentially guide HR analytic activities. As one can consider any analytics team to be positioned under the umbrella of the HR function, any ethical guidelines and principles associated with HR in general can be applied to HR analytics experts. There are no specific agreed ethical guidelines that can be drawn on to help act as an ethical guide for HR; one could, however, consider the ethical standards set out by the Chartered Institute of Personnel and Development (CIPD) in the UK as reasonable initial guiding principles (2024).

The CIPD's HR ethical standards and integrity commitment

In agreeing to be a member of the CIPD, there is an expectation that HR practitioners must:

- establish, maintain and develop business relationships based on confidence, trust and respect

- exhibit and defend professional and personal integrity and honesty at all times
- demonstrate sensitivity for the customs, practices, culture and personal beliefs of others
- advance employment and business practices that promote equality of opportunity, diversity and inclusion, and support human rights and dignity
- safeguard all confidential, commercially sensitive and personal data acquired as a result of business relationships and not use it for personal advantage or the benefit or detriment of third parties.

Whilst the CIPD standards are not specifically designed for HR analytics activities, there are some ethical standards that could be considered to govern the use of people and HR data exploration within the HR analytics team. Some of these are set out here, drawn from an article written by Professor Paul Schwartz (2011):

1 Organizations should comply with legal requirements in conducting analytics.

2 Organizations should consider whether analytics activities reflect cultural and societal norms about what is acceptable, beyond legal requirements.

3 Organizations should consider the impact of the use of analytics activities and ensure that the trust of various stakeholders is not breached, violated or lost.

4 Clear accountability should be introduced into the HR analytics process, and the organization should develop policies that govern information management. An individual should be designated to oversee the appropriateness of analytics activities.

5 Appropriate safeguards need to be introduced to protect the security of information that is used in the analytic process.

6 Organizations should consider whether analytics activities involve sensitive areas and accompany the process with safeguards proportionate to the risk.

As a set of guiding principles for an analytics team to consider adopting, these six standards seem to be wholly appropriate.

A practice sometimes used in organizations is a mutually agreed ethics charter. The one in Figure 12.1, adopted by a large mining organization, forms part of the organization's data privacy training.

Analytics Ethics Charter
A pledge

As trusted guardians of personal data and creators of tools used by leaders to inform decisions that impact our people:

We pledge to be responsible, transparent and unbiased in the work we do and to respect the individuals behind the data.

Purpose and Impact

1. We are honest and transparent about the capability and limitations of products we produce
2. We strive to use data in a way that is consistent with the intentions of the disclosing party
3. We exhaustively test products, consider different ways they might be used and strive to eliminate adversarial use
4. We limit data collection to what is needed for the purpose we are serving
5. We listen to the concerns of stakeholders, clearly explain our methods of analysis, and strive for shared understanding and informed agreement
6. We ensure our design approach incorporates transparency, explainability and fairness
7. We present our results in the most clear, transparent and open manner
8. If we feel it compromises our pledge, we question the agenda of our stakeholders and reserve the right to decline work.
9. We are accountable for the products we produce

Privacy

- Personal data is secured and is shared only on a 'need to know' basis.
- We are compliant with the Data Privacy Standard when we process, generate or create personal data.
- Our processing of personal data reflects what has been notified to the relevant individuals (eg in the Employee Privacy Statement);
- We ensure that projects involving personal data risk have passed a Privacy Impact Assessment (PIA) or are settled with E&C data privacy team (as required)

Security

- We ensure our work is covered by a relevant Security Risk Assessment (SRA) and that the data is secure.
- We seek to limit access to data and solutions to those for whom it is necessary in line with the project purpose
- We endeavor to ensure human interventions of data, including steps from data collection, consent, processing and visualization, are auditable

Fairness

- We strive to remove potential biases in the data.
- We strive to ensure automated decisions will not be made about people purely on the basis of data and analytics.
- We ensure our products do not unfairly categorize people based on incomplete data or put any person or group of people at a disadvantage

12.1   Example of an ethics charter

Data privacy

As with the cyber security function, any organization large enough to have an HR analytics function will also have a data privacy and ethics team. They are accountable for the protection of personal data of employees and usually sit within the legal department. They work in partnership with the data and analytics team as well as IT and cyber security to advise teams.

Depending on the country or countries in which the organization operates, the data privacy team will ensure the processing of data carried out by data and analytics teams is in line with the relevant legislation. Examples of this legislation include the GDPR in Europe, the Privacy Act in Australia, the Lei Geral de Protecao de Dados (LGPD) in Brazil, Canada's Digital Charter Implementation Act and China's Personal Information Protection Law (PIPL), though similar legislation is in place in many other countries and continues to evolve.

Data privacy experts will often carry out a privacy impact assessment with Data and Analytics teams to understand the business reason for the work, ensure responsible use of personal information and often to provide guardrails or parameters within which the work needs to be completed in order to remain compliant with the legislation. Successful HR Analytics teams will work hard to develop a healthy and mutually supportive relationship with the data privacy experts.

The metric and the data are linked to human beings

HR analysts work with data linked to living, breathing, feeling human beings – these are not just numbers and abstractions. It is not unusual for HR information analysts, or indeed any quantitative analyst, to become so engrossed in the analytic activity in exploring data linked to people that the human aspect is forgotten or lost. People who are used to managing people projects and conducting workforce planning can very quickly start referring to people as 'heads' (as in headcount), 'resources' and 'capacity' reduction. The authors have had anecdotal experience of HR professionals discussing employees as if there were no human beings involved and discussing the employees as 'heads' or 'resources' in a clinical fashion (e.g. 'underutilized heads'), such that the level of dehumanization was distasteful. Ultimately, the HR analytic expert needs to try to be aware that whilst there may be ways of describing analytic activities using technical jargon – and this may give the appearance of the highly technical aspect of HR analytics, which may boost one's sense of technical expertise – almost every analytic activity will be linked to human beings.

Whilst not specifically related to HR analytics, Keenoy and Anthony (1992) wrote an interesting book chapter that reflected upon the tendency for language used in relation to redundancies to become dehumanized. Instead of job lay-offs/

redundancies, the descriptions that are used by organizations might include terms such as delayering, rationalization, headcount reduction, rightsizing, workforce re-profiling – and because of the language used, the 'reality of job loss is banished from our language'. Whilst this is obviously not about HR analytics, the tendency for narratives linked to discussions of the workforce to lose some link with the human beings is something that the HR analytics expert needs to be aware of and sensitive to. When predicting sickness absence rates, for example, there are real people behind the numbers that are being analysed; what may also be linked to sickness absence is some degree of human suffering. Thus, HR analytics experts should try to ensure that they do not lose sight of the fact that the data is data about people – and not forget the 'human' in HR analytics.

References

BBC (2018) Amazon scrapped sexist AI tool, www.bbc.com/news/technology-45809919 (archived at https://perma.cc/PQ8L-Q7AB)

Birkhoff, A (2018) 9 ways the GDPR will impact HR data and analytics, AIHR, www.analyticsinhr.com/blog/general-data-protection-regulation-gdpr-impact-hr-analytics/ (archived at https://perma.cc/82EC-FKRV)

Briggs, F (2015) Shopper are put off by queues more than seven people deep, *Retail Times*, www.retailtimes.co.uk/shoppers-put-off-queues-seven-people-deep-box-technologies-intel-research-shows/ (archived at https://perma.cc/ZY29-68DY)

Brown, R (2010) *Prejudice: Its social psychology*, 2nd edn, Wiley, Chichester

Canhoto, A (2017) Ted Talk: Blind faith in big data must end, anacanhoto.com/2017/10/10/ted-talk-blind-faith-in-big-data-must-end/ (archived at https://perma.cc/685E-X8EA)

CIPD (2024) Code of conduct and ethics, CIPD, www.cipd.org/uk/membership/professional-standards/code-of-conduct/ (archived at https://perma.cc/3J22-9G74)

Edwards, M R, Charlwood, A, Guenole, N and Marler, J (2022) HR analytics: An emerging field finding its place in the world alongside simmering ethical challenges, *Human Resource Management Journal*

Eubanks, B (2022) *Artificial Intelligence for HR: Use AI to support and develop a successful workforce*, Kogan Page, London

Fiske, S T and Taylor, S E (1984) *Social Cognition*, AddisonWesley, MA

IBM (2017) Getting to the GDPR: Four key use cases to jumpstart your efforts, *IBM Security*, June

IBM (2023) Artificial intelligence and a new era of human resources, www.ibm.com/blog/artificial-intelligence-and-a-new-era-of-human-resources/ (archived at https://perma.cc/54DW-MFCC)

Keenoy, T and Anthony, P (1992) HRM: Metaphor, meaning and morality, in *Reassessing Human Resource Management*, pp 233–55, ed P Blyton and P Turnbull, Sage Publications, London

Marr, B (2018) How much data do we create every day? The mind-blowing stats everyone should read, www.forbes.com/sites/bernardmarr/2018/05/21/how-much-data-do-we-create-every-day-the-mind-blowing-stats-everyone-should-read (archived at https://perma.cc/7YMG-5AP2)

McKinsey & Company (2024) What is AI (artificial intelligence)? www.mckinsey.com/featured-insights/mckinsey-explainers/what-is-ai (archived at https://perma.cc/B6Y8-YUGM)

O'Neil, C (2016) *Weapons of Math Destruction: How big data increases inequality and threatens democracy*, Broadway Books, New York

Schwartz, P M (2011) Privacy, ethics and analytics, *Privacy Interests*, May/June, pp 66–69, paulschwartz.net/wp-content/uploads/2019/01/pschwartz_privacy-eth-analytics-IEEE-P-Sec-2011.pdf (archived at https://perma.cc/4RBJ-DQTH)

Telegraph (2018) Amazon scraps 'sexist AI' recruiting tool that showed bias against women, www.telegraph.co.uk/technology/2018/10/10/amazon-scraps-sexist-ai-recruiting-tool-showed-bias-against/ (archived at https://perma.cc/JX4L-ZSC5)

Yorkshire Post (2015) Morrisons abandons high-tech checkout system, www.yorkshirepost.co.uk/news/morrisons-abandons-high-tech-checkout-system-theyre-now-going-to-look-to-see-how-many-are-queuing-1821886 (archived at https://perma.cc/8GMY-L2G3)

INDEX

Looking for another book?

Explore our award-winning books from global business experts in Human Resources, Learning and Development

Scan the code to browse

www.koganpage.com/hr-learning-development

Also from Kogan Page

ISBN: 9781398610828

ISBN: 9781398610040

ISBN: 9781398614567

ISBN: 9780749498290

www.koganpage.com

From 4 December 2025 the EU Responsible Person (GPSR) is:
eucomply oÜ, Pärnu mnt. 139b – 14, 11317 Tallinn, Estonia
www.eucompliancepartner.com

www.ingramcontent.com/pod-product-compliance
Lightning Source LLC
Chambersburg PA
CBHW080547060326
40689CB00021B/4771